ROAD TRIPS
IRELAND

The spectacular Glengesh Pass winding past mountains

DK EYEWITNESS

ROAD TRIPS
IRELAND

Above The picturesque road curving down to Coumeenoole Bay, Co Kerry

CONTENTS

Front cover: The tree-lined Dark Hedges along Bregagh Road at sunset, Ballymoney, Northern Ireland

Above Hay bales in the pretty countryside around Skerries, near Dublin

Above The Belfry Tower, known as the Yellow Steeple, of St Mary's Abbey on the River Boyne

The rapid rate at which the world is changing is constantly keeping the DK Eyewitness team on our toes. While we've worked hard to ensure that this edition of Ireland is accurate and up-to-date, we know that opening hours alter, standards shift, prices fluctuate, places close and new ones pop up in their stead. So, if you notice we've got something wrong or left something out, we want to hear about it. Please get in touch at travelguides@dk.com

ABOUT THIS BOOK

The 25 driving tours in this guide reflect the fantastic diversity of Ireland. Although it is a relatively small island – 488 km (303 miles) long and 304 km (189 miles) at its widest point – it has an amazing variety of terrain. The landscape ranges from rolling green pastures and fertile fields to mountain peaks, dramatic coastline, sandy beaches, tranquil lakes (loughs), great stretches of blanket bog and rocky peninsulas jutting out to sea. Ireland has one of Europe's oldest cultures, glimpses of which can be found in its mysterious prehistoric sites, its quaint stone villages and its ancient native tongue. These driving routes take visitors beyond the must-see tourist sights to lesser-known places that provide a more intimate experience of the people, customs, architecture and cuisine. Expect delightful surprises around every bend, packed with the sights, sounds and flavours of the real Ireland.

Getting Started

The front section of the guide will give you all the practical information you need to plan and enjoy a driving holiday in Ireland. It includes an overview of when to go and how to get there, advice on bringing your own vehicle or hiring one and details of any documentation required. In-depth motoring advice ranges from driving rules to road conditions, from buying petrol to breakdown or accident procedures – the kind of background knowledge that helps to make a driving trip stress-free. There is information on money, opening hours, mobile phones and Wi-Fi, health and safety and other practical matters, as well as advice on accommodation and dining options, to ensure that you experience the very best of Ireland's legendary hospitality.

The Drives

The main touring section of the guide is divided into leisurely drives, ranging in duration from two to five days. All the tours can be driven in a standard vehicle, and no special driving skills are required.

The drives encompass every region of the country, from the gentle plains of Kildare to the rocky peninsulas of Cork and Kerry, from the remote and dramatic landscapes of Connemara and Donegal to Northern Ireland's stunning Causeway Coast.

Each drive begins with a list of highlights and a clearly mapped itinerary. There is advice on the best time of year to do the drive, road conditions, market days and major festival dates. The tour pages contain descriptions of each stop on the route, linked by clear driving instructions. Side panels have information on the most authentic places to stay and eat. Tinted boxes feature background information and anecdotes.

Each drive features at least one mapped town or countryside walking tour, designed to take a maximum of two hours at a gentle pace with stops along the way.

The tours are flexible: some can be linked to create a longer driving holiday; or they can be dipped into as day trips while based in a region.

Using the Sheet Map

A pull-out road map of the entire country is supplied. This map contains all the information you need to drive around the country and to navigate between the tours. All motorways, major roads, airports – both domestic and international – plus all the ferry ports are also easily identified. This makes the pull-out map an excellent addition to the drive itinerary maps within the book. The pull-out map also has a comprehensive index to help you find the places, and is further supplemented by a clear distance chart so you can gauge the distances between the major cities in Ireland.

Top far left Devil's Pass near Lough Nafooey, Connemara **Top left** Rainbow over West Cork **Centre far left** Fishing boats in Cobh Harbour, Co Cork **Centre left** Old-fashioned truck, Sheep's Head Peninsula, Co Cork **Far left** Dublin's Temple Bar area **Left** Baldoyle Beach, near Dublin **Right** Road to Rossapena on the Fanad Peninsula

INTRODUCING IRELAND

With its charming rural lanes, rolling green hills and stunning mountain vistas and seascapes, there can be few countries as rewarding for back-roads driving as Ireland. The winding lanes of Ireland run through lush pastures to the wildflower-studded pavements of the Burren and to the basalt columns of the Giant's Causeway. They weave their way into the glens of the Antrim Coast, along the wild peninsulas of Cork and Connemara and around the calm loughs of Galway and Donegal. Along their leisurely way they pass by ancient stone circles and megalithic tombs, Celtic crosses and round towers, medieval castles and stately homes. They afford ample opportunities to pause for a stroll in a pretty town or village and, for refreshment, a cosy pub is seldom far away. And, should a visitor ever stray too far off the unbeaten path, there are always friendly folk around who are more than happy to help with directions.

When to Go

The Gulf Stream ensures that Ireland enjoys a moderate climate all year round. However, summer not only has the warmest temperatures but also the longest days. With sunset as late as 11pm in midsummer, it's easy to pack in a lot more sightseeing and activities, from walking and cycling to boating and golf. If the goal of the trip is to take in the most popular attractions and beauty spots, however, there will be fewer crowds and yet still pleasant weather in both spring and autumn. Bargain-hunters will find the best deals on hotel and car hire rates in winter.

However, there's more than the weather to consider in deciding when to visit. Incorporating a music festival, a sporting event or a local celebration can turn out to be the making of a trip to Ireland.

Times to Avoid

The busiest time to visit is during the summer school holidays (late Jun–early Sep). Prices will be highest, traffic heaviest and queues longest. Dublin hotels quickly fill up during conventions and events, so check, and book, well ahead. Night falls as early as 4pm in winter, and many attractions have restricted opening times or may close entirely. Rural and smaller seaside resort hotels and restaurants often close completely from November until Easter.

Left A country road in Co Cork, flanked by dry-stone walls **Right** A stall in the market square of Macroom, Co Cork, with its Norman gateway

Climate

Summer temperatures usually range from 15–20°C (60–68°F), with spring and autumn temperatures around 10°C (50°F). Winters generally average 5–8°C (41–46°F), although rain and wind can make it feel colder. It rarely snows, but expect rain at any time throughout the year. Ireland's "soft" rain is often interspersed with sunshine, so dress in layers and be prepared for sudden changes.

Festivals

St Patrick's Day (17 Mar) is celebrated most enthusiastically in Dublin, but many fairs and festivals, from local food and livestock events to ancient festivities, to music, theatre and arts events, are held throughout the country all year round. Full details of main festivals, where they are held and when, are supplied in each drive.

Public Holidays

New Year's Day (1 Jan)

St Patrick's Day (17 Mar)

Good Friday (Fri before Easter); **Easter Monday** (Mon after Easter)

May Bank Holiday (1st Mon May); **Spring Bank Holiday** (last Mon May, Northern Ireland; 1st Mon Jun, Republic of Ireland)

July Bank Holiday (12 July, Northern Ireland only)

August Bank Holiday (1st Mon Aug, Republic of Ireland; last Mon Aug, Northern Ireland)

October Bank Holiday (last Mon Oct, Republic of Ireland only)

Christmas Day (25 Dec); **St Stephen's Day** (26 Dec, Republic of Ireland); **Boxing Day** (26 Dec, Northern Ireland)

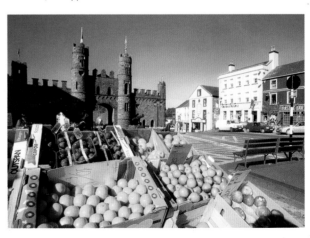

GETTING TO IRELAND

Ireland is a popular destination for travellers worldwide, and its three major airports – Dublin, Shannon and Belfast – are served by frequent, direct flights from Great Britain, Europe and North America as well as flights from major cities around the world. From these key gateways there are easy connections by air to regional airports, as well as good road and rail links throughout the country. Numerous ferry companies sail to Ireland from Britain and France, offering vehicle and foot-passenger services. Some connect with rail services to and from the ports. There are also low-cost combined coach and ferry routes to Ireland.

Above Road sign indicating the route for Belfast Airport along a main road

Arriving by Air

Ireland is served by many international airlines. The Irish national carrier, **Aer Lingus**, has non-stop flights from many British and European cities as well as quite a few in North America, such as New York, Boston, Chicago, Toronto and San Francisco. The Irish budget airline **Ryanair** offers direct flights to Ireland from many British and European cities. Ireland's major and regional airports are also served by other budget carriers from Britain and Europe. Both Irish carriers have flights to domestic destinations throughout the country. **Air Canada** has frequent flights to Ireland from Canada's main cities, but these may entail a stop in London. Flights from major cities in Australia and New Zealand to Dublin involve at least one, sometimes two, stops en route, most often in Dubai but also in Singapore, with additional stops in London or Frankfurt.

Ireland has five international airports. **Dublin Airport** is 10 km (6 miles) north of the city. Both regular city buses and the direct Airlink Express run between the airport and the city centre, with the latter stopping at Connolly and Heuston rail stations as well as the central bus station, Busaras. Many flights from North America land at **Shannon Airport**, 26 km (16 miles) west of Limerick on the west coast. There are bus connections into the city, as well as to Ennis and Galway. **Belfast International Airport**, set 24 km (15 miles) outside the centre, is the main airport in Northern Ireland. Bus 300 runs a regular service between the airport and city centre. **Cork Airport** is 7 km (4 miles) south of the city centre, with regular buses to Parnell Place bus station and then on to Kinsale. **Ireland West Airport Knock** is located about 6 km (4 miles) southwest of Charlestown, County Mayo. Taxis are available at all airports.

The Republic of Ireland has five regional airports at Kerry, Waterford, Galway, Sligo and Donegal. Northern Ireland also has George Best Belfast City Airport and City of Derry Airport.

The **Tourism Ireland** *(see p15)* website has information on travel options from each of these.

Arriving by Sea

Ireland has five main ferry ports: Dublin, Rosslare and Cork in the Republic of Ireland, and Belfast and Larne in Northern Ireland. Three ferry companies operate car and foot-passenger services between Ireland and Britain. There are also ferry services to and from ports in France. The easiest way to compare routes and prices is online at the **Direct Ferries** website.

The Liverpool to Dublin route (8 hours) is operated by **P&O Ferries**, which also has a crossing from Cairnryan, in southwest Scotland, to Larne (2 hours). There are also crossings to Belfast from Cairnryan (2 hours) and from Liverpool (8 hours) with **Stena Line**. Stena also sails to Dublin from Holyhead in North Wales (3 hours 30 minutes) and to Rosslare from Fishguard in southwest Wales (3 hours 15 minutes). **Irish Ferries** also operates crossings to Dublin from Holyhead (3 hours) as well as crossings from Pembroke in south Wales to Rosslare (4 hours).

From France, Stena Line operates an overnight route from Cherbourg to Rosslare (17–19 hours), while Irish Ferries operates a route between Cherbourg and Dublin (17 hours). Between March and October, **Brittany Ferries** runs an overnight route each Wednesday and Saturday between Roscoff and Cork (14 hours) and a Tuesday night sailing route between Cherbourg and Rosslare (15 hours).

Arriving by Rail and Coach

Trains run direct to most ferry ports, including Dublin, Dun Laoghaire, Fishguard Harbour in Wales and Stranraer in Scotland, which has bus links to Cairnryan. If travelling by rail, combination train-and-ferry tickets are usually available; these are convenient, and also often offer substantial savings. Several UK rail operators, Irish Rail and ferry companies offer SailRail tickets, a great deal whereby you can travel from any UK train station to any station in the Republic of Ireland or Northern Ireland, using most ferry routes. Tickets can be bought at most railway stations in the UK and Ireland and from the ferry operators.

Stena Line offers Rail-and-Sail fares from several British rail stations for the crossings between Fishguard and Rosslare, from Holyhead to Dublin, and from Cairnryan to Belfast. Similar fares are available on routes operated by Irish Ferries. Check for deals with **National Rail**, **ScotRail**, **Irish Rail** and **Northern Ireland Railways**.

The long-distance coach operator **Eurolines** offers a similar bus-and-ferry service, with routes to Dublin, Belfast and beyond from most of the main British cities. Journey times may be long, but the fares are relatively inexpensive. In Ireland, Eurolines operates jointly with **Bus Éireann**.

Below far left The check-in area at Dublin Airport **Below left** The modern exterior of Dublin Airport **Below centre** Sign for the Port of Belfast, Northern Ireland's biggest seaport **Below** Irish Ferries ship loading up at Rosslare Harbour

DIRECTORY

ARRIVING BY SEA

Brittany Ferries
021 4277 801 (Ireland);
www.brittany-ferries.ie

Direct Ferries
0333 300 0128 (UK);
www.directferries.co.uk

Irish Ferries
08717 300 400 (UK);
0818 300 400 (Ireland);
www.irishferries.com

P&O Ferries
0130 448 888 (UK);
01 686 9467 (Ireland);
www.poferries.com

Stena Line
03447 70 70 70 (UK);
01 907 5555 (Ireland);
www.stenaline.co.uk

ARRIVING BY RAIL AND COACH

Bus Éireann
01 836 6111 (Ireland);
www.buseireann.ie

Eurolines
www.eurolines.de

Irish Rail (Iarnród Éireann)
836 6222 (Ireland);
www.irishrail.ie

National Rail
08457 48 49 50 (UK);
www.nationalrail.co.uk

Northern Ireland Railways
028 90 66 66 30;
www.translink.co.uk

ScotRail
www.scotrail.co.uk

PRACTICAL INFORMATION

Ireland may have an idyllic rural image but its infrastructure is thoroughly up-to-date. Public services operate smoothly and efficiently, and its health system is good. Communication networks, from Internet to mobile phone services, are widespread, and most banks have an ATM outside. What hasn't changed is Ireland's respect for religion and tradition, or the affable, laid-back nature of its people. Some shops and services are closed on Sundays, and the pace of life may feel slow, especially in the countryside.

Above Traditional green cross indicating a pharmacy, illuminated for visibility

Passports and Visas

For entry requirements, including visas, consult your nearest Irish or **British Embassy** or check the **INIS** or **UK Government** websites. EU nationals and those from the United States, Canada, Australia, New Zealand and South Africa do not need a visa for a stay of up to 90 days as long as their passport is valid for at least three months beyond the end of their stay. British citizens can stay in Ireland for any length of time at the time of publication of this guide, but should check the INIS website before travelling for any further updates.

All other visitors to Ireland must have a passport that is valid for at least six months.

Government Advice

Now more than ever, it is important to consult both your and the Republic of Ireland's government's advice before travelling. The **UK Foreign and Commonwealth Office**, the **US State Department,** the **Australian Department of Foreign Affairs and Trade** and the **Irish Department of Foreign Affairs** offer the latest information on security, health and local regulations.

Travel Insurance

All travellers are strongly advised to take out travel insurance that offers cover for a broad range of possible emergencies. In addition to medical insurance, a comprehensive policy will normally cover the holder: for loss or theft of luggage and other belongings such as passports and money; damage or injury to a third party; personal accident; delayed or cancelled flights; and in some cases the cancellation of your trip due to personal illness or that of a family member. Most policies also cover legal costs up to a certain limit, as do comprehensive motor policies *(see p16)* in the event of any legal advice or action being needed, for example, after an accident. A standard policy will not cover hazardous or extreme sports; many activities can be added for a small extra premium.

Read the terms and conditions carefully as coverage, excess amounts, exclusions and deductibles vary widely. Also check to see what kind of cover, if any, is offered under your home insurance policy. Some credit card companies also offer limited travel insurance benefits if you use your card to book your trip or rental car.

Health

No vaccinations or immunization documents are required to enter Ireland, unless travelling from a country where infectious disease is widespread. Anyone planning to hike in boggy areas is advised to bring insect repellent to ward off the tiny biting insects, called midges, that are active when in dull and damp weather.

Standard remedies can be bought in pharmacies, but bring any prescription medications from home to last throughout the trip, otherwise it will be be necessary to visit a doctor for a prescription. Pack medications in carry-on luggage with their original pharmacy labels in order to avoid any problems at airport security. If any condition requires carrying a syringe when travelling by air, get a formal letter of notification of the condition from the prescribing physician.

In the event of illness while travelling, the **Irish Medical Council** can provide a referral to a doctor or dentist. Most pharmacies are open Monday–Saturday during business

Beware of the bull

Above Emergency ambulance **Above right** Main shopping street, Carlow Town

hours, and some are open 24 hours in larger towns and cities. Pharmacists can advise on minor medical matters.

Visitors from EU countries are covered for medical treatment in Ireland under the EU's social security regulations. To be eligible, identification and a **European Health Insurance Card** (EHIC) are required. UK citizens are eligible for free emergency medical care in the Republic of Ireland provided they have a valid EHIC or UK **Global Health Insurance Card** (GHIC). Apply online prior to travel. British visitors to Northern Ireland will receive treatment as they would at home. Visitors from all other countries should have private medical insurance, as Ireland does not provide publicly funded health care for foreigners.

In Ireland, general practitioners charge fees for consultations and non-emergency treatment, and this must be paid at the time. Emergency hospital treatment will not be withheld or delayed, but will be billed later. The patient is expected to settle the bill and then seek reimbursement from their insurance company.

Police and Security

Ireland is a relatively safe country, but take the normal precautions against petty crime, especially in large towns and tourist areas. Leave all passports and valuables in the hotel safe. Keep an eye on your handbag or wallet in crowds and on public transport, and do not carry large amounts of cash. Never leave anything unattended or visible in a car, even if it is locked.

Victims of crime should contact the **Irish Tourist Assistance Service** in the Republic or the local police station in Northern Ireland. In the Republic, the police force is the **An Garda Síochána**, known as the Gardaí. The **Police Service of Northern Ireland** is their counterpart in the North.

The Troubles are largely a thing of the past and any residual violence between Catholics and Protestants are occasional and seldom affect tourist areas. If in doubt, check locally. Orange marches still take place in the fortnight around July 12, commemorating the Battle of the Boyne in 1690 *(see p156)*. Avoid these gatherings, as they generate protests and sometimes violence.

Below left Uniformed Gardaí in the Republic of Ireland **Below centre** Sign warning against entering field with dangerous bull **Below** Cycling on the narrow roads around Mount Leinster, Carlow

DIRECTORY

PASSPORTS AND VISAS
INIS
www.inis.gov.ie
UK Government
www.gov.uk

EMBASSIES AND CONSULATES
American Consulate
www.uk.usembassy.gov
American Embassy
42 Elgin Road, Ballsbridge, Dublin 4; 01 668 8777; www.ie.usembassy.gov
Australian Embassy
47–49 St Stephen's Green, Dublin 2; 01 664 5300; www.ireland.embassy.gov.au
British Embassy
29 Merrion Road, Ballsbridge, Dublin 4; 01 205 3700; www.gov.uk
Canadian Embassy
7–8 Wilton Terrace, Dublin 2; 01 234 4000; www.international.gc.ca/country-pays/ireland-irlande

GOVERNMENT ADVICE
Australian Department of Foreign Affairs and Trade
www.smartraveller.gov.au
Irish Embassies Abroad
www.dfa.ie
UK Foreign and Commonwealth Office
www.gov.uk/foreign-travel-advice
US State Department
www.travel.state.gov

HEALTH
European Health Insurance Card
www.ec.europa.eu
Global Health Insurance Card
ghic.org.uk
Irish Medical Council
www.medicalcouncil.ie

POLICE AND SECURITY
An Garda Síochána
www.garda.ie
Emergency Services
112 or 999 (Republic): 999 (UK)
Irish Tourist Assistance Service
www.itas.ie
Police Service of Northern Ireland
www.psni.police.uk

Phones, Wi-Fi and Postal Services

Telephone service is provided by Telecom Éireann in the Republic, and by British Telecom in Northern Ireland. Irish phone numbers have a two- or three-digit area code beginning with 0 and followed by a local number of five to eight digits, depending on the region. When dialling within the country, use the full area code. It is only necessary to dial the local number when calling within the same area code.

When calling Ireland from abroad, dial the **international access code**, followed by the Ireland **country code**, and then the local area code (minus the initial 0) and number. The country code is 353 for the Republic and 44 for Northern Ireland. To make an overseas call from Ireland, first dial the international access code 00, then the country code, area code and local number you wish to reach.

When dialling Northern Ireland from the Republic, dial the prefix 048, and then the local number. Calls to the Republic from Northern Ireland, however, are dialled in the same way as those from the rest of the United Kingdom: 00+353+area code (minus the initial 0) and then the number.

There are still about 400 or so public pay phones in Ireland. The easiest and cheapest way to make calls is to purchase a pre-paid Callcard in the Republic or Phonecard in Northern Ireland. These are sold at newsagents, post offices, tourist offices and other outlets, in a variety of deno-minations. International phone cards are also available, and can be the cheapest way to call abroad. Some are rechargeable with

a credit card, but note that the cards may not be interchangeable between the Republic and Northern Ireland.

Visitors travelling with EU tariffs are able to use their devices in Ireland without being affected by data roaming charges. Users will be charged the same rate for data, SMS services and voice calls as they would at home. This situation may change in Northern Ireland now the UK has left the EU. Those not on EU tariffs should check roaming rates with their provider. A cheaper option may be to buy an Irish SIM card (you'll need to show ID).

Free Wi-Fi hotspots are available in all major towns, cities and public places in Ireland. Cafés and restaurants usually permit the use of their Wi-Fi if you make a purchase.

The Republic and Northern Ireland have separate postal systems. You must use Irish stamps to send mail from the Republic but British stamps to send mail from Northern Ireland. Mail boxes are painted green and red respectively. You can buy stamps at newsagents and in many shops as well as at post offices.

Currency and Cards

The currency in the Republic of Ireland is the Euro (€). One Euro is made up of 100 cents. Euro notes come in denominations of €5, €10, €20, €50, €100, €200 and €500. There are 1c, 2c, 5c, 10c, 20c, 50c, €1 and €2 coins. Sterling is the currency in Northern Ireland. One pound (£) is divided into 100 pence. There are £5, £10, £20, £50 and £100 notes, and 1p, 2p, 5p, 10p, 20p, 50p, £1 and £2 coins.

Bank debit and credit cards can be used to withdraw local currency from ATMs, which are widespread

Above Fáilte Ireland (Irish Tourist Board) shamrock sign for approved accommodation

throughout Ireland. The card provider may charge for withdrawing cash abroad, but you may benefit from better rates than when exchanging cash at a bank or bureau de change. Traveller's cheques are fast becoming obsolete, but a prepaid currency card is a safe alternative to carrying cash.

Debit cards and credit cards such as Visa and MasterCard are widely accepted everywhere, including hotels and guesthouses, restaurants and pubs, shops and petrol stations, and small businesses. Contactless payments are accepted by most major retailers. Credit card companies are ever more vigilant against fraud, so it is wise to let them know you will be travelling and using the card abroad, so they do not put a block on further use. It is also a good idea to carry a different credit card as a back-up.

Tourist Information

Fáilte Ireland (the National Tourism Development Authority of the Republic) and the **Northern Ireland Tourist Board** have offices that provide information about sights,

Above Post office and *bureau de change* in Ventry, Co Kerry **Above right** Old-style red Northern Ireland phone box by the road, Fermanagh Lakelands

activities and accommodation in their area. There are also local tourist offices in most towns and tourist areas, such as the **Dublin Tourism Centre**. **Tourism Ireland** covers the whole island. Along with general advice, its website has links to Irish Tourist Board offices worldwide.

Opening Hours

Most Irish shops are open Mon–Sat, 9am–6pm. Sunday trading hours are from noon to 5 or 6pm in the Republic, 1–5pm in Northern Ireland.
Banking hours are typically Mon–Fri, 10am–4pm in the Republic, and 9:30am–4:30pm in Northern Ireland. Post offices are generally open Mon–Fri, 9am–5:30pm, but main post offices in larger towns are also open on Saturdays, from 9am to 5pm in the Republic and from 9am to 12:30pm in Northern Ireland.

COVID-19 The pandemic continues to affect Ireland. Some museums, tourist attractions and hospitality venues are operating on reduced or temporary opening hours, and require visitors to make advance bookings for a specific date and time. Always check ahead before visiting.

Museums and galleries are usually closed on Mondays and on public holidays.

Facilities for Travellers with Specific Requirements

Many visitor attractions are now accessible to wheelchair users, and a growing number of hotels and restaurants provide facilities for guests with disabilities. For more information, contact the **National Disability Authority** in the Republic, and **Adapt NI** and **Disability Action** in Northern Ireland.

Time

Ireland is on Greenwich Mean Time (GMT), with one hour's Summer (Daylight Saving) Time in effect from late March to late October.

Electricity

The electrical current is 230/240 volts. Plugs have 3 pins. Overseas visitors will need an adaptor for their appliances. Most hotels have built-in adaptors for shavers only, and provide a hairdryer.

Below far left Republic of Ireland telephone box **Below left** Green postbox in the Republic **Below centre left** Keep our beach tidy sign, Waterford beach **Below centre** Late bar sign, Kilkenny City **Below** Signs for Waterford Treasures Museum

DIRECTORY

PHONES, WI-FI AND POSTAL SERVICES

International Access Codes
Australia: 0011; New Zealand: 0170; UK: 00; US and Canada: 011

Country Codes
Australia: 61; New Zealand: 64; UK: 44; US and Canada: 1

TOURIST INFORMATION

Fáilte Ireland
www.discoverireland.ie

Northern Ireland Tourist Board
www.discovernorthernireland.com

Tourism Ireland
www.ireland.com

Dublin Tourism Centre
www.visitdublin.com

FACILITIES FOR TRAVELLERS WITH SPECIFIC REQUIREMENTS

National Disability Authority
01 608 0400; www.nda.ie

Adapt NI
028 9023 1211; www.communityni.org

Disability Action
028 9029 7880; www.disabilityaction.org

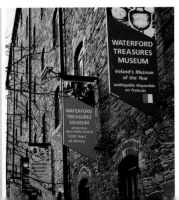

DRIVING IN IRELAND

Ireland has an extensive road network and in recent years there has been extensive upgrading and expansion of all main routes. However, it is only by driving the back roads that you'll discover the real Ireland. The relaxed pace is one of the greatest joys of driving here and the further you get from the cities, the more likely you are to have the road to yourself. To travel safely and get the most from your trip, it is vital to familiarize yourself with the rules and requirements for driving in Ireland before you set out.

Above Premium, unleaded and diesel petrol pumps by a rural roadside in Co Tipperary

Insurance and Breakdown Cover

Third-party motor insurance is compulsory in Ireland and, if you bring your own car, you must have an insurance certificate that is valid in the country. You do not necessarily need a "Green Card and Bail Bond", but you should check with your insurer prior to travelling that you are covered for the trip. Most companies give you automatic coverage in EU countries for up to 90 days. If your policy has breakdown cover, check whether it applies abroad. If not, consider purchasing additional breakdown and accident cover. Motoring organizations such as the AA *(see p19)* also offer single-trip policies of this type.

What to Take

In order to drive in Ireland, you must have a valid national driving licence, issued in your country of permanent residence. By law you must have your licence with you at all times while driving in the Republic. If your licence does not have a photograph, be sure also to carry your passport or another form of official photo ID. If you are bringing your own vehicle, including caravans and motorcycles, you should

carry the registration document with you. If it is not registered in your name (for example, if it is a company car), bring a letter of authorization from the owner.

While not compulsory, it is advisable to carry the following in your vehicle: a warning triangle, first aid kit and visibility vests (one for every occupant of the vehicle). A torch (flashlight) and a petrol container are also recommended extras.

Road Systems

In the Republic, motorway numbers are prefixed by an M. National Primary Routes have the prefix N, followed by numbers 1-50, while National Secondary Routes (also N) are 51 and above. Regional roads have an R prefix and a three-digit number; these range from stretches of dual carriageway to narrow rural roads. Local road numbers are designated with an L, but often are not shown on road signs or maps.

Northern Ireland uses the British system of road classification: M for motorways, A for major roads, B for secondary roads and C for minor ones. A barrier-free motorway toll system, called **eFlow**, operates on the M50 around Dublin. If your car is not

registered, your vehicle number plate is recorded each time you pass the toll point and you must pay according to distance travelled. Payment can be made online, through the call centre or at Payzone outlets nationwide, but the journey must be paid for by 8pm the following day. More information is available on the eFlow website. Some other motorways in Ireland also charge a fee, which is paid at toll plazas en route or as you leave.

Speed Limits and Fines

In the Republic of Ireland, speed limits are given in kilometres per hour (km/h). In Northern Ireland they are posted in miles per hour (mph). Be sure to remember the change when near the border: it is unmarked and easy to cross without realizing.

Unless otherwise stated, speed limits are as follows:
• In the Republic: 120 km/h (74 mph) on motorways; 100 km/h (62 mph) on national roads; 80 km/h (50 mph) on non-national roads; 50 km/h (31 mph) in towns and built-up areas.
• In Northern Ireland: 70 mph (112 km/h) on motorways; 60 mph (96 km/h) on the open road; and 30 mph (48 km/h) in towns and

Above Slow sign on Lough Navar Forest Drive **Above centre** Signs warning of changes in the road ahead **Above right** Double-decker buses, Dublin

built-up areas. There are both fixed and mobile speed cameras in Northern Ireland, but only mobile cameras in the Republic. In the event of a speeding violation, you will be issued with a fixed penalty notice, which must be paid within 28 days. You won't escape the penalty by driving a rental car. The car hire company will bill you for the ticket, along with an administration fee. Speed camera detectors are illegal and will be confiscated.

The laws on drink-driving are very strict and penalties are high. The legal limit is 50 mg per 100 ml of blood (about equal to a pint of beer). Police are authorized to perform a breathalyser test at any time, and the penalty for refusal may be prosecution. Any accident that occurs while the driver is under the influence of drink or drugs is automatically considered his or her fault.

Rules of the Road

Driving is on the left throughout Ireland. Most visitors get used to this quickly, but pay extra attention at crossroads and roundabouts, where it is easy (and dangerous) to forget or get confused. Always turn left into a roundabout, and give way to traffic

already in the roundabout and approaching from the right. Overtake on the right, but do not do so if there is a solid white line in the centre of the road. At a junction where neither road has priority, yield to traffic coming from your right.

Seat belts must be worn at all times, by the driver and all passengers. It is illegal to use a hand-held mobile phone while driving; this will incur a fine. The horn must not be sounded between 11:30pm and 7am.

At traffic lights, drivers must yield to pedestrians when the amber light is flashing, but if the crossing is clear they may proceed with caution.

Buying Petrol

There are plenty of petrol (gas) stations throughout Ireland, and all grades of unleaded petrol, as well as diesel, are available. While electric car charging points are now adequately widespread, LPG fuelling opportunities are increasingly hard to find. Most stations are self-service, and nearly all take major credit cards.

Below left Old-fashioned signpost near Leenane, Connemara **Below centre** Sightseeing tour bus, Belfast **Below** Sports car on the Coomakesta Pass, Iveragh Peninsula

DIRECTORY

ROAD SYSTEMS

eFlow
www.eFlow.ie

IRISH PHRASES FOR DRIVERS

Géill slí
Give way

Mall
Slow

Bóthar dúnta
Road closed

Oscailt cheilte
Concealed entrance

Coisithe amháin
Pedestrian zone

Aire
Caution

Leanaí ag trasnú
Children crossing

Rampa romhat
Ramp ahead

Trácht aon líne
Single file traffic

Dromchla sealadach
Temporary road surface

Cloichíní scaoilte
Loose chippings

An Iar
City centre

Road Conditions

Most roads in Ireland are both well-surfaced and well-maintained. Distances are shown in kilometres on signposts in the Republic, and in miles in Northern Ireland. In the Republic (and occasionally in Northern Ireland), road signs and place names are posted in both English and Irish. In the Gaeltacht (Irish-speaking areas), however, there are stretches where signs are in Irish only. Also be aware that road signs may be inadequate or confusing in rural areas and, on occasion, can be broken off or pointing in the wrong direction. It is essential to have a good road map.

Given the small size of the island, and the relatively short distances between towns, it can be easy to underestimate the time it takes to drive between two points. Back roads by their nature are often slow and winding, with reduced speeds through villages and hamlets, while traffic can become congested in busy tourist towns such as Killarney. Unexpected things can slow things down – a flock of sheep on the road, a farm vehicle, a beautiful view or even two locals stopping their cars for a chat in the middle of the road. Take extra care on blind curves and look out for pedestrians walking on the roadway. An average of 50–65 km (30–40 miles) per hour is a sensible figure when planning your route.

Many country roads are so narrow that one vehicle will have to pull over to the side to let an oncoming car pass. Courtesy dictates that the one closest to a wide spot waits. Buses always have right of way, however. It is wise to allow local drivers, who know the roads well and will drive much faster, to overtake. And be sure to give drivers who make way for you a friendly wave of thanks.

Taking a Break

If you are feeling tired or think you may be lost, it's a good idea to pull over and take a break. Many roads have signposted areas where you can pull off and stretch your legs, have a snack and consult your map. The glorious scenery can be a huge distraction so, if you find it hard to keep your eyes on the road, it's best to stop and admire the view. Parks and areas with nature trails also make good picnic stops. Ireland does not have US- or Continental-style rest areas, as distances are not great between towns with pubs, petrol stations and other public facilities.

Breakdown and Accident Procedures

If you have a breakdown or accident, move the car safely off the road and turn on hazard lights or use a warning triangle. Emergency telephones are sometimes located along the hard shoulders of the motorways, but along rural back roads it is best to have a mobile phone.

Rental car companies will supply a number to call in case of breakdown or problems with the vehicle. They will advise or arrange for assistance, and can usually provide a replacement vehicle quickly. No repairs should be undertaken on a hire car without the company's authorization. If you are a member of the Automobile Association (AA), RAC or AAA, check whether reciprocal services are available in Ireland. If you have an accident,

Above Dangerous bend warning sign

stop and exchange name, address and car registration details with the other parties involved. The police must be notified within 24 hours if anyone is injured and a report will be filed. Call the emergency services (see p13) if there are casualties. Be sure to get the insurance details of the other driver and give them yours. If your vehicle is rented, the company must be notified.

Circumstances can be confusing at the time of an accident, so do not admit fault, accept liability or give money to any party. If possible, take down details from any independent witnesses. It is also a wise idea to take photographs of any vehicle damage, as well as the scene of the accident.

Parking

Parking is allowed wherever you see a red circle with a black P. A diagonal line crossing the sign means that parking is prohibited. A red circle marked with an X means the road is a Clearway, and you may not stop on it during the hours indicated. Double yellow lines on the pavement mean no parking at any time. Car parks and other parking areas are designated by a blue P sign. It is permissable to park on the street unless signs indicate otherwise. However, check

Above Cows on the road near Kells **Above centre** Scenic drive sign, Gortin Glen Forest Park **Above right** Sign for Glenariff, Northern Ireland

in case there is a parking scheme in operation, such as Pay and Display, in which you obtain a ticket from a nearby machine and display on your windscreen. Disc parking is another system used in towns, whereby you must buy a scratch card from a nearby shop and scratch off the date and time before displaying it in your car. In many rural towns and villages, there is little room for parking in the centre, but there are car parks, usually free, situated at the edge of town. In the countryside, be sure not to block farm or other gates or private roads if you are leaving your vehicle for a walk or to explore archaeological sites. On single-lane roads, never park in designated passing places, as this is a traffic hazard.

In the cities, where space is at a premium, parking regulations are strictly enforced, often by towing or wheel-clamping. These are strong deterrents to parking illegally or overstaying the time limit on a parking meter, as it is can prove very expensive to get a car released. In the Republic, traffic wardens and police can issue on-the-spot fines for parking offences. Should you receive one, be sure to get an official receipt from the person collecting the fine. It is best to use a designated car park, and some now

accept credit cards. Drivers with disabilities can use their UK blue badge to park in designated spaces in Ireland. For further assistance and information, and for disabled drivers from other countries, contact the Disabled Drivers' Association of Ireland.

Maps

Free tourist maps are widely available, but they are seldom of much use for back roads driving. It is useful to have a map that gives place names in both English and Irish, especially if travelling in Gaeltacht areas such as Connemara and Donegal. The *Ordnance Survey Official Road Atlas Ireland* is highly recommended. This can be purchased at petrol stations, bookshops, newsagents and tourist information centres. Even with the best map in the world, you are likely to have to stop and ask directions along the way. Locals usually refer to roads by their direction rather than their number, as in "take the Limerick road", so it's helpful to know which towns are near to your destination.

Below far left Sheep on village street, Achill Island **Below left** Array of signs in the Glen of Aherlow **Below centre** Give Way sign in Irish **Below** Road through Galbally, Glen of Aherlow

DIRECTORY

MOTORING ASSOCIATIONS
Automobile Association
*01 649 7460; www.theaa.ie
(Republic of Ireland)
0800 887 766; www.theaa.com
(Northern Ireland)*

Aviva Ireland Breakdown Cover
1800 448 888; www.aviva.ie

Caravans and Motorhomes/RVs

Caravans and motorhomes are subject to the same rules of the road as any other vehicle. However, camper vans or cars towing caravans are restricted to speeds of 80 km/h 50 mph) unless signs indicate otherwise. Caravan and motorhome drivers should also leave a greater space between them and the vehicle in front, to allow for the greater stopping distance required. Many of Ireland's country roads are very narrow and winding, and they may not be suitable for caravans and motorhomes. Signs are often posted, but they are easy to miss. It is worth enquiring locally about conditions before setting out on these roads. Narrow bridges, sharp curves and bends and steep gradients can be potentially dangerous for large vehicles, so pay attention to road signs warning of such hazards.

If you are bringing your own caravan to Ireland, you must ensure that your LPG supply, used for cooking, has been turned off correctly for the ferry crossing.

You can also hire motorhomes and caravans that sleep several people, some fully equipped with sleeping bags, linens and cooking utensils. For information on rental, repairs and campsites and caravan parks throughout Ireland, contact the **Irish Caravan and Camping Council**.

Motorbikes

By law, all motorcyclists and their passengers must wear helmets, and dipped headlights must be used during the day at all times. You must have a valid driving licence to cover a motorcycle, and an insurance policy. You may not carry a passenger if you hold only a provisional licence; you must have a full licence as well as an insurance policy that allows you to do so. Motorcycles must have a white or yellow headlamp, a red rear lamp, a red rear reflector, and rear number plate lighting. Ensure that your tyres have adequate tread; the legal minimum is 1 mm. In the Republic, a current road tax disc must be displayed.

The rules of the road are the same for motorcyclists as for other drivers, though you should take additional safety precautions. Do not ride between traffic lanes, moving or stationary. Give other vehicles a wide berth when overtaking, and be alert to the fact that they may not see you.

Driving with Children

Child seats are legally mandatory for children aged between a year and 4 years 6 months. It is strongly advised that children under the age of 12 do not sit in the front seat. Babies and small children must be placed in a restraint system suitable for their height and weight, such as a child seat or baby carrier. Infants must never be placed in a rear-facing child seat in the front passenger seat if there is an active airbag fitted. Children over the age of three who are under 150 cm (5 ft) tall and weigh less than 36 kg (80 lb) must use the appropriate child or booster seat or booster cushion. Remember to request child seats in advance when making a car hire booking. It is the driver's responsibility to ensure that any passengers under the age of 17 comply with these laws.

Above Devil's Pass, near Lough Nafooey

Disabled Drivers

Drivers with disabilities who have a Disabled Parking card or UK Blue Badge can use designated disabled parking spaces around Ireland, either in their own vehicle or a hired one. The card or badge should be clearly visible on the dashboard. Contact the **Disabled Drivers' Association of Ireland (DDAI)** or the **Irish Wheelchair Association** for more details. If you are bringing your own vehicle to Ireland, you may be entitled to a discount from the ferry company on some sailings. Contact the company concerned, your motoring association or the DDIA for more information.

Car and Motorhome/RV Hire

Most of the international vehicle-hire companies have branches at airports and ferry ports and in all the larger cities, and offer a range of vehicles. A good local firm with offices around the country is **Dan Dooley Car Rentals**. To rent a car in Ireland you will need a valid driving licence and a credit card. Normally drivers must be between the ages of 21 and 70, but check with the company concerned before you make your reservation, regarding their age restrictions. It is recommended to book in advance,

Above Farmer driving cattle along an Irish country lane **Above right** Bikers stopping for a break at a café in Kinvarra, Co Galway

especially during peak season, and you will often get a better rate. Most rental cars in Ireland are standard (manual) shift. Automatic cars are available but they cost more and must always be booked in advance. Consider renting a smaller car as they are much easier to handle on narrow country roads. If you require a child seat, this should be booked well in advance as well.

Always let the rental company know, for insurance purposes, if you plan to drive between Northern Ireland and the Republic. Third party insurance is compulsory and included in the rate. Some rental agreements also include Collision Damage Waiver (CDW), which limits your liability for damages to the car, theft/loss cover and personal injury insurance; others charge additional fees for these items. Read the agreement carefully if you are at all unsure about what your coverage and liabilities are. Some drivers may be able to use insurance from a personal credit card to claim CDW, but check with your card company to make sure that they cover your trip to Ireland (many don't) and be prepared to show proof of cover. Further information about car hire is available from the **Car Rental Council** in the Republic

and the **British Vehicle Renting and Leasing Association** in Northern Ireland. For information on motor-home hire, contact the **Irish Caravan and Camping Council**. You can also rent a traditional horse-drawn caravan from **Irish Horse Drawn Caravans**.

Driving in Rain and Fog

When rain, mist, fog or cloudy conditions reduce light levels, dipped headlights should be used. Turn on fog lights whenever visibility is less than 100 m (328 ft). If you bring a left-hand-drive vehicle over for your trip round Ireland, you will need to deflect the beam of your headlights. Beam-adjusters are simple to use; you can buy them at ferry terminals, or check with your motoring organization. Snow and ice are rare in Ireland, but you still may encounter them in mountain areas in winter. Reduce your speed in adverse conditions, as you will need a far greater braking distance, and poor visibility gives you less time to react to sudden hazards.

Below far left Mountain road near Portsalon, Fanad Peninsula **Below left** Main Street, Cushendall **Below centre** Traditional horse-drawn caravan from Tralee **Below** Sheep crossing the road at the foot of Slievemore, Co Mayo

DIRECTORY

CARAVAN AND MOTORHOMES/RVS

Irish Caravan and Camping Council
www.camping-ireland.ie

DISABLED DRIVERS

Disabled Drivers' Association of Ireland (DDAI)
094 936 4054; www.ddai.ie

Irish Wheelchair Association
01 818 6400; www.iwa.ie

CAR AND MOTORHOME/RV HIRE

British Vehicle Renting and Leasing Association
www.bvrla.co.uk

Car Rental Council
www.carrentalcouncil.ie

Dan Dooley Car Rentals
01 844 5151; www.dan-dooley.ie

Irish Horse Drawn Caravans
www.irishhorsedrawncaravans.com

WHERE TO STAY

Ireland offers some of the most romantic and special places imaginable in which to stay, from historic castles to traditional horse-drawn caravans, charming rural cottages to chic boutique hotels. The warm welcome that visitors receive in Ireland is like no other, and getting to know the hosts at a farmhouse bed-and-breakfast or family-run guesthouse is part of a memorable visit. The accommodation in this guide has been specially selected to reflect the unique Irish character of its back roads.

Above Youth hostel entrance, High Street, Kilkenny City

Hotels

Ireland has a fine range of traditional hotels across the country, with properties to suit all budgets. Some might be picturesque village inns; others may have been converted from former stately homes or other landmark buildings. Whether their decor is elegant and luxurious or modest and comfortable, these hotels have great character and charm, often with lovely features such as stone fireplaces or decorative plasterwork ceilings. Many also have a pub or an acclaimed restaurant attached, making them a gathering place for the local community too. The websites of **Ireland's Blue Book** and the **Good Food Ireland** list many such traditional hotels.

Country-house hotels are set in beautiful grounds and are usually elegant and spacious. Food is often a highlight, with creative menus prepared by a top chef and served in a formal dining room. They may also offer a range of activities, from angling and horse riding to cookery courses. Some do not accept young children. The **Hidden Ireland Guide** and **Original Irish Hotels** list many of these special properties.

Ireland also has numerous resort hotels with impressive golf and other sporting activities on offer, as well as luxurious spa facilities.

Increasingly it is possible to find boutique hotels in towns and resort areas as well as in larger cities, with rooms and public areas featuring the best in modern design. Many will also have a bar and/or restaurant.

As well as all these, Ireland also has a range of national and international chain hotels with accommodation in all price ranges, which can be found in the larger towns and cities or along the more major roads.

Depending on their rating (see opposite), most hotels have rooms with en suite bathrooms, and some also offer family rooms and suites. Most include breakfast in the room rate, and larger hotels will normally have a restaurant and bar.

The **Irish Hotels Federation** publishes Be Our Guest, an annual guide to hotels and guesthouses in the Republic. The **Northern Ireland Hotels Federation** provides a similar service in the north. These properties have been inspected and approved by the tourist boards, and are identified by a green shamrock symbol.

Guesthouses

Guesthouses are smaller and usually less expensive than hotels. They are often family-run, with an emphasis on personal service. Many are set in large Georgian or Victorian houses, with all or several rooms converted for guests, often with simple but charming decor. Those with higher ratings will have en suite bathrooms; those in lower categories may have shared facilities for some rooms. Breakfast is usually included in the rate, but most guesthouses do not have a restaurant or bar, although they may have snacks and drinks available for guests.

In smaller towns and villages, pubs may have guest rooms available, and this can be an enjoyable way to experience the local nightlife without having to drive afterwards.

Bed-and-Breakfast

Bed-and-breakfast (B&B) is offered in private homes around the country, from busy town centres to remote villages. Traditional Irish farmhouse B&Bs are among the most popular. They have from one to three guest rooms, often en suite but sometimes with shared bathrooms. Facilities and

Above Picturesque café in Gowran, Kilkenny **Above right** Resort hotel with its own golf course near Lough Erne, Fermanagh Lakelands

decor vary, but are usually clean and neat. Some hosts will offer an evening meal for an additional charge, but this must be arranged in advance, and is usually taken at a large communal table with the family and other guests. B&Bs are generally cheaper than hotels and guesthouses, and are a great way to meet local people. For a range of bed-and-breakfast options, contact **B&B Ireland** and **Irish Farmhouse Holidays**.

Castles and Historic Homes

The most stunning accommodation in Ireland can be found in castles and historic homes that have opened some of their rooms to overnight visitors. Although such an experience does not come cheap, a night or two in one of these landmark buildings can be the most memorable of any trip. For listings, see Ireland's Blue Book, Hidden Ireland, **Adams & Butler**, **Elegant Ireland** and the **Irish Landmark Trust**.

Booking

You should book ahead for stays at any time of the year, with reservations best made online,

though you can always phone too. Alternatively, use direct booking websites such as www.booking.com and www.hotels.com.

Be sure to check if the rate quoted is per person or per room – B&Bs and guest houses often charge per person, as do many hotels. Also check if the hotel rate includes tax.

Facilities and Prices

Irish hotel rooms generally have a double or twin beds; if a cot or child's bed is required, request it at the time of booking. Coffee- and tea-making facilities are standard. Most places serve a full Irish breakfast, with a lighter "continental" option available.

Hotels are rated from one to five stars. Few one-star properties have en suite facilities, while a five-star rating signifies luxury. Guesthouses are classified separately, from one to four stars. Generally, the higher the star rating, the more expensive the room, but prices also vary seasonally.

Below far left Pretty thatched cottage in Skerries, Co Dublin **Below left** Historic Ardgillan Castle, Co Dublin **Below** Clonmel, set on the banks of the River Suir, Co Tipperary

DIRECTORY

HOTELS
Good Food Ireland
053 915 8693; www.goodfoodireland.ie

Ireland's Blue Book
01 676 9914; www.irelands-blue-book.ie

Hidden Ireland Guide
098 66650; www.hiddenireland.com

Original Irish Hotels
01 295 8900; www.originalirishhotels.com

Irish Hotels Federation
01 497 6459; www.ihf.ie

Northern Ireland Hotels Federation
028 9077 6635; www.nihf.co.uk

BED-AND-BREAKFAST
B&B Ireland
071 982 2222; www.bandbireland.com

Irish Farmhouse Holidays
071 982 2222; www.irishfarmholidays.com

CASTLES AND HISTORIC HOMES
Adams & Butler
01 288 9355; www.adamsandbutler.com

Elegant Ireland
01 473 2505; www.elegant.ie

Irish Landmark Trust
01 670 4733; www.irishlandmark.com

PRICE BANDS
The following price bands are for a standard double room in high season:

Republic of Ireland
Inexpensive – under €100
Moderate – €100–€200
Expensive – over €200

Northern Ireland
Inexpensive – under £100
Moderate – £100–£200
Expensive – over £200

WHERE TO EAT

With its green pastures, fertile farmland and clear coastal waters, Ireland enjoys an abundance of high-quality produce. In recent years, Ireland's restaurants have come into their own and now talented chefs are turning all that premium beef, succulent lamb and fresh seafood into New Irish cuisine in acclaimed restaurants throughout the country. For those on a budget, there are hearty pub meals as well as that Irish favourite, fish and chips, not to mention endless delicious items for a memorable picnic.

Above One of the many pubs in the Temple Bar district of Dublin

Practical Information

A cooked breakfast – commonly known as a "Full Irish" or "Ulster Fry" – at your accommodation could easily keep you going throughout the day. If not, lunch is normally served from noon or 12:30pm until 2:30 or 3pm. Restaurants and cafés in larger towns and cities have longer hours than those in smaller towns and villages. Although it was once customary in Ireland to eat a large meal at midday, dinner is now the main meal for most people. Restaurants' evening hours vary. Most open between 5:30 and 7pm. In larger towns and tourist areas they may serve until 10 or 11pm, but in smaller towns and villages they often close at 9pm, with last orders 30 minutes earlier. Many pubs serve bar food from lunchtime until around 9pm. Restaurants often close for a day or two each week (usually Mondays), but many smaller establishments in busy areas stay open seven days. Off the beaten track, they may close out of season.

Credit and debit cards are widely accepted in all establishments. Tax is always included in the bill. A service charge is often added as well; if not, leave a tip of 10–15 per cent.

Casual dress is acceptable in most restaurants, though you may want to dress smartly for more expensive establishments. Most places are wheelchair-accessible, but check in advance. Children are allowed into pubs with their parents until 9pm in winter and 10pm in summer. Smoking is banned in any indoor area, including restaurants and bars.

Menus are generally displayed outside, so you can make an informed decision before entering. Fine dining establishments usually offer a set-price menu as well as à la carte. These can be excellent value, especially at lunchtime, and allow you to enjoy a top restaurant at an affordable price.

Restaurants

Restaurants in Ireland range from cosy, casual dining to trendy bistro-style hotspots to traditional dining rooms set with crystal and fine china. Many country house hotels offer outstanding dining in an elegant setting, and they are00 often open to non-guests who book in advance. Wild salmon, fresh seafood, oysters and mussels feature on menus in season. The current trend is for New Irish cuisine, which uses accents from Europe, America and the Pacific Rim to put a fresh spin on familiar dishes. However, it is also worth seeking out local restaurants that serve traditional Irish dishes, such as boxty (potato pancakes) or the classic Irish stew. There are international dining options too, from Indian and Chinese restaurants to Japanese noodle bars to Italian restaurants and pizzerias.

Nearly all restaurants feature at least one vegetarian option, often more. Fine dining establishments usually have impressive wine lists, as well as a good selection of Irish whiskeys and other spirits. It may be necessary to book well in advance for a table in a top restaurant. In Northern Ireland, look for restaurants with the Taste of Ulster designation, a symbol of quality.

Visitors returning to Ireland will be shocked to find that restaurant prices have risen significantly in recent years, and Ireland is no longer the bargain that it once was when it comes to quality dining. It may be possible to cut costs by opting for the "early-bird" specials at some restaurants, though this will, of course, entail dining rather early (between 5:30 and 7pm).

Above A grocer's shop in the Boyne Valley **Above centre** Pavement seating at a café in Carlow City **Above right** Shops along Malahide's main street

Pubs and Bars
The most reliable option for an inexpensive but delicious meal is the traditional Irish pub. An assortment of classic dishes usually features on the menu, along with burgers, lasagne, fish and chips and other standards. Pubs serve hot meals at lunch and dinner, with table service available in most places.

Hotel bars and wine bars may also serve snacks and light meals. Eighteen is the minimum legal drinking age in Ireland.

Cafés and Takeaways
For snacks and light meals, there is an array of cafés, cafeterias and bakeries. Cafés are generally open for breakfast and lunch, but many close by 6pm. Most museums and visitor attractions have cafeterias serving light refreshments. Ireland has not escaped the coffee craze. There are branches of international chains, as well as individual coffee-shops, in larger towns and cities. Most sell sandwiches and pastries as well. Look out for traditional tea shops, where you can have a pot of tea or coffee along with homemade cakes, breads and local specialities.

Ireland has all the usual fast-food chains, but far more enjoyable is a takeaway from the local "chippy", or fish and chip shop. On the coast, this is an experience not to be missed. Bakeries often sell pasties (a thick, enclosed pastry case filled with meat and vegetables) and other baked goods that make quick, filling and inexpensive takeaway snacks.

Picnics
Most towns will have a sandwich shop, where you can grab ready-made picnic supplies. More fun are the independent food shops and delicatessens that usually offer a great range of cured meats, patés, cheeses and other local delicacies.

Best of all are the colourful farmers' markets. These are a showcase for regional producers and you should be able to stock your picnic basket with home-baked breads, local cheeses, honey and preserves, and fresh seasonal fruit. Each driving tour notes the location and days of the week for markets around the region.

Below far left Old School House Café, Inistioge, Co Kilkenny **Below left** Pavement café in Dublin's Temple Bar **Below centre** A pub in Temple Bar **Below** Fish specials at Howth Harbour

DIRECTORY

PRICE BANDS
The following price bands are based on a three-course meal for one, including a half-bottle of house wine, cover charge, tax and service:
Republic of Ireland
Inexpensive: under €25
Moderate: €25–€50
Expensive: over €50

Northern Ireland
Inexpensive: under £25
Moderate: £25–£50
Expensive: over £50

THE FLAVOURS OF IRELAND

For a small island, Ireland offers an amazing range of foods, and a high standard of both cooking and presentation. Some of Ireland's speciality dishes, such as boxty and colcannon, are based on its humble staple, the potato. Artisan breads and Irish cheeses are made to traditional recipes in time-honoured fashion. Fresh salmon, oysters and other seafood take pride of place on menus in season. And you can enjoy Ireland's best ales and stout, and its exquisite aged whiskeys, at any time of year.

Above Flower-decked shop fronts along Main Street, Cashel, Co Tipperary

Irish Specialities

Ireland has a marvellous array of traditional dishes to try. Most are based on simple ingredients – potatoes, cabbage, bacon and the like – that were important staples in the centuries when Ireland was primarily a rural country. A culinary resurgence has seen these basics being used in new ways by artisan food producers, and there is often great pride invested in their cooking.

Perhaps because they're mostly cooked at home, many traditional Irish dishes can be surprisingly hard to find on restaurant menus. They are most likely to appear as daily specials in family-run pubs or small cafés, or in independently owned restaurants that specialize in Irish home cooking.

Irish stew is the national dish, a slow-cooked casserole made with neck of mutton (mature lamb), potatoes, carrots and onions and served with fresh bread and butter. Dublin coddle is made with pork sausages, bacon and vegetables cooked in a ham or apple cider stock. The magical combination of beef and Guinness makes for a rich, dark stew, sometimes with the addition of oysters for extra luxury.

Of Ireland's many potato dishes, a favourite is boxty, a griddled pancake made of grated raw and mashed cooked potato with buttermilk. Others to look out for include champ (or poundies), a mashed potato and spring onion dish served shaped like a volcano with warmed milk and a knob of butter in the "crater", and colcannon, made with mashed potatoes, onions and cabbage.

Fish and Seafood

The abundance of fresh fish and seafood from the Atlantic, the Irish Sea and the country's many rivers is one of the delights of eating out in Ireland. Locally caught fish such as wild salmon and trout are highlights on many restaurant menus, and oak- or peat-smoked salmon is a popular starter. Herring, mackerel and eels are also served smoked or fresh. Fish chowder is sold in most pubs and restaurants in coastal villages. Seafood and shellfish are plentiful along the coast: mussels from Bantry Bay, langoustines from Dublin Bay and oysters from Galway Bay are the most renowned. Oysters are often served with Guinness at annual oyster festivals in the region.

Breads and Baked Goods

Bread is baked and served as proudly as any other food in Ireland, and there is a delicious assortment to try. A slice of warm, freshly baked bread, generously spread with butter, and a cup of tea is a traditional sign of hospitality. Home-made brown or soda bread is an accompaniment to most meals. Soda bread, which has a light texture, uses baking soda instead of yeast as a leavening agent, and also contains buttermilk. In Northern Ireland, soda bread is baked in the "farl" shape, with a cross slashed into the top of the dough, giving it a flatter form that is easily split into four sections. Soda farls are a key constituent in an Ulster fry. When made with wholemeal (rather than white) flour, soda bread is called brown bread in the Republic and wheaten bread in Northern Ireland. In Waterford, the traditional soft white doughy roll (bun) known as blaa was brought to the city by the Huguenots in the 17th century.

There is also a wide variety of sweet breads and cakes to try: scones; barm brack, a rich, fruity cake-bread traditionally eaten at Hallowe'en; and porter cake, which is made with dried fruit and stout.

Above Market in Moore Street, Dublin **Above centre** A perfect pint of Guinness **Above right** Platter of oysters **Above far right** Irish stew, the national dish

Irish Cheeses

Cheese-making is a centuries-old art in Ireland, dating back to the time of the monasteries. Today, several dozen farmhouse-made cheeses are produced as local specialities, and are worth sampling. There are two blue cheeses produced in Ireland. Cashel Blue is a semi-soft, medium-strength unpasteurized cow's milk cheese with a creamy texture. Its sister cheese is Crozier Blue, made from pasteurized sheep's milk, as delicious young and crumbly as it is when mature and creamy. Both are from Tipperary. Durrus is a round, semi-soft raw milk cheese with a coral-coloured washed rind, produced on the Sheep's Head Peninsula. Milleens is a similar style of cheese from the Beara Peninsula, as is Gubbeen, from Schull on Mizen Head. Another washed-rind cheese, with a rich, earthy flavour, Ardrahan comes from inland County Cork. Corleggy is a hard goat's milk cheese made in County Cavan. The same producers make Quivvy, a soft goat's milk cheese preserved in olive oil.

Stouts and Ales

Guinness is Ireland's most famous drink, and many believe that it tastes best on home soil, close to where it is brewed in Dublin, because the taste and texture of this dark, heavy beer, also known as "stout" is affected by how it is stored. A perfect pint is poured slowly and topped with a thick, creamy head. Other good Irish stouts are Beamish and the slightly milder Murphy's. Ales, made with malted barley, are also very popular. The best-selling brand is Smithwick's, produced at Ireland's oldest brewery, in Kilkenny. In pubs, be sure to try the excellent "real ales" that are produced by local micro-breweries.

Irish Whiskey

Whiskey has been made in Ireland since at least the 12th century. The first commercial distillery, Kilbeggan, was founded in 1757. There are currently more than 20 distilleries in operation, the most well known being Bushmills and Cooley. Several working and former distilleries offer tours that explain the Irish triple-distillation process. Irish whiskey is matured in wooden casks for at least seven years, giving it a distinctive flavour.

Below far left Traditional Irish bar signs **Below left** The Temple Bar, Dublin **Below centre** Dublin coddle **Below right** Irish coffee pudding **Below far right** High-quality Galway salmon

The Irish Pub

The archetypal Irish pub is noted for its friendly locals, genial staff and the *craic* (pronounced "crack", an Irish term for good times). Irish pubs date back to medieval taverns, coaching inns and the *shebeens*, illegal drinking dens, that flourished under colonial rule. In the Victorian era, brewing and distilling were major industries. The interiors of some city pubs are testament to these times, furnished with mahogany and marble bar counters. Snugs, or partitioned-off booths, are another feature of Irish pubs. Some rural pubs double as the village grocery. Ireland's pub scene varies greatly from one county to the next. In the southeast, Kilkenny has great pubs, while Cork and Kerry possess some of the most picturesque. The Lower Shannon region is noted for its convivial pubs, especially in County Clare where music sessions are common. The West has an abundance of typical pubs, and the many tourists and students guarantee a profusion of good ones in Galway.

The rich landscape of the Burren plateau in Co Clare

THE
ROAD TRIPS

TRIP 1

A TASTE OF EAST CORK

Cork City to Youghal

HIGHLIGHTS

Wonderful wildlife
See exotic and endangered species roaming free at
Fota Wildlife Park

Maritime history
Learn about Irish emigration, the last days of the
Titanic and Sir Walter Raleigh in the old ports of
Cobh and Youghal

Rare birds and heavenly coves
Spot rare sea and marsh birds on a walk along the cliffs
to Paradise Cove from Ballycotton fishing harbour

Golden sands
Wander along the beautiful golden sandy beach
at Youghal

Local flavours
Sample Jameson Irish whiskey and buy fabulous picnic
fare from Cork's historic English Market

A TASTE OF EAST CORK

East Cork is a relaxed and peaceful region to visit, with many beautiful places to enjoy, from the stately home and wildlife park of Fota to the golden beaches and clifftop walks of Youghal and Ballycotton. The expanse of coastline and harbours including historic Cobh has endowed the area with a rich maritime legacy. This short drive begins in Cork City itself, and follows the shores of lovely Cork Harbour to reach the spectacular bays of Ballycotton and Youghal. It also ventures inland from the fishing villages of the shore through the lush pastures that provide the fresh produce – from fine cheeses to pig's feet and oysters to corned mutton – for which the region is justly celebrated.

Above Graceful curve of the limestone Parliament Bridge in Cork City, built in 1806 and spanning the south channel of the River Lee, see pp34–5

ACTIVITIES

Follow the Titanic Trail and undergo the Titanic Experience in historic Cobh

Watch a cookery demonstration at Ballymaloe House

Set sail for a sea-angling trip in lovely Ballycotton Bay

Enjoy a swim from the 8-km (5-mile) Blue Flag beach of Youghal

Above View across Ballycotton Bay to the fishing village of Ballycotton and its sheltering island, *see p37*

KEY

— Drive route

Above The peaceful promenade and bandstand in Cobh, on Great Island, *see p36*

PLAN YOUR DRIVE

Start/finish: Cork City to Youghal.

Number of days: 2, allowing half a day to explore Cork City.

Distance: 86 km (53 miles).

Road conditions: Roads are good, with most of the drive taking place on regional roads. There are some smaller, unclassified roads towards the end of the drive. On such roads there may not be a central line marked, and drivers should take care on bends in case of oncoming vehicles.

When to go: East Cork is lovely in every season, but be prepared for mixed weather – warm sunshine, rain or cold winds – at any time of year, and pack appropriate clothing.

Opening times: Most shops and attractions open 9 or 10am–5 or 6pm. Shops open Mon–Sat; in large towns also 12–6pm on Sun. Convenience stores in villages open 8am until late.

Main market days: Cork City: Mon–Sat; **Cobh:** Farmers' Market, Fri; **Midleton:** Farmers' Market, Sat.

Shopping: In Cork City, explore the small shops of the pedestrianized Huguenot Quarter, and don't miss the English Market, Ireland's finest covered market. Midleton is home to Jameson Irish whiskey, where visitors can purchase as well as sample.

Major festivals: Cork City: Harbour Festival, Jun; Jazz Festival and East Cork Early Music Festival, Oct; Film Festival, Nov; **Cobh:** People's Regatta, Aug; **Midleton:** Food and Drink Festival, Sep.

DAY TRIP OPTIONS

For **lovers of history**, a day divided between Cork City and Cobh would be time well spent. **Epicureans** will enjoy Midleton and Shanagarry, which offer both fine whiskey and fine food, while, for **families**, the wonderful beaches, clifftop walks and historic harbours of Ballycotton and Youghal would be hard to beat. For full details, *see p37*.

Above The elegant English Market in Cork City

VISITING CORK CITY

Parking
There are plenty of multi-storey car parks in the city. Try the covered, multi-storey Grand Parade car park or park on the streets around Grand Parade, St Patrick's Street and South Mall, with a disk which can be purchased at newsagents or convenience stores.

Tourist Information
125 St Patrick's Street; 021 425 5100; www.purecork.ie

WHERE TO STAY IN CORK CITY

Hotel Isaacs *moderate*
Just minutes from the city centre, this is a pleasant hotel in a restored Victorian building, with plenty of character and elegantly furnished rooms. There's a good restaurant here, as well as a cask bar, set in a former antiques shop, located just opposite
48 MacCurtain Street; 021 450 0011; www.hotelisaacscork.com

Hayfield Manor *expensive*
This luxurious and intimate five-star hotel is very near the city centre but set on its own secluded grounds. The drawing room or library are charming for morning coffee or afternoon tea.
Perrott Avenue, College Road; 021 484 5900; www.hayfieldmanor.ie

❶ CORK CITY

Co Cork

Cork is a compact city with a lively atmosphere and plenty of historic sights. There are museums and churches to explore, and a church steeple to climb with bells to ring. Whether it's the impressive architecture of Cork Opera House, great local produce of the indoor English Market, or the little shops and cafés of the Huguenot Quarter, there's something for everyone to love in this friendly city.

A half-day walking tour

From the car park on **Grand Parade** ①, turn right. The **Cork City Library** ② *(closed Sun)* is across Grand Parade and further along on the same side is **Bishop Lucey Park** ③, which has remains of a 13th-century city wall. Cross Grand Parade again for the indoor **English Market** ④ *(closed Sun)*. At the end of Grand Parade, turn right into St Patrick Street. The pedestrianized streets of the **Huguenot Quarter** ⑤, running between St Patrick Street and Paul Street, are worth exploring, with lots of small shops, cafés and galleries. Turn left on Paul Street, then right into **Cornmarket Street** ⑥ where there is an outdoor market, especially good on a Saturday. Turn left into Kyle Street, then right into North Main Street and across the road to reach **St Peter's Cork** ⑦ *(closed Sun)*,

Sculptures at Crawford Art Gallery

with local and national exhibitions. Leaving here, turn left and, at the River Lee, turn right along the quays to the glass-fronted **Cork Opera House** ⑧ and the **Crawford Art Gallery** ⑨ *(open daily)*, with works by Jack B Yeats, Louis le Brocquy and Paul Henry. Cross the river here, turn left, then immediately right along Upper John Street, taking the first left onto Dominick Street for the historic Shandon area. Over to the right is the landmark **St Ann's Church** ⑩. The bells in its 36-m- (120-ft-) steeple, which is open to climb, are famous and, for anyone who ascends to the top, it is possible to try their hand at ringing them, and admire the views. Around the corner on O'Connell Square is the **Cork Butter Museum** ⑪ *(open daily)*, in what was the world's largest butter market, telling the story of Ireland's most important food export.

Above Tall, pastel-shaded buildings add character to the sweep of Popes Quay, Cork City

The English Market

Although there has been a market here since 1610, the current elegant covered market hall was built in 1786, and extensively restored after fires in 1980 and 1986. Despite its name (dating from the days of English rule) the best of regional and national produce is to be found here, from fine cheeses to pigs' feet, but there are also delicacies from around the world. The galleried upper level makes for great people-watching, and you can sample local fare at its cafés and restaurants.

Turn left and walk down Shandon Street to the river, turn right along North Mall and Sunday's Well Road and turn right into Convent Avenue for a tour of the 19th-century Gothic-style **Cork City Gaol** ⑫ *(open daily)*.

Return to Sunday's Well Road and cross the river via **Daly's Bridge** ⑬, a fine 1926 suspension footbridge (known as "the shaky bridge" because it moves as people cross it) into **Fitzgerald Park** for the **Cork Public Museum** ⑭ *(open Tue–Sat, Sun afternoons)*, which tells the history of Cork and its most famous citizens.

From here, walk south, crossing Western Road, and over the South Channel of the River Lee to the campus of University College Cork. Don't miss the contemporary art at the **Glucksman Gallery** ⑮ *(open Tue–Sat, Sun afternoons)*; its cantilevered concrete design is an artwork in itself.

Turn right along the River Lee and Lancaster Quay, right again at the end onto Wandesford Quay, then right into Sharman Crawford Street. **St Fin Barre's Cathedral** ⑯ was consecrated in 1870 on the site of a monastery founded by the saint in the 7th century. Its elegant spires are a city landmark. Walk back to the river, cross it and turn right into Washington Street to return to Grand Parade.

🚗 *From Cork City, take the N8, then N25 signed to Waterford. Turn right on R624 to Cobh and continue on this for 4 km (2.5 miles) to Fota Wildlife Park.*

② Fota Wildlife Park & House
Carrigtwohill, Co Cork
Founded in 1983 as an adjunct to Dublin Zoo, and situated on Fota Island, the **Fota Wildlife Park** *(open daily)* is a conservation centre where wildlife can roam free. It is home to some rare Asian species, such as red pandas, Sumatran tigers and Indian rhino, and also features one of the world's finest cheetah breeding programmes. **Fota House** *(open Mar–Oct: daily; Nov & Feb: Sat & Sun)* is the 19th-century Regency-style house at the heart of the estate, with a superb art collection and fine Neo-Classical interiors. Its arboretum includes rare trees and shrubs from around the world; the lovely gardens also feature a fernery and an orangery.

🚗 *On leaving the Fota Wildlife Park, turn right and follow the R624 over the bridge to Great Island and Cobh.*

Above Cork City's lowering Gothic-style 19th-century Gaol

EAT AND DRINK IN CORK CITY

Farmgate Café *inexpensive*
Fresh ingredients are transformed into classic regional dishes – from oysters and chowder to Irish lamb stew – in this lively market setting.
English Market; 021 427 8134; www.farmgate.ie; closed Sun

Jacobs on the Mall *moderate*
Foodies flock to this award-winning restaurant for tasty, modern European cuisine served in converted Turkish baths. Excellent three-course meals for €35.
30 South Mall; 021 425 1530; www.jacobsonthemall.com; open eves only, closed Sun & Mon

Jacques Restaurant *expensive*
This restaurant serves quality Irish dishes such as West Cork scallops with almond and raisin salsa.
23 Oliver Plunkett Street; 021 427 7387; www.jacquesrestaurant.ie; closed Sun & Mon

Above The Old Distillery at Midleton
Above right Huge copper pot still at the Jameson Experience, Midleton

VISITING COBH

Parking
Parking along the waterfront is free for the first hour, but then requires a disk available from local shops. There are two free car parks: one on the waterfront; one above the cathedral.

Tourist Information
Market House, Casement Square; 021 481 3896; www.visitcobh.com

WHERE TO STAY

AROUND MIDLETON

Barnabrow Country House *moderate*
A relaxed manor house set in its own grounds with well-designed rooms and cottages; on a clear day there are views all the way to Ballycotton Island. The walled garden supplies the kitchen.
Cloyne, Midleton (take R629 from Midleton, then left on R631); 021 465 2534; www.barnabrowhouse.ie

AROUND SHANAGARRY

Garryvoe Hotel *moderate*
This comfortable and completely wheelchair accessible hotel has views over the stunning beach at Garryvoe as well as Ballycotton Bay. A classy restaurant, a bistro and the cool Cave Pub add to the charm of this hotel.
Ballycotton Bay, Castlemartyr (on drive route taking R632 from Midleton to Shanagarry); 021 464 6718; www.garryvoehotel.com

BALLYCOTTON

Bayview Hotel *moderate*
This is a comfortable and relaxing hotel in the quiet fishing village of Ballycotton, with views over the Bay.
021 464 6746; www.thebayviewhotel.com; closed Oct–Easter

❸ Cobh
Co Cork

Cobh, once known as Queenstown, on Great Island is a pretty town with bright Victorian terraces overlooking Cork Harbour, one of the world's deepest natural harbours.

Cobh was the last port for the ill-fated *Titanic*, and the Queenstown Story at the **Cobh Heritage Centre** *(www.cobhheritage.com; closed Mon)* tells the history of the liner as well as that of Irish emigration to America – two and a half million people left from Cobh alone after the Famine. The **Titanic Trail** *(www.titanic.ie; departs Commodore Hotel daily at 11am & 2pm)*, a guided walking tour, takes in sights such as the Titanic Memorial, the White Star Line office and **Cobh Museum** *(Apr–Oct: open daily)*.
🚗 *Retrace route on R624 north to N25 junction. Here, take second exit signed N25 to Rosslare. Continue on N25, then turn left onto R627 signed to Midleton.*

❹ Midleton
Co Cork

Midleton is a busy commercial town, and a major centre of production for Irish whiskey. Find out how "the water of life" is distilled at the **Jameson Distillery** *(www.jamesonwhiskey.com; open daily)*, which has been operating since 1780. There are guided tours, ending with a sample glass or tutored tasting *(book in advance)*. En route to Shanagarry are the magnificent golden sands of Garryvoe beach.
🚗 *From Midleton, return to the N25 and follow the road to Castlemartyr. Turn right at the bridge onto the R632 for Ladysbridge. Go through Garryvoe and follow R632 to Shanagarry.*

Ballymaloe Cookery School
Ballymaloe attracts would-be chefs and keen cooks from far and wide. It was founded by Darina Allen in 1983, and the renowned chef remains at its helm today. Courses on offer range from short demonstrations to half a day or a full 12-week Certificate Course for budding professionals. The school (and restaurant) kitchen is supplied with herbs, fruits and vegetables from the 200-year-old gardens *(021 464 6785; www.cookingisfun.ie)*.

Above Gateway to Ballymaloe House

❺ Shanagarry
Co Cork

Shanagarry was the birthplace of William Penn, the founding father of Pennsylvania. His ancestral home, Shanagarry Castle, is now mostly in ruins and is off limits to the public.

Today Shanagarry is probably most famous of all as the location of **Ballymaloe House** and its celebrated cookery school (from the village follow signs to the cookery school or take the R629 towards Cloyne to the front entrance). Non-guests may visit the **gardens** *(open Mon–Sat)* and shop, which sells local produce, seasonal plants and fancy kitchenware.

🚗 *From Shanagarry, take a left turn at the petrol station onto the R629 and follow to Ballycotton.*

⑥ Ballycotton
Co Cork

Ballycotton is a quiet fishing village overlooking a pretty island with a lighthouse that shelters its harbour from Atlantic gales. Rare seabirds take shelter at the marshland bird sanctuary during stormy weather, but around 300 species of bird in all visit Ballycotton during the year. A fishing fleet and sea-angling vessels are based in the harbour. There are various coves and shore walks, and the cliff walk has great views, as well

as steep steps down to a rocky swimming cove, known aptly as Paradise. Take heed of warning signs and fenced-off areas on the walk.

🚗 *Take R629 back to Shanagarry, then turn right onto R632. On reaching Ladysbridge, turn right onto R633 to Ballymacoda. There, turn left onto R634 to Youghal, passing along its picturesque strand.*

⑦ Youghal
Co Cork

The 8 km (5 miles) of golden sandy beach at Youghal naturally play an important part in its popularity as a seaside resort. However, the town is also steeped in history and it is said that Sir Walter Raleigh planted the first Irish potato here in 1585. The ancient port retains original walls and towers from the 13th century. The Clock Gate over the main street dates from 1777; the Collegiate Church of Saint Mary the Virgin from 1220.

Above Ballycotton Island with its lighthouse, buffeted by Atlantic breakers

EAT AND DRINK

COBH
Jacob's Ladder *moderate*
Modern Irish cuisine in a lovely setting with views over Cork Harbour. Try Irish mussels in a coconut cream sauce. *WatersEdge Hotel; 021 481 5566; www.watersedgehotel.ie/restaurant*

MIDLETON
Farm Gate *moderate*
The store fronting this popular eatery gives a flavour of the delicious organic and home-baked produce on offer. *The Coolbawn; 021 463 2771; www.farmgate.ie; dinner served Thu–Sat only; closed Sun & hols*

SHANAGARRY
Ballymaloe House *expensive*
Home of celebrity chef Darina Allen *(see Ballymaloe Cookery School box)*, Ballymaloe is acclaimed for gourmet cuisine using local garden produce. Also offers luxury accommodation. *Shanagarry; 021 465 2531; www.ballymaloe.ie*

YOUGHAL
Aherne's of Youghal *expensive*
Local seafood is a speciality in this cosy restaurant and bar in historic Youghal. *163 North Main Street, Youghal; 024 92424; www.ahernes.net*

Above The beautiful golden sands at the historic port town of Youghal

DAY TRIP OPTIONS
Cork, Midleton and Ballycotton are ideal bases to explore the local history, scenery and gourmet delights.

East Cork history trail
Spend the morning exploring historic Cork City ❶, then make the short drive out to Cobh ❸ to walk the Titanic Trail.

Follow the drive instructions but, instead of turning off to Fota Island, continue on the R624 direct to Cobh.

Fine Irish food and drink
Nominate a designated driver, or hire a taxi, to travel the short distance from the Jameson Distillery in Midleton ❹ to the food-lover's paradise of Ballymaloe House at Shanagarry ❺.

Follow the drive instructions from Midleton to Shanagarry.

A day at the seaside
Go beach-hopping from Ballycotton ❻, ending the day with a seafood supper at Aherne's in Youghal ❼.

Follow the drive instructions or take the coastal road out to the rugged Knockadoon Head.

TRIP 2

ISLANDS AND LIGHTHOUSES
Kinsale to Macroom

HIGHLIGHTS

Unspoiled beaches
Escape to a tranquil island and stroll on deserted,
sandy beaches

Spectacular Sheep's Head
Walk around the tip of this peninsula for stunning vistas
and perhaps a glimpse of whales or dolphins

Breathtaking peninsulas
Explore rugged scenery, coves and mountains, stopping
off at pretty fishing villages and historic sights

Lighthouse panoramas
Visit one of the region's many lighthouses and take in
some panoramic coastal views

ISLANDS AND LIGHTHOUSES

West Cork offers some of Ireland's most scenic driving routes, with no fewer than three long, spectacular peninsulas to explore, each stretching southwest into the Atlantic. This drive encompasses a mix of wild forest and lush, cultivated farmland; unspoiled, golden beaches, rocky coves and inlets; and historic ruins and castles. There are opportunities to visit islands including Cape Clear, Sherkin, Hare, Bere, Dursey and the lonely Fastnet Rock, the most southerly point in Ireland. And all along the route are the tall, imposing lighthouses and beacons that guide ships safely to secluded harbours and bays, from the moody Fastnet lighthouse to the stunning white beacon at Baltimore or the Mizen Head Signal Station perched high on the sea-battered cliffs. As if that weren't enough, every little village on the way has its share of pubs and great regional cooking.

ACTIVITIES

Have a surfing lesson at Inchydoney Island

Look out for whales and dolphins from headlands such as Galley Head

Take a boat trip to an island such as Cape Clear, Sherkin, or the iconic Fastnet Rock

Walk part of the Sheep's Head Way, a waymarked track across rolling countryside and along rugged cliffs

Pedal a stretch of the Beara Way, a cycle route running along picturesque country roads

0 kilometres 10

0 miles 10

KEY

 Drive route

Above Pretty shops and houses lining the winding cobbled streets of Kinsale, *see p42*

PLAN YOUR DRIVE

Start/finish: Kinsale to Macroom.

Number of days: 4–5.

Distance: 340 km (210 miles).

Road conditions: Roads are generally good. However, some minor roads may not have central markings so take things slowly and watch out for oncoming vehicles.

When to go: West Cork can be busy at any time of year. It is most peaceful in the winter months, although some restaurants and sights may be closed. The climate is mild all year, but the weather can change quickly, so be prepared for sun or rain.

Opening times: Most shops and attractions open 9 or 10am–5 or 6pm. Shops open Mon–Sat; in large towns also 12–6pm on Sun. Convenience stores in villages open 8am until late.

Main market days: Kinsale: Wed; Clonakilty: Fri; Skibbereen: Sat; Schull: Sun; Bantry: Fri. These are among the country's best Farmers' Markets and an ideal way to sample the area's fine produce.

Shopping: With its temperate climate, lush farmlands and traditional farming methods, West Cork has become well-known for its excellent artisan food producers. World-class cheeses from Gubbeen and Durrus, cured meats from Gubbeen and slow-smoked wild fish from the Woodcock Smokery are just some of the treats on sale in shops and on farms.

Major festivals: Kinsale: Arts Weekend, Jul; Gourmet Festival, Oct; **Baltimore**: Fiddle Fair, May; **Skibbereen**: Taste of West Cork, Sep; **Cape Clear**: International Storytelling Festival, Sep; **Bantry**: West Cork Chamber Music Festival, Jun–Jul.

DAY TRIP OPTIONS

Based in Baltimore, spend a day on one of the **islands**. Visiting one of the three **peninsulas** would also make a perfect day trip. For full details, *see p49*.

Left Empty, silken sands of lovely Barley Cove Beach on the Mizen Head peninsula, *see p45*

Above Traditional shop sign in Clonakilty

VISITING KINSALE

Parking
Pay-and-display in the car park next to the Tourist Office and along Pier Road. Free car parks on Church Square and New Road.

Tourist Information
Pier Road; 021 477 2234; www.kinsale.ie

WHERE TO STAY

KINSALE

Acton's Hotel *moderate*
This is an old favourite in an excellent location near the harbour. Enjoy the bar and restaurant, or relax and admire sea views from the gardens.
Pier Road; 021 477 9900; www.actonshotelkinsale.com

The Old Presbytery *moderate*
This is an atmospheric former presbytery, dating back to the early 1800s. Rooms are traditional but comfortable and some have brass and iron beds and claw-foot baths.
43 Cork Street; 021 477 2027; www.oldpres.com

INCHYDONEY ISLAND

Inchydoney Island Lodge & Spa
expensive
This resort spa has rooms and apartments with sea views. Short break packages, with accommodation and treatments included, are popular.
023 883 3143; www.inchydoney island.com

① Kinsale
Co Cork
Kinsale is a pretty town set around a harbour, with narrow streets full of small, eye-catching shops. Kinsale also has a reputation for fine food and gourmet dining, with plenty of atmospheric restaurants and pubs and gourmet-themed events. The tourist office is a good place to start exploring the town, with some great craft shops nearby. **Desmond Castle** in Cork Street, built in around 1500, has been used as a Spanish arsenal and a prison, but is now closed for renovation. On leaving town the road passes the 17th-century, star-shaped Charles Fort, its two huge bastions overlooking the estuary. This lovely stretch of waterway is the venue for international sailing events.

🚗 *Take the coast road past Kinsale Yacht Club and cross the river at the bridge, following the R600. At the junction with the R604, turn left. Then turn left again at the Speckled Door pub onto the L3233 for Old Head.*

② Old Head of Kinsale
Co Cork
This is the nearest point to the spot where the *Lusitania* was sunk by a German U-boat in 1915. The event is commemorated in the **Lusitania Museum** *(open daily)*, which is located within the Old Signal Tower. The tower is one of the 81 such structures that were built during the Napoleonic wars in response to the threat of French invasion. The tower overlooks the waters in which the attack took place. There is a memorial garden too.

🚗 *Turn back along the L3233 and turn left onto the R604, passing two Blue Flag beaches at Garrylucas and Garretstown. Turn left onto the L3222, passing by Ballinspittle. At crossroads continue on R600, then turn left onto N71 (Convent Road), entering Clonakilty. Go straight across roundabout at the edge of town, down to the harbour.*

③ Clonakilty
Co Cork
Clonakilty is a delightful heritage town that is a pleasure to explore, with colourful and traditional shop fronts whose hand-painted, old-style signs reveal their contents, such as Knitwell Wools, Quirky Kitchen and Harrington's Original Recipe Black Pudding. Spiller's Lane is a pretty, enclosed lane lined with little shops and galleries. The town is also a major centre for live music.

The **Michael Collins House** *(closed Sun & Mon)* tells the story of the Irish patriot through interactive and audio-visual displays and artifacts. The town centre features a memorial to him; there is also a garden commemorating John F Kennedy, whose ancestors came from Clonakilty. The **West Cork Model Railway Village** *(open daily)* is great for children: this miniature West Cork villages linked by a 1940s-era model of the now-closed railway line.

🚗 *From the harbour, leave town with the bay on the left. On reaching a Y-junction, take the right-hand fork, then continue straight on at the next junction, following the road down to Inchydoney Beach and Island.*

Above Tranquil estuary of the River Bandon, just outside Kinsale

Above Inchydoney Beach, one of the loveliest on this stretch of coastline

Michael Collins

Michael Collins (1890–1922), the nationalist military and political leader, was born in Clonakilty at a time when West Cork was the nationalist heartland. He rose to prominence during and after the Easter Rising of 1916, but was assassinated aged 31. His monument in Clonakilty was unveiled in 2002 by Liam Neeson, who played him in the film based on his life.

④ Inchydoney Island
Co Cork

This little island is linked to the mainland by a causeway, so you can drive on to it. The focal point is Inchydoney Island Lodge & Spa, a luxury resort spa with a thalassotherapy pool. Inchydoney is also home to the **Inchydoney Surf School**, which offers surf rental and a range of surfing lessons provided the waves are good.
🚗 *Return to Clonakilty and take the N71 for Skibbereen. After Lisavaird, turn left signed for Long Strand. Take the right-hand fork at the Y-junction onto the R598. After Rathbarry, take the second exit at the roundabout by Castlefreke Post Office. Take the next right turn for Galley Head and go straight through the next crossroads, then turn right. Stop when the cliffs come into view.*

⑤ Galley Head
Co Cork

Galley Head is an attractive headland jutting out into the Atlantic Ocean. Dating from 1873, the **lighthouse** here was one of the most powerful of its day. On private property run by the Irish Landmark Trust, the lighthouse now functions as

self-catering accommodation. The rocks at the end are a good place from which to spot whales and dolphins. The drive to Dromberg passes some lovely beaches as well as the ruins, in private grounds, of Castlefreke Castle.
🚗 *Return along the road and take the first left onto the L4006, then go straight through the next crossroads. The Warren Blue Flag beach and Castlefreke Dunes are on your left. Turn left onto the R598 to Rathbarry for Castlefreke Castle and Wood. Continue on the R598, from which there is a lovely viewpoint on the left, overlooking headlands and islands. You'll also pass Owenahincha beach. Turn left onto the N71 to Rosscarbery, then left again onto the R597 towards Glandore. At Drombeg, take a left signed for the Stone Circle. There is a car park, from which the circle is just short walk away.*

Above Lighthouse at Galley Head

VISITING INCHYDONEY AND GALLEY HEAD

Inchydoney Surf School
Inchdoney Beach; 086 869 5396; www.inchydoneysurfschool.com; open Jun–Sep: daily; Oct–May: Sat–Sun

Galley Head Lighthouse
Tours run by the Irish Landmark Trust. *www.irishlandmark.com*

EAT AND DRINK

KINSALE
The Fish Market *moderate*
This restaurant, in the Blue Haven Hotel, serves modern Irish cuisine with seafood and fresh locally sourced produce both strongly featured.
3/4 Pearse Street; 021 477 2209; www.bluehavenkinsale.com; closed Oct–Mar: Sun & Mon

Fishy Fishy *moderate*
Not surprisingly, from the name, this busy restaurant and deli serves locally caught seafood with a twist in bright modern surroundings. Try pan-fried scallops with Rosscarbery black pudding.
Crowley's Quay; 021 470 0415; www.fishyfishy.ie; open mid-Mar–mid-Oct: daily

CLONAKILTY
An Súgán *inexpensive*
This bar/restaurant is renowned for its great seafood, including Bantry Bay mussels. Its open fires and child-friendly atmosphere make it a popular spot.
41 Wolfe Tone Street; 023 883 3719; www.ansugan.com

De Barra *inexpensive*
A cosy, wood-panelled pub that's a mecca for musicians, with traditional Irish music on Mondays, and live music nearly every other night.
56 Pearse Street; 023 883 3381; www.debarra.ie

AROUND GALLEY HEAD
Pilgrim's *moderate*
This pretty little restaurant, on the road to Drombeg Stone Circle, serves up fresh, inventive, modern takes on local produce, including foraged ingredients and some global flavour influences.
6 South Square, Rosscarbery; 023 883 1796; www.pilgrims.ie; open Wed–Sat eve, Sun lunch;

Above Ancient stone circle, Drombeg
Above centre Boat in the Sound at Union
Hall **Above right** Baltimore's Beacon

VISITING BALTIMORE

Sherkin Island Ferries make the
15-minute crossing from Baltimore
daily year-round (087 911 7377;
www.sherkinisland.eu; open from
7:45am Mon–Fri, 9am Sat, 10:30am
Sun, last ferry 5:30pm).

Cape Clear Island Ferry Service
departs Baltimore daily year-round
(028 39159; www.capeclearferries.com).

Heir Island MV *Tresher* makes the
crossing to Heir Island year-round (086
809 2447; www.heirislandferry.com).

WHERE TO STAY

BALTIMORE

Rolf's Country House *moderate*
This charming bed-and-breakfast is in
an old farmhouse with stone cottages
and converted outbuildings. The
whole complex, from the thriving café
and wine bar to the quiet garden with
sea views, has great character.
*Baltimore Hill; 028 20289; www.rolfs
countryhouse.com*

Casey's of Baltimore *moderate*
This popular hotel, traditional pub and
seafood restaurant (see opposite) is at
the entrance to Baltimore and makes a
great base for exploring the area. Many
of the rooms overlook the quiet bay.
*028 20197; www.caseysofbaltimore.
com; closed 20–26 Dec*

SKIBBEREEN

West Cork Hotel *moderate*
This family-run riverside hotel is a
good base from which to explore the
surrounding coastline. Many of the en
suite rooms enjoy views over the river,
as do the bar and breakfast room.
*Ilen Street; 028 21277; www.westcork
hotel.com*

6 Drombeg Stone Circle
Co Cork
Known locally as the Druid's Altar,
and in a magnificent setting with sea
views, this circle of 13 (originally 17)
pillar stones dates back to around
900 BC. During excavation in the
1950s, a pot containing the cremated
remains of a young woman was found
in the centre, dating from 150 BC.

*Drive back onto the R597 to arrive
at the attractive village of Glandore,
on a picturesque bay. Drive through
the village and around the coast. Turn
left signed for Union Hall and cross the
bridge over the Sound, turning right
signed for Castletownshend. Take the
next right, signposted for Skibbereen,
drive through Rineen and, at the
T-junction, turn left. Take a sharp
left at the next crossroads onto the
R596 for Castletownshend.*

7 Castletownshend
Co Cork
This is a pretty village set on a steep
hill. Drive down the village to the
pier at the end. There is a secluded
cove with boats moored, and to the
left, the Castle, which is now an upmarket hotel, dates back to the 1600s
and is still owned by the Townsend
family. The village was home for
many years to Somerville and Ross,
authors of *Experiences of an Irish R M.*

*Drive back through the village
and turn left onto the L4218. There
will be lovely cliff views to the left.
Toe Head, off the road to the left,
has great views, and the village of
Tragumna has a fabulous bay and
a Blue Flag beach, but beware of
the strong rip and rocks. After
Tragumna, turn left at the first*

*T-junction and take the next right,
then next left, then right again and
then a slight left at the next fork.
Keep left at the next junction and
then left again for Lough Hyne.*

8 Lough Hyne
Co Cork
Lough Hyne (also known as Lough
Ine) is a salt-water lake and Ireland's
only marine nature reserve. The lake
is fed by the sea through a narrow
channel that causes irregular tidal
movements. There are many species
of plants and animals, including sea
urchins and oysters, and the lake is
studied intensively by marine bio-
logists and scientists. An Interpretive
Centre in Skibbereen (see right) gives
more information on what is found
in the lake, which is also the subject
of poetry and local folklore.

*Follow the road left, signed for
Baltimore, and turn left at the R595.*

9 Baltimore
Co Cork
This tiny coastal village, set in lovely
scenery and with ideal conditions for
watersports, is the reason why there
are so many holiday homes in the
area. Nestled around a harbour, and
warmed by the Gulf Stream, it offers
sailing, angling, diving, kayaking,
whale- and dolphin-watching and
boat trips to the islands (Sherkin, Cape
Clear and Heir), Lough Hyne and the
Fastnet lighthouse. The harbour
bustles with boats, especially in
summer. The small central "square"
offers plenty of dining options.

Drive or walk to The Beacon (turn
left at the harbour) for fantastic views
out to sea and over to Sherkin Island.

It's a steep climb, and it is dangerous to visit the Beacon in high winds.
🚗 *Follow the R595 all the way from Baltimore to Skibbereen.*

⑩ Skibbereen
Co Cork
The busy town of Skibbereen has strong ties to the Great Famine of the 1840s, which devastated the local community. There is a large famine graveyard at Abbystrowry, nearby. The **Heritage Centre** *(open mid-Mar–Apr & Oct: Tue–Sat; May–Sep: Mon–Sat)* has an excellent exhibition on the subject. It also houses the Lough Hyne Interpretive Centre, with information on the marine nature reserve, including an aquarium.
🚗 *At the roundabout in Skibbereen take the N71 west, signed to Bantry. Bear left onto R592, entering Ballydehob, to begin the 37-km (23-mile) drive around Mizen Head.*

⑪ Mizen Head Peninsula
The first stop on the drive to Mizen Head is the village of **Schull**, with its busy harbour. Its Sunday market features crafts as well as fresh local produce.
Stay on the R592 signed to **Goleen**, then turn left onto the L4406 for the "coast road" (it actually runs a little inland). After the crossroads, keep left at the Y-junction. There are great views of Clear Island and the Fastnet Rock and lighthouse. After Toormore, stay on the R591 for Mizen Head. Just after Goleen is **Spanish Point**, where there is a lighthouse. Further on, the pretty village of **Crookhaven** can be seen

Skibbereen's famine memorial, in the form of a Celtic Cross

Fastnet Rock
Fastnet Lighthouse, 7 km (4.5 miles) out in the Atlantic from Cape Clear Island, is visible from much of West Cork's coastline, and is the tallest and widest lighthouse in Ireland and Great Britain. The Rock is Ireland's most southerly point, and is the rounding marker for the gruelling Fastnet yacht race.

across a lovely sound. Ships stocked up on provisions here before setting sail for America. In 1837, there were 424 residents – now there are around 40. On the left you'll pass the secluded **Galley Cove**. Keep left onto the L4402 for Mizen Head. Further along on the left is the car park for **Barley Cove Beach**, a short walk away along a boardwalk through the dunes. This is a conservation area, full of birds, flora and fauna. Turn left at the next junction, signed for **Mizen Head**, Ireland's most south-westerly point. There are great views down to Barley Cove and across to Brow Head. The 1909 **Mizen Head Signal Station** *(open mid-Mar–Oct: daily; Nov–mid-Mar: weekends)* is linked to the mainland by a 52-m (172-ft) suspension bridge and has a fascinating exhibition on its history as well as the building of the **Fastnet Rock** lighthouse. The surrounding cliffs are spectacular.
Leaving Mizen, take the first left turn for Dunlough and **Three Castle Head** which has some great Atlantic views.
🚗 *Take main road back to Toormore and turn left onto the R591 to Durrus. Turn left here for Sheep's Head.*

Above Clear tidal stream and pristine sands of Barley Cove Beach

EAT AND DRINK

BALTIMORE
Casey's of Baltimore *inexpensive*
Choose from an extensive menu of fresh seafood, including lobster dishes and mussels from their own farm in Roaringwater Bay. The bright restaurant aside, the hotel also has its own craft brewery and an organic garden. *028 20197; www.caseysofbaltimore.com; closed 20–26 Dec*

The Lookout *moderate–expensive*
This smart French restaurant specializes in seafood including fresh lobster and Sherkin Island oysters. Stunning views of both the harbour and the islands. *The Square; 028 20600; www.waterfrontbaltimore.ie; open Easter–Oct*

AROUND SKIBBEREEN
Island Cottage *moderate–expensive*
A short ferry journey from Cunnamore is Hare (or Heir) Island and The Island Cottage restaurant, with set menus only, run by chef John Desmond. The ferry must be booked in advance. *Hare Island, Skibbereen; 028 38102; www.islandcottage.com; open mid-Jun–mid-Sep: Wed–Sat eve; Apr, May & Jun: Sat & Sun lunch*

AROUND MIZEN HEAD PENINSULA
Heron's Cove B&B *moderate*
Enjoy fresh fish, game and other local produce in a secluded tidal cove with lovely views, and choose your own wine from the collection on the rack. *The Harbour, Goleen (on R591 between Toormore and Crookhaven); 028 35225; www.heronscove.com*

Left Rocky cliffs at Mizen Head

Above Traditional shop front in Kilcrohane on Sheep's Head Peninsula

VISITING BANTRY

Tourist Information
The old courthouse, The Square, Bantry; 027 50229; www.visitbantry.ie

Parking
Parking in the town centre is free but limited to 2 hours. Unlimited parking is towards the sea end of the square.

WHERE TO STAY

SHEEP'S HEAD PENINSULA

Blairscove House
inexpensive–moderate
Dating from 1760, this relaxed country house is surrounded by lush gardens. It offers B&B, self-catering cottages and apartments, and has an atmospheric restaurant in a converted stable.
Durrus (located 2.5 km/1.5 miles south of Durrus on R591 to Golleen); 027 61127; www.blairscove.ie; open mid-Mar–Oct

BANTRY

Bantry House *moderate*
Staying in this historic stately home (*see p47*) is a treasured experience. There are just six rooms, all in the east wing overlooking the splendid gardens.
Bantry Bay; 027 50047; www.bantry house.com; open Apr–Oct

GLENGARRIFF

Glengarriff Park Hotel
inexpensive–moderate
Comfortable, modern hotel at the start of the Beara Peninsula, with a smart bistro and a warming bar too.
The Village, Glengarriff; 027 63000; www.glengarriffpark.com

⑫ SHEEP'S HEAD PENINSULA

At the start of the drive out to the end of Sheep's Head from Durrus, the road runs through Ahakista, which has a peaceful waterside memorial to those who died in the Air India disaster of 1985. From Kilcrohane onwards, the road narrows and becomes more scenic, with stone walls, heather, craggy hills and breathtaking views left to Three Castle Head and the Mizen Peninsula, and right over to the Beara Peninsula. On the way, there are lots of little side turnings and stopping-off points to explore the lakes, churches, beaches, holy wells, burial grounds and secluded coves. Follow any of the brown signs. The road ends at the Tooreen Turning Table, where there is a car park and a Visitor Centre with a small café. From here, there is a marked, circular walking trail out to the Sheep's Head lighthouse on the point and back. If the keeper is there, it may be possible to see inside the lighthouse.

A two-hour walking tour

This walk is a small part of the Sheep's Head Way, a stunning long-distance walk which runs around the entire peninsula. The walk goes around the very tip of the peninsula to the lighthouse, with spectacular panoramas of the neighbouring peninsulas along the way.

Information is available from **Bernie's Café ①**, but the path is marked all the way along with blue arrows, and the signposts are made from local stone or Irish oak, in keeping with the beauty of the surroundings.

The trail passes rocky outcrops until it reaches **Lough Akeen ②**. The easiest and safest way to cross the lough is via the wooden boardwalk to the right, but it can be skirted along the cliff edge as well. The path then goes up a rocky incline and across a helicopter pad. The views from here over the sea and over to Mizen Head are breathtaking, and whales and dolphins can often be spotted, especially between July and September.

At this point, follow the steps down to reach the **lighthouse ③** at the tip of the headland. On the return from the lighthouse, halfway up the steps, go around to the left-hand side of the green container and follow the path, which leads to the northern side of the Sheep's Head peninsula. The path passes along a scenic route, but the first part can be boggy, with a slightly uneven surface. Upon reaching the top, the path runs close to the cliff edge and could be dangerous, so extreme care is needed along this stretch of the route. There are spectacular views over to the Beara Peninsula as well

0 metres 500

0 yards 500

Cliffs ④

Lough
Akeen
②

③ Lighthouse

Bernie's
Cafe
①

as the chance of seeing whales or dolphins. The cliffs, which rise to some 120 m (400 ft), are home to nesting seabirds, and visitors might be lucky enough to spot the rare chough, which frequents Sheep's Head in significant numbers.

After the **cliffs** ④, turn right at the arrow, taking the signposted path back across the headland to return to the car park and the café, which serves delicious home-baked treats.

🚗 *Drive back to Kilcrohane and then turn left onto Goat's Path Road, which winds up through the mountains. From the top of the hill pass, there are spectacular views over Roaringwater, Dunmanus and Bantry bays and over to Castletownbere, Bere Island and Dursey Island. Turn left on the N71 to reach Bantry, where there is free parking at the sea end of the square.*

⑬ Bantry
Co Cork

This large market town and fishing port is set at the head of picturesque Bantry Bay. There is an elegant open square in the centre with seating, trees and a fountain. One of Bantry's loveliest attractions is **Bantry House and Gardens** *(open Jun–Aug: daily; Apr, May, Sep & Oct: Tue–Sun; www.bantry house.com)*, a Georgian stately home built in the 18th century, with some magnificent artwork on show. Even more impressive are the formal gardens, with wonderful bay views; two woodland walks and a tea room complete this delightful visit.

Take a ferry from Bantry pier to **Whiddy Island** for walking or cycling. There are some interesting historical remains on the island, as well as a pub-restaurant.

🚗 *Follow the N71 all the way to Glengarriff via Ballylickey.*

⑭ Glengarriff
Co Cork

Glengarriff is set in a lush, green area with lovely gardens and islands. The **Glengarriff Bamboo Park** *(open daily)* is an exotic coastal garden featuring bamboo and palms, with splendid views. From Glengariff harbour, boat trips operate to **Garnish Island** *(open Apr–Oct: daily)*, where there are delightful sub-tropical Italian gardens with rare plants and a miniature temple. There is a seal colony on the island's rocky shore.

🚗 *Turn left onto R572, signed for Castletownbere. At Adrigole, continue on R572 onto the Beara Peninsula.*

West Cork Garden Trail
This marvellous trail comprises 27 different gardens around the region, each of which has its own opening times; a few are open year-round. They range from country gardens, lakes and seaside gardens to mature and historical gardens. A leaflet, detailing when the gardens are open, is available from any of the area's tourist offices or see www.westcorkgardentrail.com.

Above left Rainbow over Bantry Bay
Above Reen Point, near Ahakista on the Sheep's Head Peninsula

VISITING WHIDDY ISLAND AND GARNISH ISLAND

Whiddy Island Ferries cross from Bantry Pier to Whiddy Island several times daily. The crossing takes 10–15 minutes *(www.whiddyferry.com; 086 862 6734)*.

Harbour Queen Ferries cross from Glengarriff Pier to Garnish Island every 30 minutes daily Apr–Oct *(www. harbourqueenferry.com; 027 63116)*.

EAT AND DRINK AROUND SHEEP'S HEAD PENINSULA

Bernie's Cupan Tae *inexpensive*
This proves to be a great spot to try sandwiches, soups, tea and scones before heading towards Sheep's Head lighthouse. *Tooreen, Co Cork; 027 67878; open mid-Mar–Oct*

Below Majestic Bantry House with its marvellous view over Bantry Bay

Above Dramatic Dunboy Castle, set on the bay in Castletownbere

VISITING BERE ISLAND

Bere Island Ferries makes the crossing from Castletownbere daily year-round *(027 75009; www.bereislandferries.com).*

VISITING DURSEY ISLAND

The **Dursey Island Cable Car** shuttles back and forth every day of the year except 25–26 Dec & 1 Jan *(027 73851; www.durseyisland.ie).*

VISITING BEARA PENINSULA

Tourist Information
St Peter's Grounds, Castletownbere, Beara; 027 70054; www.beara tourism.com

WHERE TO STAY

BEARA PENINSULA
Rodeen Country House *inexpensive*
Set within sub-tropical gardens in a secluded location, this guesthouse offers panoramic views of Bere Island and Bantry Bay.
Castletownbere; 027 70838; www.rodeencountryhouse.com

GOUGANE BARRA FOREST PARK
Gougane Barra Hotel *moderate*
The setting of this family-run hotel has to be one of the most picturesque in West Cork, with views out over the tranquil lake to St Finbarr's Oratory on the island, and surrounded by forests and national parklands. Rooms are very comfortable and the home-cooked food is delicious.
Gougane Barra, Macroom; 026 47069; www.gouganebarrahotel.com; closed Nov–Mar

⑮ BEARA PENINSULA

Co Cork

The Ring of Beara is a scenic driving route that runs around the Beara Peninsula from Glengarriff to Dursey Sound and then back to Kenmare in County Kerry. Along the way are stunning coves, picturesque villages, islands, forests and mountains. Whether the weather is sunny and warm or moody and misty, this peninsula leaves a lasting impression on visitors. For archaeology enthusiasts, there are stone circles, cairns and burial grounds, some dating back to 2500 BC, while walkers and cyclists will find plenty of routes, trails and mountain paths on the Beara Way. Sea angling is also very popular. Visitors should take their time driving around the peninsula, stopping off at beaches, harbours or historical sights along the way.

On the route from Glengarriff to Castletownbere the route passes through **Adrigole** ①, whose harbour affords plenty of opportunities for water sports such as sailing, kayaking and powerboating.

Castletownbere ② is the main town on the Beara peninsula, with a busy port full of fishing trawlers. Its large natural harbour, Berehaven, is overlooked by the ruins of Dunboy Castle. Across the harbour lies **Bere Island** ③, accessible by ferry. It has an interesting military history, with parts of the island still used by the Irish army for training. There is a choice of places to eat, drink and stay on the island, and panoramic views from its Ardnakinna lighthouse.

Further along, at the very tip of the Beara Peninsula, lies **Dursey Island** ④, a rugged, almost treeless place accessible only by cable car – strong tides make it unsafe for boats. Only about ten people live here and there are no cafés or shops, but it is a peaceful spot for walks and birdwatching, and there are great Atlantic views.

The area around **Allihies** ⑤, the last village on the peninsula, used to be dotted with copper mines and there is a Copper Mine Museum *(open Easter–Oct: daily)* that tells the history of copper-mining in the area. Allihies is on lovely Ballydonegan Bay, which has a quartz strand. Many artists are drawn to the area by its scenic beauty.

The village of **Eyeries** ⑥, with its brightly painted houses, overlooks the Atlantic. The surrounding area is rich in historic sights, including an Ogham Stone (a granite pillar carved with ancient writing) at **Ballycrovane** ⑦ standing over 5 m (17 ft) high.

At Lauragh, take the **Healy Pass** ⑧ though the Caha Mountains, back to Adrigole and on to Glengarriff, or continue on the R571 to Kenmare in County Kerry *(see p54)*.

🚗 *Return to Glengarriff on the R572, then take the N71 to Ballylickey. Turn left onto the R584 and head upwards and through the spectacular Pass of Keimaneigh. At the end of the pass, turn left onto the L4643 following the signs for Gougane Barra.*

Coastal Landscapes
A driving tour around this part of the world is lovely not only for the pretty towns and villages along the way, but for its stunning coastal scenery. Cliffs and peninsulas are almost sculpted, dotted by grazing sheep or cows. The lush green pastures and hedgerows here are in contrast to the more desolate scenery of the coastline further west. Mild Gulf Stream temperatures cause everything to flourish. It is no wonder that there are so many local artisan foods produced in this area, many of which can be sampled in atmospheric pubs and restaurants along the route.

🔟 Gougane Barra Forest Park
Co Cork
This is a stunning, peaceful national park set in a lake-filled valley and surrounded by mountains and forests. It is also home to the source of Cork's River Lee. In the centre of the lake you'll see **St Finbarr's Oratory**, set on the island where St Finbarr, the founder of Cork city, built his monastery in the 6th century. The current chapel was built around 1900. The island is accessible by causeway and there are also circular cells and a well to be seen.

For those who do not have time to explore on foot, there is also a circular drive through the forest (5 km/3 miles). Follow the road with St Finbarr's to the right. But to fully

appreciate the 140 ha (350 acres) of forest park, leave the car and try one of the many signposted nature trails. In summer, the hotel *(see left)* stages a series of events down by the lake.

🚗 *Return to the R584 and turn left following signs for Macroom.*

🔟 Macroom
Co Cork
Macroom is a busy market town on the River Sullane. It has several historical features, such as the remains of a gateway and Norman tower, both of which were part of Macroom Castle. The gate gives access to the castle grounds, with fine riverside walks. Nearby, **Bealick Mill Heritage Centre** *(open Apr–Sep: daily)* is a working corn mill with a water-powered wheel.

Above Colourful façades and market cross in Macroom's main square

Above St Finbarr's Oratory, on the lake in Gougane Barra Forest Park

EAT AND DRINK AROUND BEARA PENINSULA

The Copper Kettle *inexpensive*
An atmospheric café offering sandwiches, salads and hot dishes, plus mouthwatering desserts and home-baking.
The Square, Castletownbere; 027 71792; open daytime only; closed Sun

MacCarthy's Bar *inexpensive*
Lively grocery-pub made famous following its appearance on the cover of Pete McCarthy's eponymous book; bar food is available during the day.
The Square, Castletownbere; 027 70014; www.maccarthysbar.com

DAY TRIP OPTIONS
Baltimore is a great base to visit one of West Cork's lovely islands. Take a trip to Sherkin, Cape Clear, Garinish, Whiddy, Dursey or Bere Island to sample the relaxed pace of life, or take one of the peninsula drives.

Sherkin Island
Sherkin Island, just 5 km (3 miles) long and 2 km (1 mile) wide, is a peaceful and relaxed haven, with stunning beaches such as Silver Strand and Trabawn, which are safe for swimming, as well as the ruins of O'Driscoll Castle and a Franciscan Abbey dating back to 1460 to explore. There are places to stay on

the island, and the two pubs, the Jolly Roger and Murphy's Bar, often have live music sessions. The island is also well-known for its artists.

Take the ferry from Baltimore ⑨ *(see p44).*

Cape Clear Island
This is a wild, rugged and unspoiled island and, with plenty of wild flowers, birds and beaches, it is a haven of solitude. There are breathtaking views in all directions, from the Atlantic and Fastnet Rock, to Roaringwater Bay and Baltimore. Historic sights include St Kieran's Church and O'Driscoll Castle. Walk to the 19th-century lighthouse and watchtower at the

southern end of the island – you may see whales and dolphins from here. Ireland's southernmost inhabited island is also home to a Gaeltacht (Irish-speaking area), with two Irish summer colleges. There are also craft shops, a café, two pubs and a club that often hosts music sessions.

Take the ferry from Baltimore ⑨ *or Schull; the journey time is 45 minutes.*

Peninsula drives
Explore one of the peninsulas – Mizen Head ⑪, Sheep's Head ⑫, or Beara ⑮ – from Baltimore ⑨ or Bantry ⑬.

Follow the drive instructions.

TRIP 3

THE MAJESTIC RING OF KERRY
Kenmare to Killarney

HIGHLIGHTS

Charming Kenmare
Soak up the atmosphere of this heritage town, gateway to the Ring of Kerry, and shop for fine local crafts

Remote monastic settlements
Go on a boat trip out to the island of Skellig Michael to view the early Christian monastery there, a UNESCO World Heritage Site

Island adventures
Admire awesome vistas from the Fogher Cliffs and the Martello tower at Bray Head on Valentia Island

Dramatic mountain drives
Take the high road through gaps in the Macgillycuddy Reeks range

THE MAJESTIC RING OF KERRY

The Ring of Kerry is on the Iveragh Peninsula, the largest of five peninsulas jutting out into the Atlantic from the southwest of Ireland. The scenic promontory is famed for its vistas of sea and mountains – visitors have been coming here for centuries, drawn by the sheer abundance of natural beauty. It is a popular tourist route, so don't expect splendid isolation, but this drive offers plenty of opportunities to veer off the beaten track into a dramatic landscape of coves, cliffs, broad bays and rugged countryside, all set against the Macgillycuddy Reeks, Ireland's highest mountain range. This ancient landscape is richly endowed with remnants of early Christian settlements and megalithic sites.

ACTIVITIES

Visit Iron Age Staigue Fort, the best-preserved in Ireland, set in a beautiful valley

Take a boat trip out to the island of Skellig Michael, a UNESCO World Heritage Site, to see the superb monastic ruins

Walk around Muckross Lake, through ancient forests, and have tea in an 18th-century hunting lodge

Go for an invigorating swim in the blue waters of Castlecove Bay, and canoe in nearby Derrynane Harbour

KEY

▬▬ Drive route

0 kilometres   5

0 miles   5

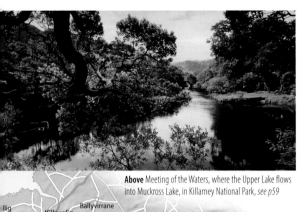

Above Meeting of the Waters, where the Upper Lake flows into Muckross Lake, in Killarney National Park, *see p59*

PLAN YOUR DRIVE

Start/finish: Kenmare to Killarney.

Number of days: 3, allowing half a day for Valentia Island and a trip to Skellig Michael island, and half a day for Killarney National Park.

Distance: 210 km (130 miles).

Road conditions: Roads are paved and signposted, but there are some steep inclines on the passes. Turns off the main Ring of Kerry are not always as well signposted.

When to go: July and August can be crowded, with tour buses dominating the main routes. The best months in which to visit are June and September. In the winter, many places beyond Kenmare and Killarney will be closed.

Opening times: Shops are generally open 9 or 10am to 5 or 6pm, but most close on Sundays except corner shops. Catholic churches stay open all day.

Main market days: Kenmare: Wed; Milltown: Sat; Killarney: Fri.

Shopping: Kenmare is renowned for its wide range of individual shops and galleries selling top-quality local art and crafts. Look out in particular for fine linen and lace.

Major festivals: Killorglin: Puck Fair (coronation of goat king), 10–12 Aug; Cahersiveen: Cahersiveen Festival of Music, Jun/Jul–Aug.

DAY TRIP OPTIONS

For **nature and history lovers**, a day spent exploring Killarney and the National Park, with beautiful lakes and historic buildings, is a perfect choice. **Outdoor enthusiasts** will enjoy the rugged cliffs of Valentia Island and then a boat trip to the ancient monastery of Skellig Michael. If time allows, finish with a walk up to the Geokaun Mountain or Fogher Cliffs. For full details, *see p59*.

Left One of many attractive cafés in the village of Sneem, *see p54*

Above Handsome Derrynane House, set in subtropical gardens where flax grows

VISITING KENMARE

Parking
Park on either side of Main Street or in the Square opposite the Tourist Office.

Tourist Information
The Square; 064 664 1233; open Mar–Oct: daily; www.kenmare.ie

WHERE TO STAY

KENMARE
Lissyclearig Thatched Cottage *inexpensive*
Charming thatched cottage featuring four rooms with lovely countryside views.
Moll's Gap Road; 064 664 2562; www.lissyclearigthatchedcottage.com

Lansdowne Arms *moderate*
A welcoming family-run hotel set in a handsome late-18th-century building.
Main Street; 064 664 1368; www.lansdownearms.com

The Park Hotel *expensive*
This chateau-style hotel offers modern comforts, in a traditional setting.
High Street; 064 664 1200; www.parkkenmare.com

SNEEM
Parknasilla Hotel *expensive*
Set in swathes of subtropical parkland overlooking Kenmare Bay, this hotel may have the best location in Ireland.
Parknasilla Resort; 064 667 5600; www.parknasillaresort.com; closed Jan–Mar

WATERVILLE
Butler Arms Hotel *moderate*
One of Ireland's best-known hotels. Charlie Chaplin was once a regular.
Waterville; 066 947 4144; www.butlerarms.com

❶ Kenmare
Co Kerry

The picturesque heritage town of Kenmare on the mouth of the River Sneem regularly comes top of many Irish people's list when asked to nominate their favourite town. It isn't completely in thrall to tourism and goes about its business in a dignified and discreet manner. Its Irish name, Neidín, translates as "little nest", and is an apt description. It lies at the head of the River Kenmare, flanked by the Ring of Beara *(see p48)* and the Ring of Kerry, making it an ideal base from which to explore either peninsula.

The town centre is compact, and its X-shaped street pattern converges in a triangular square at the junction of Henry Street and Main Street. Its narrow streets are lined with great shops and galleries, live music pubs and some excellent restaurants and cafés. The library now houses the **Carnegie Arts Centre** *(www. carnegieartskenmare.ie)*, whose state-of-the-art theatre stages a wide range of top-quality drama and concerts. It is worth dawdling a while to make the most of this delightful town. An advantage to starting the drive around the Ring from here is that there is less chance of getting stuck behind a convoy of tour buses, as the majority of tours set off from Killarney, following an anti-clockwise route around the peninsula.

Kenmare is also renowned for its traditional lace. During the famine years, nuns from the local convent, St Clare's, introduced lace making to create work for the women and girls.

🚗 *Take the main N71 from the Square and over the Cromwell Bridge, signposted for Moll's Gap and Killarney. Very shortly after the bridge, turn left onto the N70, signposted to Sneem. The drive from Kenmare to Sneem along the banks of the River Kenmare affords lovely views of the Caha and Slieve Miskish mountains on the opposite shore.*

❷ Sneem
Co Kerry

This quaintly pretty village, located at the head of an estuary flowing into Kenmare river, is built around a picturesque green on which stands a statue to the local hero Steve "Crusher" Casey, a world champion wrestler. This is a good place to stop for a quick bite or coffee. There are some nice shops, galleries and cafés off the main square.

🚗 *Continue west on the N70 in the direction of Castlecove. At a junction just before the village, there is a tea room and visitor centre for Staigue Fort. Turn right here, taking the narrow road as indicated, which leads to the fort itself, and park by the fort.*

❸ Staigue Fort
Castlecove, Co Kerry

This is an impressive ring fort, thought to date from 300–400 AD, set in a beautiful, remote valley. One of the best preserved Iron Age forts in Ireland, Staigue Fort has 5-m (16-ft) high dry-stone walls surrounded by a bank and a ditch. Access the two vaulted chambers within and climb up the ramparts. It's also well worth

Above The River Sneem before it flows into the estuary at Kenmare

walking a little way up the slopes of the valley to get a proper sense of the scale of the fort set against the surrounding landscape.

🚗 *Return to the N70 and turn right for Castlecove, then left for the beach.*

④ Castlecove
Co Kerry
The main attraction of this little resort is the beautiful white sandy beach that looks out across the River Kenmare towards the Slieve Miskish Mountains. This sheltered cove is ideal for safe swimming and is understandably popular with families. Children will also love to explore the deep rock pools for sea life when the tide is out.

🚗 *Return to N70 and continue to Caherdaniel. Turn left here, signposted to Derrynane House.*

⑤ Derrynane Bay
Co Kerry
The village of Caherdaniel sprawls along Derrynane Bay's eastern flank. You will find the excellent Blind Piper bar located at the heart of the village.

A little way beyond the village is **Derrynane House** *(open mid-Mar–mid-Dec: daily; gardens all year)*, set in a 120-ha (300-acre) wooded National Park. The former home of Daniel O'Connell *(see p58)*, it is now a museum dedicated to "The Liberator" as he is sometimes called. A hugely popular and non-violent campaigner, he championed the rights of the poor and helped bring

about Catholic emancipation in 1829. The house contains much important memorabilia, such as his triumphal chariot, state chair and deathbed. The lush subtropical gardens run down to the bay where there is a wide, sandy beach backed by dunes.

🚗 *Return to the N70 and turn left. Beyond Caherdaniel, the Ring of Kerry climbs steeply to the Coomakista Pass, with stunning views of Scariff Island and the mouth of the River Kenmare. Carry on to Waterville.*

Blind Piper pub sign, Caherdaniel

⑥ Waterville
Co Kerry
Near Waterville, on the descent from the Coomakista Pass, the jagged silhouette of Skellig Rock *(see p56)* can be seen far out to sea. The town itself is located on a long strip of land between Lough Currane and Ballinskelligs Bay. Many visitors are attracted by its extensive beach, **Waterville Strand**; a championship golf course and superb angling are other notable attractions. The beach is on the eft of the town, backed by a grassy promenade. Keep an eye out for the bronze statue of Charlie Chaplin, who was a regular visitor, staying at the Butler's Arms with his trademark bowler hat and cane. Waterville boasts many good places to eat and is an ideal stop off.

🚗 *Continue in the same direction on the N70, signposted for Cahersiveen. After New Chapel Cross turn left onto the R567, signed to Ballinskelligs.*

Above left White sands and rocky outcrops of Castlecove **Above** Sturdy remains of the impressive Iron Age Staigue Fort

EAT AND DRINK

KENMARE

No 35 Restaurant *moderate*
The menu at this informal restaurant features rare breed Saddleback pork from the owners' farm and fresh fish delivered daily.
35 Main Street; 064 664 1559; www.no35kenmare.com; closed Wed & Thu

Lime Tree Restaurant *expensive*
One of Kenmare's best restaurants, with a loyal following. The food is classic Irish with a contemporary approach. Try the shepherd's pie with a confit of garlic and thyme *jus*.
Shelbourne Street; 064 664 1225; www.limetreerestaurant.com; closed Nov–Mar: Mon–Fri

SNEEM

Sacre Coeur Restaurant *moderate*
Fresh fish features on the menu but local lamb is also a speciality.
North Square; 064 664 5186; open dinner only

WATERVILLE

Old Cable House *inexpensive*
The Old Cable House is blessed with clear views across the Atlantic, where the first transatlantic telegraph cable was laid from here to the USA in 1866. A guesthouse, it also welcomes non-residents for unfussy seafood with an emphasis on freshness and flavour. Local lamb and beef also on the menu.
Old Cable Station; 066 947 4233; www.oldcablehouse.com

Smuggler's Inn *moderate*
The watchword at this smart restaurant adjacent to the golf course overlooking Ballinskeligs Bay is sustainable seafood, such as monkfish and black sole.
Cliff Road; 066 947 4330; www.smugglersinn.ie

Above Puffin Island, seen from Coonanaspig Pass on the Skellig Ring Drive

VISITING SKELLIG MICHAEL

The **Skellig Experience Centre** organizes cruises to Skellig St Michael (Great Skellig) and Small Skellig when the sea is not too rough. For details visit the centre or its website, *www. skelligexperience.com*. Several independent boat owners can take you to the Skelligs too. On Valentia Island, try **Skellig Boat**, *087 290 6168, www. skelligboat.com*; **Skellings Rock**, *087 236 2344, www.skelligsrock.com* (Apr–mid-Oct); and **Casey's Skellig Island Tours**, *www.skelligislands.com*.

WHERE TO STAY IN BALLAGHBEAMA GAP

Blackstones House *inexpensive* Situated at the foot of Carruntuohill, Ireland's highest mountain, and overlooking the Caragh River, this friendly family-run B&B enjoys a splendid location. All rooms are en suite with views of the river and the soothing sound of its soft gurgling. *Blackstone Bridge, Glencar; 066 976 0164; www.blackstoneshouse.com*

Carrig Country House and Restaurant *moderate–expensive* A former hunting lodge, owned by Lord Brockett, this manor house is the perfect hideaway – relaxed, and with a charming atmosphere. There are wonderful views over Caragh Lake, and a restaurant, which offers exceptional cooking (non-residents are welcome). *Killorglin, Caragh Lake; 066 976 9100; www.carrighouse.com; open Mar–Oct*

⑦ Skellig Ring Drive
Co Kerry

Since there are no coach tours allowed on this stretch of the road – known as the Skellig Ring Drive – it is easy to enjoy the scenery in relative isolation. Where the R567 joins the R566, turn left and follow the road as it curves around the bay, leading to Ballinskelligs village, where there is a magnificent stretch of sandy beach. After the village, the road inclines sharply towards Bolus Head, before turning northwards, skirting Bolus Mountain. Soon the landscape opens up into thrilling vistas of a patchwork of fields sweeping down to the headland and the jagged diamond of the Skellig Rocks, rising up from a vast expanse of sea. The road continues around, skirting the edge of Saint Finan's Bay before climbing again to Coonanaspig Pass. There follows an exhilarating descent into the harbour village of Portmagee. At the foot of the hill, on the left, is the fabulous Smugglers Café. From here, it is a 20-minute walk to the nearby cliffs, which offer a spectacular view across to Valentia Island.

🚗 *From the café turn left onto the minor road and follow it onto the R565 to the left to drive over the bridge that crosses the channel to Valentia Island. Coming off the bridge, the Skellig Experience Centre is on the left.*

⑧ Valentia Island
Co Kerry

Valentia Island has an enthralling mix of towering cliffs, rolling hills and wild seascapes, and is noted for the variety of subtropical plants that have taken root here. History was made here in 1866 when the first transatlantic telegraph to the United States was laid here. Be aware that the car ferry used for part of this route runs Apr–Oct only; winter visitors will have to return from the island using the road bridge.

① **Skellig Experience Centre**
Housed in a striking, prize-winning stone building with a grass roof, the Skellig Experience Centre *(open May–Sep: daily; Mar, Apr, Oct & Nov: Mon–Fri)* has displays on every facet of Skellig Michael (Sceiig Mhichíl), which is now a UNESCO World Heritage Site. This remote and rocky outcrop contains one of the best-preserved early Christian monastic sites in the world. The audiovisual presentation is full of fascinating detail on the centuries in which the monastery thrived on the island and on the way of life of its remarkably resilient monks. There are also displays on the bird and underwater life of the island. The Centre is able to arrange boat trips to Skellig Michael.

🚗 *On leaving the car park, turn left up the hill. At the first junction turn left again, following the signs for the Skellig Drive, and continue to a fork in the road. To access the path to Bray Tower, fork left and drive until a lay-by at the end of the road is reached. Park here.*

② Bray Tower

Bray Tower is an 18th-century signal tower standing on the promontory of Bray Head. It is thought originally to have been a Martello lookout tower, many of which were built around Ireland in response to the threat of an invasion by Napoleon. From the car park, head out on foot along the track that leads out to the headland and the tower. On a clear day, the sweeping vistas of the surrounding headlands and islands are truly magnificent. Allow an hour for the whole walk.

🚗 *Return to the fork in the road and this time take the other fork. Continue until you see a left sign for Geokaun Mountain and Fogher Cliffs. Drive to the top or park at the foot of the mountain and walk (20 minutes).*

③ Geokaun Mountain and the Fogher Cliffs

These are the highest points on the island and indeed on the whole Ring of Kerry. The views from the top are certainly worth the short trek up. On **Geokaun Mountain** there is a viewing platform and information plaques explaining what you can see. Before reaching the top, walk the short path on the left to the **Fogher Cliffs** and take in the panoramic landscape from the viewing deck.

🚗 *Continue to Knightstown for the car ferry that runs continuously to Renard Point. From there drive east to Cahersiveen. If the ferry is not running (Nov–Mar), head back to Portmagee. Take the R565 to Oghermong, then the N70 north to Cahersiveen.*

Monastic Miracle

In the 6th century, a group of monks established a monastery on the island Skellig Michael – nothing short of a miracle of devotion and ingenuity. Having withstood the forces of the Atlantic for nearly 1,500 years, the chapel and beehive huts are still remarkably preserved. The hardy monastic community remained there for 600 years.

Above Rossbehy Beach at Glenbeigh, on the road from Cahersiveen to Caragh Lake

EAT AND DRINK

SKELLIG RING DRIVE

The Moorings *moderate*
Looking out over the harbour, this guesthouse, restaurant and bar caters for all needs. The award-winning Bridge Bar is ideal for a light lunch before venturing onto Valentia Island. There's traditional Irish music and dancing every Friday and Sunday evening.
Harbour Front, Portmagee; 066 947 7108; www.moorings.ie

VALENTIA ISLAND

The Coffee Dock *inexpensive*
This welcoming coffee shop offers superb coffee as well as cakes and light snacks. The views of Valentia Harbour are great too.
The Seafront, Knightstown; 087 298 0199; closed Oct–May

CAHERSIVEEN

O'Neills The Point *moderate*
Near to where the ferry disembarks from Valentia Island, this place is an institution and a great spot for a pint outdoors on a summer's evening. However, the real draw here is the fresh seafood, which typically includes crab claws, monkfish, Atlantic lobster and salmon.
Renard Point, Cahersiveen; 066 947 2165; www.oneillsthepoint.ie; closed Dec–Feb

Above A panoramic view of Bray Head and its steep cliffs, Valentia Island

⑨ Cahersiveen
Co Kerry

Cahersiveen is the main service town for this part of the peninsula. Its chief claim to fame is that Daniel O'Connell, who agitated for Catholic emancipation, was born here. The Heritage Centre has exhibits about his life and the ill-fated Fenian uprising of 1867.

🚗 *Take the N70 north. It dips down to sea level at Glenbeigh. Beyond this, turn right for Glencar and Caragh Lake. Turn right over a bridge and drive round the lake to Blackstone Bridge over the River Caragh, a picturesque picnic spot.*

⑩ Ballaghbeama Gap
Co Kerry

From Blackstone Bridge, a narrow road winds its way up in the shadow of the Magillicuddy Reeks to Ballaghbeama Gap. On a clear day there are sweeping views across the lonely, windswept landscape. Take a right fork 1 km (half a mile) after the bridge to a T-junction (2 km/1 mile), then turn right for Cahersiveen, past the Climber's Inn, then sharp left for Ballaghbeama Gap (signposted). From the top, the road descends to join the R568, skirting the southern flanks of the Reeks.

🚗 *On the R568 turn left to Moll's Gap.*

VISITING KILLARNEY

Tourist Information
Beech Road, Killarney; 064 663 1633;
www.killarney.ie

Killarney National Park Information
Muckross House; 085 801 7973;
www.killarneynationalpark.ie

Parking
There is a car park next to the Tourist
Information centre, but this may be
full in high season. An alternative is
Glebe car park on College Road.

WHERE TO STAY

KILLARNEY

Killarney Lodge *moderate*
Just a stroll from the town centre yet
beautifully secluded in its own walled
garden, this family-run guest house
offers excellent accommodation.
Countess Road; 064 663 6499;
www.killarneylodge.ie; closed Nov–Feb

KILLARNEY NATIONAL PARK

Cahernane House Hotel *moderate*
Set in its own parklands on the edge of
the national park, this has a charming
old-world atmosphere and open fires.
Muckross Road (off N71); 064 663 1895;
www.cahernane.com; closed Nov–Feb

Coolclogher House *moderate*
This early Victorian house on a working
farm is a haven of tranquillity. Four
rooms have mountain and sea views.
Mill Road (third left off N71 from
Killarney); 064 663 5996;
www.coolclogherhouse.com

Muckross Park Hotel
moderate–expensive
Dating from 1795, this is Killarney's
most beautifully located hotel, opposite
Muckross Abbey. Elegant bedrooms.
Muckross Village; 064 662 3400;
www.muckrosspark.com

Below Lovely Muckross House, in the heart
of Killarney National Park

Above Majestic Upper and Muckross lakes and Lough Leane, seen from Ladies' View

⑪ Moll's Gap
Co Kerry

Moll's Gap is where the R568 meets
the N71, which runs between Killarney
and Kenmare. There are spectacular
vistas from here, but sadly many good
viewing places have been fenced off.

🚗 *Continue on the N71 to Ladies'*
View, pausing at the lay-by just before
it for more splendid views.

⑫ Ladies' View
Killarney, Co Kerry

Ladies' View takes its name from one
of Queen Victoria's ladies-in-waiting
who, accompanying the monarch
on a visit to Killarney in 1861, pronounced it "the finest view in the
realm". It would be hard to disagree
with her. From here it seems as if
the whole of Kerry is laid out directly
below. Upper Lake stretches away
to link up with the two lower lakes,
Muckross and Leane. On the far side
is the dramatic Carrauntoohil massif.

🚗 *Continue on the N71 to Killarney*
National Park and Muckross.

The Liberator

Daniel O'Connell (1775–1847), "The
Liberator", campaigned for equal
rights and religious tolerance. His
goal was partially achieved in 1829,
when Catholics were at last admitted
to Parliament in Westminster, and
he became the first Irish Catholic
MP in the House of Commons.

---

⑬ KILLARNEY NATIONAL PARK
Co Kerry

Killarney National Park covers approximately 10,000 ha (25,000 acres)
and encompasses three lakes – Upper, Muckross and Leane – and the
surrounding mountains. It contains Ireland's largest area of ancient
oak forest and its only remaining herd of indigenous red deer.

A two-hour walking tour

This circular tour, known as the Dinis
Walk, is a lovely stroll around Muckross
Lake, through ancient woodlands of
oak and mountain ash. It starts at
Muckross House ① *(open daily)*, next
to the car park. The focal point of the
park, the house is a fine Victorian residence, completed in 1843 to designs
by Scottish architect William Burn.
Queen Victoria herself visited in 1861
as a guest of the Herbert family, who
landscaped the gardens in her honour,
planting them with azaleas and rhododendrons. Today, the main rooms
have been renovated in period style.

Next door, the working farm project
at the Traditional Farms *(open Apr–Sep:*
daily; Mar & Oct: weekends) has recreated Irish rural life of the 1930s, before
electrification. Mucros Pottery and
Weaving can be seen in action next
to the craft shop in the Walled Garden
Centre. From the house there are
several alternative walks around the
lakes and through the woods or, for a
different touring experience, trips in
a horse-drawn jaunting car are also
possible (pick one up outside the
house). To continue the Dinis Walk,
follow the marked trail down to the
great 20 m (60 ft) **Torc Waterfall** ② – a

30-minute walk. From here, follow the Torc Trail along the base of Torc Mountain to the **Old Weir Bridge** ③, where Muckross Lake and the Upper Lake first meet. Soon afterwards the path arrives at the thrilling **Meeting of the Waters** ④, where the Upper Lake actually flows into Muckross Lake. It's worth pausing here to watch the boatmen negotiate the turbulent flow of water. A little way further along on the right is **Dinis (Dinish) Cottage** ⑤ (open May–Sep daily), an 18th-century hunting lodge, now an eco-friendly tea room. Continue along the narrow stretch of land between Muckross Lake and Lough Leane to the picturesque arches of **Brickeen (Bricin) Bridge** ⑥. Cross the bridge and carry on past Colleen Bawn Rock, following the path along Lough Leane to **Muckross Abbey** ⑦, founded in 1448. Return to the car park, finishing the circuit. Back in the

car, turn left out of the main entrance onto the N71. Turn left before Killarney to the 15th-century Ross Castle, on a peninsula in Lough Leane. From here boats cross to Innisfallen Isle, home to the ruins of another abbey.

🚗 *Return to the N71 and continue to Killarney.*

⑭ Killarney
Co Kerry

Killarney is a convenient base from which to explore the natural splendours of the national park. **St Mary's Cathedral**, designed by Pugin and built in 1842, is considered Ireland's finest example of High Gothic, and is worth a visit. The little Victorian lanes that branch off the main street are also enjoyable to wander. There are plenty of pubs – many playing live music – and restaurants in the town, and a good choice of accommodation.

Stained-glass pub window

Above Riding in a traditional jaunting car through the woods in Killarney National Park

EAT AND DRINK IN KILLARNEY

Bricin *inexpensive*
Bricin is Gaelic for small trout so it's no surprise that fish dishes feature in this family-run restaurant and high-quality craft store. Also worth trying is boxty, a traditional potato pancake. *26 High Street; 064 663 4902; www.bricin.ie; closed Jan, Feb, Sun & Mon*

Gaby's Seafood Restaurant *moderate*
At this excellent seafood restaurant you can choose from a wide selection of fish, cooked in a variety of ways. The lobster and wild Atlantic salmon steaks are particularly succulent. Cosy, rustic decor, with an open fire. *27 High Street; 064 663 2519; closed Sun*

DAY TRIP OPTIONS
Killarney or the area around Valentia Island are ideal bases from which to explore the glorious Kerry landscape.

Lakes and abbeys
Stroll around Killarney ⑭ and have a look at the cathedral, then head to Killarney National Park ⑬. After doing the Dinis Walk, take a jaunting-car trip up to Muckross Abbey and on to the pier at Ross Castle, where boat

trips set off across Lough Leane to visit the lovely 6th-century ruined abbey on the heavily wooded island of Inisfallen.

From Killarney, take N71 to the Killarney National Park and park in Muckross House or Muckross Abbey car park (just before house on the right).

Islands and monasteries
Explore Valentia Island ⑧, starting the day at the Skellig Experience Centre to find out about the Skellig

Michael UNESCO World Heritage Site – a monastery established in the 6th century on the remote island of Great Skellig. The drystone beehive huts built by the monks can be seen on a cruise from the centre or on an independent boat trip from Valentia Island or Portmagee. Back on dry land, continue to Bray Tower or Geokaun Mountain and the Fogher Cliffs for bracing clifftop walks.

Follow the drive instructions from Ballinskelligs and Valentia Island.

TRIP 4

THE DINGLE PENINSULA
Tralee to the Maharees Peninsula

HIGHLIGHTS

Lively musical town
Discover the vibrant, colourful harbour town of Dingle, situated in the heart of an Irish-speaking region

Culinary delights
Sample the freshest seafood and other produce to see why the local cuisine is held in such high regard

Dramatic headland
Explore the wild scenery of Slea Head, one of Europe's most westerly fringes

Historic landscapes
Delve into countryside rich in atmosphere and studded with Neolithic and early Christian sites

The Dingle Peninsula

Of the five peninsulas in southwest Ireland, the Dingle is perhaps the connoisseur's choice. This is a drive through an ancient landscape, dotted with remnants of early Christian churches, monastic settlements and Neolithic structures. It runs through the most westerly landscape in Europe, and the dramatic scenery of Slea Head, the brooding presence of Mount Brandon and the marvellous chain of precipitous cliffs and sandy beaches will remain etched in the memory. Food-lovers will enjoy the famed seafood of Dingle, part of the burgeoning culinary scene that has seen its reputation soar in recent years.

Brandon Point

Brandon Head

Brandon (Cé Bhréanainn)

Brandon Bay

R550

Stradl

BRANDON CREEK

Ballyroe (Baile Reo) **14**

Brandon Mountain 953m

Tiduff (An Tigh Dubh)

Cloghane (An Clochán)

Ballydavid (Baile na nGall)

FEOHANAGH (An Fheothanach) **13**

Ballyduff (An Baile Dut

Beenoskee 827m

Strad Mour

15 MOUNT BRANDON

Smerwick (Ard na Caithne)

Ballybrack (An Baile Breac)

Murreagh (An Mhuiríoch)

R549

R560

Sybil Head

12 KILMALKEDAR CHURCH

CONOR PASS **16** (An Chonair)

Coumduffmo

BALLYFERRITER (Baile an Fheirtéaraigh) **10**

11 GALLARUS ORATORY

R559

R549

Lisdargan (Lios Deargáin)

Clogher Head

R559

Milltown (Baile an Mhuilinn)

VENTRY (Ceann Trá) **11**

Blasket Island Centre

DUNQUIN (Dun Chaoin) **9**

Caherbullig (Cathair Boilg)

6

R559

DINGLE **5** (An Daingean) **11**

N86

Lispole (Lios Póil)

Kilmur (Cill Mh

Mount Eagle 516m

Ventry Harbour

R559

Dingle Harbour

Great Blasket Island (An Blascaod Mór)

Dunmore Head

7 DUNBEG FORT

Bull's Head

Minard Point

Tearaught Island (An Tiaracht)

Coumeenole Bay

8 SLEA HEAD (Ceann Sléibhe)

11 Fahan (Fán)

Dingle Bay

Inisbnabro (Inis na Bró)

0 kilometres   5

0 miles   5

Inisbvickillane (Inis Mhic Aoibhleáin)

KEY

Drive route

Above A prehistoric beehive hut, or *clochan*, in the Fahan Group near Dunbeg Iron Age Fort, overlooking Dingle Bay, *see p66*

ACTIVITIES

Savour delicious seafood chowder in Dingle and finish off with a gourmet Irish whiskey ice-cream

Stroll along a white sandy beach at Ventry Bay and take a refreshing dip in its clear waters

Walk among prehistoric homes, the *clochans*, or beehive huts, of Fahan

Take a ferry ride out to Great Blasket Island and spend time exploring this lovely, now-uninhabited island

Cross the Conor Pass, Ireland's highest, and enjoy splendid views over the Brandon and Tralee bays

be Seven Hogs or
Tagbaree Islands

Rough Point

gane Bay

Fahamore

Ardfert

Chapeltown — R551

Towlaght

Kilfenora — R558

Fenit

Spa

TRALEE ❶

THE MAHAREES PENINSULA ⑰

Castlegregory

Killiney

Aughacasla

R560

Blennerville

N70

Tralee Bay

Derrymore — N86

Camp

Killelton

Glanteenassig

K E R R Y

Baurtregaum 852m △

Slieve Mish Mountains

❷ **PASS OF CAHERCONREE**

N86

White Gate Roads

Boolteens

Fybagh

Keel

Castlemaine

Aughils — R561

N70

NASCAUL

Inch

R561

Castlemaine Harbour

Milltown

❸ **INCH POINT**

Inch

Tullig

Killorglin

Knockaunaglashy

N70

Above Vivid orange swathes of montbretia flowers lining the quiet country roads of the Dingle Peninsula

PLAN YOUR DRIVE

Start/finish: Tralee to the Maharees Peninsula.

Number of days: 2, allowing half a day for a trip to Great Blasket Island.

Distance: 180 km (110 miles).

Road conditions: Roads are well paved and signposted but, in places, narrow with some steep inclines.

When to go: April to October are the best months to explore the Dingle Peninsula, when hedgerows and fields glow with wild fuchsias and montbretia. Many places close in winter. In peak season, be sure to book accommodation well in advance.

Opening times: Most shops and attractions open from 9 or 10am to 5 or 6pm. Shops are usually open Mon–Sat and from 12 to 6pm on Sun. In most villages there are convenience stores, open from 7 or 8am until late.

Main market days: Tralee: Sat; Dingle: Fri.

Shopping: Dingle has delightful little shops selling lovely artisan jewellery, crystalware, pottery and other crafts. Traditional Blasket Islands weaving can be seen, and items bought, on Great Blasket in summer, or articles woven on the islands can be bought in Dingle year-round.

Major festivals: Tralee: Rose of Tralee Festival, Aug; Dingle: Animation Dingle Film Festival, Mar; Regatta, Aug; Dingle Races, Aug; Food Festival, Oct; Folk Festival, Oct; Other Voices Festival, Nov.

DAY TRIP OPTIONS

Families might enjoy a day of **water-based activities**, starting with an early morning **dolphin-swim** at Dingle, then **kayaking** or **windsurfing** at Ventry or Sandy Bay and **bodyboarding** at Coumeenole Bay. A visit to the Blasket Islands Centre in Dunquin, followed by a trip out to Great Blasket, will appeal to **history enthusiasts**, and **movie-lovers** may spot locations used in the David Lean film *Ryan's Daughter*. For full details, *see p69.*

Above Steam train that once ran from Tralee

VISITING DINGLE

Parking
There is a pay-and-display car park on the waterfront, adjacent to the pier.

Tourist Information
Strand Street; 066 915 1188; www.dingle-peninsula.ie; open Mon–Sat

WHERE TO STAY

AROUND TRALEE

Camp Junction House *inexpensive*
This B&B, 5 minutes' walk from the beach, has six en suite bedrooms and two apartments. Rooms at the front overlook Tralee Bay; those at the back have views of the Slieve Mish mountains.
Camp; 087 243 0704; www.camp junctionhouse.com; closed Nov–Feb

INCH POINT

Inch Beach Guest House *inexpensive*
Smart B&B in a lovely scenic location with spectacular views across the bay; cottages and camping are available too.
Inch Beach, Dingle; 087 256 5700; www.inchbeach.com

DINGLE (AN DAINGEAN)

The Hideout Hostel *inexpensive*
Located in the heart of Dingle, this friendly, well-run hostel caters for the independent traveller and for families. There is a mix of private and dormitory rooms. Michael, the owner, is a fount of wisdom on the whole area.
Dykegate Street; 066 915 0559

Ballintaggart Manor House *moderate*
Affording beautiful views across the harbour, Ballintaggart House is an ideal base from which to explore the peninsula. This family-run manor house manages to combine boutique hotel style with homely charm.
Race Course Road; 066 915 1333; www.ballintaggarthouse.com

① Tralee
Co Kerry
Tralee (Trá Lí) is the administrative capital of County Kerry. A busy market town, it is probably best known for the international pageant, the Rose of Tralee, celebrating Irish womanhood, which takes place here each August. Though the town is principally 19th-century in character, there are some Georgian buildings too. For a pleasant family outing, visit the Tralee **Bay Wetland Centre** *(open daily)*, which offers an Activity Zone (with rowing boats and a climbing wall) and a Nature Zone (with viewing towers and safari boat tours).

🚗 *From Tralee take the N86 along the northern flank of the peninsula. Cross the stone bridge by the Blennerville Windmill, follow the undulating road and fork left after Camp. On reaching a farm building, head up the narrow road to its left. At the next junction turn left, which leads over the Pass of Caherconree.*

② Pass of Caherconree
Co Kerry
This is a little-known pass through the Slieve Mish Mountains to the southern flank of the peninsula. Near the summit of the pass is a sign for the Caherconree Iron Age Fort. It's worth a scramble up a boggy path to see it on a fine day. At the brow of the pass there are fantastic views over Castlemaine Harbour to the south.

🚗 *Descend into Aughils and turn right on the R561 for Inch.*

③ Inch Point
Co Kerry
The setting for much of David Lean's 1970 movie *Ryan's Daughter*, Inch (Inse) Point is a splendid sand and dune spit that curves out into Dingle Bay – popular for water sports and swimming. When the tide is out, it is the perfect place for a bracing walk along its 6-km (4-mile) strand. Look out for sea otters, seals and dolphins in the bay. There are splendid views across the bay to the Macgillycuddy Reeks, the highest mountain range in Ireland *(see p57)*.

🚗 *From Inch Point continue west on the R561 signed for Anascaul. Soon after leaving Inch, look out for a lay-by from which there are great views of Dingle Bay. Further along, there will be a T-junction. Turn right here onto the N86 for Anascaul.*

South Pole Inn pub sign

④ Anascaul
Co Kerry
In Anascaul is a pub called the South Pole Inn. Its former owner was Tom Crean, a member of both Scott's and Shackleton's expeditions to the Antarctic, known to locals as "Tom the Pole". The pub is full of memorabilia, as well as photographs of visiting dignitaries. There is a Memorial Garden, with a bronze statue of Crean holding the sled dog puppies of which he was so fond.

🚗 *Return to the main road and turn right, following the N86 to Dingle. Park in waterfront car park by pier.*

Above Fishing boats moored in front of St Mary's Church in Dingle's pretty harbour, seen from the bay

⑤ DINGLE (AN DAINGEAN)

Co Kerry

Dingle, the westernmost town in Europe, is located in the heart of a Gaeltacht – an Irish-speaking area *(see p178)*. Though hardly undiscovered, it is nonetheless a gem. Dingle's most famous resident was Fungie the dolphin who, until his disappearance in 2020, had been attracting the tourists for around 40 years. The town's characteristic features are brightly painted houses, traditional shop fronts and tightly bunched, narrow streets, all of which run down to the harbour. Good restaurants and traditional pubs tempt visitors to linger.

A one-hour walking tour

From the car park, turn right along Quay Street, with the harbour on your right. The **Tourist Office** ① and Visitor Centre is at the foot of the pier. Continue into Strand Street and up the hill into Green Street, lined with shops, restaurants, pubs and cafés. On the left is **St Mary's Church** ②, and in its grounds is the Diseart Cultural Centre, housed in an old convent. Here in the chapel there are 12 stained-glass windows by the celebrated stained-glass artist Harry Clarke. Opposite is the famous pub **Dick Mack's** ③, which doubles up as a hardware store. Only a few of these store-cum-pubs now remain in Dingle. At the top of Green Street you come to Main Street, with its many traditional pubs and restaurants. To the right on Main St is

Live music sign written in Irish

Lord Baker's Restaurant ④ *(see right)*, which has a cosy dining area around a turf fire. Turn right into Lower Main Street, past **Ashes Bar** ⑤, where the seafood chowder enjoys renown. Turn right down Dykegate Lane, looking for **An Café Liteartha** ⑥ on the left, a café-bookshop specializing in books of local interest. Continuing further on, turn left into Bridge Street for **O'Flaherty's Pub** ⑦. Here, a lively musical session usually commences when the landlord picks up his accordion. Retrace your steps and turn left into Strand Street to return to the car park. Stop in at the turquoise building on the left for at least one scoop of **Murphy's** ⑧ delicious, award-winning ice cream.

🚗 *Leave Dingle with the harbour on your left and follow signs for Ventry, heading due west on the R559, to the start of the drive around Slea Head.*

Above Colourful frontage of Dick Mack's combined pub and hardware store

EAT AND DRINK

INCH POINT

Sammy's *inexpensive*
A popular seafront restaurant, which looks out across Inch Beach. Casual dining with steak and chips the pick.
Inch Beach; 066 915 8118

ANASCAUL

The South Pole Inn *inexpensive*
This historic, family-run pub serves excellent home-cooked food, including some terrific burgers and curries.
Main Street; 066 915 7388; www.southpoleinn.com

DINGLE (AN DAINGEAN)

John Benny's Pub *inexpensive*
A traditional Irish music pub, serving good food in a friendly atmosphere.
Strand Street; 066 915 1215; www.johnbennyspub.com

Ashes Bar and Restaurant *moderate*
A marvellous seafood restaurant, Ashes offers dishes such as seared scallops with poached apple, and steamed mussels in a Thai broth.
Lower Main Street; 066 915 0989; www.ashesbar.ie

Grey's Lane Bistro *moderate*
Seafood forms the mainstay of an exciting menu in this modern, family-run bistro.
Grey's Lane; 066 915 2770; www.greyslanebistro.com; closed Sun

Lord Baker's Restaurant *moderate*
This well-known Dingle venue serves mainly seafood – lobster often features.
Main Street; 066 915 1277; lordbakers.ie; closed Thu

Global Village *expensive*
Outstanding seafood restaurant offering one of the best dining experiences in town.
Upper Main Street; 066 915 2325; www.globalvillagedingle.com; open Mar–mid-Nov

0 metres 250
0 yards 250

St Mary's Church ②
Dick Mack's ③
Lord Baker's Restaurant ④
Ashes Bar ⑤
An Café Liteartha ⑥
O'Flaherty's Pub ⑦
Murphy's ⑧
Tourist Office ①

Town Park

UPPER MAIN ST
SPA ROAD
GREEN STREET
STRAND ST
QUAY STREET
HOLY GROUND
THE MALL
THE TRACKS
DYKEGATE LANE
JOHN STREET
BRIDGE STREET

Above Rocky headland overlooking Dingle Bay, site of the Iron-Age fort of Dunbeg

VISITING THE BLASKETS

Blasket Island Ferries cross from Dunquin Harbour roughly every half hour from 10am to dusk Easter-end Sep. *066 915 6422; www.blasketislands.ie*

WHERE TO STAY AROUND VENTRY (CEANN TRÁ)

Moriarty's Farmhouse *inexpensive*
This friendly guesthouse is set on a working farm in an idyllic location near Ventry. Its six en suite rooms have stunning views across Ventry Harbour. Owners Ted and Brid Moriarty are experts on the history of the region. *Rahanane (1 km/2 miles from Ventry at the start of the Slea Head Drive); 066 915 9037; www.dinglevacation.com*

Milltown House *moderate*
Robert Mitchum stayed in this award-winning period guesthouse during the filming of *Ryan's Daughter*. The 10 rooms, each one named in honour of people (or animals) of signficance to the house, are furnished to a high standard. *Ventry Road, Milltown (at the start of the Slea Head Drive between Dingle and Ventry); 066 915 1372; www. milltownhouse.com*

⑥ Ventry (Ceann Trá)
Co Kerry
Cushioned up against the slopes of Mount Eagle, Ventry perches alongside a wonderful crescent of white sandy beach, backed by sand dunes and hills. Here, upturned *currachs* (traditional Irish fishing boats of black-tarred canvas) are a common sight. The beach, one of the safest in the region, is popular with water sports enthusiasts and is ideal for swimming. On hot summer days, the pier at Ventry is also a popular swimming spot.
🚗 *Continue along the R559 to Dunbeg Fort.*

⑦ Dunbeg Fort
Fahan, Co Kerry
Just beyond Ventry, on a promontory looking out across Dingle Bay, is the Iron Age fort of Dunbeg. Surrounded by sea on three sides, this fortress has walls 7 m (23 ft) thick, surrounded by earthen trenches. Though much of the original construction has long since tumbled into the sea, including a large section of the western wall during the ferocious storms of 2014, it is still an imposing sight. Opposite is the **Visitor Centre** *(open Mar–Nov: daily)*, where there is a car park.
A little further along the R559 is the first set of *clochans*, or beehive huts, with the **Fahan Group** a short walk or drive away (there is ample parking at the site). It is estimated there are up to 400 of these huts on the southern slopes of Mount Eagle. Many of these prehistoric dwellings, constructed in unmortared stone, are

still in good watertight condition. Some are on private land, and farmers may charge a small fee to view them.
🚗 *Continue west on the R559 to Slea Head and round into Coumeenole Bay. This is an exhilarating stretch of cliff-hugging road, high above Dingle Bay. On the right, the western flanks of Mount Eagle slope down to the sea, on the left you can see the Blaskets.*

The Blasket Islands
Once the most westerly settlement in Europe, Great Blasket was finally abandoned in 1953, when its dwindling population could no longer be sustained. Nevertheless, the Blasket Islands remain, for many Irish people, a potent symbol of an ancient Irish-speaking culture. Three books by islanders recount a lost way of life: Muiris O'Suilleabhan's *Twenty Years a'Growing*; Peig Sayer's *A Woman's Reflections*; and Tomas O'Criomhthain's *The Island Man*. English translations retain much of the local flavour and evocative phrasing of the original Irish.

⑧ Slea Head (Ceann Sléibhe)
Co Kerry
Offering exhilarating views across Dingle Bay and over to Great Blasket Island, **Slea Head** is the westernmost point in Europe, and the focal point of the Dingle drive. The sweep of sea, craggy coves and outlying islands that come into view as you round the headland is a spectacular sight. The dramatic confluence of sea and land can be appreciated from the viewing point – a much

Above Road curving down from Dunmore Head, with views over Blasket Sound to the Blaskets photographed scene. A short distance further on, the road sweeps around to **Coumeenoole Bay** (Trá an Choma) popular with surfers and bathers. The bay has an organized picnic area which affords breathtaking vistas across the bay. Behind the picnic area is a stone stile. On the other side of it is a grassy path leading out to Dunmore Head, which overlooks the Blasket Sound.

🚗 *Stay on the R559, which now begins to turn north as it rounds the peninsula's headland and heads slightly inland for Dunquin.*

Above Looking across Smerwick Harbour between Ballyferriter and Ballydavid

⑨ Dunquin (Dun Chaoin)
Slea Head, Co Kerry

Dunquin is famous as the setting for David Lean's epic 1970 drama *Ryan's Daughter*. While the film was not a critical success upon release – though acclaimed today – the breathtaking scenery certainly did wonders for regional tourism.

Dunquin was also the place where the Blasket Islanders came ashore to trade or buy provisions, which is why it has a certain historical resonance with local people. Some still speak of the crossing from Dunquin to the Blaskets as the "authentic one" – the one from Dingle to Great Blasket actually takes longer. In Dunquin, the **Blasket Islands Centre** (open mid-Mar–mid-Oct: daily) has exhibitions and audiovisual displays that show life as it was once lived on the Blaskets.

Here also is Kruger's bar, a popular landmark, and the last pub this side of the Atlantic. From the bar can be seen the island known as Skellig Michael (see p57) in the distance.

🚗 *Follow the R559 north, then east, towards Ballyferriter.*

⑩ Ballyferriter (Baile an Fheirtéaraigh)
Slea Head, Co Kerry

As remote a spot as it gets on the peninsula, this comely village offers a fine beach at Wine Strand and bracing walks towards the twin peaks of Sybil Head and Three Sisters. At the end of the village, on the left, is the **West Kerry Museum** *(open Jun–mid-Sep: daily; mid-Sep–May: by appointment)*, dedicated to the peninsula's archaeology. The area between Ballyferriter and **Ballydavid** (Baile na nGall) has retained its traditional way of life. Here, and in the villages around Smerwick Harbour, *Gaelige* (Irish) is widely spoken.

🚗 *Continue on the R559 which turns sharply left after the Smerwick Hotel. Further along, turn right at the signpost for Gallarus Oratory.*

⑪ Gallarus Oratory
Slea Head, Co Kerry

Often compared to an upturned boat in appearance, the Gallarus Oratory is one of the best-preserved early Christian churches in Ireland. Just as impressive are the dry-stone corbelling techniques that meant it has been able to withstand the elements for nearly 1,300 years. There is a **Visitor Centre** *(open Easter–Oct: daily; rest of year: by appointment)* with a café and an audiovisual exhibition. The centre also provides information on Kilmalkedar Church *(see p68)*, the other important early Christian site in the area.

🚗 *Leaving the Oratory, rreturn to the R559 and turn right in the direction of Murreagh (An Mhuirioch). From here, turn sharp right staying on the R559, signed for Kilmalkedar Church.*

Above The simple but stunning early Christian Gallarus Oratory, whose dry-stone walls have survived 1,300 years

OUTDOOR ACTIVITIES

Longs Horse Riding in Ventry is an excellent outfit offering a variety of mountain and beach trail rides for both beginners and more experienced riders *(Kilcolman; 087 225 0286; www.longsriding.com)*.

EAT AND DRINK

VENTRY (CEANN TRÁ)

Páidi Ó Sé's *inexpensive*
Named after, and once run by, the late former Kerry Gaelic football star, this jolly country pub is a terrific spot to tuck into comfort food like chowder or beef lasagne, best enjoyed with a pint. *Near the church, Ventry; 066 915 9011; www.paidiose.com*

DUNBEG FORT

Stone House Restaurant *inexpensive*
Husband-and-wife team David and Michelle run this lovely family restaurant located opposite Dunbeg Fort. Try some steamed mussels in lemongrass or Dingle Bay scampi. *Fahan, Ventry; 066 915 9970; www.stonehouseventry.com*

BALLYFERRITER

Tigh Uí Chathain *moderate*
A restaurant brimful of local character, this offers excellent value for money. With some of the best produce in Ireland on their doorstep, they cook simply, seasonally, and extremely well. *Ballyferriter; 066 915 6359*

WHERE TO STAY

FEOHANAGH (AN FEOTHANACH)

An Riasc Guest House *moderate*
This charming stone farmhouse is
located just outside Feohanagh,
amid breathtaking scenery. Its four
rooms have original artworks and
eco-friendly products.
*Feohanagh; 066 915 5446;
www.anriasc.ie*

AROUND CONOR PASS (AN CHONAIR)

O'Connor's Guesthouse *inexpensive*
In a stunning location at the foot of
Mount Brandon, overlooking Brandon
Bay, this family-run guesthouse in the
village of Cloghane is popular with
walkers. It has seven bedrooms,
including family rooms, plus a three-
bed townhouse. There is also a good
restaurant and a convivial bar with
occasional live music.
*Cloghane (turn left on R585 as you
descend the Conor Pass); 066 713
8113; www.oconnnorskerry.com*

THE MAHAREES PENINSULA

Tigh Beagh *moderate*
This compact, beautifully restored
farmhouse – the "small house" – is set
in 17 acres of native woodland, and
comes with its own mountain river
and waterfall. It should appeal to
those seeking peace and solitude.
The cottage is fully equipped with
all mod cons and has a geothermally
heated tiled floor, as well as a wood-
burning stove. Two large bedrooms
can accommodate six guests.
*Glanteenassig, Castlegregory (take
R560 from Castlegregory and right
turn uphill to Glanteenassig); 087 779
3126; www.tighbeag.com*

Below Ancient crosses near the Irish
Romanesque Kilmalkedar Church

⑫ Kilmalkedar Church
Slea Head, Co Kerry

This early Christian and medieval site
is spread over 4 ha (10 acres) and is
associated with St Brendan. At the
centre is the 12th-century Kilmalkedar
Church, an excellent example of Irish
Romanesque style. Near the chancel
door is an early Christian Alphabet
Stone, and there are several ancient
crosses here, as well as an Ogham
Stone (marked with ancient script).
The Pilgrim's Way walk to the top of
Mount Brandon starts behind the
church. Even a short 20-minute
stretch of the walk is rewarded with
fine views across Smerwick Harbour.
🚗 *Return on R559 towards Murreagh.
Before the village is a school house.
Turn right here but, if the turning is
missed there is another right turn onto
the R549 in Murreagh itself. Either
road will take you into Feohanagh.*

Local Flavours

In the last decade or so a culinary
renaissance has taken place on the
Dingle Peninsula. Some of the local
delicacies worth sampling are
Blasket Island lamb, highly regarded
for its fine flavour; black (blood) and
white pudding made in Anascaul;
award-winning Dingle Peninsula
seaweed-flavoured cheese from
Castlegregory; Dingle's smoked fish
and Murphy's ice cream *(see p65)*.

---

⑬ Feohanagh (An Feothanach)
Slea Head, Co Kerry

As you arrive in Feohanagh, pull into
the car park to admire stupendous

views across Smerwick Harbour and
the ragged headland of Ballydavid.
Below you is Dooneen pier, which is
accessible on foot. There you may
see the remains of old *currachs*,
once the main fishing vessels here.
Though they are still built on the
peninsula, their use has declined.
🚗 *Just past Feohanagh turn sharp
left and take the minor road signed
to Ballyroe and Tiduff.*

Above Steep-sided cliff walls form a sheltering
harbour at lovely Brandon Creek

⑭ Brandon Creek
Slea head, Co Kerry

Brandon Creek is believed to be
the spot from which St Brendan the
Navigator set out on his epic voyage
to Newfoundland in the 6th century.
His journey is recounted in *Navigato
Brendan*, the earliest copies of
which, in Latin and dating from the
11th century, were once housed in
medieval libraries across Europe.

It is not advisable to drive down to
the pier at Brandon Creek. Leave the
car in the small parking area above,
and walk the short distance. At the
end of the pier is a rock within which
is a large crevice. This creates an air
pocket that, depending on the roll
of the tide, makes a booming sound
when trapped air is released.

Brandon Creek nestles in the
shadows of imposing Mount
Brandon, the second-highest
mountain in Ireland and one
of the country's holiest places.
🚗 *From Brandon Creek, drive
due south on a minor road which
eventually joins the main R549 road
back towards Dingle. Just before it
joins the main road there is a sign
pointing left for Mount Brandon.
Take this narrow road.*

⑮ Mount Brandon
Co Kerry

According to legend St Brendan climbed to the top of this 952-m-(3,123-ft-) high mountain to view the Americas before starting out on his voyage. Near the Mount Brandon car park, a gateway, a grotto and a stream mark the starting point for the annual pilgrimage to the summit, which takes place on the nearest Sunday to 29 June. On this day a special mass is celebrated on top of the mountain. A well-trodden path, punctuated by the Stations of the Cross, winds its way to the summit. It's well worth walking as least as far as the early markers for panoramic views of Dingle Harbour.

🚗 *Return to the R549, turn left and follow the road to Dingle. On leaving Dingle, turn first left at the first roundabout to the R560 for the Conor Pass.*

⑯ Conor Pass (An Chonair)
Co Kerry

Ireland's highest route, the Conor Pass road rises quickly, winding its way to the summit at 460 m (1,500 ft). On a clear day there is a view of some of the most spectacular scenery in Ireland, with a panorama of mountains, sea, lakes and boulder-strewn valleys. To the south is Dingle Bay, while to the north are sweeping views over the Maharees Peninsula to Tralee Bay (on the right), and across Brandon Bay to Brandon Point (to the left).

🚗 *From the summit, continue on the R560, which winds down between Brandon and Stradbally mountains to the coast. It is narrow in places, so exercise caution, especially in poor weather. At Stradbally, turn left onto a minor road towards Killiney and go on from there to Castlegregory.*

⑰ The Maharees Peninsula
Co Kerry

Castlegregory is the gateway to the Maharees Peninsula, a sandy spit that divides Brandon and Tralee bays. It is a pretty village with narrow streets and gaily coloured little houses. The Maharees itself has mile upon mile of sandy beaches, and is one of Ireland's main water sports centres. Bird-watchers may want to stop at Lough Gill, outside Castlegregory, which is famed for the variety of bird species.

From Castlegregory, follow the main road along the central spine of the spit to the village of **Fahamore**. This is one of the few places in which *currachs* are still made. Carry on to **Scraggane Bay**, at the tip of the peninsula. It is popular with windsurfers, and its harbour is home to a small fishing fleet. From the pier there are views across to the **Magharee Islands**, known as the Seven Hogs. On the largest, Illauntannig, there are three stone huts and two oratories, the remnants of an early Christian monastery. Occasionally, local fishermen will ferry people across.

Above Road leading to Brandon Creek, in the shadow of Mount Brandon

EAT AND DRINK

AROUND FEOHANAGH (AN FEOTHANACH)
Gorman's Clifftop House and Restaurant *moderate*
A top-notch restaurant with an emphasis on local produce, organic when possible, and robust Irish cooking. The owners are very knowledgeable about the local area. *Glashabeg (just outside Feohanagh); 066 915 5162; www.gormans-clifftop house.com; closed mid-Oct–mid-Mar & Sun*

THE MAHAREES PENINSULA
Spillane's *moderate*
Run by Marilyn and Michael Spillane, this popular bar and restaurant is one of the landmark eating houses on the Maharees Peninsula. It has a wide-ranging menu, designed to suit all tastes. Try the Irish lamb stew and fresh steamed mussels. Also offers self-catering accommodation. *Fahamore; 066 713 9125; www.spillanesbar.com; closed Nov–Feb*

DAY TRIP OPTIONS

This drive never strays far from the sea or from history, so make the most of both. One day trip links up a range of water-based activities, while, for those caught up in the romance of Irish history and culture, there's a chance to step back in time.

Watery wonders
Start the day in Dingle ➎ with a stroll around its colourful streets or take a scenic boat trip, then head out to Ventry ➏ and try windsurfing or kayaking on the Blue Flag beach. After lunch, join the surfers at Coumeenoole Bay ➑ and stay on for a fabulous sunset view over the Blasket Islands.

Follow the itinerary from Dingle to Ventry. From Ventry, take the coastal R559 to Coumeenoole, and use the same road to return to Dingle.

Irish history
With Dunquin ➒ as the base, first visit the Blasket Islands Centre to learn about the history of the Islands, then take the boat to Great Blasket to explore this lonely place. On returning, head to Ballyferriter ➓ for a lively pub music session. Movie fans will feel they have stepped right into *Ryan's Daughter*.

Follow the drive instructions.

TRIP 5

VIKING COUNTRY
Waterford City to Ballymacarbry

HIGHLIGHTS

Viking city
See Waterford glass being made and walk in the footsteps of the Vikings in Waterford City

The colourful Copper Coast
Find out about the fascinating geology of the coast between Tramore and Bunmahon

Fairytale castle
Visit Lismore Castle, the Duke of Devonshire's Irish retreat in the Blackwater Valley

Exhilarating pass
Tackle the exhilarating Vee, a dramatic high pass through the Knockmealdown Mountains

VIKING COUNTRY

The large county of Waterford in southeast Ireland has fine stretches of coastline, gently indented with small coves, the big strand and holiday resort of Tramore, the beautiful Copper Coast beyond, and the stirring seascapes of Helvick Head. At the eastern end of the county is Waterford City, founded by the Vikings in the 10th century. Inland are the pretty towns of Lismore and Cappoquin in the languid Blackwater Valley. Two wild mountain ranges stretch north to the borders of Tipperary – the Knockmealdown Mountains, with their dramatic high passes, and the Comeragh Mountains, accessed along the beautiful Nire Valley Drive.

ACTIVITIES

Experience a Waterford pub that bottles its own whiskey

Body surf in huge Atlantic rollers on Tramore's long sandy beach

Visit the Anglo-Norman castle on Dungarvan's quayside

Stroll through the riverside gardens of Cappoquin House

Enjoy afternoon tea in the peaceful setting of Mount Melleray Abbey

0 kilometres   5

0 miles   5

KEY

Drive route

Left The Anglo-Norman fortress of Dungarvan Castle, *see p76*

PLAN YOUR DRIVE

Start/finish: Waterford to Ballymacarbry.

Number of days: 3.

Distance: 175 km (109 miles).

Road conditions: Generally well paved and well signposted. Steep inclines and hairpin bends through the Knockmealdown Mountains.

When to go: Spring and summer are warm, autumn is bright and colourful, winter is mild. Southeast Ireland is sunnier than other regions.

Opening times: Most shops and attractions open from 9 or 10am to 5 or 6pm. In towns shops stay open late on Thu and 12–6pm on Sun.

Main market days: Waterford City: Sat; Dungarvan: Thu; Lismore: Sun.

Shopping: Waterford City is the main shopping centre. World-famous hand-cut Waterford Crystal can be bought at shops and the visitor centre there.

Major festivals: Waterford City: Waterford New Music Week, Mar; Spraoi, Aug; **Tramore:** Horse Racing Festival, Aug; **Dungarvan:** West Waterford Festival of Food, Apr; **Lismore:** Immrama Festival of Travel Writing, Jun.

DAY TRIP OPTIONS

Explore the Copper Coast, which combines fine **beaches** and unusual **geology**. For contrasting **scenery** visit the idyllic towns of Cappoquin and Lismore, with their **stately homes** and **riverside gardens**, then take a **rollercoaster ride** through the Knockmealdown mountains. For full details, *see p77*.

Left Yachts, fishing trawlers and pleasure craft moored in Waterford marina, *see p74*

Above Reginald's Tower, a 13th-century landmark on Waterford's riverfront

---

VISITING WATERFORD CITY

Parking
There is ample pay-and-display car parking along the quays beside the River Suir.

Tourist Information
Waterford Discover Ireland Centre, 120 Parade Quay; 051 875 823; www. visitwaterford.com; open Mon–Sat

Shopping
The Quays and their narrow side streets contain a number of long-established shops, including **Shaws** department store *(The Quay; 051 872 977; www.shaws.ie)* and **Kelly's** *(75 Meaghers Quay; 051 588 000)*, selling Waterford crystal, linen and ladies' fashion. Barronstrand Street has smaller independent shops.

WHERE TO STAY IN WATERFORD CITY

Granville Hotel *moderate*
Long-established and independent hotel on the river. Elegant public rooms, furnished with paintings and antiques, and a range of comfortable guest rooms, some with river views.
Meagher Quay; 051 305 555; www.granvillehotel.ie

❶ WATERFORD CITY

Co Waterford

The capital of County Waterford is a handsome cathedral city set on the estuary of the River Suir. Founded by the Vikings in 914, by the 18th century it was southeast Ireland's main port as well as a centre for glass-making. The Mall, with its elegant Georgian buildings, is testament to this period, while the old quays are now part of a revitalized historic quarter.

A one-hour walking tour

Start at **Reginald's Tower** ① *(open Jan-mid-Mar: Wed-Sun; mid-Mar-Dec: daily)*. This squat 13th-century tower forms the east corner of the Norse and medieval city – a rough triangle of streets between The Mall, Garden Alley, Michael Street, Broad Street, Barronstrand Street and the Quays. A stronghold of the Anglo-Norman kings, the tower is said to be the oldest civic structure in the country. It now holds a collection of Viking artifacts.

From the tower, turn right onto The Mall. Here is the **City Hall** ②, incorporating Theatre Royal, designed in 1788 by John Roberts, a local man, and remodelled in the 19th century. Turn right on Palace Lane, leading into Cathedral Square. On the right, two medieval buildings housing Waterford's medieval collection make up the 13th-century **Chorister's Hall** ③. To the left is the Protestant **Christ Church Cathedral** ④ *(open daily)*, also designed by Roberts and built on the site of a 12th-century church. Its remnants include a crypt containing the 1481 cadaver tomb of James Rice, a former mayor of Waterford. Showing

Waterford city coat of arms

a badly decayed corpse crawling with worms, it is inscribed: "I am what you will be; I was what you are now".

From the cathedral, go back down Palace Lane, then turn right onto The Mall. On the right is the **Bishop's Palace** ⑤, an 18th-century building housing the world's largest collection of historic Waterford glass. From here, turn right up Colbeck Street, then up Henrietta Street, and finally left into High Street and **John Roberts Square** ⑥, named after the architect whose influence is everywhere in the city. One of his last works was the **Catholic Cathedral** ⑦ *(open daily)* on Barronstrand Street, which has a rich Neo-Classical interior. From here, return to John Roberts Square and turn right into Great George's Street. On the left, a palatial townhouse built in 1795 for the Morris family, also by Roberts, now contains the **Waterford Chamber of Commerce** ⑧. Head along O'Connell Street and left into Thomas Street to **Henry Downes** ⑨, a famous pub *(see right)*. Walk down to Merchants Quay and along the river back to the start.

🚗 *Leaving the city, take the R675 to Tramore. Park near the Lifeguard Station by Tramore Strand.*

Far left Waterford City Hall and Christ Church Cathedral **Left** Boats in Waterford Marina

EAT AND DRINK

WATERFORD CITY

Henry Downes *inexpensive*
This atmospheric old pub has been in the same family since 1797. Try the whiskey Downes No 9, which is blended on the premises.
10 Thomas Street; 051 874 118

Bodega *moderate*
Bright and lively with a varied menu. Try crispy pork belly with black pudding or Lebanese cous-cous and Bodega fish pie.
54 John Street; 051 844 177; www.bodegawaterford.com; closed Mon & Tue

La Bohème *moderate–expensive*
Stylish restaurant in the basement of one of the city's finest buildings. Dishes include foie gras parfait, pan-seared Barbary duck breast, and pear and almond clafoutis.
2 George's Street; 051 875 645; www.labohemerestaurant.ie; closed Sun & Mon

TRAMORE

The Victoria *inexpensive*
This veteran pub's creditable menu includes all the classics alongside some tempting wok and curry dishes.
12 Queens Street; 051 338 144; www.thevic.ie

❷ Tramore
Co Waterford

Due to its long sandy beach, Tramore has been a popular holiday resort for generations. There is a lively seafront, with an amusement park, miniature railway and other attractions, plus good swimming and surfing. Its Horse Racing Festival in August is a fashionable four-day event.

On the east side of town, an 8-km (5-mile) circular walk passes along the **Cush Sandspit** to **The Burrow** and back along the beach. It is a lovely stretch with opportunities to see a large variety of birds on the **Back Strand**'s mudflats, including Brent geese, golden plover, black-tailed godwit, red-throated diver, little egret, kingfisher and fulmar.

Accessible by car on the west side of the bay is **Great Newtown Head** (leaving Tramore, take the first left after 4 km (2 miles), along the coast, then signposted) where the **Metal Man** can be seen pointing shipping safely through the sand bars. Park at Newtown Cove for a short, tricky walk to the headland.

🚗 *Carry on, turning left onto the R675 to Annestown. Park by the beach.*

Heart of Glass

Waterford has been famous for its delicate cut glass since 1783, when George and William Penrose started the crystal manufacturing business. The industry prospered until 1851, when a lack of capital and crippling taxes caused business to fail. In 1947 a new factory opened, with crafts-men brought in from Europe to teach what had become a lost art. In 2009, the factory closed again, a vic-tim of the credit crunch, but a major visitor centre, factory and shop have now opened on the historic Mall.

The Metal Man

High on the cliffs on the west side of Tramore Bay are three pillars, one topped by the Metal Man, a 19-m (61-ft) high figure dressed in the colourful uniform of a 19th-century petty officer. The Metal Man's out-stretched right arm points to the safe channel for ships. He is one of four such figures cast in London in 1819 following a shipping disaster in the bay; another is in Sligo Bay *(see p204).*

❸ Annestown
Co Waterford

The cluster of houses at Annestown lies on the so-called **Copper Coast** between Tramore and Dungarvan, an area known for its copper mining in the 19th century. It is a beautiful drive past unspoiled beaches, coves and grassy headlands. Annestown has a good **beach**, popular with surfers.

🚗 *Continue along R675 to Bunmahon. Park in town centre car park.*

❹ Bunmahon
Co Waterford

The Copper Coast has been designated a European Geopark for its geological heritage. Bunmahon's **Geological Garden** (*www.coppercoastgeopark.com; open daily*) explains the volcanic and sedimentary rock that remains after two continents collided, creating Ireland. There is also a standing stone inscribed with ogham, an early Irish script in use from the 3rd century. Some 19th-century copper mine workings are still visible in the area.

🚗 *Leaving Bunmahon, take a left turn off the R675 and follow L3025 to Stradbally, which has a good beach. Stay on the road as far as Ballyvoyle crossroads (looking out for neolithic remains), then rejoin the R675 left to Dungarvan. Park on the street.*

Below Secluded cove near Bunmahon on County Waterford's Copper Coast

Above Boats at Helvick Head pier **Above top
right** Brightly painted shopfront in Lismore
Above right Barrels outside a pub in Dungarvan

WHERE TO STAY

HELVICK HEAD

Gortnadiha Lodge *moderate*
Family farm with beautifully appointed
rooms. Serves exceptional breakfasts.
*Ring (An Rinn); 058 46142;
www.gortnadihalodge.com*

CAPPOQUIN

Richmond House *expensive*
Built by the Earl of Cork in 1704, this
charming country house offers
exceptional comfort and fine food.
*Cappoquin (just east of town); 058
54278; www.richmondhouse.net*

LISMORE

Ballyrafter Country House Hotel
moderate
Small hotel built in the 1800s for the
Duke of Devonshire's estate manager.
Elegant rooms are complemented by
beautiful public areas.
*Lismore; 058 54002;
www.ballyrafterhouse.com*

AROUND BALLYMACARBRY

Hanora's Cottage *moderate*
Country house hotel featuring well-
furnished rooms with Jacuzzi baths
and a fine restaurant. Adults only.
*Nire Valley (a short drive east of
Ballymacarbry on a minor road); 052
613 6134; www.hanorascottage.com*

⑤ Dungarvan
Co Waterford
Set around a large harbour and looking
out to Helvick Head, this old market
town retains much of its original charm.
For centuries it was protected by its
Anglo-Norman **castle** (1186), the history of which is told in its 18th-century
barracks *(open Jun–Sep daily)*. Dungarvan
blossomed in the early 19th century
when the 5th and 6th dukes of
Devonshire modernized its centre. In
the Old Town Hall on Augustine Street,
Waterford County Museum *(open
Mon–Fri)* charts its maritime history.
🚗 **Take the N25 south from
Dungarvan and then the first left onto
the R674 to Helvick Head. There are
car parks at the end of the head.**

⑥ Helvick Head
Co Waterford
The road to Helvick Head passes
through Ring (An Rinn), in Waterford's
Gaeltacht (Irish-speaking) area. Rising
70 m (230 ft) above a harbour, the
headland has fine views.
🚗 **Return inland to Dungarvan and
turn left onto the R672 and from then
again turn left from the junction on
the N72 to Cappoquin, which has
ample street parking.**

⑦ Cappoquin
Co Waterford
This town on the River Blackwater is
famous for fly fishing and has a salmon
and trout run. Day tickets issued by

the Cappoquin Anglers' Association
can be bought from Titelines tackle
shop on Main Street. The town's
other attraction is **Cappoquin House**
*(for opening times see www.cappoquin
houseand gardens.com)*, an 18th-century
mansion. Following a fire in 1923
the house was rebuilt back to front
to take better advantage of its riverside location. The lovely gardens *(open
Mon–Sat year-round)* are particularly
noted for their rhododendrons in May.
🚗 **Continue on the N72 to Lismore.
There is pay parking on the street.**

Local Specialities
Dungarvan's market is a good
place to find local produce and
specialities. These include
Knockanore farmhouse cheese and
Knockalara sheep's milk cheese.
Also look for Gallwey's chocolates,
handmade in Waterford. Ardkeen
Quality Food Store, on Dunmore
Road in Waterford, is a source of
artisan food from all over Ireland.

⑧ Lismore
Co Waterford
Situated in the Blackwater valley
beneath the Knockmealdown
Mountains, Lismore was once
famous for its double monastery
(housing both nuns and monks),
founded in the 7th century by
St Carthage. It was a world-renowned
centre of learning. Its **castle** *(closed
to public)*, dominating the approach to
the town, is the Irish seat of the Duke
of Devonshire. It is largely 19th-century,

Below Lismore Castle, the Irish seat of the
Duke of Devonshire

though there has been a castle on this spot since the 12th century. Fred Astaire's sister Adele, who married the second son of the 9th Duke of Devonshire, lived here for some years. The gardens *(open mid-Mar–mid-Oct daily)* contain a collection of modern sculpture and a lovely riverside walk.

The town has two cathedrals dedicated to St Carthage, the late 19th-century **Catholic Cathedral**, and the Protestant **Cathedral of St Carthage** (1633), which has Gothic vaulting and a stained-glass window by the Pre-Raphaelite artist Edward Burne-Jones.

🚗 *Return to Cappoquin and take the R669 towards Tipperary. Turn right at the Cats Bar to Mount Melleray.*

⑨ Mount Melleray
Co Waterford
Set on the bare slopes of the Knockmealdown Mountains, the Cistercian abbey at **Mount Melleray** *(open daily)* was founded in 1832 by Irish monks expelled from France. The monks observe a rule of silence but keep a tradition of hospitality; it is usual to make an offering. Visitors can view most areas in the abbey and have tea in the restaurant *(closed Mon)*.

On leaving Mount Melleray, return to the R669 and turn right to join the R668 for an exhilarating drive through the **Gap**, the road's highest point, and the **Vee**, a series of hairpin bends, to Clogheen. On the way, look out for the beehive-shaped tomb of Samuel Grubb (1750–1815) on Sugarloaf Mountain. One-time owner of Castle Grace, near Clogheen, Grubb was buried upright in order, it is said, to overlook his land.

🚗 *Carry on to Clogheen and park on the street.*

⑩ Clogheen
Co Tipperary
A small market town on the River Tar, Clogheen was a prosperous mill town in the 18th and 19th centuries, as a smattering of fine Georgian townhouses testifies. Three kilometres (2 miles) east of town, off the R665, are the remains of **Castle Grace**, an Anglo-Norman castle with a tower at each corner; 8 km (5 miles) west, also on the R665, is **Ballyporeen**, where former US president Ronald Reagan came to celebrate his Irish roots in 1984.

🚗 *From Clogheen, go back along the R668 and take the first left, following signs to Newcastle. Pass through Goats Bridge and Newcastle to Ballymacarbry.*

⑪ Ballymacarbry
Co Waterford
This village is an ideal base for exploring the majestic **Comeragh Mountains**, either on foot or by car. The **Nire Valley Drive** (signposted off the R671 east of town) into the mountains is a spectacular route flanked by the Comeragh range to the right and the dramatic Punchbowl formation to the left.

Above Mount Melleray abbey at the foot of the Knockmealdown Mountains

EAT AND DRINK

DUNGARVAN
Quealy's *moderate*
Busy and friendly, Quealy's is a traditional Irish pub with a cosy cocktail bar.
O'Connell Street; 058 24555

The Tannery *expensive*
This is regarded as one of the country's finest restaurants, reinventing many Irish classics using the best local produce. Booking advisable.
Quay Street; 058 45420; www.tannery. ie; closed Mon & Tue

HELVICK HEAD
An Seanachaí *moderate*
A thatched cottage has been converted to a cosy bar, with good food, on the road from Dungarvan.
Pulla Cross, An Rinn (Ring); 058 70957; www.anseanachai.com

LISMORE
Summer House Cafe *inexpensive*
Hidden away to the rear of a gift shop, this sweet little place has all manner of baked goodies, as well as simple lunches.
Main Street; 058 54148; closed Mon

DAY TRIP OPTIONS
Spend a day on the coast or in Waterford's inland valleys.

Tramore and the Copper Coast
Begin at Tramore ②, taking in the beach and seafront attractions, and a walk along the sandspit east of town. Afterwards head along the Copper Coast to Dungarvan ⑤ via

Annestown ③ and Bunmahon ④, stopping at the Geological Garden. In the late afternoon, the sun brings out the colours of the cliff face.

Leaving Waterford City take the R675 all the way to Dungarvan. Return by the same route or cut inland along the N25.

Mountains and valleys
Combine a gentle drive along the lovely Blackwater Valley, stopping in

picturesque Cappoquin ⑦ and Lismore ⑧, with an exciting ride through the Knockmealdown Mountains to Clogheen ⑩.

From Cappoquin take the N72 to Lismore. From there take the R668 to join the R669 and head north through the Knockmealdown Mountains to Clogheen. Return to Cappoquin on the R669, making a detour to Mount Melleray if there is time.

TRIP 6

KILKENNY'S MEDIEVAL TREASURES
Kilkenny City to Carlow Town

HIGHLIGHTS

Kilkenny's commanding castle
Explore the interior of Kilkenny's magnificent castle and stroll through its grounds

Rural Kells
Walk through the haunting ruins of Kells fortified priory

Delightful details
Discover the elaborate carvings adorning the cloister of Jerpoint Abbey, a Cistercian masterpiece

Granary of the Monks
Visit the ecclesiastical centre of Graiguenamanagh, for centuries dominated by Duiske Abbey

KILKENNY'S MEDIEVAL TREASURES

On the fringes of well-heeled Leinster, beyond the gravitational pull of Dublin, Kilkenny City has a keen sense of its own worth. For 500 years the powerful Earls of Ormonde held sway here, and for a time in the 17th century it even challenged Dublin as the centre of power in Ireland. Running through the city and County Kilkenny is the River Nore, a lovely waterway that laps ivy-clad priories, stone castles, round towers and picturesque villages such as Inistioge and Thomastown on its course south. This route stops off at many of the Kilkenny's medieval treasures, from Dominican Black Abbey in the county capital to Cistercian Jerpoint Abbey and Duiske Abbey in Graiguenamanagh, the "Granary of the Monks".

Above The picture-perfect town of Inistioge nestled on the River Nore, *see p85*

ACTIVITIES

Climb St Canice's Round Tower, in Kilkenny, for splendid views

Buy some of Ireland's finest crafts in the Kilkenny Design Centre, opposite Kilkenny Castle

Savour a pint of Kilkenny ale, the velvety local brew, in Kyteler's Inn, the former home of a so-called witch

Wander through the monkey puzzle walk in Woodstock Gardens

See the Romanesque remains in Duiske Abbey, Graiguenamanagh

Stand in the ruins of Carlow Castle, a stronghold besieged by Oliver Cromwell

0 kilometres   5

0 miles   5

KEY

Drive route

PLAN YOUR DRIVE

Start/finish: Kilkenny City to Carlow Town.

Number of days: 1–2 days.

Distance: 170 km (91 miles).

Road conditions: Well paved and signposted.

When to go: The weather is better in summer, and some places are closed Nov–Feb. There is plenty to see and do all year, especially in Kilkenny City.

Opening times: Shops and attractions are open from 9am to 6pm, Mon–Fri, and shorter hours on Sunday.

Main market days: Kilkenny City: Farmers' Market, Thu; **Carlow Town:** Sat.

Shopping: Visit the Kilkenny Design Centre for high-quality crafts.

Major festivals: Kilkenny City: Roots Festival, May; The Cat Laughs Comedy Festival, Jun; Kilkenny Arts Festival, Aug.

DAY TRIP OPTIONS

Art and architecture buffs are richly served by Kilkenny City's **medieval heritage**. For **12th-century ruins** nestling in **lush river valleys**, head for Kells Priory and Jerpoint Abbey, and then relax in the **romantic gardens** at Inistioge. For full details, see p85.

Below The 13th-century early English Gothic-style St Canice's Cathedral, Kilkenny City, see p82

Above Kilkenny Castle, an impressive Norman fortress **Above centre** The choir of St Canice's Cathedral, Kilkenny **Above right** St John's Bridge and the River Nore

VISITING KILKENNY CITY

Parking
Park in Market Yard off Bateman's Quay, or in one of the central car parks on Ormonde Street or James Street.

Tourist Information
Rose Inn Street; 056 775 1500; www.visit kilkenny.ie; open Mon–Sat year-round.

Shopping
Kilkenny Design Centre stocks a superb range of high-quality crafts including jewellery, knitwear, china and glass. The Crafts Council of Ireland is in the same complex.
Castle Yard, The Parade; 056 772 2118; www.kilkennydesign.com; open daily

WHERE TO STAY IN KILKENNY CITY

Laragh House inexpensive
Modern, family-run guesthouse within walking distance of the city centre.
Waterford Road; 056 779 6691;
www.laraghhouse.com

Butler House moderate
Part of the castle estate, this upmarket Georgian townhouse boasts 17 plush rooms, some overlooking the gardens.
16 Patrick Street; 056 7722 828;
www.butler.ie

Kilkenny Hibernian Hotel moderate
Housed in a former bank, this hotel has spacious rooms and a bar mixing traditional and modern styles.
Ormonde Street; 056 777 1888;
www.kilkennyhibernianhotel.com

Kilkenny River Court Hotel moderate
Set on the banks of the Nore, this fine hotel has beautifully appointed rooms and a sunny riverside terrace.
The Bridge, John Street; 056 772 3388;
www.rivercourthotel.com

① KILKENNY CITY
Co Kilkenny
Ireland's only inland city, Kilkenny is also one of its finest. It brims with medieval treasures and has narrow alleyways, gaily coloured shop fronts and a vibrant atmosphere. Set on the west bank of the River Nore, the historic centre is book-ended by its two main landmarks, St Canice's Cathedral and Kilkenny Castle.

A two-hour walking tour
From Market Yard **car park** ① follow the walkway onto St Kieran's Street and then Parliament Street. On the right, in the yard of the **Smithwicks Experience** ②, which offers tours of the Kilkenny Brewery (daily), are the ruins of 13th-century St Francis' Abbey (closed to public). Leaving the yard, turn right onto Irish Town. Ahead is **St Canice's Cathedral** ③ (open daily), a 13th-century Protestant cathedral in the Early English Gothic style; it sits on the site of a pre-Norman church dedicated to St Canice – Cill Chainnigh (Church of Canice), from which Kilkenny derives its name. Inside, look out for the 16th-century carved effigies of Kilkenny's powerful Butler family (see box), a model of the town in its Elizabethan heyday and the 13th-century east window. Climb the cathedral's tower (847) for sweeping views.

Leaving the cathedral, turn right down Dean Street. After 200 m (656 ft), cross the road and turn left, following

Dukes of Ormonde
In 1391 Edmund Butler, the third Earl of Ormonde bought Kilkenny Castle, a move designed to consolidate the family's power in Kilkenny and Tipperary. Butlers of various branches influenced life in the region for nearly 500 years. Their strength lay in their loyalty to the English Crown, their disdain of Irish ways and their success in dismantling the power of the Catholic Geraldines.

signs for **Black Abbey** ④ *(open daily)*, a 13th-century Dominican Friary with fine stained-glass windows. From here, head down Abbey Lane, through Black Freren Gate. On the right are remnants of the city walls. Turn right onto Parliament Street to arcaded **Rothe House** ⑤ *(open Tue–Sun)*, a medieval merchant's house. Continuing up Parliament Street, veer left down St Kieran's Street, past **Kyteler's Inn** ⑥, a good place to enjoy a pint of ale. It was once the home of Alice Kyteler, convicted of witchcraft in the 14th century. Kyteler fled the country, but her maid was sent to the stake. The presiding judge, Bishop Ledrede, is buried in St Canice's graveyard.

Continue along St Kieran's Street and turn right up the Butter Slip, the old butter market, to Main Street. On the left is the **Tholsel** ⑦, a Georgian remodelling of the medieval exchequer and subsequent Town Hall. Turn left up High Street and fork left up the Parade to the castle, stopping to look at Irish crafts in the **Kilkenny Design Centre** ⑧ *(open daily)* in the castle's stable block. The **Castle** ⑨ *(open daily)* was the seat of the Dukes of Ormonde for 500 years. Inside, the Long Gallery (1820s) has a hammer beam roof painted with motifs from the *Book of Kells*. From the castle gates,

follow the path around the lawn, turning right at the end. Turn down a slipway and through a gate in the castle walls. Turn left to follow the canal (which merges with the river) to St John's Bridge. Turn left up Rose Inn Street, where the **Tourist Information Office** ⑩ *(open Mon–Sat)* occupies a medieval almshouse, and take St Kieran's Street to the car park.
🚗 *Leave the city centre by Patrick Street (N10) and turn right at Kells Road (R697). In Kells, drive to top of village and turn left to Kells Priory.*

② Kells

Not to be confused with the more famous Kells Monastery in Meath, 13th-century **Kells Priory** lies at the end of a sloping field, accessed through a kissing gate. Its fortified towers and connecting walls date from the 15th century.
🚗 *Turn left onto the L023 from the priory. After 3 km (2 miles) turn right at a T-junction, signed for Mount Juliet. At the junction with the R448, turn left. Jerpoint Abbey is just before Thomastown.*

③ Jerpoint Abbey

Founded in 1180, this Cistercian abbey is a daughter house of Mellifont Abbey *(see p159)*. Its tower and battlements stand out, and there is still a sense of its former grandeur. Most of the buildings still standing date from the 15th century, but the abbey's principal attraction lies in its details. The carvings in the cloister are the most ornate of any religious building in Ireland, with knights, courtly ladies, bishops and dragons. Enjoy a scone at Jerpoint Park, a heritage site that is only a few minutes away by car.
🚗 *Turn right onto the R448 leaving the abbey and drive into Thomastown.*

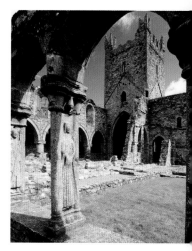

Above The 15th-century cloisters of Jerpoint Abbey, one of Ireland's finest Cistercian ruins

EAT AND DRINK IN KILKENNY CITY

Kyteler's Inn *inexpensive*
The former home of convicted witch Alice Kyteler in the 14th century, this historic inn serves Smithwick's beer, brewed in Kilkenny since 1710.
Kieran's Street; 056 776 1064; www.kytelersinn.com

Mocha's Vintage Tea Room *inexpensive*
Lovely old world decor and top-notch tea, coffee, cakes and savoury snacks.
4 Gas House Lane; 056 777 0565; closed Sun

Kilkenny Design Centre *moderate*
Self-service restaurant in the castle's former dairy and stables. Consistently good food at reasonable prices.
The Parade; 056 772 2118; www.kilkennydesign.com

Rinuccini *moderate*
One of Ireland's finest Italian spots, Rinuccini offers superb fare such as seared scallops with fresh green pea risotto and pancetta.
Parade; 056 776 1575; www.rinuccini.com

La Campagne *expensive*
This Michelin-starred restaurant delivers seriously good modern French food in a relaxed setting. Menus start from €40.
5 Gas House Lane; 056 777 2858; www.campagne.ie; closed Sun dinner, Mon & Tue

Far left Mullins Mill Museum, next to Kells Priory **Left** The 15th-century fortified towers of Kells Priory

Above View over the small market town of Graiguenamanagh

WHERE TO STAY

THOMASTOWN

Ballyduff House
inexpensive-moderate
Handsome and elegant 18th-century house overlooking the River Suir. Guests are free to avail themselves of the gorgeous library and drawing room.
Thomastown; 056 775 8488; www.ballyduffhouse.ie

GRAIGUENAMANAGH

Waterside Guesthouse *inexpensive*
Originally a corn store for the local boatmen, this has been sensitively converted into a delightful guesthouse. All the rooms overlook the River Barrow.
The Quay; 059 972 4246; www.waterside guesthouse.com; closed Nov–Feb

AROUND GRAIGUENAMANAGH

Mulvarra House *inexpensive*
Perched on a hill overlooking the picturesque St Mullins village, 6 km (4 miles) south of Graiguenamanagh, this retreat centre offers comfortable rooms and delicious vegetarian meals.
St Mullins, Co Carlow; 051 424 936; www.mulvarra.com

CARLOW TOWN

Barrowville Townhouse *inexpensive*
This period house near the town centre has seven rooms and serves hearty breakfasts.
Kilkenny Road; 059 914 3324; www.barrowville.com

Right Riverside garden in the attractive village of Inistioge

④ Thomastown
Co Kilkenny

Strategically important in medieval times, this market town gives few hints of the walled town it once was, save for its old stone bridge over the River Nore and the 13th-century ruins of **St Mary's Church**. A pleasant, 2 km (1 mile) walk along the river leads to the 13th-century shell of **Grennan Castle**.
🚗 *Turn left onto The Quay and follow signs for the R700 towards New Ross and Inistioge.*

Statutes of Kilkenny

In 1366 the English Crown decided that the Anglo-Norman rulers of Ireland were becoming too enamoured of Irish ways and customs. Fearful of losing its grip, it enacted the much-hated "Statutes of Kilkenny". Under the new laws, intermarriage between Anglo-Normans and Irish was an act of high treason, and settlers speaking Irish, adopting Irish dress or wearing their hair long in the Irish style risked forfeiting their lands.

⑤ Inistioge
Co Kilkenny

Picture-perfect Inistioge sits elegantly on the River Nore, the ideal setting for an Irish country drama. It's no surprise then that *Circle of Friends* (1995), starring Minnie Driver, and *Widow's Peak* (1994), with Mia Farrow, were both filmed here. There is a lovely riverside walk, and the nine-arch stone bridge – the largest in Ireland – is a source of local pride. Unusually in Ireland, the Catholic and Anglican churches stand side by side.

Just above the town lie the beautifully restored **Woodstock**

Gardens *(open daily)*, which feature an arboretum, a monkey puzzle walk, dovecote and grotto. Derelict Woodstock House, burnt down in the civil war of 1922, gives an extra poignancy to the garden.
🚗 *Leaving Inistioge, cross the arched bridge and take the first left onto the L4209 to Graiguenamanagh (11 km/ 7 miles) almost immediately after the bridge. Arriving in Graiguenamanagh, drive up the hill, past Duiske Abbey, to the car park on right.*

⑥ Graiguenamanagh
Co Carlow

Once a place of significant ecclesiastical importance, Graiguenamanagh (Granary of the Monks) is a small market town on the River Barrow. Occupying centre stage is **Duiske Abbey** *(open Mon–Fri)*, founded in 1204 by Cistercian monks. After the Dissolution of the Monasteries in 1536, it was abandoned and fell into gradual decline, the tower finally collapsing in 1774. In the early 19th century parts of the church were roofed and mass was celebrated here once again. Most of the present building dates from this period. However, it retains some original features, in particular a Romanesque doorway, an effigy of a Norman knight and by the main entrance the original fleur-de-lis paving stones. A second restoration was undertaken in the 1970s, and the abbey is now a working parish church.
🚗 *Exiting the abbey's car park drive uphill to the roundabout. Take the third exit onto Borris Road (R705). At the junction with the R702 turn right for Borris (2 km/1 mile).*

7 Borris
Co Carlow
Nestling in the Barrow valley below the Blackstairs Mountains, this is a pretty village with a cluster of Georgian houses. Its two main landmarks are the Regency-styled **Borris House** *(tours May–Sep: Tue–Thu; www.borrishouse.ie)*, ancestral home of the High Kings of Leinster, and the 16-arch **viaduct** at the bottom of the town. In the 1800s Borris experienced a period of prosperity, thanks to its sawmills and lace industry. For a time Borris lace enjoyed an international reputation.

Above Borris House, ancestral home of the High Kings of Leinster

Exiting Borris, follow the R702 as far as Gowran. Just before the village, turn right onto the R448, signposted Carlow (19 km/12 miles).

8 Carlow Town
Co Carlow
The county town of Ireland's second- smallest county, Carlow was an Anglo-Norman stronghold guarding the River Barrow. Its position on the fringes of the English Pale, the protected area around Dublin, gave it a significant role in the history of Ireland. During the 1798 rebellion 600 rebels were massacred here after attempting to take the town. The Liberty Tree sculpture off Hanover Street commemorates this event.

Standing next to the River Barrow are the ruins of **Carlow Castle**. It survived many sieges, including one by Oliver Cromwell, but was finally laid to waste by a Dr Middleton in 1814. Determined to convert the castle into an asylum, he set about reducing the thickness of its walls with explosives, eventually causing their demolition. Other buildings of note are the Neo-Gothic Catholic **Cathedral** and **St Mary's Church of Ireland**, both dating from the early 19th century.

Above left Traditional bar at Graiguenamanagh **Above** Colourful narrow boats moored on the River Barrow at Graiguenamanagh

EAT AND DRINK

INISTIOGE
Footlights *inexpensive*
A riverside bistro offering pretty views, light dining and evening meals.
The Square; 086 361 9411; www.footlights.ie

The Otter *inexpensive*
The best of Inistioge's several pubs, with summer barbecues, superb ales and live music at weekends.
High Street; 087 061 9015

GRAIGUENAMANAGH
Waterside Restaurant and Guesthouse *inexpensive*
Stone warehouse on the bank of the River Barrow. Smoked eel from the river is a signature dish.
The Quay; 059 972 4246; www. watersideguesthouse.com; closed Nov–Feb

BORRIS
The Stephouse Hotel *moderate*
Smart hotel with a classy restaurant and brasserie, both offering classic Irish cooking with a modern twist.
66 Main Street; 059 0773209; www.stephousehotel.ie

DAY TRIP OPTIONS
Kilkenny City is a good base to explore the area. Kilkenny City can be quickly accessed along the M9 from Waterford City and the M7 (then N8 and N77) from Dublin.

Kilkenny's castle and cathedral
The highlights of Kilkenny City 1 can easily fill a whole day. Climb the cathedral's round tower, find the

grave of the judge who convicted Alice Kyteler of witchcraft in the 14th century, and admire the 13th-century east window. Afterwards head for the castle, seat of the Butler family for 500 years.

Kilkenny City can be explored on foot.

Abbeys and gardens
Just a few kilometres apart are Kells Priory 2 and Jerpoint Abbey 3, set in countryside south of Kilkenny

City. Kells has fortified walls and towers; Jerpoint is known for its carvings. Afterwards head to Inistioge 5 to see Woodstock Gardens and have lunch overlooking the River Nore.

From Kilkenny City, head south along the R697 Kells Road (or faster N10 to Stonyford and turn right), then cut east to Jerpoint via Mount Juliet, and then south along the R700 to Inistioge.

TRIP 7

TIPPERARY'S HOLY GLEN
Cashel to Clonmel

HIGHLIGHTS

The Ancient Rock of Cashel
Marvel at the solitary glory of Ireland's finest
ecclesiastical site

Tranquil Athassel Priory
Discover this hidden Augustinian priory on the banks of
the River Suir

The verdant Glen of Aherlow
Strike out on one of the many hiking trails or explore the
leafy lanes of this resplendent river valley in the shadow
of the Galtee Mountains

Stronghold of Cahir
Explore the formidable castle of the medieval dukes of
Ormonde, and their *cottage ornée* from a gentler era

The striking ruins of Hore Abbey, near the Rock of Cashel

TIPPERARY'S HOLY GLEN

Bordered by the Galtee and Knockmealdown mountains to the south, this fertile, landlocked county is often overlooked by visitors, eager to move on to the more dramatic landscape of the western coastal counties. This is a pity, as Tipperary's many captivating sights warrant far more than a cursory glance. Chief among them is the resplendent Glen of Aherlow, studded with holy wells and ruined abbeys. Also here is Ireland's most fascinating ecclesiastical site – the totemic Rock of Cashel, a lofty citadel that soars above the surrounding vale. To the east are the vibrant former Anglo-Norman strongholds of Cahir and Clonmel, quintessential Irish market towns that are ideal for a leisurely wander.

Clonkelly

Dundrum

Ballymore

Newtown

Knockavilla

R505

Donohill

Moanmore

Ballynahi

R497

Gorteen

Mulleen

R661

Donaskeagh

Cullen

Monara

Thomastown

N24

Kilfeakle

G

Tipperary

N74

ATHASSEL
PRIORY **2**

Lattin

R515

Shronell

Bawnbrack

Lagganstown

R664

Ballinleenty

R662

Brookville

Bansha

Rathdermot

Ara

GLEN OF AHERLOW
NATURE PARK **3**

Kilross

Foxfort

Ballygorteen

R663

Glen of Aherlow

N24

Aberlo

Newtown

Lisvernane **4**

Rossadrehid

THE KYLE **6**

Galbally **5**

CLONBEG
CHURCH

Ballydre

R663

MOORE
ABBEY

Spittle

Barna

Galty Mountains

R662

△ Galtymore
920m

△ Greenane
804m

Clonmore

11

ACTIVITIES

Walk out to Hore Abbey for an outstanding view of the soaring Rock of Cashel

See red squirrels and spring flowers on the Bianconi Forest Walk in the Glen of Aherlow

Climb up to Darby's Bed, a megalithic passage tomb on a hillside near Galbally

Visit Cahir's curious Swiss Cottage, a *cottage ornée* designed by Georgian architect John Nash

Left Celtic cross in Cashel's broad Main Street, *see p90*

Above The town of Cashel, below the famous Rock, *see p90*

PLAN YOUR DRIVE

Start/finish: Cashel to Clonmel.

Number of days: 2–3.

Distance: 240 km (154 miles).

Road conditions: Well paved and signposted.

When to go: Mar–Oct is best. Many of the holy wells and monastic sites are wet and boggy in winter.

Opening times: Shops are generally open 9 or 10am to 5 or 6pm, but closed Sun. Sights may be closed in winter.

Main market days: Cahir: Farmers' Market, Sat am (car park beside Craft Granary on Church Street).

Major festivals: Cashel: Art Festival, Sep; **Clonmel**: National Coursing Meeting, Feb; Junction Arts Festival, Jul; **Cahir**: Trad Fest, Sep.

DAY TRIP OPTIONS

For fascinating insights into Irish **history and culture**, dramatic **views** and outstanding **Romanesque architecture**, head to the Rock of Cashel, Cahir Castle and the old market town of Clonmel. Keen walkers can explore the many **hiking trails** in the Glen of Aherlow, taking in the **wooded hillsides**, **ruined abbeys** and **holy wells**. For full details, *see p91*.

Below the Glen of Aherlow, ideal walking country, *see p91*

KEY

Drive route

0 kilometres 5

0 miles 5

Above The dramatic Rock of Cashel tops a craggy limestone outcrop

VISITING CASHEL

Parking
There is a pay car park at the foot of the Rock of Cashel, next to the Tourist Information Office.

Tourist Information
Main Street, Cashel; 062 61333; www.cashel.ie; open daily; Nov–Feb: Mon–Fri only

Brú Ború Cultural Centre
Cashel; 062 61122 ; http://bruboru.ie; open mid-Jun–Aug: Tue–Sat, Sep–mid-Jun: Mon–Fri

WHERE TO STAY IN CASHEL

Aherlow House Hotel *moderate*
Former hunting lodge set in acres of woodland. Elegant and comfortable with beautiful views over the Galtee mountains. Frequently has special offers. Situated just off the R663, a short distance west of Newtown.
Glen of Aherlow; 062 56153; www.aherlowhouse.ie

Cashel Palace Hotel *expensive*
Set within peaceful gardens, the former archbishop's palace has been spectacularly revamped. Sumptuous bedrooms are complemented by a fine restaurant.
Main Street; 06262002; www.cashel palacehotel.ie

① Cashel
Co Tipperary
All royal and ecclesiastical ruins in Ireland fade into insignificance when compared with the **Rock of Cashel** *(closed 24–26 Dec)*. Visible from afar, this tight cluster of turrets and towers soars majestically above the vales of Tipperary. From the 4th or 5th century it was the seat of the Kings of Munster, whose kingdom extended over much of southern Ireland. Legend has it that St Patrick baptized Aengus, King of Munster, here in AD 448. In 1101, Cashel was handed over to the Church. It flourished as a religious centre until Cromwell's army sacked it in 1647.

From the car park, Bishop's Walk leads to the 15th-century **Hall of the Vicar's Choral**, built for Cashel's top choristers. It now houses the ticket office and an audiovisual presentation on the site. In the museum on the lower floor, look out for **St Patrick's Cross**; its base is believed to be the coronation stone of the Munster kings, and the carving on the east face shows St Patrick on his visit to Cashel in 450. Opposite the **Dormitory of the Vicar's Choral** is **St Cormac's Chapel**, a Romanesque masterpiece with carvings on the tympanum, containing the sarcophagus of Cormac the Bishop, a 12th-century King of Munster.

The largest building on the Rock is **St Patrick's Cathedral**, burned in 1495 by the Earl of Kildare and again by a Cromwellian army, when 3,000 townfolk seeking sanctuary were roasted to death by Lord Inchoquin, one of Cromwell's generals. Look out for the panels of three 16th-century tombs in the north transept, decorated with intricate carvings of vine-leaf designs and stylized beasts. Next to the cathedral, the 28-m (92-ft) **Round Tower** dates from the early 12th century.

Beyond the ramparts of the Rock (a 2-km/1-mile walk across the fields) is **Hore Abbey**, which affords one of the best views of the Rock.

In Cashel itself, in the grounds of the Protestant cathedral on John's Street, is the **Bolton Library**, named after the 18th-century bishop of Cashel. Owing to the poor conditions within, the library's rich collection of antiquarian books was transferred to Limerick University in 2016.Back in the car park at the foot of the rock, the **Brú Ború**

Cultural Centre – named after Brian Ború, a 10th-century king of Munster – charts the history of Irish culture, and holds traditional music, song and dance performances.

🚗 *From the car park, turn left and then left again onto the main Dublin–Cork road. Turn right and drive through Cashel. At the end of the High Street turn right and left onto the R505. At the first roundabout turn left onto the N74. After 6 km (4 miles), past the village of Golden, turn left just after Bridge House pub on the L3101. Shortly after the priory comes into view, 1.5 km (1 mile) from the turning, pull into a lay-by on the left, just past some stone pillars.*

② Athassel Priory
Co Tipperary
From the stone pillars a path leads over a bridge and through the old gate lodge of the priory. Founded in 1192 by the Anglo-Norman knight William de Burgh, this Augustinian priory *(open daily)* was once the largest in Ireland. Its walls still stand, and the church has an aisled nave, a choir and transepts with a 15th-century tower over the crossing. Look for a carved face protruding from the tower.

🚗 *From the stone pillars, retrace the route to Golden, then take a left turn onto the N74, following signs towards Tipperary. Once in Tipperary, take the R664 off Main Street. Follow the road for a short distance then turn right at a traffic island, following signs for the Tipperary Golf Club. Continue to the Christ the King statue and the entrance to the Glen of Aherlow Nature Park. Park at the foot of the statue.*

Above The ruined 15th-century tower, nave and choir of Athassel Priory

③ Glen of Aherlow Nature Park

The Glen of Aherlow, a 25-km (15-mile) long valley dotted with megalithic and early Christian sites, runs from Galbally in the west to Bansha in the east. Within the valley, the Christ the King statue is a major landmark and the starting point for a network of hiking trails in the Glen of Aherlow Nature Park. It is said that the statue's raised hand bestows a blessing on all who pass.

A two-hour walking tour

One of several trails in the nature park, Bianconi Forest Walk is a 7-km (4-mile) loop. It is glorious at all times of the year, but especially in spring, when the woods – a habitat for red squirrels – are filled with bluebells and primroses.

From the car park near the **Christ the King statue** ①, walk up to the display board above the picnic area. The Bianconi Walk is marked by a blue arrow. Entering the forest, follow the path down stone steps, over a wooden bridge and turn right. When the path divides after about 300 m (984 ft), veer left, pausing to read the first of a series of poems on a tree trunk.

Continue along the path to a stone stile. Cross this and turn left along a broad path, shaded by oak and ash trees – once part of the old Bianconi coach route from Tipperary to Limerick, named after Charles Bianconi, who founded public transport in Ireland with a carriage service from Clonmel to Cahir in 1815. Walk down the hill

The Christ the King statue

to a beautiful forest glade, mountain stream and **stone bridge** ②. Cross the bridge and follow the wide track as it snakes to a T-junction. Turn right and follow the path to a paved road. To the left is the **Aherlow House Hotel** ③, a good stop for refreshments. Turn right, follow the road up a steady rise for 1 km (half a mile), taking in the views of the glen. At the T-junction turn right and walk downhill, with a clear view of Galtymore, the highest peak in the Galtee Mountains. Leave the road and re-enter the forest. The path leads down to a crossroads. On the left, stone steps lead up to the ruins of an old **stone cottage** ④ from the famine era (1845–70). Follow the path back to the start.

🚗 *From the Christ the King statue follow the R664 to Newtown (3 km/ 2 miles). At the T-junction, turn right onto the R663, signposted Galbally. Just outside Newtown, after the Glen Hotel, follow the left sign for Clonbeg Church.*

VISITING GLEN OF AHERLOW NATURE PARK

Parking
There is a car park at the Christ the King Statue, the entrance to the Glen of Aherlow Nature Park.

Glen of Aherlow Information Centre
Maps and information on the Glen. *Glen of Aherlow Fáilte Society, Coach Road; 062 56331; www.aherlow.com; open Jun–Aug: Mon–Sat; Sep–May: Mon–Fri*

EAT AND DRINK IN CASHEL

The Bakehouse *inexpensive*
A bakery with a café upstairs, opposite the Tourist Information Office. Offers well-prepared unfussy food.
Main Street; 062 61680; closes 5:30pm

Feehan's Bar *inexpensive*
This pleasant pub serves up home-made soups, steak sandwiches and more. Takeaway also available.
Main Street; 062 61929

Chez Hans *expensive*
Fine food served in the unusual setting of an old church. A signature dish is the cassoulet of seafood. Next door, Café Hans offers more informal dining.
Moor Lane; 062 61177; www.chezhans. net; closed Mon & Tue

Below View over the glorious Glen of Aherlow with the Galtee Mountains in the background

Above The Swiss Cottage at Cahir, a *cottage ornée* designed by John Nash

WHERE TO STAY

AROUND CLONBEG CHURCH

Ballinacourty House and Restaurant *inexpensive*
Eighteenth-century building with rooms and restaurant overlooking an inner courtyard. Camping and self-catering cottages attached. Located a short distance north of Lisvernane on a minor road.
Glen of Aherlow; 062 56224; www.ballinacourtyhouse.com

CLONMEL

Hotel Minella *moderate*
Swish, sprawling hotel with a range of rooms overlooking the River Suir towards the mountains. Comprehensive leisure facilities here include a superb indoor pool.
Coleville Road, Clonmel; 052 612 2388; www.hotelminella.com

CAHIR

Cahir House Hotel *moderate*
The former home of the Butler family, this is a popular hotel complete with a landscaped garden in the middle of Cahir. The hotel bistro is well regarded too.
The Square; 052 744 3000; www.cahir househotel.ie

④ Clonbeg Church
Co Tipperary
This 18th-century Church of Ireland chapel is unusual in having both a Catholic and Anglican burial ground. It is built on the site of a church founded by St Sedan – the ivy-clad remains of an earlier church can still be seen – and is notable for **St Sedan's Well**, situated in the far right-hand corner of the graveyard. The water from the well is noted for its healing properties, in particular for treating eye ailments. People visiting the well tie "clooties" – pieces of clothing belonging to the sick – to the birch tree behind the well.

🚗 Return to main road (R663) and turn left towards Galbally and Lisvernane. Moore Abbey is 4 km (2 miles) beyond Lisvernane. As the road approaches the abbey it swings right over a stone bridge. There is a small parking bay on the right-hand side just past the abbey.

Above The cemetry of the 18th century Clonbeg church

⑤ Moore Abbey
Co Tipperary
On the western end of the Aherlow Valley, **Moore Abbey** was founded in 1204 by Donough O'Brien, King of Thomond (North Munster). Repeatedly destroyed by the Desmond and Ormonde dynasties, it took 300 years to build. The remains date mainly from the 15th century.

Carry on along the R663 to **Galbally**, a town centring on a large square with a statue commemorating those who lost their lives in the struggle for Irish Independence. Just outside town on Duntryleague Hill is **Darby's Bed**, a megalithic passage tomb. To get there take the narrow road (behind the statue) off the main square. It is a 15-minute walk from the car park.

🚗 From Galbally return to Newtown and continue east on the R663 towards Bansha. After 3 km (2 miles) turn right onto an unclassified road signposted Rossadrehid (7 km/4 miles). Immediately after the first crossroads, pull in and park in front of cottage on the right-hand side of the road. To find the Kyle, follow the path to the right of the cottage, climb over a stile and follow a rough path across the field.

Holy Wells
The Glen of Aherlow has many holy wells, many of them pre-dating Christianity in Ireland. Druids were said to draw their power from them. They continue to be considered holy and to possess miraculous healing powers. Pilgrims often use a piece of cloth to wash the afflicted part of their body and then tie it to the tree overhanging the well – usually an ash or whitethorn – as a prayer offering.

⑥ The Kyle
Co Tipperary
The oval enclosure known as the **Kyle** was created to preserve a collection of Celtic relics – grinding stones, fragments of a cross and carvings – found on the site here. It has also been used as a burial place for unbaptized children.

To reach **St Berrihert's Well**, walk past the Kyle, through the wooden gate and along a causeway over marshy ground. Follow the path to some wooden steps and a bridge,

Above The Main Guard in Clonmel, built as a courthouse by the Earl of Ormonde

and turn left towards a second gate. Through the gate veer right. The well is marked by a "rag tree". According to local legend, water from the well will not boil; it also protects from fire. 🚗 *Continue in the same direction to the N24. Turn right for Cahir. Park just past Cahir Castle, across the bridge.*

7 Cahir
Co Tipperary
The main attraction of this market town is **Cahir Castle** *(open daily)*, an Anglo-Norman stronghold of the Butler dynasty, Earls of Ormonde. It was a formidable defence, although Cromwell's army breached its walls in 1650. The foundations, curtain walls and keep are 13th-century; much of the rest dates from the 15th and 16th centuries. Don't miss the magnificent Great Hall and the ramparts.

A 2-km (1-mile) walk along the River Suir (signposted from the back of the car park) leads to the **Swiss Cottage** *(open mid-Mar–Oct)* a *cottage ornée* designed by Regency architect John Nash for Richard Butler in 1810, and conceived as an ornamental retreat where the earl could entertain guests. By the car park, **Inch Field** has

a fine view of the castle. From here turn right along Castle Street to the main square, designed by the Victorian architect William Tinsley, and turn left along **Church Street** for a medley of shops and cafés. **St Paul's**, a Church of Ireland chapel also designed by John Nash in the early 1800s, is at its end. 🚗 *Turn right from the car park and drive to the top of Castle Street and the main square. Turn left onto the R640 at the junction, following signs for Clonmel (16 km/10 miles).*

8 Clonmel
Co Tipperary
This is Tipperary's most important market town and its bustling atmosphere makes it a pleasant place to stroll around. Like many towns in the area, it was besieged by Cromwell in 1650, but was one of the few places that put up serious resistance. The medieval **West Gate** (rebuilt in 1831) leads to **O'Connell Street**, the main thoroughfare. A stone plaque in the gate commemorates Laurence Sterne, author of the early comic novel *Tristram Shandy*, who was born in Clonmel in 1713. Halfway down O'Connell Street, in Mary Street, **St Mary's Church** contains one of the oldest organs in Ireland, stained-glass windows by William Tinsley and remnants of the original city walls.

At the east end of O'Connell Street, **Main Guard**, built as a courthouse in 1675, houses the **Tourist Information Centre** *(open Mon–Fri)*. Nearby, off pedestrianized Mitchell Street, Abbey Street leads to the **Old Quay**, where the **Franciscan Friary** retains a 15th-century tower. At the end of Mitchell Street, Emmet Street leads to Mick Delahunty Square, with a statue of Clonmel's favourite son, the tenor Frank Patterson (1938–2000), and the **Museum of Hidden History** *(open Tue–Sat)*.

EAT AND DRINK

CAHIR
The River House
inexpensive–moderate
Opposite the castle, this restaurant offers breakfast, lunch and takeouts in a relaxing setting. Good for home-made soups and salads. There is also a bar onsite.
1 Castle Street; 052 744 1951; closes 5pm; www.riverhouse.ie

Lava Rock *moderate*
Modern and bright restaurant offering mouthwatering plates such as monkfish tagine and venison shoulder croquette.
Castle Street; 052 744 5359; www.lava rockrestaurant.com; closed Mon–Wed

CLONMEL
Befani's Mediterranean & Tapas Restaurant *moderate*
Stylish restaurant that is popular with locals and discerning diners. The food is bold and flavoursome with such mainstays as cassoulet sausage and duck confit, in addition to small plates like crispy crab meat arancini. Also provides accommodation.
6 Sarsfield St; 052 617 7893; www.befani.com

Below Quayside walk in Clonmel, a market town on the River Suir

DAY TRIP OPTIONS
Cashel is the ideal base to explore the area's two highlights.

Fortified rock
One of Ireland's top attractions, the Rock of Cashel 1 is a fortified cathedral with towers, turrets and a

round tower rising straight out of the rock. Be sure to get there early to avoid the crowds. Afterwards take in Cahir 7, a market town with a superb castle, or the historical town of Clonmel 8.

From Cashel take the M8 to Cahir and then the N24 to Clonmel.

Holy glen and holy wells
Combine a walk through the Glen of Aherlow Nature Park 3 with a drive through its main valley, stopping at ruined abbeys, holy wells, villages and megalithic tombs.

Follow the drive instructions from Cashel.

TRIP 8

THE SUNNY SOUTHEAST
Enniscorthy to the Saltees

HIGHLIGHTS

Miles of beach
Wander Curracloe's uncrowded sandy beach, the
longest in Ireland, keeping an eye out for seals

Rebel town
Explore the rebellious history of Wexford, a handsome
town now famed for its opera festival

Wildlife havens
Go bird-watching at Lady's Island and Tacumshane lakes,
and on rugged Great Saltee Island

THE SUNNY SOUTHEAST

Wexford's mild maritime climate yields Ireland's best strawberries and potatoes and has made the county a favourite haunt of Dubliners who want a retreat away from home. This drive includes a good stretch of the coastline, with long and unspoiled beaches and two world-class sites for bird-watchers. There are many links along the route with the 1798 Rebellion, which took place largely in Wexford (*see p106*). The southern end of the county is very rural, with thatched cottages and one of the last original windmills in Ireland.

Above Tacumshane's lovingly preserved windmill, dating from 1846, *see p101*

ACTIVITIES

Walk the ridge of Oulart Hill, site of an important rebel victory in 1798

Have a go at bodyboarding on Curracloe, Ireland's longest beach

Listen to uplifting music during the Wexford Festival Opera

Take a short boat ride to Great Saltee Island to see its colony of puffins

0 kilometres   4

0 miles   4

KEY

▬▬ Drive route

PLAN YOUR DRIVE

Start/finish: Enniscorthy to Kilmore Quay for the Saltee Islands.

Number of days: 3, allowing half a day for a visit to the Saltee Islands.

Distance: 75 km (47 miles).

Road conditions: Larger roads are in good condition and well signposted. Smaller roads are often winding, so take care on bends.

When to go: All year round – Wexford is famous for its mild climate. Opera-lovers should go in October for the Wexford Festival Opera.

Opening times: Shops open Mon–Sat from 9 or 10am to 5 or 6pm.

Main market days: Enniscorthy: Sat; Wexford Town: Fri.

Shopping: Fresh produce such as artisan cheeses, hand-pressed apple juice and dry-cured bacon are widely available. Wexford Town's shops include a craftsman silver- and gold-smiths established in 1647.

Major festivals: Enniscorthy: Strawberry Festival, Jun; Wexford Literary Festival, Jul; **Wexford Town:** Viking Fire Festival, Sep; Wexford Festival Opera, Oct.

DAY TRIP OPTIONS

Fans of **Irish history** will want to visit Vinegar and Oulart hills, important sites of the 1798 rebellion; while **bird-watchers** and **nature lovers** should not miss the chance to visit Lady's Island and Tacumshane lakes. For full details, see p101.

Below Wexford Town Harbour, with fishing boats and pleasure craft, see p100

Above Enniscorthy, with the spire of its magnificent cathedral **Above top right** Pastoral landscape near Curracloe **Above right** Enniscorthy's 13th-century castle

WHERE TO STAY

AROUND ENNISCORTHY

Anam Cara *inexpensive–moderate*
High-end guesthouse located half a mile (1 km) northwest of town, with five beautifully appointed rooms, some of which overlook the lush gardens. Enjoy wonderful hospitality and several acres of woodland paths. *Carraigabruce, Enniscorthy; 087 223 0332; www.anamcaraguesthouse.com*

Monart *expensive*
A most luxurious destination spa, set in 40 ha (100 acres) just northwest of Enniscorthy, Monart encourages its guests to connect with themselves and the landscape by immersion in relaxation therapy, wandering in the gardens and eating sumptuous meals. *The Still, Enniscorthy; 053 923 8999; www.monart.ie*

① Enniscorthy
Co Wexford

An attractive market town on the hilly west bank of the River Slaney, Enniscorthy was a focal point of the 1798 Rebellion. After a victory against the British here, insurgency spread through the region. **St Aidan's Cathedral** *(open daily)*, by Augustus Welby Pugin, is a mid-19th-century Gothic Revival building of superb quality. The 13th-century castle on which the town was founded has been restored as a local history **museum** *(open daily)*.

🚗 *Leaving Enniscorthy, cross the river to the eastern side and follow the signs for Vinegar Hill, which overlooks the town.*

② Vinegar Hill
Enniscorthy, Co Wexford

This was the principal camp for the insurgents who took the town of Enniscorthy in May 1798. In June, they were surrounded by 20,000 troops; many were massacred, and the rest escaped through a gap in the British lines. The windmill used as a fort still stands, and there are great views across the country, to Enniscorthy and over to Oulart Hill.

🚗 *Return towards Enniscorthy and take the R744 in the direction of Blackwater. When the road veers right, take the fork to the left, signposted for Oulart. The narrow road passes through pleasant farming country to the village of Oulart. Turn left, then left again before the church, then up a long straight road to the top of the hill, where there is a car park.*

Artisan Food

Enniscorthy and Wexford markets are the best places to find artisan produce from the county's farmers. Carrigbyrne's St Killian (voted Best Irish Cheese at the 2007 World Cheese Awards) and Irish Brie, made in Adamstown west of Wexford Town, are excellent, as are the juices from Ballycross Apple Farm, in Bridgetown near Kilmore Quay.

③ Oulart Hill
Oulart, Co Wexford

In May 1798, the day before the rebels stormed Enniscorthy, a small insurgent force under Father John Murphy defeated the British on

Above View over Enniscorthy towards Oulart Hill from Vinegar Hill

Oulart Hill. A short walk from the car park passes along the brow of the hill, on a path marked with stones engraved with the names of people and places associated with the 1798 Rebellion in Wexford. At the end is *Tulach a' tSolais* (meaning "mound of light"), a grassy mound bisected by a striking and austere concrete memorial, erected to commemorate the bicentenary of the Rebellion, designed by leading architect Ronald Tallon and enclosing an oak sculpture by Michael Warren. The central shaft of the monument, cut through the hill, is aligned with Vinegar Hill. There are great views of the surrounding countryside and Wexford Bay.

🚗 *Return to Oulart village and turn left. At the junction with the R741 turn right. At the junction with the R744 turn left, heading for Blackwater.*

④ Blackwater
Co Wexford

This village features many of the thatched cottages for which County Wexford is famous, some decorated in patterns with seashells. Turn left, then right, down a pretty road with more thatched cottages, to reach **Ballyconnigar**. The beach here runs all the way to Wexford Town.

🚗 *Return to Blackwater, head south on the R742, signed Curracloe. Take a left turn signed to Bently Cottage/ Ballinesker down a narrow road through sand dunes to Curracloe Beach.*

Below The dunes behind sandy Curracloe Beach, location for the film *Saving Private Ryan*

NEW POTATOES HOME GROWN

Curracloe village farm sign

⑤ Curracloe Beach
Co Wexford

The D-Day landing scenes in Steven Spielberg's *Saving Private Ryan* were shot on Curracloe's 16 km (10 miles) of golden sands. The waymarked **Raven Point Loop** trail here passes through an area that is home to grey seals and wild orchids. Allow at least two hours. The **Wexford Wildfowl Reserve** *(open daily)*, where thousands of birds overwinter, is nearby.

🚗 *Take the R742 to the junction with the R741 (signposts point left to the Wildfowl Reserve). Cross the bridge at Wexford, turn right on the R730 towards the N11, then take the left turn signed to the Irish National Heritage Park.*

⑥ Irish National Heritage Park
Ferrycarrig, Co Wexford

A trail within the 14 ha (35 acres) of the park *(open daily)* takes visitors through reconstructions of Irish settlements dating from the Stone Age to the arrival of the Normans in the 12th century.

🚗 *Return to the R730 towards Wexford Town. Turn left for Wexford Town and park on the quayside.*

Wexford Wildfowl
Around 10,000 Greenland white-fronted geese overwinter here, but others to look out for in the marshes and grasslands include dunlins, godwits, plovers, scoters, pochards and shovelers, and listen out for warblers and cuckoos in season.

Above Typical Wexford-style thatched cottage near Blackwater village

EAT AND DRINK IN ENNISCORTHY

The Wilds *inexpensive*
Attached to a craft shop, this daytime café-cum-deli has bright and breezy interiors and serves all-day brunches.
23 Wheafer Street; 053 923 7799; www.thewilds.ie; closed Mon

Via Veneto *moderate*
A good, authentic Italian restaurant offering fish and rice dishes, polenta, broths and stews as well as pasta and pizza, along with top-class wine. Stylish and informal.
58 Weafer Street; 053 923 6929; www.viaveneto.ie; closed Mon & Tue

Above Striking statue of a Pikeman of the 1798 Rebellion, Wexford Town

VISITING WEXFORD TOWN

Parking
Paid parking on Paul Quay near the Tourist Office.

Tourist information
Crescent Quay; 053 912 3111; visitwexford.ie; open Mon–Sat

VISITING GREAT SALTEE ISLAND

Boats to Great Saltee leave Kilmore Quay mid morning in fine weather.

WHERE TO STAY

WEXFORD TOWN

Clayton Hotel Whites *moderate*
This well-loved hotel has been renovated with first-class facilities such as an indoor pool and a tranquillity spa.
Abbey Street; 053 912 2311; www.claytonwhiteshotel.com

AROUND WEXFORD TOWN

Killiane Castle *moderate*
At this stunning castle and working farm guests can watch cows being milked, lambs being born, and even use the golf driving range. Lovely rooms. Excellent breakfasts are served.
Drinagh, Wexford; 053 915 8885; www.killianecastle.com

KILMORE QUAY

Quay House *inexpensive*
This pleasant, bright B&B is especially popular with fishermen.
087 231 5470; www.quayhouse.net

Coast Kilmore Quay *inexpensive*
The rooms here are smart and there is a top-notch restaurant onsite.
053 914 8641; www.coastkilmore quay.com

⑦ WEXFORD TOWN

Co Wexford

This handsome walled town at the mouth of the River Slaney was founded by the Norsemen in the 9th or 10th century and, in the 12th century, it was the first Irish town to be captured by the Anglo-Normans. The charming quays of Wexford's once-thriving port are now given over to recreation, and the pretty, narrow streets tucked behind it are full of shops, museums, and sights of historic interest.

A one-hour walking tour

From the **Tourist Office** ① walk along Crescent Quay to the statue of Commodore John Barry, father of the US Navy, who was born near here in 1745. Go back to the tourist office, turn up Oyster Lane and then right, left and right again, onto High Street. On the right is the **Opera House** ②, *(see box)* hidden behind a façade of terraced houses. Turn back to the first corner, then right into Mary Street and up to School Street, where the mainly 18th-century **Franciscan Friary** ③ holds a relic of St Adjutor, the Roman boy-martyr. Walk along School Street and turn right to Rowe Street. The **Church of the Immaculate Conception** ④ was built in 1858 to a design by architect Robert Pierce. Walk down Rowe Street to North Main Street and turn left. At the junction of North Main, Abbey and Common Quay streets is the **Bullring** ⑤, scene of bull-baiting in Roman times, and of a massacre in 1649 by Cromwell's men. The impressive figure of a 1798 **Pikeman** ⑥, erected in 1905, is by Oliver Sheppard.

Carry on up North Main and Selskar streets into Westgate to the **Abbey of the Holy Sepulchre** ⑦ *(open daily)*, the remains of a 14th-century church of the Augustinian Priory. It was here that the English king Henry II is said to have spent Lent of 1172 doing penance for the murder of Thomas à Becket. To return to the car park, walk down Westgate to Wellington Place, and along the quays, pausing to admire the striking modern bridge on the way.
🚗 *Leave Wexford on the R730, then take the N25 south to Tagoat, then turn right onto the L0360 and follow the signs to Lady's Island Lake.*

Wexford Opera Festival

Each autumn, Wexford Town's streets are packed with opera fans from around the world. Founded in 1951, the Festival often showcases little-known or neglected works. In 2008, a superb new dedicated opera house opened, reinforcing the Festival's status as a musical event of global stature and importance.

Above The Wexford Town's quays, as seen from across the estuary of the River Slaney

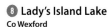

Above The Gothic Revival mansion of Johnstown Castle, with its glorious gardens

EAT AND DRINK

WEXFORD TOWN

Westgate Design *inexpensive*
The restaurant in this superb crafts and design centre serves tasty, generous, home-cooked local dishes. There's a takeout-only café too.
22 North Main Street; 053 912 3787; www.westgatedesign.ie; closed Sun

Cistin Eile *moderate*
Cosy, informal restaurant serving rustic Irish fare such as Wicklow venison. Good spot for a glass of wine too.
80 South Main Street; 053 912 1616; closed Sun

TACUMSHANE

The Millhouse *inexpensive*
Next to the windmill, this family-run pub offers hearty fare and, intriguingly, a Peking Asian street food menu.
053 913 1700; www. meylersmillhouse.com

KILMORE QUAY

Silver Fox Seafood Restaurant *moderate*
This first-rate restaurant serves a wide range of locally sourced seafood, such as Dublin Bay prawns, black sole and lobster, which is complemented by a stellar wine menu.
053 912 9888; www.thesilverfox.ie

8 Lady's Island Lake
Co Wexford

Lady's Island Lake is a saltwater lagoon, separated from the sea by a barrier of sand and shingles. It is an internationally important site for breeding terns and home to many species of migrating birds. The island, linked to the mainland by a causeway, is named for an abbey dedicated to the Virgin Mary. Now in ruins, it has for centuries been a place of pilgrimage. Off the coast to the east is Tuskar Rock, with its 19th-century lighthouse.

The roads are narrow, winding and rarely signposted. To avoid getting lost, return to Tagoat, turn left on R736, left again signed to for Tacumshane.

9 Tacumshane
Co Wexford

Tacumshane Lake is another salt-water lagoon, cut off from the sea by a storm beach. There is a diverse waterfowl population here and rare breeds can be seen all year. In Tacumshane village, a fine windmill dating from 1846 is the only surviving one that is complete. Ask for the key to see inside it at the friendly pub nearby, the Millhouse.

Return to the R736 and turn left onto it, then left onto the R739 signposted for Kilmore Quay.

10 Kilmore Quay
Co Wexford

This pretty seaside village, with many old thatched cottages, is an important fishing port and holiday resort. It is also the departure point for **Great Saltee Island**, Ireland's most important bird sanctuary, just off the coast. The Saltees are home to important colonies of gannet, guillemot, puffin, razorbill and fulmar. There is also a breeding colony of around 120 grey seals. The islands are privately owned but day visitors are welcome on Great Saltee, and boat trips run daily in good weather from Kilmore Quay.

DAY TRIP OPTIONS

This region offers the country's best birdwatching opportunities.

Rebel views
From a base in Enniscorthy 1, Vinegar Hill 2 and Oulart Hill 3, two important sites of the 1798 Rebellion, are close together, and offer panoramic views. The drive is on pretty country roads.

Follow the directions in the itinerary.

Wexford wander
Take a stroll around the city of Wexford, with a trip to the Irish Heritage Park.

Birders' paradise
For rich wildlife, visit Lady's Island Lake 8, Tacumshane 9 and then Kilmore Quay 10 for a trip to Great Saltees.

Follow the directions in the itinerary from Wexford Town to Kilmore Quay.

TRIP 9

CARLOW'S HIDDEN TREASURES
Tullow to Bagenalstown

HIGHLIGHTS

Ancient earthworks
Explore atmospheric Rathgall hill fort, burial place of the Kings of Leinster

Castle life
Step back in time at Clonegal's 17th-century castle

Mountain wilderness
Drive the narrow mountain road around Mount Leinster and leave the modern world behind

Natural wonders
Enjoy a woodland walk at Altamont, one of the most magical gardens in Ireland

Pathway in the lush Altamont gardens in Ballon

CARLOW'S HIDDEN TREASURES

County Carlow is out of the way of the usual tourist trails and is rarely explored by foreign tourists, or even visitors from elsewhere in Ireland, but there are secrets to be discovered on this drive through lushly wooded countryside. The county is crossed by lovely waterways, including the rivers Barrow, Slaney and Derry, affording ample opportunities for peaceful walks or even a spot of fishing.

Above Tullow Museum, in a former chapel beside the River Slaney, *see p106*

KEY

- Drive route

ACTIVITIES

Stroll around the hilly town of Tullow where leaders of the 1798 Rebellion were executed in the square

Play a round of golf at Tullow's magnificent Mount Wolseley course

Get inspiration for your garden from the romantic landscapes of Altamont

Take to the River Barrow for a fishing trip

PLAN YOUR DRIVE

Start/finish: Tullow to Bagenalstown.

Number of days: 2 days.

Distance: 72 km (45 miles).

Road conditions: Most roads are in good condition, with larger roads well signposted. Mostly flat country, with modest hills near Tullow and an open mountain road around Mount Leinster.

When to go: Spring and summer are mild and frequently sunny; this is a lovely time to visit Altamont Garden. Autumn is quieter, with spectacular colour in the trees.

Opening times: Opening hours are generally 9 or 10am to 5 or 6pm. Most shops close on Sundays, except convenience stores. Catholic churches are usually open all day.

Main market days: Carlow Town: Sat.

Major festivals: Carlow: Carlow Arts Festival, Jun; Carlow Garden Festival, Jul; **Tullow:** Tullow Agricultural Show, Aug; **Bagenalstown:** Carlow Farmers' Point-to-Point Races, May; Bagenalstown Festival, Jul.

DAY TRIP OPTIONS

Garden enthusiasts could spend a whole day at Altamont. More **active visitors** will enjoy the challenge of climbing Mount Leinster, while Shillelagh to Clonegal is a pleasant river drive, with a castle to visit at the end, for those interested in **nature and history**. For details, *see p109*.

Below The River Slaney in lush countryside outside Bunclody, *see p107*

Above Tullow Museum, which tells the events of the 1798 Rebellion in Tullow

VISITING CARLOW AND WICKLOW COUNTIES

Carlow Tourist Office
College Street; 059 913 1554;
www.carlowtourism.com

Wicklow Tourist Office
Fitzwilliam Square; 404 69117;
www.visitwicklow.ie; open Mon–Fri

Shillelagh Sticks
Olde Shillelagh Stick Makers, Main
Street, Shillelagh; 086 272 2913;
www.oldeshillelagh.webs.com

WHERE TO STAY IN TULLOW

Ballyderrin House *inexpensive*
Offering a comfortable place to stay, this beautifully renovated old house is situated just east of Tullow. Its nine bedrooms – four in the main house and five garden rooms – all have luxurious facilities.
Shillelagh Road, Tullow; 059 915 2742;
www.ballyderrinhouse.ie

Mount Wolseley Hotel *expensive*
To the southeast of Tullow, this luxury hotel with spa is popular among golfers who play the adjoining 18-hole championship course
Mount Wolseley, Tullow; 059 918 0100;
www.mountwolseley.ie

① Tullow
Co Carlow

A handsome small market town by the River Slaney, with some fine old stone town houses and shops, Tullow is known locally as "the granite town". On the hilly main street is a monument to two leaders of the 1798 Rebellion, John Gallagher and Father John Murphy, "most cruelly and barbarously put to death by English soldiers on the square of Tullow". The **museum** *(Apr–Sep: Mon–Fri pm; volunteer-staffed so hours may vary),* in a former chapel beside the River Slaney, tells their story. The Tullow Agricultural Show in August is a major livestock show, famous for its enormous prize bulls.

🚗 *From Tullow take R725 (Shillelagh Road) east. After 2 km (1 mile) turn left onto a narrow side road. After 2 km (1 mile), Rathgall stone fort is on the right, a short walk across a field. Park at the gate and climb over it. Be careful of cattle and be sure to close any gate that is opened en route.*

② Rathgall
Co Carlow

Unrestored and overgrown with briars, this impressive prehistoric four-ring stone hill fort appears much as it has stood for thousands of years. The medieval outer walls encircle earlier fortifications from the Bronze and Iron Ages, when spears, swords and shields were fashioned here. North of the fort are the impressive Haroldstown Dolmen, while a stone circle to its east is said to be the birthplace of the 5th-century Kings of Leinster.

🚗 *Carry on along the side road until it rejoins the R725. Continue through lovely wooded country to the estate village of Shillelagh.*

The 1798 Rebellion
The revolutionary United Irishmen planned a national revolt against British power in May 1798, when sporadic uprisings took place in parts of Leinster and Ulster. The only substantial rebellion occurred in Wexford, where the insurgents displayed great fortitude and the fighting lasted until July.

③ Shillelagh
Co Wicklow

Shillelagh is an attractive planned village with stone cottages and a courthouse. **Coolattin Park**, 2 km (1 mile) east, in whose estate Shillelagh was set, was built in 1804 for Earl Fitzwilliam, a former Lord Lieutenant of Ireland. It is now a golf course. In **Tomnafinnoge Wood** (3 km/2 miles northeast on the R749) are remnants of one of the great ancient Irish oak forests, which provided the roof timbers for St Patrick's Cathedral in Dublin and Westminster Hall in London. Shillelagh gives its name to the famous Irish oak cudgel, now more usually made of blackthorn. It is possible to visit a traditional stickmaker's yard in the village to see how they are made.

🚗 *From Shillelagh take R725 east. Turn right after 4 km (2½ miles) on a minor road along the Derry river valley towards Watchhouse village, where you turn right and cross River Derry for Clonegal.*

Above Cycling the peaceful, empty mountain roads that skirt Mount Leinster

④ Clonegal
Co Carlow

Clonegal, a pretty and particularly well-preserved village, marks the end of the Wicklow Way, a mountainous 127-km (79-mile) trail that starts in Dublin. The surrounding countryside of wooded hills is very beautiful, and the banks of the River Derry here are popular for fishing. The 17th-century Jacobean **Huntington Castle** (open Mar & Apr: weekends; May–Sep: daily) that adjoins the village can be visited, and is said to be haunted. Within the grounds are a prehistoric megalith, an ancient yew walk and a temple to Isis.

🚗 *Go back across the River Derry to Watch House and take the road right along the river through fine wooded country; on reaching the R746 (Carnew Road), turn right for Bunclody.*

⑤ Bunclody
Co Wexford

Bunclody, site of a bloody battle in the 1798 Rebellion, is a small and charming town situated where the River Slaney meets the River Clody at the foot of the Blackstairs Mountains. A narrow canal from the Clody flows down the middle of its main street. The town is the best base for climbing 795-m (2,610-ft) **Mount Leinster**. To reach Mount Leinster, leave Bunclody heading uphill and turn left opposite the Wexford Farmers' Co-op. After 10 km (6 miles), near Corrabut Gap, turn left for Nine Stones. The road crosses a cattle grid and there is fine scenery on both sides. Park at the Nine Stones megalithic alignment for the walk to the top. It's a steep climb, but the surfaced road goes all the way, with spectacular

views of the surrounding mountains, valleys and sea. Watch out for cloud.

🚗 *From Nine Stones retrace the route and drive back across the cattle grid to the junction with the main road. Turn left and follow the road as it descends. On the descent, take a right turn at the T-junction and continue on to Myshall.*

⑥ Myshall
Co Carlow

This little village is noted for the beautiful Adelaide Memorial Church built in 1912 by John Duguid of Dover, around the graves of his wife and daughter. It is designed as a miniature of Salisbury Cathedral and, among the exquisite features of the interior, the design of the floor was taken from St Mark's in Venice.

🚗 *Take R724 heading northeast and take first road (L2023) left, after 2 km (1 mile). After crossing the N80 Altamont Garden is on the right.*

Above left Lush watermeadows and woods along the banks of the River Derry **Above** Bicentennial memorial to those who died in the 1798 Rebellion in Bunclody

EAT AND DRINK

TULLOW

Rathwood *moderate*
The café-restaurant in this award-winning garden centre is a goodplace to take a break, and the food is wholesome and fresh. Pleasant outside sitting area.
Rath, Tullow; 059 915 6285; closes 5:30pm; www.rathwood.com

CLONEGAL

Sha-Roe Bistro *expensive*
This small restaurant in a fine 18th-century house in an unspoilt village provides exceptional food and comfort. Imaginative cooking features Wexford lamb, local aged beef, fish and cheeses. Booking recommended.
Main Street; 053 937 5636; www.sha-roe.ie; closed Mon–Wed

Above Icons in niches on the pebble-dashed exterior of the Adelaide Memorial Church, Myshall

⑦ Altamont Garden
Ballon, Co Carlow

Altamont *(open daily)* is a natural woodland garden of some 16 ha (40 acres). The woodland walks and granite steps leading up from the River Slaney are thought to have been designed by William Robinson. Called "the most romantic garden in Ireland", it is now managed by the state according to the principles of Corona North, the last member of the family to live there. There are many mature trees, both native and exotic, and walks take visitors along the lawns and paths, by the pond and down to the river. A highlight in spring is one of Ireland's largest snowdrop collections.

🚗 *Continue along the road to the N81. Turn left, then right at the N80. Before reaching Ballon, turn left, heading south. At the R724, turn right to Bagenalstown.*

Above Entrance of Altamont Garden **Above right** Colourful herbaceous border in the Robinsonian garden **Above top right** Overgrown doorway, Altamont Garden

VISITING BAGENALSTOWN (MUINE BHEAG)

Parking
There is ample parking in town.

Tourist Information
www.ireland.com

WHERE TO STAY

AROUND BAGENALSTOWN (MUINE BHEAG)

Kilgraney House *moderate*
A Georgian, adults-only house overlooking the Barrow valley. Two courtyard suites complement the elegant rooms in the main house, and there are also two cottages. The Drawing Room is a delight too.
Kilgraney (6 km/4 miles on the R705 from Bagenalstown); 059 977 5283; www.kilgraneyhouse.com

Lorum Old Rectory *moderate*
A former Victorian rectory with elegant rooms and four-poster beds, this old residence also features delightful public areas including the dining room, a sitting room and a study.
Kilgraney; 086 828 1644; www.lorum.com

⑧ Bagenalstown (Muine Bheag)
Co Carlow

This pretty market town on the River Barrow is now officially called Muine Bheag, meaning "small thorn tree", but is still widely known by its old name. It was founded in the 18th century by Walter, Lord Bagenal, who intended it to bear the name New Versailles. While not achieving this level of magnificence, the town does have notable buildings, including a courthouse modelled on the Parthenon in Athens – the only part of Bagenal's grand plans to be realized – and a handsome 19th-century Neo-Classical railway station.

A two-hour walking tour

This 8-km (5-mile) walk from Bagenalstown to Leighlinbridge (pronounced "lock-lin-bridge") and back is along a stretch of the Barrow Way, a walk trail that covers 120 km (75 miles) in total, following the canal and river towpaths of

Above Picturesque ruins of medieval Ballymoon Castle, with its thick granite walls, standing majestically in fields to the east of Bagenalstown

the Barrow, the second-longest river in Ireland. The walk is best enjoyed in the early morning or at dusk. Be sure to look out for herons and kingfishers along the tranquil waterway. Follow Barrow Way signs north out of **Bagenalstown** ①. Pass the charming "lifting bridge" linking the quayside with a wooded island bird sanctuary and ruined watermill. The river sweeps on round to picturesque **Rathellin Lock** ② and, further along, a brick-arched bridge leads to another island. The path then follows the side of the canal until a weir where the route rejoins the river.

Approaching Leighlinbridge there are views of Mount Leinster to the right. By the splendid seven-arched bridge in Leighlinbridge, the **Black Castle** ③ is a 14th-century tower, all that remains of a castle built to command the river crossing. Return to Bagenalstown, along the same

The Barrow Way

The 120-km- (75-miles-) long Barrow Way extends from Lowtown near Dublin in the north to St Mullins near Wexford in the south. At its southern end it rejoins the even longer and more mountainous Wicklow Way (see p135). A well-marked walk through the counties of Carlow and Kildare in eastern Leinster, it wends its way from start to finish along the banks of canals and rivers through this largely flat region. Its charms are both natural – walkers may well spot hawks and hares as they meander through fields of daisies, yarrow and mint – and man-made as the tow-path skirts pretty Georgian towns and mansions, Norman castles and Cromwellian battle sites. Waymarked Ways of Ireland (www.sportireland.ie) lists suggestions for day- and half-day-long walks along the route.

river- and canal-side route, and finish the walk with the finest view of the Grecian courthouse, along with the town's church spire and tower.

In the fields east of Bagenalstown are the ruins of Ballymoon Castle (a 3-km/2-mile drive along the R724 towards Fenagh), thought to have been built around 1300 by Roger Bigod, one of the 12th–13th-century Earls of Norfolk, and later occupied by the Knights Templar. Thick granite walls, two storeys high, surround a huge courtyard 25-m (80-ft) square.

Above Typically pretty local granite cottage at Fennagh, between Ballon and Bagenalstown

EAT AND DRINK

AROUND BAGENALSTOWN (MUIN BHEAG)

Lord Bagenal Hotel *moderate*
This well-known pub (4.5 km/3 miles on the R705 from Bagenalstown) has expanded into a chic, modern hotel, but retains its original, cosy wood-panelled bar, complete with open fires. Hearty pub food is available, but there is also a more formal restaurant in a lovely setting beside the River Barrow. *Main Street, Leighlinbridge; 059 977 4000; www.lordbagenal.com*

DAY TRIP OPTIONS

Tullow, Bunclody and Ballon are ideal bases to visit the highlights of this area.

Romantic gardens

Explore the delights of Altamont Garden ⑦, with a break for a delicious, home-cooked lunch in the delightful Walled Garden Café.

Altamont is signposted from the N81 (left from Tullow, right from Ballon) and the N80 (right from Bunclody).

Mount Leinster

See Bunclody ⑤, then make the steep but exhilarating climb to the top of Mount Leinster for spectacular views of the surrounding mountains, the valleys below and the sea in the distance.

From Bunclody, follow the itinerary to Nine Stones, then park and walk.

Derry valley drive

The road from Shillelagh ③ to Clonegal ④ runs through gorgeous scenery. End the day with a visit to fascinating Huntington Castle.

Follow the directions in the itinerary.

TRIP 10

LOUGHS AND LIGHTHOUSES
Portumna to Tarbert

HIGHLIGHTS

Formidable Norman fortress
Climb the battlements of King John's Castle in Limerick,
Ireland's finest Norman fortress

Treasure island
Follow in the footsteps of pilgrims and plunderers on a
boat trip to Lough Derg's Holy Island

Megalithic mysteries
Visit Grange Stone Circle and the banks of Lough Gur,
the source of important archaeological finds

Pioneering flights
Recapture the excitement of early transatlantic air travel
at the Foynes Flying Boat Museum

Scenic expanse of Lough Gur in County Limerick

LOUGHS AND LIGHTHOUSES

Follow the majestic Shannon as it snakes towards the ocean, from the jagged shores of Lough Derg to the broad estuary that opens out at Limerick. This is an extraordinarily rich region, with pretty lakeside villages, smart marinas, a splendid city with medieval and Georgian quarters, and grand 18th-century country estates. This fertile valley has a long and illustrious history; it was widely settled in megalithic times; the base of Brian Boru, King of Ireland, in the 10th century; and in modern times the birthplace of Eamon de Valera, the founder of the Irish Free State.

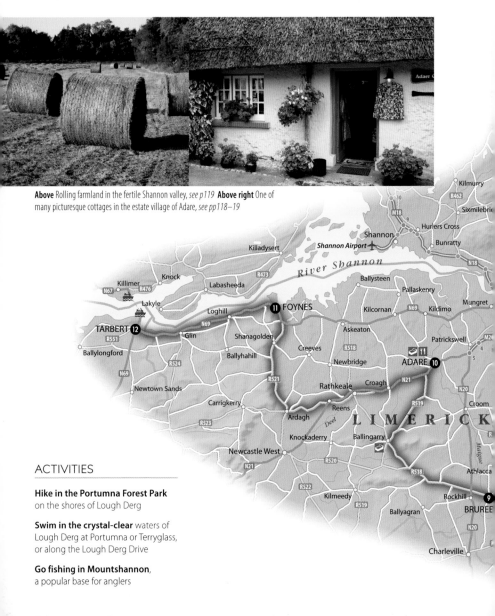

Above Rolling farmland in the fertile Shannon valley, *see p119* **Above right** One of many picturesque cottages in the estate village of Adare, *see pp118–19*

ACTIVITIES

Hike in the Portumna Forest Park
on the shores of Lough Derg

Swim in the crystal-clear waters of
Lough Derg at Portumna or Terryglass,
or along the Lough Derg Drive

Go fishing in Mountshannon,
a popular base for anglers

PLAN YOUR DRIVE

Start/finish: Portumna to Tarbert.

Number of days: 2–3.

Distance: 302 km (188 miles).

Road conditions: Main roads are well paved and signposted. Some smaller roads are potholed.

When to go: Although winters are mild in southwest Ireland, May–Oct is the best time to visit. To swim in Lough Derg, visit in Jun–Aug.

Opening times: Most sights and attractions are open from 9 or 10am to 5 or 6pm, or dusk if earlier.

Main market days: Limerick: Riverside Market, Sun 11am–4pm, Bedford Row; Milk Market, Sat am, Cornmarket Row.

Major festivals: Limerick: River Fest, Apr/May; **Adare:** Village Festival, mid-May.

DAY TRIP OPTIONS

Enjoy a lazy day **swimming** and **boating** in Portumna. **Families** can take in a **forest walk** or view the **lakeside gardens** at Portumna Castle. For **history and culture**, spend a morning in **medieval and Georgian** Limerick, and the afternoon seeing the **megalithic sites** around Lough Gur. For a scenic drive, focus on the Shannon's south bank from Foynes to Tarbert. Take a **picnic** and visit two **museums**. For full details, *see p119*.

Below A roadside sculpture forms part of the scenery near Adare, *see pp118–19*

Above Portumna Friary, a Dominican Friary built over a Cistercian chapel

VISITING MOUNTSHANNON

Boat Trips to Holy Island
Between April and September, boat trips to Holy Island are operated by Gerard Madden and leave from Mountshannon Harbour. Tickets can be bought from a kiosk on the pier. *Gerard Madden; 061 921 615; www.holyisland.ie*

VISITING KILLALOE AND BALLINA

Tourist Information
Brian Boru Heritage Centre, Killaloe; 360 788; www.discoverkillaloe.ie; open May–mid-Sep: daily

WHERE TO STAY

MOUNTSHANNON

Hawthorn Lodge B&B *inexpensive*
A charming, family-run guesthouse located near the village, Hawthorn has homely, well-furnished rooms as well as a cosy lounge and lovely gardens. *Main Street; 061 927 120; www. mountshannon-clare.com*

KILLALOE

Lakeside Hotel *inexpensive–moderate*
Popular for its location beside the lake, this hotel features an indoor pool, steam room and sauna. *061 376 122; www.lakesidehotel.ie*

① Portumna
Co Galway
Surrounded by open farmland and forests, Portumna lies at the head of Lough Derg, its bridge straddling the Tipperary and Galway banks of the Shannon. In summer, it plays host to small groups of holidaymakers cruising on the river. It has a **lakeside bathing spot**, with picnic tables and a lifeguard *(Jun–Aug)*, less than a kilometre (half a mile) from the centre (signposted "Swimming Area" from the Bank of Ireland).

Portumna's main sight is **Portumna Castle and Gardens** *(open Apr–Oct)*, reached by turning left opposite Portumna Catholic Church in the centre of town (the entrance to the castle is 300 m (984 ft) along on the right; fork right after the Gate Lodge). A fortified mansion built in the early 17th century for the De Burgo family, the castle is undergoing continual restoration, but the ground floor is open to visitors. The gardens are known for the Renaissance Sun Garden, laid out in a geometric design in front of the house, a rare 17th-century rose and a fully restored kitchen garden.

Return to the Gate Lodge and this time take the left fork to the **marina** where there are picnic tables looking across Lough Derg. Nearby are the ruins of **Portumna Friary**, a Cistercian chapel extended by the Dominican order in the 15th century.

From the marina, it is possible to continue on foot to **Portumna Forest Park** *(open daily)*, a public forest park along the shore of Lough Derg.

Alternatively drive there (2 km/ 1 mile) along the Gort Road (R353). Maps of its marked trails can be picked up at the entrance. There is a wide variety of birdlife in the park, as well as red squirrels and fallow deer.

While visiting Portumna, it is also worth taking a look at **Terryglass**, a pretty boating village with a couple of good restaurants *(see right)*, just around the bay, off the N65.

🚗 *Exit Portumna on Shannon Road, then follow R352 along the lakeshore.*

② Lough Derg
Co Galway and Co Clare
The section of Lough Derg between Portumna and Mountshannon (around 40 km/21 miles) is sparsely populated. Views of the lake are largely obscured by trees, but two scenic detours off the R352 make the drive worthwhile. Ten kilometres (6 miles) from Portumna, at a crossroads, turn right at the sign for **Lough Derg Drive** leading to higher ground away from the lake but offering better views. It reaches the quaint village of Woodford before returning to the R352.

Continue through Gorteeny and 2 km (1 mile) before Whitegate, where the road bends sharply left, leave the main road by veering right onto a narrow country lane. Drive straight for 2 km (1 mile) and turn left at a cottage, crossing the R352 again. Continue to the shore of the lake, where there is a shallow area that is good for swimming.

🚗 *Return to the R352, turn left and drive on to Mountshannon.*

Above The quay at Killaloe, a pleasant town on the banks of Lough Derg

③ Mountshannon
Co Clare

Picturesque Mountshannon has an elevated position overlooking Lough Derg. Long and linear, it was conceived as a plantation town, intended for Protestant settlers; even by the 1830s it didn't have a single Catholic resident. Today it is a good base for exploring the surrounding area and is popular with anglers. Solid 18th-century cottages line the harbour, and it has several good pubs, including Cois na h'Abhna bar on Main Street *(see right)*, which sometimes holds traditional music sessions in summer. Information on angling can be obtained in any of the town's tackle shops.

Boats to **Holy Island**, just 2 km (1 mile) offshore, in Scarriff Bay, leave from the pier *(see left)*. St Caimin founded a monastery on the island in the 7th century. The ruins include monastic cells, five churches and 80 marked graves pre-dating the 12th century. Dominating the island is an 80-m (260-ft) high round tower.

The island has been a draw for both pilgrims and plunderers through the centuries. Lured by the prospect of monastic wealth, the Vikings ransacked the island in 836 and again in 922. It is also associated with Brian Boru, the powerful High King of Ireland ("Ard Ria"). His brother Marcan, an abbot, is said to have rebuilt one of the island's churches on the orders of Boru.

🚗 *Follow the R352 along the lakeshore as far as Tuamgraney, bypassing Scarriff, and carry on along the lake, now on the R463, into Killaloe. It is possible to swim in the lough at Two Mile Gate, and walk in Cragg Wood. In Killaloe, park on the street.*

Brian Boru

King of Munster and High King of Ireland, Brian Boru is credited with uniting Ireland's clans and routing the Vikings. Born in Killaloe, he earned his nickname Brian of the Tribute (Boru), for the tributes he exacted, used mainly to rebuild monasteries ransacked by the Vikings. In 1014 – at the ripe old age of 74 – the great warrior was slain by a Viking as he prayed in his tent at the Battle of Clontarf.

④ Killaloe
Co Clare and Co Tipperary

The twin towns of Killaloe and Ballina are actually in different counties, but they face one another on opposite banks of the River Shannon, linked by a 17th-century bridge. **Killaloe** is the more interesting of the two. Brian Boru, the High King of Ireland, was born here and built his palace, Kincora, on the site of the Catholic church at the top of the hill. It was the centre of power in Ireland until his death at the Battle of Clontarf in 1014. Learn more about this totemic Irish figure at the **Brian Boru Heritage Centre** *(see left)* on the bridge over the Shannon.

The other building of note is **Flannan's Cathedral**, dating from around 1182, on Royal Parade at the bottom of the hill. Inside, look for the Romanesque doorway, the Thorgrim Stone, a bilingual rarity inscribed with both Nordic runes and Ogham markings, and the 13th-century font.

Ballina has less to offer in the way of historical sites, but has a pleasant riverside and a lively pub scene.

🚗 *From Killaloe, cross the bridge into Ballina and take the R494 south until it meets the M7. Turn right onto the M7 and leave at junction 29, following the signs to Limerick.*

Above left Motor cruisers in Portumna Marina, a popular springboard for boating on the Shannon. **Above** The 17th-century bridge linking the twin towns of Ballina and Killaloe

EAT AND DRINK

AROUND PORTUMNA

Paddy's Bar *inexpensive*
Congenial spot for good fish and chips, steaks, burgers, and seafood chowder. The Sunday lunch is recommended.
Terryglass; 067 22147

Derg Inn *moderate*
Laid-back bar with comforting food in the pretty village of Terryglass, 12 km (7 miles) from Portumna (head south on the N65; turn right onto the R493).
Terryglass; 067 22037

MOUNTSHANNON

Cois na h'Abhna *inexpensive*
Popular local pub known for its music sessions (Sat & Sun eves). Sit in the beer garden in summer or by an open fire in winter.
Main Street; 061 927 881

KILLALOE AND BALLINA

Ponte Vecchio *inexpensive*
Italian deli and wine store. Eat in, grab a coffee or stock up for a picnic.
Royal Parade House, Killaloe; 061 622 845; closed Mon

Wooden Spoon Café *inexpensive*
Freshly baked foods including scrumptious sausage rolls. Takeaway bakery upstairs.
5 Abbey Street, Killaloe; 061 622 2415

AROUND KILLALOE

Larkin's Lakeside Pub and Restaurant *inexpensive*
Landmark pub on the Tipperary shore of Lough Derg. Wide choice of dishes, from fish chowders to T-bone steaks. Renowned for its music sessions.
Garrykennedy (turn left at Portroe, 13 km/8 miles north of Ballina on the R494); 067 23232; www.larkins.ie

Above The medieval tollgate on Thomond Bridge in Limerick

VISITING LIMERICK

Tourist Information
*20 O'Connell Street; 061 317 522;
www.limerick.ie; open Mon–Sat*

Parking
The best place to park in is in
Arthur's Quay Centre, a multi-storey car park on Arthur's Quay, just off Patrick Street. For on-street parking, discs are available from shops and service stations.

WHERE TO STAY IN LIMERICK CITY

Clayton Hotel *moderate*
One of the country's tallest hotels, Clayton's distinctive structure offers superlative views from its plush rooms, health club and swimming pool.
*Streamboat Quay; 061 444 100;
www.claytonhotellimerick.com*

Absolute Hotel *moderate*
Overlooking the confluence of the Abbey and Shannon rivers, this stylish modern hotel has a waterside bar and restaurant with an outside terrace. For a small premium, guests have access to the spa.
*Sir Harry's Mall; 061 463 600;
www.absolutehotel.com*

No 1 Pery Square Hotel and Spa
moderate–expensive
Luxurious boutique hotel (20 rooms) in an immaculately restored 18th-century property on one of Limerick's finest squares. There is a great restaurant and spa too.
*1 Pery Square; 061 402 402;
www.oneperysquare.com*

⑤ LIMERICK CITY
Co Limerick
Limerick city centre has two distinct areas, divided by the Abbey River. North of the river is King's Island, the medieval quarter clustered around the 12th-century castle, and south is the Georgian development of Newtown Pery, laid out in the 18th century on a grid plan by the Italian architect Davis Ducart.

A two-hour walking tour
Start at the **Tourist Information Centre** ①, where you can pick up maps and details of events in the city. Continue up O'Connell Street and along Rutland Street to the **Hunt Museum** *(open daily)* ②. Occupying the 18th-century Customs House, this private museum is crammed with antiquities and art, from Neolithic bronze artifacts to works by Picasso, Renoir and Henry Moore. From the museum, turn left across Matthew Bridge, over the Abbey River, and left into Merchant's Quay. Here you'll find the glass-and-steel **City Hall and Civic Centre** ③. Walk through its foyer to the courtyard, which leads onto an embankment with river views.

Return to Merchant's Quay and turn left up St Augustine's Place. On the right the 12th-century **St Mary's Cathedral** ④ *(open daily)* has exquisite barrel-vaulted ceilings, stained-glass windows and, in the Jebb Chapel, Ireland's only surviving misericords. Continue to Nicholas Street and turn left into it, passing **King John's Castle** ⑤

(open daily) on the left, which dates from 1210. Guided tours take in the extant walls and towers. Cross Castle Street onto the Parade. On the left corner is the Neo-Classical façade of the old **Bishop's Palace** ⑥ *(open Mon–Fri)*. It is free to enter. Adjacent is **St Munchin's Garden** ⑦ (part of St Munchin's Protestant Church), the picturesque graveyard of Church of Ireland St Munchin's church, with some very old tombstones. It has fine views down to Villiner's Alms Houses below.

Leaving the palace, turn right down Castle Street, cross Thomond Bridge to the west bank and turn left onto Clancy's Strand and the riverside walkway. On the corner of the bridge is Catholic **St Munchin's Church** ⑧. Further along the walkway is the **Treaty Stone** ⑨, on which the treaty that ended the Second Siege of Limerick was signed in 1691. It promised religious freedom to the Irish Catholics, but within two months England reneged on the treaty and the stone came to symbolize hatred of English rule. Just along on the right is **Curragower Seafood Bar** ⑩, known for its Irish oysters. Continue along the river as far as **Sarsfield Bridge** ⑪ and cross back to the east bank. At the end of the bridge turn right into Harvey's Quay then left down Bedford Row to the **Limerick Museum** ⑫ *(open Mon–Fri)*, which relates the city's history. Continue down Bedford Row towards the Tourist Information Centre.

🚗 *From the car park, turn right onto Patrick Street, left up William Street and Upper William Street, and veer right along Roxboro Road. Take the first exit off the roundabout and at the next roundabout take the R512 for Lough Gur and Killmallock. Grange Stone Circle is 20 km (12 miles) from Limerick. Park in the lay-by in front of the entrance.*

Above A sheltered backwater on Lough Gur, an area rich in archaeological sites

⑥ Grange Stone Circle
Co Limerick
Though not as imposing as Stonehenge in the UK, Grange Stone Circle packs a significant punch, not least because of its isolation. Dating from 2000 BC, the ring consists of 113 standing stones and has an internal diameter of 46 m (150 ft), making it Ireland's largest stone circle. In Irish it is called *Lios na Grainsi* (Stones of the Sun), suggesting that it had a ritualistic function. The largest stone, the Rounach Croim Dubh (Prominent Black Stone), is over 2 m (6 ft) high and weighs 40 tons. Entrance to the site is free, but visitors are asked to leave a small contribution in the donation box.

🚗 *Continue in same direction on the R512 and turn left at Holycross, where*

Lough Gur is signposted (5 km/3 miles) left. On the left immediately after the turn are the ruins of the old church of Tempall Nua (New Church) and further along on the right Giant's Grave, a megalithic wedge tomb. Follow signs to Lough Gur and the visitor centre.

⑦ Lough Gur
Co Limerick
Horseshoe-shaped and cupped in the limestone hills, Lough Gur is one of Ireland's richest archaeological sites. The whole area is dotted with megalithic remains, including burial chambers and ring forts. When the lough was partially drained in the 19th century many artifacts were revealed, the most significant of which was the magnificent Lough Gur Shield, dating from 700 BC (now in the National Museum in Dublin). Many other finds are in the Hunt Museum in Limerick *(see left)*.

On the shores of the lake are the ruins of two castles, both of which once stood on islands in the lake: 15th-century **Bourchier's Castle**, near the car park, and on the far side of the lake ivy-mantled **Black Castle**, dating from the 13th century, where the Earls of Desmond periodically resided. (It can be reached along a path on the east side of the lake.)

Overlooking the lake, in two replica Neolithic huts, the **Heritage Centre** *(open daily)* sheds light on the history of the area with exhibits and information boards. It also sells light refreshments.

🚗 *Return to Holycross and rejoin the R512, following the signs to Kilmallock (15 km/9 miles). On reaching Kilmallock, take an immediate right after John's Gate and park in the public car park.*

Above Grange Stone Circle, a remote and atmospheric spot shaded by oak trees

Above The old stone mill in the market town of Bruree, near Kilmallock

OUTDOOR ACTIVITIES

Located behind the Hunt Museum in Limerick, **Nevsail Watersports** offers kayaking and stand-up paddleboarding on the Shannon, plus an indoor climbing wall *(Rutland Street, Limerick; 086 330 8236; www.nevsailwatersports.ie)*.

EAT AND DRINK IN LIMERICK CITY

The French Table *moderate*
This fancy riverside restaurant produces stunning plates such as civet of rabbit and Atlantic hake with Champagne beurre blanc.
Steamboat Quay; 061 609 274; www.frenchtable.ie; closed Mon & Tue

The Locke Bar *inexpensive–moderate*
Reputedly Limerick's oldest pub (1724), Lockes has a lovely location overlooking the Abbey River. During the summer a barbecue is served on the terrace out front. Also worth a try is the Oyster House and Seafood Bar. There are live music sessions nightly.
3 George's Quay; 061 413 733; www.lockebar.com

Curragower Seafood Bar *moderate*
Cosy, unpretentious seafood bar with a loyal following. Choose from chowder, crab claws, sea bass, salmon, oysters and much more.
Clancy's Strand; 087 701 4723; www.curragower.com

Above Kilmallock's Dominican Friary, a testament to the town's medieval prosperity

WHERE TO STAY

KILMALLOCK
Deebert House Hotel *inexpensive*
Located on the site of an old mill on the edge of town, this charming, family-run hotel has good-value rooms and a restaurant. Walkers and cyclists are particularly welcome – there's a drying room and bike storage facilities.
Kilmallock; 063 31200; www. deeberthousehotel.com

AROUND KILMALLOCK
The Old Bank *inexpensive*
Pleasant family-run B&B in a former bank building in the village of Bruff, just off the R512 between Lough Gur and Kilmallock. Two rooms have four-poster beds.
Bruff; 061 389 969; www.theoldbank.ie

AROUND BRUREE
Echo Lodge *moderate–expensive*
This is a spacious Victorian country residence that was converted from a 19th-century convent. Set in extensive gardens, it is also home to the highly acclaimed Mustard Seed Restaurant. Non-residents welcome to dine by reservation. Overlooks Ballingarry, on the R519, 13 km (8 miles) south of Adare.
Ballingarry; 069 68508; www.mustard seed.ie

ADARE
Dunraven Arms Hotel
moderate–expensive
Established in 1792 and still retaining the ambience of a country inn. Though luxurious, it has a lovely informal elegance.
Main Street; 061 605 900; www. dunravenhotel.com

⑧ Kilmallock
Co Limerick
In medieval times Kilmallock was one of the most important towns in Munster. But from the mid-17th century, having suffered badly in the confederation wars of 1641, it went into decline, and it never really recovered. Nevertheless, it is one of the most intact medieval towns in Ireland. A substantial portion of the old walls survive, as well as **John's Gate** and **Blossom Gate**. Notable buildings include the 13th-century **Collegiate Church of Saints Peter and Paul**, and down by the river the **Dominican Friary**, attacked and destroyed by Cromwellian forces under Lord Inchiquin in 1648. The **Ballyhoura Heritage Centre** *(open Mon–Fri)* near the Friary is home to the Friar's Gate Theatre and **Kilmallock Museum** *(open daily pm)*, which traces the history of the town in the 19th and 20th centuries. Daily tours of Kilmallock leave from outside the museum at 2pm.
🚗 *From Kilmallock drive to the top of the town and turn right onto the R518 towards Bruree (6 km/4 miles). Drive through the centre of Bruree and just before the road swings left over a stone bridge veer right and park across the road from an old school house.*

⑨ Bruree
Co Limerick
The market town of Bruree has two main attractions, both on the outskirts of town, facing one another off the road to Ballingarry. They are the **De Valera Museum** *(closed Mon)*, in the school where Eamon de Valera was educated, and the **Genesius Theatrical Museum** *(visits by appointment, 087 926 8481)* dedicated to Vic Loving. They were two very different figures in

Irish history. Eamon de Valera, one of the leaders of the 1916 uprising, founder of the Irish Free State and keen advocate of Catholic values, was a colossal figure in post-independent Ireland. Vic Loving, performer, actress, and impresario was also a famous male impersonator. The De Valera Museum is also home to the **Bruree Heritage Centre** recounting the town's history. Across the road, the Genesius Theatrical Museum – a hidden gem – includes costumes from 1860, posters, old programmes, photographs and other memorabilia. Vic Loving's granddaughter runs the museum; entry is free but donations are gratefully accepted.
🚗 *Return to the stone bridge and turn right, follow the R518 to Ballingarry (18 km/11 miles) and then turn right onto the R519 for Adare. At the T junction at the N21 turn right. Park by the village green.*

Irish Coffee
Irish coffee, almost as symbolic of Ireland as a shamrock or harp, was invented in the 1940s by Joseph Sheridan, head chef at Foynes International Airport, forerunner of Shannon Airport. During World War II all transatlantic flights flew under the cover of darkness and this invigorating concoction of black coffee, cream and Irish whiskey warmed up chilly passengers before they set off. The drink gained further favour in 1950s Los Angeles.

Above Kilmallock's beautifully kept 13th-century Collegiate Church of Saints Peter and Paul

⑩ Adare
Co Limerick
With its thatched cottages and spruce green, Adare prides itself on being Ireland's prettiest village.

In fact, the beautification of this estate village was the personal project of the third Earl of Dunraven. An "improving landlord", he wished to create a bucolic haven and indulge his passion for early Irish architecture.

For a village intended to be an Irish idyll, it feels quite English. Nonetheless, it is hard to resist its quaint charm. It has an array of medieval buildings, including three monasteries, two in use and the third a ruin. In the middle of the village the **Heritage Centre** (open daily) runs guided tours (Jun–Sep) of 15th-century **Desmond Castle**. Next to the centre is the 15th-century **Catholic parish church**, once part of the Trinitarian Abbey, which has an unusual stone dovecote.

Just south of the river, an **Augustinian Friary** is now an Anglican church and school (limited access after 3pm). On the golf course beyond the castle, the **Franciscan Friary** has a fine cloister and the tombs of the Desmonds (permission to visit from the clubhouse). **Adare Manor**, ancestral home of the Earls of Dunraven, is now a luxury hotel.

🚗 *Take the N21 west towards Newcastle West. Four km (2 miles) after the turn for Rathkeale take the R523 to Ardagh and then turn right onto the R521 and then- onto the N69 for Foynes (14 km/9 miles). Park at the Flying Boat & Maritime Museum in the centre.*

⓫ Foynes
Co Limerick

During the late 1930s and early 1940s this sleepy port overlooking the Shannon estuary was the focal point of transatlantic air travel. On 9 July 1939, Pan Am's luxury flying boat, the *Yankee Clipper*, landed at Foynes, the first direct commercial passenger flight between the United States and Europe. In the centre of town, the **Flying Boat & Maritime Museum** (open daily mid-Mar–mid-Nov) recreates these pioneering days. See the original terminal building, the radio and weather room, an early commercial passenger plane and a 1940s tea room. Foynes is also where Irish coffee was invented.

🚗 *Turn left from the car park and drive along the N69 to Tarbert. A roadside picnic spot near Foynes offers good views of the estuary and access to a forest walk.*

⓬ Tarbert
Co Limerick

The N69 between Foynes and Tarbert is one of the best riverside drives in Ireland, with sweeping views of the estuary and **Tarbert Lighthouse**. In Tarbert itself, the **Tarbert Bridewell Courthouse and Jail** (open Apr–Sep: daily; Oct–Mar: Mon–Fri) recreates the plight of early 19th-century convicts. The town also operates regular **car ferries** across the Shannon to Killimer in County Clare.

Above The Blue Door Restaurant in Adare, a village beautified by the Earl of Dunraven

EAT AND DRINK IN ADARE

Blue Door Restaurant *moderate*
Bistro-style restaurant in archetypal thatched cottage. Also serves morning coffee and, in summer, afternoon tea in the pretty cottage garden.
Church View; 061 396 481; www.bluedooradare.com

The Wild Geese Restaurant *moderate*
Acclaimed restaurant in cottage setting. Uses locally sourced meat, fish and cheese and organic vegetables. Renowned for its seafood, such as Castletownbere scallops and Atlantic cod with crabmeat.
Rose Cottage, Main Street; 061 396 451; www.thewild-geese.com; closed Sun & Mon

---

DAY TRIP OPTIONS
Spend a leisurely day on Lough Derg enjoying simple lakeside pleasures, explore the many sites around Limerick or take the lovely drive along the River Shannon.

Messing about on the lake
For boating, swimming and riverside drinking and eating, concentrate on Portumna ❶ at the northern tip of Lough Derg. There are bathing spots and a marina, as well as forest walks and Portumna Castle and Gardens to explore. At the end of the day, drive to Garrykennedy for dinner in lakeside Larkin's (see p115).

Portumna and Limerick are ideal bases for these day trips.

Limerick loop
Spend a morning exploring medieval and Georgian Limerick ❺, visiting the eclectic Hunt Museum, the Cathedral and King John's Castle, then have lunch at Curragower Seafood Bar (see p117). Afterwards head out to Grange Stone Circle ❻ and Lough Gur ❼, a peaceful lake and valley packed with megalithic sites. From there, drive on to Kilmallock ❽, a medieval gem, and then to Adare ❿, Ireland's prettiest village, stopping for afternoon tea

at the Blue Door (see above), before returning to Limerick.

Follow the drive instructions from Limerick to Adare and return to the city on the N21.

Foynes to Tarbert
Combine a lovely riverside drive with a picnic, a forest walk and visits to two museums – the Flying Boat & Maritime Museum at Foynes ⓫ and the Tarbert Bridewell Courthouse and Jail in Tarbert ⓬.

From Limerick take the N69 direct to Foynes, then follow the drive instructions to Tarbert.

TRIP 11

LYRICAL CLARE

Ennis to the Burren

HIGHLIGHTS

Musical Ennis

Soak up the atmosphere of this vibrant medieval market
town, famous for its folk music

Lovely Shannon Estuary

Savour the rolling pastoral land where the gentle waters
of the Shannon meet the driving force of the Atlantic

Dramatic Cliffs of Moher

Experience the Atlantic Edge, where the plateau plunges
into the sea, at the Cliffs of Moher Visitor Experience

The Stony District

Survey the wild beauty of the Burren's unusual limestone
landscape, with its flagstones fissured by grikes

Interior of the well-known McGann's Pub in Doolin

LYRICAL CLARE

County Clare can be broadly separated into two geographical regions: in the south, the gently rolling countryside along the course of the River Shannon; and in the north, a rugged and stony land with vertiginous coastal cliffs. Cutting across the county, northwest to southeast, is the magical region of the Burren, a limestone plateau crisscrossed by deep fissures sprouting a dizzying array of plant life. Then there is the music. Many of the towns on the coast and around the edges of the Burren live and breathe traditional music, perhaps more than any other county.

Above The soaring Cliffs of Moher, where the limestone plateau of the Burren meets the sea, *see p126*

ACTIVITIES

Spot bottlenose dolphins in the Shannon Estuary

Tune in to Clare's music scene, which takes place in characterful pubs all over the county

Follow the exhilarating coast road around Black Head

Delight in the wildflowers of the Burren landscape

Visit one of the megalithic tombs and 5th-century ring forts that pepper the Burren

KEY

Drive route

PLAN YOUR DRIVE

Start/finish: Ennis to the Burren.

Number of days: 2–3 days.

Distance: 195 km (121 miles).

Road conditions: Well paved and well signposted except on some non-classified roads.

When to go: May–Oct are the best months to come, but May, when the flowers on the Burren are in bloom, is particularly lovely.

Opening times: Pubs and music venues stay open until 11pm or later.

Main market days: Ennis: Fri/Sat; Kilrush: Thu.

Shopping: Ennis has a variety of small independent shops – from fashion boutiques to antiques and specialist food shops – while Doolin is known for its music shops, selling traditional Irish instruments and music. Burren Perfumery sells lotions inspired by the wildflowers.

Major festivals: Ennis: Trad Fest, Nov.

DAY TRIP OPTIONS

Walkers will love the spectacular north coast of Clare, with the **cliff path** at the vertiginous Cliffs of Moher; finish with a visit to the **music village** of Doolin or head up the coast to Black Head. Alternatively, devote a whole day to exploring the Burren's **landscape**, **villages**, **ring forts** and **megalithic sites**. For full details, see p127.

Below The lighthouse at Loop Head, on the southwest tip of County Clare, see p125

VISITING ENNIS

Parking
Ennis is a small town and its narrow streets get congested. All town-centre parking is metered. There is a multi-storey car park near Market Place.

Tourist Information
Arthur's Row (off the main square); 065 682 8366; open Tue–Sat; www.visitennis.com

VISITING SCATTERY ISLAND

Dolphin Discovery sails from Kilrush Creek Marina Apr–Oct, subject to tides; 065 905 1327; www.discoverdolphins.ie

WHERE TO STAY IN ENNIS

Newpark House *moderate*
A stylish period house dating from 1650, in a beautiful woodland setting, Newpark has well-appointed rooms. It is 2 km (1 mile) east of Ennis, off the R352. *Roslevan; 065 682 1233; www.newparkhouse.com*

Temple Gate Hotel *moderate*
Modern hotel off Ennis main square. Comfortable, convenient, good value. *The Square; 065 682 3300; www.templegatehotel.com*

Old Ground Hotel *moderate*
An 18th-century building in the centre of Ennis with spacious, elegant rooms and superb dining as well as the wonderful Poet's Corner Bar, which features regular live music. *O' Connell Street; 065 682 8127; www.oldgroundhotelennis.com*

Below The creeper-clad ruins of Ennis Friary, dating from the 14th century

Above Vandeleur Walled Garden, the last remnant of Kilrush House

❶ Ennis
Co Clare
This is Clare's largest town, located midway between the Shannon Estuary and the Burren. Straddling the River Fergus, it retains a winding medieval street pattern either side of O'Connell Street, named after Daniel O'Connell, the first Catholic MP to sit in Westminster, in 1828. His statue stands in O'Connell Square.

The ruins of 14th–15th-century Franciscan **Ennis Friary** *(open Apr–Oct)* on Abbey Street are noted for their rich carvings and decorated tombs – above all, the McMahon tomb. On the corner of Francis Street, is the Queen's Hotel, featured in James Joyce's *Ulysses*. The town is also renowned for its painted shopfronts and folk music festivals or *fleadhs*. To find out more visit **Glór Arts Centre**, on Causeway, or the **Tourist Information Centre** and **Clare Museum** *(open Jun–Sep: Mon–Sat; Oct–May: Tue–Sat)*.

🚗 *Take the R473 towards Clarecastle, turning right 2 km (1 mile) before the town. Follow signs for Ballynacally along the Shannon Estuary. Continue on the R473, through Labasheeda, Kilmurry and Knock on the R486, until Killimer, then join the N67 to Kilrush.*

Colourful mural on a pub in Ennis

❷ Kilrush
Co Clare
Cill Rois ("church of the promontory") is a designated Heritage Town, in recognition of its legacy as an 18th-century estate town with strong maritime traditions. Its **Heritage Centre** *(open May–Sep: daily)* has an exhibition about the Great Famine.

Vandeleur Walled Garden *(open daily)*, just outside the town (drive clockwise around the main square and turn right off Moore Street, following signs for the garden) was once part of Kilrush House, seat of the Vandeleur family. The house was demolished in 1973. Enclosed by lovely old stone walls, the garden was restored to its former glory in the 1990s and is now noted for its tropical plants.

Drive back to the main square in Kilrush and take Frances Street off the square. This long broad street leads down to **Kilrush Creek Marina**, from where there are boat trips on the Shannon Estuary to see Ireland's only resident bottlenose dolphins and excursions to Scattery Island, 2 km (1 mile) offshore.

🚗 *Board a boat at the marina (see left).*

❸ Scattery Island
Co Clare
This tiny island boasts a 6th-century monastery, founded by St Senan, five churches and a 300-m- (100-ft-) high round tower, still relatively intact (unusually, its main door is at ground level). On the north of the island are the remains of a gun rampart from the Napoleonic Wars (1799–1815).

🚗 *Return to Kilrush. From the town's square, take the N67 west, signed to Kilkee (23 km/14 miles).*

4 KILKEE

Co Clare

In summer, Kilkee is popular with out-of-towners, mostly from Limerick, who come for its splendid crescent-shaped beach. When the tide is fully out, deep rock pools known as the Pollock Holes can be explored at the southern end of the sands; they are favourite swimming and snorkelling spots. The cliffs on either side of the beach offer good walks with stunning views.

A 45-minute walking tour

The cliffs above Kilkee offer scenery almost as dramatic as that of the Cliffs of Moher *(see p126)*, but are less visited. This walk begins to the left of Kilkee beach in the so-called West End. From the public car park next to the **Diamond Rocks Café** ①, where there is a life size statue of the actor Richard Harris, who was a frequent visitor to Kilkee as a child, a paved path gently ascends to the top of the cliffs. To the right, just beyond the café, are flat, lime-stone slabs known as the **Diamond Rocks** ②, a natural amphitheatre used for musical and theatrical events in summer. About 50 m (164 ft) further on is a shelter with seating and a look out. On a clear day, the hazy silhouettes of the three Aran Islands are visible to the north, and the outline of the Kerry coastline can be discerned to the south. To the west is the tapering finger of Loop Head.

The paved path continues for about 1.5 km (1 mile) to **Foohagh Point** ③, where it curves left, away from the cliff edge. The final section, which gets progressively steeper, overlooks Intrinsic Bay, named after a Liverpool-bound cargo ship which sank in a gale here in 1830. Heading away from the cliff edge, take the first left down Dunlicky Road and into Kilkee. Along the way are views across Kilkee and over the bay. For a longer walk, adding a further 4 km (2 miles), turn right instead of left on Dunlicky Road and follow it to Goleen Bay.

Back in the West End, explore the delights of Kilkee's beach. If the tide is out scramble over the rocks in front of the car park to the three **Pollock Holes** ④, deep tidal pools popular with snorkellers. For snacks or lunch, the Diamond Rocks Café has a terrace with views to George's Head. In sum-mer, vendors on the seafront sell periwinkles and dillish – an edible sea grass gathered from the rock pools.

🚗 *From Kilkee, either take a scenic drive around Loop Head (23 km/ 15 miles) on the R487, or head direct to Milltown Malbay on the coastal N67. From there it is possible to continue towards Ennistimon (an attractive market town with painted shop fronts). To experience the full drama of Clare's coastline, however, turn left off the N67 at Lehinch, taking the R478 to the Cliffs of Moher.*

Above The cliffs at Loop Head, along the scenic drive from Kilkee

VISITING KILKEE

Parking
Park by the beach in the town's West End, next to the Diamond Rocks Café.

EAT AND DRINK

ENNIS

Rowan Tree Café Bar *inexpensive*
Mediterranean-style food is on offer at this café in a lovely old manor house with an outdoor terrace. Accommodation is available in the hostel next door.
Harmony Row; 065 686 8669; www. rowantreecafebar.ie; closed Mon

Town Hall Bistro *moderate*
Set in the old town hall, and now part of the Old Ground Hotel, this excellent restaurant offers a con-temporary dining experience with an emphasis on bistro-style dishes such as medallions of monkfish with Katafi prawns.
O'Connell Street; 065 682 8127; www.oldgroundhotelennis.com

KILKEE

The Strand Restaurant and Guesthouse *moderate*
Family-run restaurant and guesthouse on the seafront overlooking Kilkee Bay. The menu leans towards seafood but also includes mainstays such as rack of lamb and fillet steak. Has six en suite rooms above the restaurant.
Strand Line; 065 905 6177; www.thestrandkilkee.com

Above The majestic Cliffs of Moher rising from the Atlantic Ocean

SHOPPING IN DOOLIN

The **Traditional Music Shop** on Fisher Street sells recordings of musicians from the area, sheet music and locally made musical instruments *(065 707 4407)*.

WHERE TO STAY

DOOLIN
Ballinalacken Castle Country House Hotel *moderate–expensive*
Period-style grandeur is the watchword for this fabulous manor house with views of the Aran Islands. *Doolin; 086 361 3719; www.ballinalackencastle.com*

BALLYVAUGHAN
Hyland's Burren Hotel *inexpensive*
An 18th-century hotel with 32 individually designed, en suite rooms and turf fires in the public area. The Burren Bar is a lovely spot for a drink. *Ballyvaughan; 065 707 7037; www.hylandsburren.com*

THE BURREN
Fergus View *inexpensive*
Neat farmhouse well located for exploring the surrounding area. *Killinaboy, Corrofin; 065 683 7606; www.fergusview.com*

Gregan's Castle Hotel *expensive*
A charming manor house hotel. Turf fires and sweeping views of the Burren. *Corkscrew Hill, 4 km (2 miles) south of Ballyvaughan; closed Nov–mid-Feb; 065 707 7005; www.gregans.ie*

⑤ Cliffs of Moher
Co Clare
One of Ireland's most remarkable natural features, the Cliffs of Moher are where the limestone plateau of the Burren plunges 300 m (1,000 ft) into the sea. They stretch for 8 km (5 miles) along the coast of Clare. Park at the northern end, by the **Cliffs of Moher Visitor Experience** *(open daily)*. The state-of-the-art visitor centre offers interactive exhibits and virtual experiences, including the Atlantic Edge, which simulates the sensation of stepping onto the cliff edge.

To view the cliffs in relative isolation, take the cliff path to the southern extremity of **Hag's Head**. On a clear day there are views of the Aran Islands and the mountains of Connemara.

🚗 *From the Cliffs of Moher, a winding coastal road leads to Doolin. However, this gets congested, especially in summer, so take the R478 north and turn left at the junction with the R479 at the sign for Doolin.*

⑥ Doolin
Co Clare
If County Clare is the heartland of traditional Irish music, the village of Doolin is its music capital, brimming with music pubs and shops. These days some of them cater more to the tourist industry than for genuine music lovers, but there are several authentic music pubs where visitors can still pull up a seat and experience the full force of a rousing session.

McGann's, McDermott's and **Gus O'Connors**, are highly recommended, the last especially for rollicking ballads.

🚗 *Take the R479 north and then turn left at the junction with the R477. This rejoins the coast, eventually rounding Black Head.*

⑦ Black Head
Co Clare
The drive around Black Head to Ballyvaughan is thrilling, sweeping close to the shore with a succession of glorious views. Pull in and stretch your legs on **Fanore Beach** or stop at the **lighthouse**, from where there are far-reaching views across Galway Bay.

🚗 *Continue along the R477 to Ballyvaughan.*

⑧ Ballyvaughan
Co Clare
A fishing village dotted with slate-roofed cottages, Ballyvaughan bustles with visitors in summer. It is often described as the gateway to the Burren, for this is where the limestone plateau at the heart of the Burren begins. The town has a range of good hotels, pubs and restaurants. Bicycle hire and guided walks to view the area's geology and botany can be arranged through the **Tourist Information Centre** *(see right)*.

🚗 *Take the N67 inland towards Lisdoonvarna, famous for its matchmaking competition. Look back for stunning views over Galway Bay. After 1.5 km (1 mile), turn left onto the R480 for the heart of the Burren.*

Above Stunning views over Galway Bay from Black Head Lighthouse

⑨ THE BURREN

Co Clare

This massive plateau covers the whole of northwest Clare. Its name derives from the Irish *An Bhoieann*, meaning "The Stony District", for it is covered with huge flagstones called clints broken by deep fissures called grikes, through which millennia of rainfall have drained to form underground caves and rivers. One of Cromwell's surveyors declared it a savage land, yielding little. In fact, it is astonishingly rich in plant life, and it abounds in stone forts and megalithic tombs.

Heart of the Burren

The characteristic karst landscape of the Burren unfolds as the R480 heads south. On the left is the western flank of **Aillwee Rock** and **Aillwee Cave**, a series of spectacular showcaves *(www.aillweecave.ie; open daily)*. Go south for 7 km (4 miles) to **Poulnabrone Dolmen**, a large portal tomb dating from 2500–2000 BC and one of some 70 in the area. A further 2 km (1 mile) south is **Caherconnell Stone Fort** *(www.caherconnell.com; visitor centre open mid-Mar–Oct)*. Such ring forts were common from the 5th century.

Turn right on leaving the fort, then left at the next junction, up **Magga Hill** and down into **Carran** (5 km/3 miles). Turn left after Cassidy's pub and then right, signposted to Boston Gort. After 1 km (half

Sign at the Burren Perfumery

a mile) turn left for **Burren Perfumery** *(www.burrenperfumery.com)*, an artisan perfumery inspired by the local flora.

Leaving here, continue in the same direction. After about 4 km (2 miles) the road descends steeply. After it levels out, look left for the entrance to **St Colman's Well**, a 20-minute walk along a path. This healing well is overhung by an ash tree that has "clooties", rags tied for a wish or a blessing.

After 4 km (2 miles), turn right on the Kinvarra road, then left at the next junction (4 km/2 miles). After a further 2 km (1 mile) turn right for Killinaboy and Corrofin, staying left when the road forks. After 4 km (2 miles), a large grey house with bay windows was the location for the popular TV sitcom *Father Ted*, and serves tea and cakes by appointment. Leaving here, turn right and at the next junction turn left to skirt the southern flank of **Mullaghmore**. This area is rich in plants and a walk is recommended (a full circuit of the mountain will take about 2 hours). Later, return to the first junction after Father Ted's and turn left to **Killinaboy** (4 km/2 miles), with a round tower and church. From here, turn left onto the R476 to **Corrofin**, for the 14-km (9-mile) drive to Ennis.

The Burren

The vast limestone pavement of the Burren – what Cromwell's surveyor described as "yielding neither water enough to drown a man, nor tree to hang him in, nor soil enough to bury" – extends across the whole of northwest Clare until it gives way to the black shale and sandstone of the Cliffs of Moher in the southwest.

Above Poulnabrone Dolmen, one of many megalithic portal tombs on the Burren

VISITING THE BURREN

Tourist Information
Village Stores, Main Street,
Ballyvaughan 065 707 7464;
www.discoverballyvaughan.com

The Burren Centre
Kilfenora, 065 708 8030; www.
theburrencentre.ie; open Mar–Oct

EAT AND DRINK

BALLYVAUGHAN

Monk's *moderate*
A cosy place with several small bars. Has a well-deserved reputation for seafood, with dishes such as fried Atlantic fishcakes and Island Eddy clams. Great views over Galway Bay.
Old Pier, Ballyvaughan; 065 707 7059;
www.monks.ie

THE BURREN

Vaughan's Pub *moderate*
Landmark pub known for its music in Kilfenora. Traditional menu featuring seafood chowder, bacon and cabbage, and a splendid beef and Guinness pie.
Main Street, Kilfenora; 065 708 8004;
www.vaughanspub.ie

DAY TRIP OPTIONS

Ennis or Ballyvaughan make ideal bases to explore the dramatic north coast and rocky land of the Burren.

Coastal drama
Head to the northeast tip of Clare's coastline for a bracing walk at the Cliffs of Moher ⑤, then stop in Doolin ⑥ for traditional music or continue to Black Head ⑦ for stunning views.

Take the N85 from Ennis and follow the drive's instructions around the coast.

A day in the Burren
Ballyvaughan ⑧ is the gateway to the Burren ⑨, and it is possible to hire a bike, walk or drive through the stark scenery, prehistoric remains and unusual geological features of the region from the town. Stop off at Aillwee Rock and the showcaves at

Aillwee Cave, then head on to the 5th-century ring fort at Caherconell. Pause at the Burren Perfumery for restorative floral scents and make a wish at St Colman's Well. Then take tea at Father Ted's house to gain energy for a walk on Mullaghmore – a chance to appreciate the flora.

From Ballyvaughan take the R480 and R476 to reach the heart of the Burren.

TRIP 12

THROUGH THE SALLY GAP
Enniskerry to Mount Usher Gardens

HIGHLIGHTS

Great gardens
Admire two of Ireland's finest gardens – formal
Powerscourt and romantic Mount Usher

The Wicklow Mountains
Explore spectacular high passes, deep wooded valleys
and rolling foothills

Monastic serenity
Contemplate the tranquillity of lakeside Glendalough
and the ruins of its 6th-century monastery

Great statesmanship
Discover more about Irish political history at Avondale
House, home of statesman Charles Stewart Parnell

Superb beaches
Stride along dune-backed Brittas Bay, Wicklow's loveliest
stretch of coast

THROUGH THE SALLY GAP

County Wicklow is known as the Garden of Ireland, and with its forests, lakes and waterfalls, and its country estates, it lives up to its reputation. As you enter the county from Dublin to the north, abundant trees give way to the rolling Wicklow Mountains. Two notable valleys – Glendalough, one of the loveliest in the country, and the Sally Gap, a remote pass flanked by heather and blanket bog – are wildly beautiful. In contrast are the formal gardens of Powerscourt, the romantic gardens of Mount Usher beside the River Vartry and the lush farmland in the Vale of Avoca. The coastal part of the drive takes in the sweeping beaches of Brittas Bay and rugged Wicklow Head topped by its three lighthouses.

Above Powerscourt House, a Palladian mansion famous for its garden, see p132

ACTIVITIES

Picnic by Powerscourt Waterfall, the highest waterfall in Ireland

Trek through the foothills of the Wicklow Mountains on horseback

Hike into the hills above Glendalough or walk beside its lakes

Let the kids run wild at the Clara Lara Funpark, an outdoor adventure centre for under-12s

Tee off at Woodenbridge Golf Course, noted for its scenic setting

GLENCREE

R759

SALLY GAP 4

Mountains

R115

Lough
Dar

Glenmacnass

R756

GLENDALOUGH
5

Wicklow

Drumgoff
Ballinde

Avonbeg

Greenan

Balli

Macreddin

Aughrim

Roddenagh

R747

Aughrim

Kilpipe

Ballinagore

| 0 kilometres | 5 |
| 0 miles | 5 |

KEY

Drive route

PLAN YOUR DRIVE

Start/finish Enniskerry to Mount Usher Gardens.

Number of days: 3–4 days.

Distance: 100 km (62 miles).

Road conditions: Roads are mostly good although unclassified roads are narrow and have no central markings. Mountain roads may be impassable in bad weather; check the forecast and make sure you have enough fuel.

When to go: Spring, summer and autumn are the best times to visit.

Opening times: Most shops and attractions open 9 or 10am–5 or 6pm. Shops open Mon–Sat; in large towns also 12–6pm on Sun. Convenience stores in villages open 8am until late.

Main market days: Enniskerry: 2nd and 4th Sun; **Glendalough:** Crafts and Country Market, 2nd Sun; **Arklow:** Sat am; **Aughrim:** Farmers' Market, Sat.

Shopping: Buy colourful woollen scarves, throws and rugs at Avoca Handweavers, or browse Enniskerry's quaint crafts and antiques shops.

Major festivals: County Wicklow: Gardens Festival, May–Sep; Wicklow Town: Regatta Festival, Jul; Arts Festival, May.

DAY TRIP OPTIONS

Take the R115 over the dramatic **Wicklow Mountains** or down the lush **Vale of Avoca. Gardeners** may want to focus on **Powerscourt** and **Mount Usher. Beach lovers** should head for **Brittas Bay.** For full details, *see p137.*

Below Monument to Wicklow's lost seafarers, Wicklow Harbour, *see p137*

Above Clocktower in the main square of the picture-postcard estate village of Enniskerry

1 Enniskerry

Co Wicklow

Set around a square in the foothills of the Wicklow Mountains, this picture-postcard estate village – originally built to house the tenants who worked the land hereabouts – is a good starting point for exploring the northern reaches of the hills. In summer it bustles with tourists, who come to visit nearby Powerscourt House and linger in Enniskerry to browse its crafts, design and antiques shops. *Head uphill from the village square, taking the road (R760) on the left-hand side of the square. Powerscourt House and Gardens are a short way up on the right-hand side.*

2 Powerscourt Estate

Enniskerry, Co Wicklow

Approached along an avenue lined with more than 2,000 beech trees, Powerscourt Estate is set in magnificent formal gardens below the Great Sugar Loaf Mountain. An exhibition inside reveals its origins as a 13th-century Anglo-Norman castle, but the current house, Palladian in style, was commissioned by Richard Wingfield, the 1st Viscount Powerscourt, in the 1730s and designed by architect Richard Cassels. Gutted by fire in 1974, the renovated building now houses an upmarket shop with an excellent café and restaurant – all part of the Avoca Handweavers enterprise *(see p137)*.

VISITING THE WICKLOW MOUNTAINS

Parking in Enniskerry
Park in or around the main square.

Powerscourt Estate
Enniskerry; 01 204 6000; www.powerscourt.com; house, gardens and waterfall open daily

Trekking and Horse Riding
Several companies offer guided trekking and horse riding in the foothills of the Wicklow Mountains. For details visit *www.visitwicklow.ie*. One alternative is **Clissmann Horse Caravans**, from Rathdrum or Avoca *(Cornybyrne Farm; 0404 46920; www.clissmannhorsecaravans.com)*, who organize donkey-walking trips.

WHERE TO STAY IN ENNISKERRY

Ferndale *inexpensive*
This is a charming Victorian House, furnished in period style and located right in Enniskerry village. Scrambled eggs and smoked salmon with home-made breads for breakfast. *Enniskerry; 01 286 3518; www.ferndalehouse.com; closed Dec–Jan*

Summerhill House Hotel *moderate*
This beautiful period house in its own wooded grounds right opposite the entrance to the Powerscourt Estate has distinguished rooms in the main house and in adjacent townhouses. *Enniskerry; 01 286 7928; www.summerhillhousehotel.com*

The gardens at Powerscourt are probably the finest in Ireland, both for their design and for their dramatic setting. The grounds were remodelled along with the house in the mid-18th century, in a design created to blend into the landscape. A century later the 6th Viscount asked architect Daniel Robertson to draw up new designs for the gardens. He redesigned them – from a wheelbarrow, fortified by sherry to relieve his gout – in an Italian style, adding the terraces leading down from the house. The new ornamental gardens were finally completed in 1858–75 by the 7th Viscount, who added gates, urns and statues collected during his travels in Europe. He brought back the gilded wrought-iron **Bamberg Gate** from a church in Bavaria.

The centrepiece of the garden today is the **Triton Lake**, dug out for the first garden, which takes its name from the central fountain – modelled on a 17th-century work by Bernini in Rome. The **Perron**, a beautiful Italianate stairway added in 1874 and flanked on either side by the terraced **Italian Garden**, leads down to the lake. It is guarded by two **statues of Pegasus**, the mythical winged horse and emblem of the Wingfield family. A **mosaic** at the top was made of pebbles from nearby Bray beach.

Next to the secluded **Dolphin Pond** is a **Pets' Cemetery** containing the graves of Wingfield family cats, dogs and even horse and cattle.

Powerscourt Waterfall is a 3-km (2-mile) drive from the house (turn right onto the R760 and after a humpback bridge sharp right). Cascading into the River Dargle from a height of 122 m (400 ft), it is Ireland's highest waterfall and a popular picnic spot.

Above Italianate statues and urns added to Powerscourt Gardens by the 7th Viscount

🚗 *Return to Enniskerry and take the right-hand road (L1010) uphill from the square. Continue past Kilgarron Cottages and Glen View and follow the L011 to Glencree.*

The Wicklow Mountains

Wicklow Mountains National Park extends over 20,000 ha (50,000 acres) of scenery southwest of Enniskerry. The product of the interaction of man and nature through turf-cutting over thousands of years, it is a rugged wilderness of unpopulated heath and extensive bogland. Although no peak exceeds 915 m (3,000 ft), the mountains can be dangerous in bad weather. The roads are narrow, winding and bumpy in summer, and may be impassable after snow in winter.

❸ Glencree
Co Wicklow

The Valley of Glencree is home to the **Glencree Centre for Peace and Reconciliation**, established in the 1970s in response to the Northern Ireland conflict, but now concerned with global peace-building. It is housed in an 18th-century British barracks. There is a **Visitor Centre** *(open daily)* and café. Further along the valley is the **German Cemetery** containing graves of servicemen killed in the world wars.

🚗 *Leaving Glencree visitor centre, turn left onto the R115 and drive south through the Sally Gap.*

❹ Sally Gap
Co Wicklow

One of the most spectacular drives in Wicklow, this remote mountain pass is surrounded by blanket bog and heather, dotted with pools and streams. It follows the Military Road, built through the mountains to flush out rebels after the 1798 Rebellion. Now the road provides easy access to the Wicklow Mountains National Park, which has open access for walkers. The landscape changes colour with the seasons from bright green in spring to purple in summer and russet-brown in autumn, and snow-white in winter. Towards the end of the pass there is a viewpoint over the Wicklow Gap, another scenic route.

🚗 *Continue south on the R115 and turn right at Laragh onto the R755. After the sign for Wicklow Gap, turn left onto the R757 and then into the car park at Glendalough Visitor Centre.*

Above Powerscourt Waterfall cascades into the River Dargle from a height of 400 ft (122 m)

Above left Patchwork fields in the foothills of the Wicklow Mountains **Above** Johnnie Fox's, a pub with plenty of character and good food

EAT AND DRINK

ENNISKERRY

Poppies *inexpensive*
With wholesome country cooking, this friendly and cosy café is a great place to stop for breakfast, morning coffee or lunch. Plenty of choice for vegetarians.
The Square; 01 282 8869; open daytime only; www.poppies.ie

Emilia's Ristorante *moderate*
This friendly spot offers Italian fare such as homemade lasagne and more.
Enniskerry; 01 276 1834; closed Mon

AROUND ENNISKERRY

Johnnie Fox's *moderate*
From Enniskerry drive towards Dublin through the Scalp (R117 north) to reach Johnnie Fox's, Ireland's highest pub, with nightly music, crackling turf fires and excellent steaks and seafood.
Glencullen; 01 295 5647; www. johnniefoxs.com

POWERSCOURT ESTATE

Avoca Café *moderate*
Typical fare includes imaginative salads, Mediterranean tarts and hearty casseroles (beef and Guinness a speciality). Views over the gardens and Sugar Loaf mountain.
Powerscourt House; 01 204 6066; www.avoca.com; open daytime

Above The two granite arches of the gatehouse at Glendalough

VISITING GLENDALOUGH

Glendalough Visitor Centre
Glendalough, Bray; 0404 45352; www.glendalough.ie; open daily

Wicklow Mountains National Park Information Office
Upper Lake, Glendalough; 0404 45425; www.wicklowmountains nationalpark.ie; open Apr–Sep: daily; Oct–Mar: Sat & Sun

Clara Lara Funpark
Outdoor adventure playground 6 km (4 miles) from Glendalough off the R755, between Laragh and Rathdrum. Designed for children under 12.
Vale of Clara, Rathdrum; 0404 46161; www.claralara.ie; open May weekends, Jun–Aug daily

WHERE TO STAY IN GLENDALOUGH

Glendalough Hotel *moderate*
A welcoming, family-run hotel popular with passing tours. It offers lovely rooms and a fabulous bistro/bar.
Glendalough; 0404 45135; www.glendaloughhotel.com

⑤ Glendalough
Co Wicklow

Glendalough (*Gleann Da Locha* in Irish), or "valley of the two lakes", was carved out by glaciers during the Ice Age. A place of great beauty and tranquillity, it is the setting for a monastic settlement founded in the 6th century by St Kevin, a descendant of the royal house of Leinster who rejected his privileged life to become a hermit in a cave in this valley. It would be easy to spend half a day here, exploring the monastery ruins and walking around the two lakes, perhaps stopping to picnic. There are two information points – the Glendalough Visitor Centre, which tells the story of the monastery, and the Wicklow Mountains National Park Information Office, at the Upper Lake, where visitors can find out more about the park, valley and walking trails in the area.

A two-hour walking tour
Most of the monastic ruins (*open daily*) lie between the entrance and the Lower Lake. From the **Visitor Centre** ① follow the path behind the centre and cross the bridge. Turn right onto the Green Road, which leads around the complex, and walk through the **main gateway** ②, originally two storeys, with two granite arches. To the right is the landmark Round Tower, one of the finest towers of its type: 30 m (100 ft) high and with its entrance 3 m (11 ft) from the ground (it would have been reached by ladders that could be hauled up from inside), it served as a belfry and a beacon for approaching

Round Tower at Glendalough

visitors, and was a place of security for the monks during times of attack.
Straight ahead are the **monastic buildings** ③, including the Cathedral, dating from the 12th century and the largest building in the complex; just to the south is St Kevin's Cross. Behind these is The Priest's House, reconstructed from the original stones, which was a place of burial for local clergy. Further along the path is St Kevin's Church, known as St Kevin's Kitchen, as well as the remains of St Kieran's Church, commemorating the founder of Clonmacnoise. From here, take the path back across the river and turn right towards the Lower Lake.

Above The tranquillity of Glendalough, which attracted the 6th-century hermit St Kevin

Walk along the Green Road, leaving the Lower Lake on the right. Just before the Upper Lake is the **National Park Information Office** ④.

From here, follow the Poulanass Walk to **Reefert Church** ⑤, dating from 1100. A little further on, up some steps, is **St Kevin's Cell** ⑥, a beehive-shaped hut where the saint is said to have lived and prayed. Little is known about the saint, but legend has it that he lived to the age of 120, and that a blackbird once laid an egg in the saint's outstretched hands as he prayed, which he held until it hatched. Further along the lake is a small cave known as St Kevin's Bed. It is not accessible, but can be seen from Miner's Road on the far shore.

From the hermit's cell follow the Poulanass Walk to the **Poulanass Waterfall** ⑦ – a steep climb through woodland – and views over the Upper Lake. Descend from the waterfall to the information office and return to the car park along the far side of the Lower Lake.

🚗 *From the car park bear right onto the R756, passing through Laragh. Turn right onto the R755 to Rathdrum and then right onto the R752 for Avoca. After 1.5 km (1 mile) take left and next left at the sign for Avondale House. Park in the car park.*

The Wicklow Way

This is a self-guided walking trail running 127 km (79 miles) from Marlay Park in South Dublin to the village of Clonegal in County Carlow, taking in mountains, lakes, rivers, forests and farmland on the way. The entire trail takes 7–10 days and requires a good level of fitness, equipment and a proper map. Alternatively it is possible to walk short segments of the trail. For more information on the trail, visit *www.wicklowway.com*.

❻ Avondale House and Forest Park

Rathdrum, Co Wicklow

Lying just south of Rathdrum, this is the birthplace and home of Charles Stewart Parnell (1846–91), one of Ireland's best-known political leaders. Avondale House *(closed for renovation)* has an important place in Irish history. Tours of its impressive interior recount the tale of Parnell's fight for Home Rule and the founding of the Irish Parliamentary Party. The house, built in 1179 by Samuel Hayes, is set in an extensive forest park *(open daily year-round)* along the west bank of the Avonmore River with marked trails, picnic spots and children's play areas.

🚗 *Leaving Avondale, return to the R752 towards Avoca, stopping at the Meeting of the Waters.*

EAT AND DRINK AROUND GLENDALOUGH

Glendalough Green Café *inexpensive*
Come to this café/deli for a great selection of freshly baked breads, soups and hotpots, as well as artisan chocolates. There are also outdoor tables for alfresco dining. *Laragh; 0404 45151; www. glendaloughgreen.com*

Wicklow Heather Restaurant *moderate*
This restaurant offers à la carte menus featuring dishes such as venison loin. *Glendalough Road, Laragh; 0404 45157; www.wicklowheather.ie*

Above Avondale House, birthplace of the Irish nationalist leader Charles Stewart Parnell

Above Pretty garden at Hunter's Hotel, a former coaching inn, Rathnew

WHERE TO STAY

VALE OF AVOCA
Woodenbridge Hotel and Lodge *moderate*
Established in 1608 as a coaching inn, this is Ireland's oldest hotel and a charming and intimate place to stay.
Arklow; 0402 35146; www.woodenbridgehotel.com

WICKLOW HEAD
Wicklow Head Lighthouse *expensive*
This restored lighthouse, originally built in 1781, is now run by The Irish Landmark Trust and can be hired on a self-catering basis. Sleeping four, it has six octagonal rooms and stunning views of the Irish Sea. A special place to stay.
Dunbur Head; 01 670 4733; www.irishlandmark.com

AROUND WICKLOW TOWN
Ballyknocken House *moderate*
This 19th-century country house is a guesthouse, farm, cookery school and restaurant (for residents only), overseen by celebrity chef Catherine Fulvio. It is 1.5 km (1 mile) from Glenealy on the road to Ashford.
Glenealy, Ashford; 0404 44627; www.ballyknocken.ie

Hunter's Hotel *moderate*
A romantic 18th-century coaching inn (on R761 to Newcastle) combining old-style elegance with modern comforts. Run by the same family since 1820.
Newrath Bridge, Rathnew; 0404 40106; www.hunters.ie

Tinakilly Country House *moderate*
An old-fashioned country house set in elegant gardens. Some period rooms with four-poster beds and sea views.
Main Street, Rathnew; 0404 69274; www.tinakilly.ie

⑦ Vale of Avoca
Avoca, Co Wicklow
The **Meeting of the Waters** is a tranquil spot where the Avonmore ("large river" in Irish) and Avonbeg ("small river") merge to form the River Avoca. The poem "The Meeting of The Waters" by Thomas Moore (1779–1852) commemorates "that vale in whose bosom the bright waters meet". The Avoca eventually flows into the Irish Sea at Arklow. Continue on the R752 to Avoca and the Vale of Avoca.

Nestling in the wooded Vale of Avoca, an area that once had gold, copper, lead and zinc mines – dating back to 1720 – is the village of **Avoca**. The last mine closed in the early 1980s, but Avoca Handweavers has the oldest working woollen mill in Ireland, established in 1723, and is still thriving, with stylish modern designs to buy *(see right)*. To see the weaving process, drive through the village, pass the church and go down the hill; it is on the left-hand side. From Avoca, continue south along the R752, bearing right onto the R747 for Aughrim.

At the meeting point of the Avoca and Aughrim rivers, **Woodenbridge** is the scenic setting for the Woodenbridge Golf Course *(0402 35202; www.woodenbridge.ie)*, and Ireland's oldest hotel, the Woodenbridge Hotel and Lodge

Many options in the Wicklow Mountains

(see left), founded in 1608. Trout fishing is popular in the River Aughrim.

🚗 *After Woodenbridge, take the R747 towards Arklow. Entering Arklow, take first exit at roundabout and follow signs towards M11/Dublin. Leave the M11 at Jack White's Cross Roads, turning right onto the R773 for Brittas Bay.*

⑧ Brittas Bay
Co Wicklow
Running for 5 km (3 miles) and backed by rolling sand dunes, Brittas Bay is a stunning beach with Blue Flag status, ideal for swimming. In summer, it is busy with day-trippers and second-home-owners from Dublin, but there is enough space to absorb the crowds. Lifeguards are on duty from mid-June through August. Out of season it is ideal for bracing walks along the sand, which provide a chance to spot some of the rare wildlife in the dunes backed by extensive marsh and fen. Wild asparagus, sea rocket and sea parsley grow among the marram grass, where dune rabbits may be seen. At different times of year it is possible to spot little tern and ringed plover, sedge warbler and reed bunting, dunlin and sanderling.

🚗 *Drive north along Brittas Bay, following the R750, which runs parallel to the beach, passing bathing beaches at Jack's Hole and Silver Strand, to Wicklow Head.*

Above Glorious expanse of Brittas Bay, fringed by dunes that are a haven for wildlife

9 Wicklow Head
Co Wicklow

This headland, rising 84 m (276 ft) above the sea, has been watched over by two lighthouses since 1781, when they were built to aid ships' navigation through channels between the sand banks in the Irish Sea. The rear lighthouse on Long Hill remains intact, and has been restored as holiday accommodation, while the front one was rebuilt in 1816. The third lighthouse, the only one currently in use, was built further down the cliff for greater visibility.

🚗 *Follow the R750 into Wicklow Town and park near the Gaol.*

10 Wicklow Town
Co Wicklow

The main attraction of Wicklow Town is its **Historic Gaol** *(open daily; www.wicklowshistoricgaol.com)*. Built in 1702 and now a museum, it details important episodes in Irish history, such as the 1798 Rebellion and the Great Famine. Visitors can climb aboard a reconstructed prison ship and learn about prisoners' harsh

conditions inside the dungeon. The building is supposed to be haunted, so brave souls could try a night tour, held on the last Friday of every month.

🚗 *Follow the R750 out of Wicklow to Rathnew and pass two roundabouts, following signs for Ashford. Mount Usher Gardens are on the right-hand side on entering Ashford.*

11 Mount Usher Gardens
Ashford, Co Wicklow

Beautifully set along the River Vartry, these gardens *(open daily; www.mountushergardens.ie)* were designed in 1868 by Edward Walpole in the Robinsonian informal style made famous by the Irish gardener William Robinson (1838–1935). Meandering walks and pretty bridges afford romantic views framed by rare shrubs and trees, from Chinese conifers and bamboos to Mexican pines and pampas grass. Seasonal highlights include crocuses, bluebells and magnolias in spring, azaleas and rhododendrons in early summer, and the glorious Maple Walk in autumn.

Above left The River Vartry cascading through Mount Usher gardens **Above** Ruins perched on the clifftop at Wicklow Head

SHOPPING IN THE VALE OF AVOCA

Avoca Handweavers
Brightly coloured handwoven woollen scarves and throws can be bought at the original Avoca mill. The **Avoca Café** serves delicious homemade baked beans with garlic and rosemary on toasted ciabatta, pancakes with fresh berries and similar delicacies. *The Mill, Avoca; 0402 35105; www.avoca.com; closes 5pm*

EAT AND DRINK

AROUND THE VALE OF AVOCA
The Strawberry Tree *expensive*
Award-winning organic restaurant in an upmarket resort hotel, 15 km (11 miles) from Woodenbridge. *Brooklodge Hotel, Macreddin; 0402 36444; www.brooklodge.com; closed Oct–Feb: Mon & Tue*

AROUND WICKLOW TOWN
Ballyknocken House and Cookery School *moderate*
See "Where to Stay", left

DAY TRIP OPTIONS
Mountains, coast, vale or gardens, there are plenty of day trips that can be taken from Enniskerry or Wicklow.

Dip into the mountains
To sample the Wicklow Mountains, follow the Military Road, the R115, from Glencree 3 to Laragh, turning off at Glendalough 5 to picnic by the lakes and see the ruins.

From Enniskerry follow signs to Glencree and then join the R115

towards Laragh. Return on the R755 via Roundwood and Vartry reservoir.

The Vale of Avoca
This valley has several interesting stops, including Avondale House 6, the Meeting of the Waters and Avoca Handweavers in the Vale of Avoca 7.

Take the R750 from Wicklow, then the R752 towards Avoca.

For gardeners
Compare and contrast two gardens by combining a morning at the

Powerscourt Estate 2 with an afternoon at Mount Usher Gardens 11.

Follow directions to Powerscourt from Enniskerry. Mount Usher is 26 km (16 miles) along the scenic coastal R761.

The Wicklow coast
Drive around Wicklow Head 9 to spend the day at Brittas Bay 8, the finest beach on the east coast.

Take the R750 from Wicklow Town, avoiding holidays when roads are busy.

TRIP 13

THE PLAINS OF KILDARE

Celbridge to Kilcullen

HIGHLIGHTS

Georgian splendour
Take a tour of Castletown House, the grandest Georgian house in Ireland

Walk in the woods
Wander the waymarked trails of Donadea Forest Park, a delightful old woodland estate

Kildare Town
Explore the wealth of historic monuments in this charming town

Sport of kings
See how some of the world's finest bloodstock is raised, at the Irish National Stud

The restored Red Drawing Room at Castletown House

THE PLAINS OF KILDARE

The county of Kildare is within easy reach of Dublin but still retains its traditional rural character. Ireland's world-famous bloodstock industry is largely based here, on some of the best grassland in the country. This drive follows the leafy roads beside the River Liffey and the Grand Canal, past such diverse attractions as writer James Joyce's boarding school, a prehistoric hill fort, a great Irish Palladian house and one of the world's most prestigious racecourses.

Above The Japanese Gardens at the Irish National Stud, *see p45*

ACTIVITIES

Listen to a recital of chamber music in a great 18th-century house

Savour a pint on a peaceful stretch of the Grand Canal

Visit St Brigid's Cathedral in Kildare Town and climb the round tower for spectacular views

Unwind in the tranquillity of the Japanese Gardens, in the grounds of the Irish National Stud

Place a bet on the horses at the Curragh Racecourse

Newp
Derrycrib
DONADEA
L1018
Timahoe
Staplestown
Bog of Allen
Hodgestown
L1021
Coolcarrigan
Garvage
Coolearagh
Blackwood
Prosperous
Allenwood
Slate
4 ROBERTSTOWN
Goat
R415
KILDAR
Kilmeage
Allen
C
Hill of Allen
206m
Lattensbog
Thomastow
Dunbyrne
Morristown
Upper
11
Milltown
R415
Friarstown
R416
R445
R401
Newbridge
THE CURRAGH
RACECOURSE
Kilbelin
Connellmo
Redhills
7
R413
12.
KILDARE
TOWN **5**
M7
R413
Athgarvan
M9
13
The Curragh
Silliothill
6 IRISH NATIONAL
STUD
R415
KILCULLE
Martinstown
Old Kilcullen
0 kilometres 3
0 miles 3
R418
M9

KEY

Drive route

PLAN YOUR DRIVE

Start/finish: Celbridge to Kilcullen.

Number of days: 2.

Distance: 60 km (37 miles).

Road conditions: The roads are in good condition, larger roads well signposted.

When to go: Summer is the best time for horse-racing and musical events. The autumn colours of the county's woodlands are spectacular.

Opening times: Shops and attractions open 9am–6pm. Shops open Mon–Sat; also 12–6pm on Sun. Convenience stores in villages open 8am until late.

Main market days: Celbridge: Sat; Kildare Town: Thu.

Major festivals: Celbridge: Castletown Concerts (Castletown House), summer; The Curragh: Irish Derby, Jun; Punchestown: National Hunt Festival, Apr; Kildare Town: Medieval Festival, Aug.

DAY TRIP OPTIONS

Lovers of **history and nature** could combine a visit to Castletown House with a stroll in Donadea Forest Park. **Walkers** might prefer to walk a stretch of the Grand Canal and climb the Hill of Allen. And, if the timing is right, a **day at the races** at The Curragh is unmissable. *For details, see p145.*

Below St Brigid's Cathedral in Kildare Town, with its striking 9th-century Round Tower, *see p144*

Above The 13th-century fortified tower of Barberstown Castle

WHERE TO STAY AROUND CLANE

Westgrove *moderate*
Top-class hotel with luxurious rooms, comprehensive leisure facilities – including swimming pools – and a fine restaurant and bar. You can also take afternoon tea in the library. *Abbeylands; 045 989 900; www. westgrovehotel.com*

Barberstown Castle *moderate-expensive*
This long-established country house hotel, the oldest part of which dates from the 13th century, is set in its own extensive grounds, with lovely gardens; rooms furnished with antiques; a fine-dining restaurant and comfortable public areas with log fires in winter. *Straffan, Clane (located off the R403 between Celbridge and Clane, 7 km/4 miles from Clane – well signposted); 01 628 8157; www. barberstowncastle.ie*

① Celbridge
Co Kildare
This well-preserved village on the Liffey has long associations with he author and Dean of St Patrick's, Dublin, Jonathan Swift (1667–1745). His beloved Esther Van Homrigh, whom he immortalized as "Vanessa", lived at Celbridge Abbey. At the end of the Main Street, the gates of **Castletown House** *(open mid-Mar–Oct: daily; Nov–mid-Dec: Wed–Sun; www. castletown.ie)* open onto a long driveway to the house, now accessible only on foot (cars must turn left at the gate and follow the signs around to the right and find the back entrance and car park). The house was built in 1722 for William Conolly, the Speaker of the Irish House of Commons, and is the largest private house in Ireland. It is a masterpiece of Georgian architecture in the Palladian style. The interiors were created by Lady Louisa Lennox, wife of Conolly's great-nephew, and include the only intact 18th-century print room in Ireland. A portrait of Lady Louisa can be seen in the superb stuccowork on the staircase. Castletown is set in a stately park of mature trees. Also within the park is Conolly's Folly, built by Richard Castle, commissioned by Conolly's widow, Katherine, in 1740 as a memorial to him and to provide employment on the estate after a harsh winter.

🚗 *Leaving Celbridge, take the R403 to Clane.*

Conolly family crest, Castletown House

② Clane
Co Kildare
The Neo-Gothic **Protestant church** (1884) on elegant Main Street stands on the site of one of the earliest monasteries in Ireland. Founded around the 5th century, it predated the arrival of St Patrick. Nothing of it remains today. Just outside the village, on the R407 heading north, is **Clongowes Wood College**, a long-established Jesuit boarding school, set in a beautiful estate of ancient woods and playing fields, the latter evoked by former student James Joyce in the opening pages of *A Portrait of the Artist as a Young Man*. The main building is Castle Browne, which was a border fort of the Pale, that part of Ireland around Dublin controlled by the English until the 17th century.

🚗 *Continue along the R407; take the side road (L009) to the left signposted Donadea, follow the signs to Donadea and park in the car park.*

③ Donadea
Co Kildare
The Aylmer family lived at **Donadea Castle** from the 15th to the 20th century. The property is now owned by the state. The imposing castle still stands but is derelict. Visitors can walk on waymarked trails of varying lengths around the 240-ha (590-acre) **Donadea Forest Park** *(open daily)* with its mixed woodland, walled garden, streams, lake and boat house. In a grove of

Above Interior of Castletown House, Celbridge, decorated in the Pompeiian style
Above right Exquisite mahogany bureau flanked by 18th-century portraits in Castletown House

Above The impressive former Grand Canal Hotel in Robertstown, at the centre of canalside activity

oak saplings, a limestone replica of the World Trade Center's twin towers commemorates members of the American emergency services who died in the attacks of 11 September 2001, including Sean Tallon, a young firefighter whose family was from Donadea. In the nearby **St Peter's Church** (open for services) is a fine 17th-century canopied tomb with effigies of Sir Gerald Aylmer and his wife Dame Julia Nugent.

Leaving Donadea Forest Park, turn left, left and left again onto the L1018, in the direction of the small village of Prosperous. Turn right on the R403, then take a left turn on to a smaller road for Robertstown.

❹ Robertstown
Co Kildare

The Grand Canal, which links Dublin in the east to the River Shannon in the west of Ireland, is now used only for leisure purposes. The highest point on its route is at picturesque Robertstown at the Hill of Allen. In 1804, the Grand Canal Company built one of its grand hotels here, though today it sadly stands derelict. There are also several good pubs, often with live music sessions in the evenings. A little further to the west is Lowtown, whose marina is one of the most popular mooring spots in Kildare. Here the canal divides, with an offshoot towards Athy and the River Barrow.

From Robertstown follow signs for the pleasant hamlet of Kilmeage.

Join the R415 and proceed along it with the Hill of Allen on the right-hand side, passing Milltown, on a feeder line to the canal. There is paid parking in and around Kildare's Market Square.

The Grand Canal Way

This waymarked canalside trail runs for 138 km (86 miles) from Dublin to Shannon Harbour. Robertstown is situated at the 45-km (28-mile) mark. The path is well-maintained along its entire route, making it safe for walkers and cyclists of all ages. Visit the website of the Inland Waterways Association of Ireland (www.iwai.ie) or Sport Ireland (www.sportireland.ie) for details of this and other waymarked trails. Alternatively, see Waterways Ireland (www.waterwaysireland.org) for information about day trips and boat hire on the canal.

EAT AND DRINK

CELBRIDGE

Courtyard Cafe *inexpensive*
An excellent café based in the high-ceilinged former kitchen of Castletown House, serving lunches of soups, tarts and salads; a good place in which to start or finish a tour of the house.
Castletown House; 01 627 9498; closes 5pm

CLANE

Mode Tapas & Grill *moderate*
Located behind Jones Bar, this smart tapas spot offers treats such as crispy brie fritters and Spanish meatballs cooked in garlic.
Main Street; 045 861 188; www.modetapas.com

AROUND ROBERTSTOWN

Hanged Man's *inexpensive*
A traditional country pub and restaurant on the canal at Milltown. The restaurant specializes in meat and seafood dishes such as surf 'n' turf pasta and New York strip sirloin.
Milltown (9 km/5.5 miles from Robertstown on the R415); 045 431 515; www.hangedmans.ie

Below Imposing Donadea Castle, set in its own forest park

Above Kildare Town Heritage Centre, in the fine 18th-century Market House

VISITING KILDARE TOWN

Parking
There is pay-and-display parking in and around Market Square.

Tourist Information
Kildare Town Heritage Centre, Market Square; 045 530 672; www.kildare heritage.com; open 9:30am–1pm & 2–5pm Mon–Fri, 10am–2:30pm Sat

WHERE TO STAY

KILDARE TOWN

Cherryville House *inexpensive*
Charming bed-and-breakfast with two gorgeous en suite rooms, in an old farm-house on a working farm, just off the R445 heading towards Monasterevan from Kildare Town.
Kildare; 045 521 091; www.kildare bedandbreakfast.com

AROUND THE CURRAGH RACECOURSE

Martinstown House *expensive*
This Gothic-style *cottage ornée*, designed in the 1830s by the English architect Decimus Burton, is set in extensive grounds with wonderful trees and even two rescue donkeys. It is well signposted a few kilometres (miles) south of the Curragh Racecourse on minor roads. Six luxurious bedrooms and a friendly, comfortable ambience. Five-course gourmet dinner, for guests only or groups of eight or more. Exceptional breakfast.
Martinstown, The Curragh; 045 441 269; www.martinstownhouse.com

⑤ KILDARE TOWN

Co Kildare

Kildare is a pretty, well-preserved small cathedral and market town, where St Brigid, one of the three great Irish saints (the other two were Patrick and Colmcille), founded a monastery in the 6th century. It later became the principal church in Leinster, and was unusual in being a double monastery (for both nuns and monks). A fine Round Tower, built as a place of refuge from the Norse raids of the 9th–10th centuries, stands beside the cathedral. Kildare is the main town serving the army camp and the racecourse, set in the great plain of The Curragh, and is the centre of the Irish bloodstock industry.

A one-hour walking tour

Start in the **Market Square** ① in the centre of the town, at the Heritage Centre, formerly the Market House. According to the Statutes of Henry VI (1458) a market has been held in Kildare "from time whereof memory runs not", but the present building is from the 18th century. As well as a place of business, the Market Square was a venue for town gatherings, and it is still the social hub, with its bars, restaurants and shops. In the Heritage Centre *(open daily)*, as well as the tourist office, is a multimedia exhibition recounting the history of the town. Opposite is the St Brigid's Flame monument, by Alex Pentek, unveiled in 2006 as a memorial to the sacred flame kept alive by St Brigid as a perpetual fire of Christianity, which burned until the suppression of the monasteries in the 16th century. At the top of Martket Square is **St Brigid's Cathedral** ② *(open May–Sep: daily)*. There has been a church on the site

Lord Edward Fitzgerald statue

since the 6th century; it may have been a pagan sanctuary before that. The present building, dating from the 13th century, has undergone much destruction and restoration, but contains some interesting medieval relics and modern stained-glass windows. On the north side of the cathedral are the restored foundations of St Brigid's Fire Temple, where a small fire is still lit on the saint's feast day (1 Feb). Behind the cathedral, is the 32-m (106-ft) **Round Tower** ③. It is possible to climb to the top, for wonderful views. To the east of the Market Square, behind the Silken Thomas pub, is a remaining 15th-century tower from **Kildare Castle** ④. Lord Edward Fitzgerald (1763–98), leader of the United Irishmen, lived in an adjoining house, now gone. Walk up Market Square back to the car park.

🚗 *From Market Square, follow Tully Road over the M7 motorway, then turn left onto the L7024, signed for the National Stud.*

⑥ Irish National Stud

Co Kildare

Established in 1946 to develop Irish bloodstock, this is the home of some of the finest thoroughbred horses in the country *(open mid-Feb–early Nov: daily)*. The guided tour includes a visit to the stableyard to see mares and foals, as well as some retired champions. The **Horse Museum** tells the history of Irish horses, shows films of some classic races and exhibits include the skeleton of the great Arkle.

Above St Fiachra's Garden at the Irish National Stud, a peaceful place of rock and water

In the grounds of the National Stud are two superb gardens *(open mid-Feb–early Nov: daily)*. St Fiachra's Garden, established in 1999 and named after the patron saint of gardeners, is a spiritual place reflecting the Irish landscape. The beautiful Japanese Gardens, laid out 1906–10, symbolize the Life of Man, and are regarded as the finest such gardens in Europe.

🚗 *Turn right out of the National Stud, then right again and continue through Kildare Town. Turn right onto R413 to the Curragh Racecourse. Ample parking.*

⑦ The Curragh Racecourse

Co Kildare

Set in a great plain, where sheep graze freely and horses from the surrounding stud farms are exercised, **The Curragh** *(open race days only)* is where all five Irish Classics are raced – the 2,000 and 1,000 Guineas in May, the Irish Derby in June/July, the Oaks in July and the St Leger in September. A place to see Irish racing at its best, in a terrific atmosphere.

🚗 *Leaving the racecourse, turn right onto R413. At the first roundabout take the second exit, signposted Newbridge. Follow signs for Kilcullen through two roundabouts, crossing the M9 motorway, to the village of Kilcullen.*

Horse Sense

The Curragh is the home of Ireland's best flat racing, while Punchestown, near Naas, is where the National Hunt Festival takes place over the jumps. Ireland is famous for its thoroughbred racehorses, and the bloodstock industry flourished for many years thanks to tax exemption on stallion profits.

---

⑧ Kilcullen

Co Kildare

This is a winding village on the river Liffey in the midst of horse country, with good restaurants and bars and a pleasant riverside walk. There are many antiquities nearby, including an early monastery at **Old Kilcullen**, where St Patrick founded a bishopric. The base of a round tower and portions of three carved stone crosses survive. The hill to the northwest, Knockaulin, is topped by an important prehistoric circular hill fort, **Dún Áilinne**. It is on private land, so enquire about visits at the Kildare Town Heritage Centre.

Above Statue of Irish thoroughbred legend Vintage Crop at the Curragh Racecourse

EAT AND DRINK

KILDARE TOWN

Silken Thomas *inexpensive–moderate*
A refurbished traditional pub in the centre of town, a popular place with a bright and busy restaurant serving breakfast, lunch and dinner.
Kildare Town; 045 522 232; www.silkenthomas.com

Dunne & Crescenzi *moderate*
This Italian restaurant is in the Kildare Village shopping outlet, not far from Kildare Town. Inventive, authentic cooking, and lovely views.
Kildare Village shopping outlet, Kildare Town; 045 535 850; www.dunneand crescenzi.com

KILCULLEN

Fallons *moderate*
The owners of this long-established eating house bring a warm atmosphere and excellent food. Try seafood chowder, fish 'n' chips, a rib eye steak, or just enjoy a pint of Guinness by the turf fire.
Main Street; 045 481 260; www. fallons.ie; closed Mon

DAY TRIP OPTIONS

Places of interest are all within easy reach of Celbridge, Robertstown and Kildare Town.

History and nature

Pass the morning exploring lovely Castletown House at Celbridge ❶, then continue to Donadea ❸ for a meander through the tranquil woodlands of Donadea Forest Park.

Take the R403 from Celbridge towards Clane, then the R407 north and follow signs to Donadea Forest Park. Return along the same route.

Walking trails

Combine a stroll – or a boat trip – along the Grand Canal at Robertstown ❹ with a walk up the Hill of Allen, for marvellous views. End the day with a music session.

Follow the route from Robertstown; turn right to the Hill after Barnacrow.

A day at the races

Walk around Kildare Town ❺ and visit the National Stud ❻ and The Curragh Racecourse ❼ for a day of equine action *(see www.curragh.ie for the dates of race meetings)*.

Follow the drive's instructions.

TRIP 14

DUBLIN'S NORTH COAST
Dublin to Ardgillan Demesne

HIGHLIGHTS

Georgian Dublin
Explore elegant Georgian terraces, and museums
and art galleries

Spectacular views
Enjoy breathtaking panoramas from Howth Head

Sweeping strands
Stride out along Portmarnock's golden,
dune-fringed beach

Country life
Learn about 19th-century rural life on Newbridge
traditional working farm

Historic houses
Tour ancient castles whose lovely grounds hold
delightful surprises

DUBLIN'S NORTH COAST

From the bustle and buzz of Dublin itself to some beautiful, unspoiled shores north of the city, this drive offers a wealth of choice in just a small number of miles. Along its route you can visit elegant castles and stately homes, wander along a dune-backed beach and admire panoramic views of the city, bay and mountains from rugged Howth Head. Pause along the way for a memorable meal at one of the region's many fine seafood restaurants, and golfers should seize the chance to play on a championship course.

Above Sturdy 19th-century Baily Lighthouse, perched atop the rugged southeastern tip of Howth Head, *see p152*

ACTIVITIES

See puffins from Howth or spot seals at Skerries

Play a round of golf at Portmarnock's famous links

Take a boat trip around Dublin Bay from Malahide

Explore a Georgian stately home at lovely Newbridge House

See traditional windmills and watermills in action at Skerries Mills

PLAN YOUR DRIVE

Start/finish: Dublin to Ardgillan Demesne.

Number of days: 2, allowing half a day to explore Dublin.

Distance: 72 km (45 miles).

Road conditions: County Dublin roads are generally good.

When to go: Summer is a lovely time to visit, but busy. Good weather in spring and autumn. The St Patrick's Day weekend is busy, so book ahead.

Opening times: Most shops and attractions open 9am–6pm. Shops open Mon–Sat; also 12–6pm on Sun.

Main market days: Dublin: Temple Bar, Sat; Powerscourt Townhouse, Sat; Docklands, Wed; Howth Harbour: Sat, Sun and public holiday Mon; Malahide: Sat; Skerries Mills: Sat.

Major festivals: Dublin: International Film Festival, Feb/Mar; St Patrick's Festival, Mar; Forbidden Fruit, Jun; Taste of Dublin Food Festival, Jun; Dublin Theatre Festival, Sep/Oct; Howth: Dublin Bay Prawn Festival, May; Malahide: Malahide Has It Festival, Jul; Skerries: Traditional Music Weekend, May.

DAY TRIP OPTIONS

History-lovers should explore the region's stately homes and gardens; in summer, **families** may prefer a day at the seaside, with boat trips and lovely beaches. For full details, see p153.

Below Dublin's elegant, high-arched Ha'penny Bridge, spanning the River Liffey, see p151

Above Frontage of The Quay's Bar, a pub in the Temple Bar district

VISITING DUBLIN

Parking
For parking near the Dublin Tourism office there is a car park at St Stephen's Green Shopping Centre (accessed from Mercer Street Lower), Drury Street car park, Brown Thomas car park (accessed from Clarendon Street) or Trinity Street car park, or at pay-and-display spaces on the street.

Tourist Information
Visit Dublin Centre, Suffolk Street, Dublin 2; 1 850 230 330; www. visitdublin.com; open daily

WHERE TO STAY IN DUBLIN

The Mont *moderate*
Located near Trinity College and Grafton Street, this terrific hotel has designer rooms, a fine Italian restaurant and a cool bar.
Merrion Street Lower, Dublin 2; 01 607 3800; www.themonthotel.ie

Merrion Hotel *expensive*
Experience Georgian grandeur in this beautifully restored luxury hotel in the heart of Georgian Dublin. It's also the venue for Patrick Guilbaud's two-Michelin-starred restaurant.
Upper Merrion Street, Dublin 2; 01 603 0600; www.merrionhotel.com

Shelbourne Hotel *expensive*
This elegant hotel overlooking St Stephen's Green is one of the city's most famous and distinguished hotels. Rooms offer unbridled luxury and the attention to detail is first class.
27 St Stephen's Green, Dublin 2; 01 663 4500; www.theshelbourne.com

❶ DUBLIN

Dublin

Dublin is a compact city and easy to explore on foot, ideal for wandering around the cobbled streets of Temple Bar or admiring the grandeur of elegant Georgian squares and parks. From its fine museums, majestic cathedrals and beautiful university buildings, redolent of Dublin's history, to modern art galleries and shopping arcades, there is plenty to see and do along this walk.

A three-hour walking tour

Start at the **Dublin Tourism office** ① in Suffolk Street. Turn right and carry on along Nassau Street. Take the fourth right into Kildare Street, passing Leinster House, seat of the Irish Government and the **National Library of Ireland** ② *(open Mon–Sat)*. The **National Museum of Ireland – Archaeology** ③ *(open Tue–Sat, Sun & Mon pm)*, further along the street, has more than two million archaeological artifacts from all Ireland. At the top of the street, turn left along Merrion Row and left again into Merrion Street Upper, to reach the **National Museum – Natural History** ④ *(open Tue–Sat, Sun & Mon pm)* and the **National Gallery** ⑤ *(open daily)*, with a fine collection of Irish and European old masters, opposite Georgian **Merrion Square's** ⑥ charming gardens. Cross the square for a fine view down Mount Street Upper to the distinctive looking **St Stephen's Church** ⑦, affectionately known as the Pepper Pot Church.

Return to Merrion Row and walk to the large Victorian park, **St Stephen's Green** ⑧, on the left. Walk diagonally across the green to Harcourt Street, and up it to Clonmel Street, on the left, at the end of which is **Iveagh**

Gardens ⑨ *(open daily)*, a secluded park with grottoes, cascades and mazes. Retrace the walk and continue along the west side of the green into **Grafton Street** ⑩, the city's main, pedestrianized shopping street. Walk down it and take the little lane beside Bewley's café on the left to **Powerscourt Townhouse Centre** ⑪, which has Irish fashion designer and antique shops. Behind this, the **George's Street Arcade** ⑫ has eclectic stalls.

Back on Grafton Street, at the far end, is the **Molly Malone statue** ⑬, which commemorates the legendary Dublin fishmonger. Further along on the right is the arched entrance to **Trinity College Dublin** ⑭ *(open daily)*, Ireland's oldest university, founded in 1592. Here the *Book of Kells* is on display in the Old Library. Walk down Dame Street, opposite, passing Bank of Ireland College Green, the former houses of parliament, on the right. Ahead on the left is **Dublin Castle** ⑮ *(open daily)*, where it is possible to tour the State Apartments and also visit the **Chester Beatty Library** ⑯ *(open Mar–Oct: daily; Nov–Feb: closed Mon)*, a gem-like collection of Asian and European manuscripts. Carry on and turn right into Werburgh Street, then

Above Georgian townhouses overlooking the charming gardens of Merrion Square

The Book of Kells

The most lavishly decorated of Ireland's illuminated manuscripts, containing the four Gospels in Latin, the *Book of Kells* was written by monks from Kells in AD 806. The text is in a beautifully rounded Celtic script, with brightly ornamented initial letters and embellishments of intricate spirals and animal and human forms.

left to **Christ Church Cathedral** ⑰, founded here in 1030. Cross over into Nicholas Street, which becomes Patrick Street, for **Saint Patrick's Cathedral** ⑱, adjacent to the well where St Patrick baptized converts. First built in 1191, the present building dates from 1220. Just behind it on St Patrick's Close is **Marsh's Library** ⑲ *(closed Tue and Sun)*, Ireland's first public library, founded in 1707. At the end of the Close is Kevin Street: walk along it and cross at the curve into Bishop Street; at the far end is Aungier Street. Turn left to visit **Whitefriars Street Church** ⑳, housing the relics of Saint Valentine, patron of romantic love. Carry on down Aungier Street into South Great Georges Street and cross into the cobbled streets of

A Georgian doorway

Temple Bar ㉑ to explore its arts centres and cafés. From here walk up Dame Street towards Trinity College; turn right at College Green to return to the start.

To extend the walk, head down Westmoreland Street to cross the O'Connell Bridge over the Liffey into O'Connell Street. Pass the General Post Office (GPO), the postal headquarters and a significant building during the 1916 Rising. Opposite it is the 120-m (400-ft) monument, The Spire. At the end of the street is Parnell Square, home to Dublin Writers Museum *(open daily)*, with memorabilia from Irish writers such as Swift, Shaw, Wilde, Yeats, Joyce and Beckett. Further along Parnell Square north is Dublin City Gallery, **The Hugh Lane** *(closed Mon)*, with Impressionist masterpieces and contemporary art.

🚗 *From O'Connell Bridge follow the river east. At the Customs House turn left onto R105, signposted Malahide. Turn left onto the R807 and pass through Clontarf, with Dublin port on the right. At Sutton Cross (12 km/8 miles out of the city), turn right up Carrickbrack Road (R105). Turn right at Summit Inn, then left up Baily Green Road, past the Summit. Park at the end of the road.*

EAT AND DRINK IN DUBLIN

McDaid's Pub
The old-style character and ambience make this one of Dublin's best-loved pubs. Beloved of some of Dublin's greatest writers, it hosts regular jazz and blues sessions.
3 Harry Street, Dublin 2; 01 679 4395

The Brazen Head *inexpensive*
Ireland's oldest pub, which dates back to 1198. Traditional Irish music live in the bar every night, and classic dishes such as Irish stew washed down with Guinness in its restaurant.
20 Bridge Street Lower, Dublin 8; 01 679 5186; www.brazenhead.com

L'Gueuleton *moderate*
A French-style bistro whose dishes, such as roast duck breast with *pomme boulangere* (baked potatoes) and cherry juice, and foie gras parfait with grape chutney, are sure-fire winners.
1 Fade Street, Dublin 2; 087 939 3608; www.lgueuleton.com

Chapter One Restaurant *expensive*
With a Michelin star, this is one of Dublin's smartest restaurants, with a popular pre-theatre menu (*moderate*). Be sure to book well in advance.
Basement of Writers' Museum, 18–19 Parnell Square, Dublin 1; 01 873 2266; www.chapteronerestaurant.com; open lunch: Tue–Fri; dinner: Tue–Sat

Above Martello tower near Howth Head

WHERE TO STAY

HOWTH

King Sitric *moderate*
A distinctive red-painted building with
eight nautically styled rooms with sea
views, and a well-known fish restaurant.
East Pier; 01 832 5235; www.kingsitric.ie

AROUND HOWTH

Clontarf Castle *moderate–expensive*
This urban castle dates back to 1172.
Its historic exterior conceals a stylish
fusion of ancient and modern.
*Castle Avenue, Clontarf, Dublin 3
(follow R105 Howth Road to Clontarf);
01 833 2321; www.clontarfcastle.ie*

MALAHIDE

The Grand *moderate–expensive*
The Grand Hotel, set amid its own
grounds in the pretty seaside village of
Malahide, was built in 1835 but today
offers every modern luxury. With easy
access to the sea and amenities, it's a
good base for exploring the area.
01 845 0000; www.thegrand.ie

② Howth
Co Dublin

The views from **Howth Summit**
across Dublin Bay to the city and the
Wicklow Mountains are unrivalled in
the whole county. From the car park
a cliff walk to the right leads to the
Baily lighthouse. Return to the main
road and turn right down Carrickbrack road to the village. Park in the
car park at the pier or on the seafront.

Dominated by a harbour with a large
marina and yacht club, **Howth** is a
pretty village with a thriving fishing
industry. Climb its hilly streets to the
abbey ruins for views over the harbour
and nearby islands, or take a boat trip
out to Ireland's Eye, a bird sanctuary
where a colony of puffins nests.

🚗 *Leave Howth and follow the
coast road (R105). Turn right at
Sutton Cross. Follow the R106 through
Baldoyle, then the coast road through
one roundabout, turning right at the
second. After Portmarnock Hotel,
turn right for Portmarnock Beach.*

③ Portmarnock Beach
Portmarnock, Co Dublin

Portmarnock Beach, also known as
The Velvet Strand, is 5 km (3 miles)
long, backed by sand dunes, with
sweeping views of Ireland's Eye,
Lambay Island and Howth Head.
To the north, a striking limestone
sculpture of a globe marks Australian
aviator Charles Kingsford Smith's
departure from the beach to fly the
Atlantic in 1930.

🚗 *Continue along the coast road
(R106) to reach Malahide.*

④ Malahide
Co Dublin

Malahide is a pretty heritage town
with interesting shops and cafés.
Both this and its large, ultra-modern
marina village are perfect for a stroll.

One of the main attractions of
the area lies just outside the village.
Malahide Castle and Demesne *(open
daily; www.malahidecastleandgardens.ie)*
was home to the Talbot family from
1185 until 1973. The Talbots were
staunch supporters of James II. On
the day of the Battle of the Boyne
in 1690, 14 members of the family
breakfasted here. However, none of
them returned for supper. A tour
of the castle's interiors, reveals highlights such as the oak-beamed Great
Hall, and a collection of 18th-century
Irish furniture and an impressive
Portrait Collection . The interpretive
centre and exhibition of local and
Irish history give further information.
The visitor centre has an exhibition
on the history of the Talbot family.

Within the 100-ha (250-acre)
landscaped grounds of the Demesne
are walks and picnic areas as well as
the **Talbot Botanic Gardens**, which
feature a collection of southern
hemisphere plants. There is also a
secret garden, a café and craft and
souvenir shops.

🚗 *From Malahide Demesne, turn right
onto Back Road and then right onto the
R107. At the next junction, turn left onto
the R106, signed for Swords. Turn right
onto the R132, then right again onto
the R126 signed for Donabate. Turn left
at the sign for Newbridge Demesne.*

Above Huge kitchen of Newbridge House, with its magnificent display of historic cooking equipment
and crockery set out on original antique furnishings

Above Thatched and whitewashed cottage in the fishing town of Skerries

⑤ Newbridge Demesne
Donabate, Co Dublin
The elegant Georgian **Newbridge House** *(open Apr–Sep: daily; Oct–Mar: Tue–Sun)* is set within the 145 ha (360 acres) of Newbridge Demesne. The tour includes the striking Red Drawing Room, one of the best-preserved Georgian rooms in the country; the huge kitchen, full of antique utensils; and a quaint Cabinet of Curiosities.

Outside the house, the cobbled courtyard features a museum of country life including an 18th-century blacksmith's forge and carpenter's workshop. Within the Demesne is a traditional farm with vintage machinery and rare-breed animals, as well as a walled garden sheltering traditional Irish apple varieties and two 19th-century glasshouses.

🚗 *Turn right onto Hearse Road (R126), at the roundabout take the third exit onto R132. Cross the next roundabout. Turn right onto R127. At the next roundabout take the first exit, drive through Lusk village. At the Skerries Road roundabout take the first exit onto R127. At the next roundabout take the first exit to Skerries.*

⑥ Skerries
Co Dublin
The fishing town of Skerries, with its long golden beach on one side and harbour dotted with yachts on the other, culminates in the peninsula of Red Island. Walk up past the Martello Tower for panoramic views as far as Northern Ireland's Mountains of Mourne. A colony of seals resides nearby, and they can often be seen accompanying fishing boats back to the harbour.

Skerries Mills *(open daily)* comprises a watermill, a five-sail Great Windmill and a thatched four-sail windmill. All date from the 16th century and have been restored to working order. There is also a millpond, cornfield and a museum of industrial heritage. As part of the tour, visitors can try their hands at milling and climb to the top of a mill for spectacular views.

🚗 *From Skerries Mills, turn right out of the car park and take second right onto Sherlock Terrace. Take the first right and right again, signed for Ardgillan Castle Demesne.*

⑦ Ardgillan Demesne
Balbriggan, Co Dublin
The name Ardgillan means "high wooded area", and the Demesne *(open daily)* enjoys magnificent views of Drogheda Bay and the north Dublin coastline. Its 78 ha (195 acres) of parklands, woods and formal gardens include a rose garden, walled kitchen garden, haunted yew walk and Ice House. In the grounds stands **Ardgillan Castle** *(open daily)*, a large, castellated house built in 1738 and lovingly restored. The guided tour takes visitors through Georgian and Victorian styled rooms. Upstairs is a collection of maps from the 17th-century Down Survey of Ireland.

EAT AND DRINK

HOWTH

Aqua *moderate– expensive*
A magnificent waterside location on Howth's Old Pier for fresh seafood. Try the hot shellfish, prepared in black bean sauce.
1 West Pier; 01 832 0690; www.aqua.ie; closed Mon

Beshoff's *moderate–expensive*
Oyster bar, café and market from the traditional fishmonger family, the Beshoffs. Great atmosphere.
West Pier; 01 839 7555; www.beshoffs.ie

King Sitric *expensive*
The best Howth Harbour's catch, and game dishes with a creative twist such as seared scallops with sweet corn purée.
East Pier; 01 832 5235; www.kingsitric.ie; closed Mon & Tue

MALAHIDE

Fowler's *inexpensive*
A traditional Irish pub with regular music sessions and pub grub.
New Street; 01 845 0960; www.fowlers.ie

Above Crenellated Ardgillan Castle, set in the lovely grounds of its Demesne

---

DAY TRIP OPTIONS
Dublin is the perfect base to visit the magnificent Demesnes or spend the day exploring the coast, perhaps ending with a boat trip.

Historic houses
Start with a walk around Georgian Dublin ① before heading out to Newbridge Demesne ⑤ with its elegant Georgian house. Continue to Ardgillan Demesne ⑦ for more Georgian-styled rooms in the castle.

From Dublin take the M1 (toll road). Take Donabate exit for Newbridge Demesne. Follow R126 back towards motorway and turn right on R127 to Balbriggan for Ardgillan Demesne.

Beside the sea
Start at Howth ② and walk around Howth Head to the Baily Lighthouse or pretty Howth village. Follow the coast to the beach at Portmarnock ③ and pretty Malahide ④ for its fascinating castle.

Follow driving tour instructions from the car park at Howth Head.

TRIP 15

VALLEY OF THE KINGS

Drogheda to the Hill of Tara

HIGHLIGHTS

Cistercian abbey
Trace the ruins of tranquil Mellifont Abbey, the first
Cistercian monastery to be built in Ireland

Ancient tombs
Explore Brú na Bóinne, home to the extraordinary
5,000-year-old passage tomb at Newgrange

Norman castle
Visit Trim to see one of Ireland's most spectacular
medieval castles, featured in the film *Braveheart*

Seat of the High Kings
Climb the Hill of Tara, a site of mythical importance as
the political and spiritual centre of Ireland

The grand tower of Jerpoint Abbey near Thomastown

VALLEY OF THE KINGS

The Boyne Valley is considered to be the cradle of Irish history and civilization. Among the remarkable heritage sites located in this rolling river valley are the medieval monastery of Monasterboice; the Boyne battlefield – setting for the most significant battle in Irish history; the world-famous Stone Age passage tombs of Newgrange; the Hill of Slane where St Patrick proclaimed the arrival of Christianity, and the Hill of Tara where Ireland's ancient High Kings were crowned. Important in shaping the country's destiny, these ancient sites have become tranquil beauty spots, where history and legend meet.

Above Oldbridge House tells the dramatic story of the Battle of the Boyne, *see p159*

ACTIVITIES

Shop for crafts in the attractive town of Drogheda, gateway to the Boyne

Explore the mysterious passage tombs at Loughcrew

Visit the battle site of the pivotal Battle of the Boyne

Follow St Patrick's footsteps on the Hill of Slane

Stroll beside the River Boyne at Trim, taking in the majestic castle and ruined abbeys on its banks

Above Trim on the banks of the Boyne. The ruined Belfry Tower on the left-hand side is one of several medieval monuments in the town, *see p161*

PLAN YOUR DRIVE

Start/finish: Drogheda to the Hill of Tara.

Number of days: 3.

Distance: 137 km (85 miles).

Road conditions: Some surfaces of minor roads are poor and uneven (for example, the road to Mellifont Abbey).

When to go: Most of the main sights on this drive are outdoors, so spring, summer or autumn are preferable. Whatever the season, rain gear and comfortable walking shoes are a must.

Opening times: Most shops and attractions open 9 or 10am–5 or 6pm. Shops open Mon–Sat; in large towns also 12–6pm on Sun. Convenience stores in villages open 8am until late.

Main market days: Drogheda: Sat; Kells: Farmers' Market Sat am.

Major festivals: Drogheda: Arts Festival, Apr/May; Irish Maritime Festival, Jun; **Loughcrew**: Opera Festival, May/Jun; **Trim**: Swift Festival, Jul.

DAY TRIP OPTIONS

Visit three of Ireland's **best historical sights,** all within a short distance of each other. Those fascinated by Ireland's Celtic **High Crosses** and **round towers** should head for Monasterboice for impressive examples of both. Romantics can spend a day exploring the **medieval town** of Trim. For full details, *see p161*.

Below The area around Newgrange is dotted with underground passage tombs, *see p160*

KEY

— Drive route

0 kilometres   5

0 miles   5

VISITING DROGHEDA

Parking
There is on-street pay-and-display parking throughout town but especially near the river, on The Mall. Central car parks include Bolton Square; O'Reilly's, off Fair Street; King Street; and Abbey and Murdoch's, both behind the Abbey Shopping Centre.

Tourist Information
The Thosel, West Street; 041 987 2843; www.drogheda.ie; open Mon–Sat

WHERE TO STAY IN DROGHEDA

The D Hotel *inexpensive–moderate*
Stylish modern hotel right in the centre of Drogheda, on the banks of the Boyne and next to the Scotch Hall shopping complex. The riverside restaurant and bar are popular local meeting places.
Scotch Hall; 041 987 7700; www.thedhotel.com

Scholars Townhouse Hotel *moderate*
This splendid townhouse, built in 1867, has some fine original features as well as a superb restaurant. There are 16 modestly sized but comfortable rooms, most of which have retained the original furnishings.
King Street; 041 983 5410; www.scholarshotel.com

Below The historic town of Drogheda viewed from Millmount

❶ DROGHEDA

Co Louth

Near the mouth of the River Boyne, Drogheda is one of Ireland's finest medieval towns and the gateway to the Boyne Valley. A mix of old and new, it has abundant history and colour, with quiet lanes and busy shopping streets. High on a hill overlooking the town is Millmount, a former military complex that is now a museum – there are splendid panoramic views from its Martello tower.

A one-hour walking tour
Start at the corner of Mayoralty Street and Bachelor's Lane ①; turn right into Bachelor's Lane, then left onto Constitution Hill. At the top is **St Laurence's Gate** ②, dating from 1234, the only surviving gate of an original 10. Walk left along Laurence Street to **Highlanes Gallery** ③ *(open Mon–Sat)*, once a Franciscan church and now an art gallery with works by eminent 20th-century Irish artists. Note the site of old **Drogheda Grammar School** ④, attended by the first Duke of Wellington.

At the intersection with Shop Street, **The Thosel** ⑤ is a pretty tower (1770) with a large four-sided clock. Cross over and walk ahead along West Street to Gothic **St Peter's Church** ⑥, containing the preserved head of the Irish martyr St Oliver Plunkett, Archbishop of Armagh. Turn right up Duke Street and left onto Fair Street, site of the old **Corn Exchange** ⑦. Return along Fair Street and cross over Peter Street into William Street. **St Peter's Church of Ireland** ⑧ has a medieval font and ancient grave stones. From the church, turn left down Peter Street, becoming Shop Street, and cross the river at **St Mary's Bridge** ⑨ for a view of the impressive Boyne Viaduct (1855), with its 18 arches. Across the road an alley leads up to **Millmount** ⑩, the 18th-century military barracks, now a museum *(open daily, Sun pm only)*. The Martello Tower (1808) is built over a Norman motte.

To return to the start, cross the bridge, turn right for North Quay and The Mall, and left to Mayoralty Street.
🚗 *Leave Drogheda from South Quay, turn right for M1/Belfast. Cross the river, follow signs for R132. At the roundabout take R132 for Dunleer, follow for 5 km (3 miles). At the roundabout turn left, then after 1 km (half a mile) turn left again to Monasterboice. Park by the round tower.*

② Monasterboice
Drogheda, Co Louth

Founded by St Buite in the 6th century, this monastic settlement is one of Ireland's most famous religious sites. It includes two churches and one of Ireland's tallest round towers at 33 m (110 ft) high, but its greatest treasure is the three 10th-century Celtic High Crosses. **Muiredach's Cross**, carved with biblical scenes, is the finest of its kind in Ireland.

Turn left from the car park and at the T-junction turn right. At the R168 turn left and then take the second right for Mellifont Abbey. Go over the small crossroads and into the car park.

③ Mellifont Abbey
Tullyallen, Drogheda, Co Louth

The first Cistercian abbey in Ireland, Mellifont *(open site)* was founded by St Malachy, Archbishop of Armagh, in 1142. He introduced the formal style of architecture used in Europe, and Mellifont became a model for other Cistercian centres in Ireland. It is now a ruin, but it is possible to trace the original ground plan, including the octagonal lavabo (washing house) with four of its Romanesque arches intact. The visitor centre *(open Jun–Aug: daily)* has a display on medieval masonry.

Return to the crossroad, turn right, then turn right at the end of the road. At the crossroads, go straight over the L2321, down the hill and over the main road. Cross the river, drive alongside the canal and after a small bridge turn right for the Battle of the Boyne site at Oldbridge.

④ Battle of the Boyne site
Oldbridge Estate, Drogheda, Co Meath

Oldbridge, on the banks of the River Boyne, is the site of the most iconic battle in Irish history– the Battle of the Boyne in1690 – between the Protestant King William of Orange and the deposed Catholic King James II of England, who sought to regain his Crown by enlisting Catholic support in Ireland. Over 61,000 troops took part. William's victory led to Protestant ascendancy in Ireland and became the source of bitter religious divisions for more than 300 years. The visitor centre *(open daily)* in **Oldbridge House** has multimedia presentations, and living history displays take place at the weekends in summer.

Turn right on leaving Oldbridge and then right again for Donore village. In Donore, turn right for Newgrange. After 2 km (1 mile), turn right for Brú na Bóinne Visitor Centre.

Above left A 12th-century Romanesque arch, Mellifont Abbey **Above** The entrance to the main burial chamber at Newgrange

SHOPPING IN DROGHEDA

As well as being a light and contemporary space for Drogheda's municipal art collection and temporary exhibitions, **Highlanes Gallery** also houses the **Louth Craftmark**, selling ceramics, jewellery, leatherware, candles and textiles by over 50 craftworkers. **Millmount** incorporates a Craft Quarter which, among others, sells the work of a silversmith, knitwear designer, quilter and ceramicist who have studios in Millmount.

EAT AND DRINK IN DROGHEDA

Brú Bar Bistro *moderate*
This contemporary building beside the River Boyne has a good bistro on the ground floor and a stylish cocktail bar on the first floor. Its floor-to-ceiling windows offer great riverside views.
8 Dyer Street, Lagavooren; 041 987 2784; www.bru.ie

Goodwins *moderate*
The D Hotel's upscale steakhouse serves beautifully prepared Irish meats, grilled seafood and more. The early bird menu is of great value at €25.
Scotch Hall; 041 987 7700; www.thedhotel.com

Eastern Seaboard *moderate*
This restaurant serves up wonderful dishes such as smoked haddock tempura with pickled fennel.
Bryanstown Cross Route; 041 980 2570; www.glasgow-diaz.com

Above The River Boyne, near the site of the Battle of the Boyne of 1690

Above Slane Castle, where Irish rock band U2 recorded the *Unforgettable Fire* album

VISITING BRÚ NA BÓINNE

Access to Newgrange and Knowth is by guided tour only (2 hours 45 mins), from the **Brú na Bóinne Visitor Centre** *(open daily; 041 988 0300; www.heritageireland.ie)*. Advance booking is highly recommended. There is no access to Dowth.

WHERE TO STAY

SLANE

Conyngham Arms Hotel *moderate*
Attractive 18th-century coaching inn offering classically styled rooms, and also a stylish restaurant.
Main Street, Slane; 041 988 4444; www.conynghamarms.ie

TRIM

Trim Castle Hotel *moderate*
A great hotel directly opposite the castle offering contemporary rooms, as well as excellent eating and drinking options in the restaurant, café or bar.
Castle Street, Trim; 046 948 3000; www.trimcastlehotel.com

AROUND HILL OF TARA

Bellinter House *moderate*
An elegant and comfortable Georgian country house in extensive grounds a couple of kilometres (a mile) from the Hill of Tara. Restaurant, pool and spa.
Bellinter, Navan; 046 903 0900; www.bellinterhouse.com

⑤ Brú na Bóinne
Donore, Co Meath
This incredible archaeological landscape, comprising Newgrange, Dowth and Knowth, is a UNESCO World Heritage Site. As well as its famous prehistoric passage tombs, it has 49 burial mounds and many other examples of megalithic art. The focal point is **Newgrange**, a passage tomb and temple dating back to 5000 BC. It is supported by 97 large kerbstones, including an elaborately carved stone in front of the entrance. Inside the mound, a 19-m (60-ft) long passage leads to a cross-shaped chamber that is penetrated by sunlight during the winter solstice.
🚗 *Leaving Brú na Bóinne, turn right. After 2 km (1 mile), look to the right for a view of the outside of the Newgrange mound. At the next Y-junction, turn right for Slane/N2, then right again for Slane.*

⑥ Slane
Co Meath
The village of Slane has many attractive features including a bridge over the River Boyne and fine 18th-century buildings. **Slane Castle** *(open May–Aug Sun–Thu pm)* can be viewed along with the new Slane Distillery on a guided tour. Rock concerts are often staged in the Capability Brown grounds, which have hosted the likes of U2 and David Bowie.

Head up to the **Hill of Slane**, just north of the village. It was here that St Patrick, Ireland's patron saint, is reputed to have lit a Paschal (Easter) fire as a challenge to the pagan High King, symbolizing Christianity's triumph over paganism.
🚗 *From Slane, drive down the hill and turn right onto the N51. After a few kilometres turn right onto the R163 for Kells and take the next left. At the junction in Kilberry turn right, then left to stay on the R163.*

⑦ Kells
Co Meath
A centre of Christian settlement since the earliest years of Christianity in Ireland, Kells is famous for the *Book of Kells*, an illuminated manuscript produced by the monks of **Kells Monastery** in around 800. The original is in Trinity College, Dublin

(see pp150–51), but there is a copy in **Kells' Heritage Centre** *(open daily, Sun pm only)*. The monastery also has a 25-m (82-ft) high round tower surrounded by carved High Crosses. Just outside the Heritage Centre is the **Market Cross**, dating from the 9th century and used as a gallows during the 1798 uprising.
🚗 *Drive up through the town and turn left and then right into Cannon Street for the round tower. Take the R163 for Loughcrew (signposted Oldcastle). After 15 km (9 miles) turn right for Loughcrew Passage Tombs.*

⑧ Loughcrew Cairns
Loughcrew, Oldcastle, Co Meath
This group of 25 passage tombs, spread over three hills, dates from around 3000 BC. According to one legend, they were created by a witch, hence the Irish name *Slieve na Calliagh* (Mountain of the Witch) for the highest hill. To enter Cairn T, Loughcrew's largest passage tomb, pick up the key from the coffee shop at **Loughcrew Gardens** *(open mid-Mar–Oct: daily; Nov–mid-Mar Sat & Sun; ring in advance; 049 854 1356; www.loughcrew.com)*, 1 km (half a mile) further along the Oldcastle road. Take a torch and prepare for a steep walk up to the cairns from the car park. The gardens are known for their yew walk.
🚗 *From Loughcrew, drive back along R163 and turn right onto R154, following signs for Trim through Athboy. In Trim, park at the visitor centre near the castle.*

Above The round tower and one of several High Crosses in the grounds of Kells Monastery

9 Trim
Co Meath

This pretty, historical town hugs the River Boyne and is dominated by **Trim Castle** (open Feb–Oct daily; Nov–Jan weekends only), Ireland's largest Anglo-Norman castle, founded by Hugh de Lacy in 1173. Extensively restored, the castle is a breathtaking sight and was used as the set for the 1995 film *Braveheart*.

Across the Millennium footbridge over the Boyne stands the **Belfry Tower** (38 m/125 ft high), which is also known as the Yellow Steeple. Built in 1368 for the original Augustinian Abbey, it later served as a watchtower. Beside the steeple is **Talbot Castle** or St Mary's Abbey, built in 1415 over the original abbey. In the 18th century, it became an exclusive Protestant school. **Sheep Gate** is the last surviving gateway of the medieval town and further east along the river are the remains of the 13th-century Gothic cathedral, **Newtown Abbey**.

St Peter's Bridge, thought to be the second oldest bridge in Ireland, leads to the ruins of the **Hospital of St John the Baptist**, founded by monks in the 13th century. **Trim Visitor Centre** (open Mon–Sat; Sun pm only) is on Castle Street. Nearby **St Patrick's Cathedral** on Loman Street is built on the site of a medieval church reputedly founded by St Patrick. The stained glass in the west window is the first ever designed by Pre-Raphaelite artist Edward Burne-Jones.

🚗 *Take R154 (for Athboy), then turn right onto R161. After 5 km (3 miles), follow signs for Bellinter House, turning right onto the L4010. About 1 km (half a mile) past the abbey turn left, then right after another 5 km (3 miles), and left after a further 1 km (half a mile). Turn right for the Hill of Tara after 700 m (750 yards).*

10 Hill of Tara
Co Meath

The **Hill of Tara** (guided tours May–mid-Sep daily) was, according to tradition, the seat of Ireland's High Kings, who ruled until the Norman takeover in the 12th century. Some 142 kings were supposedly crowned here. The tour explains the myths and legends around the hilltop enclosure and its Stone of Destiny, said to cry out when touched by the new king. The hill offers outstanding views and it is said that on a clear day 23 of Ireland's 32 counties can be seen.

Above left Cairn T, Loughcrew's largest cairn
Above centre View of Trim across the Boyne
Above Ruins of 12th-century Bective Abbey, visible on the way to the Hill of Tara

EAT AND DRINK

SLANE
George's Patisserie *inexpensive*
A terrific spot to rest up with a cup of coffee and slice of sachertorte, or light meals of soups and sandwiches.
Chapel Street; 041 982 4493; www. georgespatisserie.com; closed Tue

TRIM
Marcie Regan's
Well-known pub beside one of the oldest bridges in the country. Traditional music on Friday evenings.
Lackanash Road, Newtown; 087 310 4304

HILL OF TARA
O'Connells Pub
Characterful village pub that once featured in a Guinness Christmas advert.
Skryne Hill, near Tara; 046 902 5122; open from 4pm, Sun also lunch

---

DAY TRIP OPTIONS
Drogheda is a good base for these excursions into the Boyne Valley.

Historical trio
Combine three sites charting key periods in Ireland's history – the Battle of the Boyne site 4, the passage tombs at Brú na Bóinne 5 and the Hill of Slane 6, where St Patrick challenged the High Kings.

Take R132, then N51 to the Boyne battle site. Next follow the drive instructions to Brú na Bóinne, then on to Slane, and return to Drogheda on the N51.

High Crosses and round towers
Monasterboice 2 has one of Ireland's tallest round towers and its finest High Cross: 5.5 m (18 ft) high and richly carved with biblical scenes.

Follow drive instructions there and back.

Medieval Trim
Explore Trim's 9 medieval churches, castle and monastic hospital.

Take R132 and N51 to Navan, then R161 to Trim. Retrace route to Drogheda.

TRIP 16

HEART OF THE LAKELANDS
Athlone to Strokestown Park House

HIGHLIGHTS

Spiritual Clonmacnoise
Experience the ethereal beauty of this great 6th-century religious site

Scenic walks
Hike into the foothills and forests of the Slieve Bloom Mountains in the south of the region

Ancient peat bogs
Discover the magic of the bogs, their flora and fauna and the archaeological remains preserved within them

Stately homes and gardens
Explore the grounds of Birr Castle, Belvedere House and Strokestown Park House

HEART OF THE LAKELANDS

Though often overlooked by visitors to Ireland, the Lakelands has plenty of history, scenery and character, its special highlight being the medieval monastic settlement of Clonmacnoise, a European centre of trade and learning founded in 545. It also has heritage towns containing age-old whiskey distilleries, Norman castles and grand Georgian estates. Its landscapes include ancient boglands, rich in wildlife and archaeolgical finds, and the Slieve Bloom Mountains, undulating wooded hills crisscrossed with hiking trails.

Above The Jealous Wall, a folly with an intriguing history, in the grounds of Belvedere House, *see pp168–9*

ACTIVITIES

Take a boat trip from Athlone and listen to tales of Nordic valour

Explore seven ruined temples at the ancient monastic complex of Clonmacnoise

See the Great Telescope in the grounds of Birr Castle

Tour haunted corridors at Charleville Forest Castle, near Tullamore

Taste fine Irish whiskey at Tullamore Dew Visitor Centre

Stroll down the longest herbaceous border in all of Britain and Ireland in the grounds of Strokestown Park House

0 kilometres   10

0 miles   10

KEY

Drive route

PLAN YOUR DRIVE

Start/finish: Athlone to Strokestown Park House.

Number of days: 2 days.

Distance: 210 km (130 miles).

Road conditions: Some minor roads, particularly on the way to Clonmacnoise and Keenagh, are narrow with no road markings.

Opening times: Most shops and attractions open 9am–6pm. Shops open Mon–Sat, also 12–6pm on Sun. Convenience stores open 8am–late.

When to go: Spring through autumn is best. Roads may be icy in winter.

Main market days: Athlone: Farmers' Market, Sat; **Tullamore:** County Fair (food and drink), Sat.

Shopping: Buy Tullamore Dew whiskey in the distillery where it was first made.

Main festivals: Athlone: All Ireland Drama Festival, Apr/May; Trifest (music, sport), Jul; **Slieve Bloom Mountains:** Slieve Bloom Walking Festival, Apr/May.

DAY TRIP OPTIONS

Combine **scenery**, **culture** and **family fun** by travelling to Clonmacnoise on a **Viking boat**. Or learn about Ireland's **industrial heritage** at Tullamore, then explore the **wooded slopes** of the Slieve Bloom Mountains and admire **Georgian** Birr. For full details, see p169.

Above Birr Castle Gardens, one of Ireland's grandest 18th-century estates, see p166

Right The Grand Canal, a tranquil waterway that crosses County Offaly

WHERE TO STAY

ATHLONE

Bastion B&B *inexpensive*
A former draper's shop, this charming townhouse offers simple rooms and excellent breakfast in the neighbouring Bastion Kitchen.
2 Bastion Street; 090 649 4954; www.thebastion.net

AROUND ATHLONE

Wineport Lodge *moderate–expensive*
Lodge on Lough Ree with good food, lake views and outdoor hot tubs. From Athlone, take the N55 to Ballykeeran and fork left at the Dog & Duck pub.
Glasson, Athlone; 090 643 9010; www.wineport.ie

BIRR

Townsend House *inexpensive*
Guesthouse in a 19th-century townhouse in the centre of Birr. There is also a weekend-only tapas and wine bar.
Townsend Street; 057 912 1276; www.townsendhouse-guesthouse.com

AROUND BIRR

Charlotte's Way *inexpensive*
This restored 17th-century townhouse on Banagher Hill in the Midlands, has associations with 19th-century writer Charlotte Brontë, who stayed here and whose husband lived here after her death. There are great views of the surrounding countryside.
The Hill, Banagher (take R439 from Birr), Co Offaly; 057 915 3864

Below The terraced gardens at Birr Castle
Below right Clonmacnoise's 9th-century round tower on the banks of the Shannon

① Athlone

Co Westmeath
Set on a ford on the River Shannon, **Athlone Castle** *(open Mar–Oct: daily; Nov–Feb: Wed-Sun)* was built in 1210 for King John of England. An important military barracks, it twice came under siege from Williamite troops after the Battle of the Boyne *(see p159)*, falling in the second siege of 1691.

Athlone is a departure point for boat trips on the Shannon and Lough Ree. Viking Tours Ireland offers boat trips from Easter to October to Clonmacnoise aboard a Viking-style boat, accompanied by tales of Viking battles and treasure.

🚗 *From Athlone, take the N6 (Dublin) road and then the N62 towards Birr. At Ballynahown, turn right onto the R444 to Clonmacnoise.*

② Clonmacnoise

Shannonbridge, Co Offaly
Founded by St Ciarán in around AD 549, this monastic complex *(open daily)* lies on an important medieval crossroads. With the Shannon flowing north–south and a glacial ridge forming the main road east–west, it became a hub of scholarship and trade, and many kings of Tara and of Connaught were buried here. Plundered by Vikings and Anglo-Normans, it was finally devastated by the English in 1552.

The ruins comprise two **round towers**, a **cathedral** and seven **churches** (temples). Look for the carvings of saints Francis, Patrick and Dominic above the cathedral's north doorway, known as the **Whispering Door** on account of its acoustics. The **Visitor Centre** contains early grave slabs and crosses, including the **Cross of the Scriptures**, a 9th-century high cross carved with biblical scenes.

🚗 *Take the R444 to Shannonbridge and then turn left onto the R357 to Cloghan. Here, turn right onto the N62 for Birr. The entrance to Birr Castle Gardens is in the centre of Birr.*

③ Birr

Co Offaly
This handsome estate town retains its original Georgian layout and architectural details. **Birr Castle** *(tours May-Aug: Mon–Sat)*, seat of the Earls of Rosse, is famous for its landscaped **grounds** *(open daily)*, containing 8 km (5 miles) of footpaths and thousands of rare trees and plants. Also in the grounds are the **Great Telescope**, the largest in the world when it was built in the 1840s, and the **Science Centre** *(open daily)*, devoted to engineering, astronomy, botany and photography, passions of the 19th-century earls.

🚗 *From Birr, take the R440 to Kinnitty. Drive 3 km (2 miles) beyond Kinnitty and follow signs for the entrance to Kinnitty Forest in the Slieve Bloom Mountains.*

❹ Slieve Bloom Mountains
Co Offaly

The Slieve Bloom Mountains rise unexpectedly from the flat landscape of Offaly. Crisscrossed with walking trails and dotted with picnic areas and viewpoints, they include blanket boglands, forests and farmland, and are rich in wildlife. Kinnitty Forest offers a variety of signposted walks from the entrance in the northern foothills.

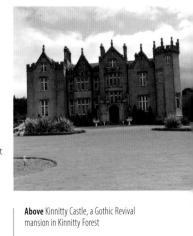

A three-hour walking tour in Kinnitty Forest

From the **car park** ① at the entrance to Kinnitty Forest, follow the path into the forest. At the Y-junction keep left, following the Glinsk Castle Loop Walk, the trail marked with the blue arrow (the green arrow is for the shorter Kinnitty Castle Loop and the yellow arrow marks the Slieve Bloom Way, an 84-km/52-mile loop). After about 1 km (half a mile), the trail reaches a three-way junction with a wooden gate to the left. Pass through the gate and into the grounds of **Kinnitty Castle** ②, a Gothic Revival castle in extensive parkland, for a long time run as a luxury hotel.

Returning to the gate, follow the trail right, walking uphill along a forest track for 1 km (half a mile) to a right bend and then to a Y-junction. Keep right, following the green and blue arrows.

Turn left after a short distance heading uphill through mature woodland, following the blue arrow and the Slieve Bloom Way.

On reaching a forestry road, turn right and after 200 m (656 ft) turn left at a three-way junction, veering left almost immediately afterwards, still following the Slieve Bloom Way.

Climb the hill and turn right at the track junction. After another 600 m (1,968 ft) leave the Slieve Bloom Way and turn right onto a woodland trail leading to **Glinsk Castle** ③, now little more than stone pillars and walls.

Follow the trail through the pillars and over the hill, and keep on downhill through the trees, rejoining the Slieve Bloom Way at a forest track. Turn right here and, after a short distance, turn left onto a forestry trail. Follow the track downhill, through mature trees, and cross two forestry tracks back to the starting point.

🚗 *Return to Kinnitty and turn right onto the R421 for Tullamore, passing through Cadamstown.*

The stables at Kinnitty Castle

Above Kinnitty Castle, a Gothic Revival mansion in Kinnitty Forest

VISITING ATHLONE

Parking
Plentiful pay-and-display on-street parking is available.

Tourist Information
Athlone Castle; 090 644 2130; open Easter–Oct

River Cruises
Viking Tours Ireland, The Quay; 086 262 1136; www.vikingtoursireland.ie

EAT AND DRINK IN ATHLONE

Sean's Bar *inexpensive*
Dating back to 900 AD, this is the oldest pub in Ireland. It has a cosy atmosphere and lots of interesting features, including a sloping floor in case of flooding from the river. *13 Main Street; 090 649 2358; www.seansbar.ie*

Left Bank Bistro *moderate*
Sophisticated restaurant on the banks of the Shannon near the Athlone lock. Loads of great seafood alongside some Asian-influenced dishes. *Fry Place; 090 649 4446; www. leftbankbistro.com; closed Sun & Mon*

Above Iron-studded portal, Charleville Forest Castle **Above right** Gothic-style crenellations, Charleville Forest Castle

WHERE TO STAY AROUND STROKESTOWN PARK HOUSE

Gleesons Townhouse *moderate*
Pretty 19th-century townhouse in the centre of Roscommon, with a popular restaurant and café. Situated 20 km (12 miles) south of Strokestown (take the R368 south and turn left at the junction with the N61).
Market Square, Roscommon; 090 662 6954; www.gleesonsroscommon.ie

Castlecoote House
moderate–expensive
Romantic and luxurious Georgian house with four-poster beds, roll-top baths, tennis courts, a croquet lawn and an orchard. Situated 28 km (17 miles) southwest of Strokestown.
Castlecoote, Co Roscommon; 090 666 3794; www.castlecootehouse.com; closed Nov–Apr

⑤ Tullamore
Co Offaly
On the outskirts of Tullamore, a gate lodge on the left marks the entrance to **Charleville Forest Castle**, a Gothic-style mansion that is said to be haunted. Ring the bell for guided tours *(on the hour in summer; pre-book by email the rest of the year: info@ charlevillecastle.com)*.

This Midlands town is also the birthplace of Tullamore Dew Irish whiskey. The **Tullamore Dew Visitor Centre** *(open daily)* on Bury Quay (in the centre of town) offers guided tours and tastings in the old distillery buildings.

🚗 *Follow the R421 north to join the N52. Follow signs to Kilbeggan, turning right at the second roundabout onto the R389. At the roundabout turn right onto the R446 for Kilbeggan Distillery.*

⑥ Kilbeggan
Co Westmeath
Established in 1757, **Kilbeggan Distillery** *(open daily)* is thought to be the oldest pot-still distillery in the world. Harnessing local resources – pure water, grain and turf (used for power), it produced malt whiskey for 200 years until, unable to compete with Scottish whisky manufacturers, it went bankrupt in 1954. The restoration of the watermill was completed in 1983, though it wasn't until 2007 that distilling recommenced. The distillery museum now offers guided tours of the grain grinding and casking equipment and the steam engine and waterwheel that powered the mill.

🚗 *Take the M6 towards Dublin. At Tyrellspass, turn left onto the N52 for Mullingar. Belvedere House is on the left, 5 km (3 miles) after Dalystown.*

⑦ Belvedere House and Gardens
Mullingar, Co Westmeath
The Palladian villa *(open daily)*, built in 1740 by Richard Castle for the Earl of Belvedere, is set in grounds beside Lough Ennell. The interior is known for its Rococo plasterwork, while

Peat Bogs
The Lakelands has an abundance of peat bogs, formed up to 10,000 years ago from compressed vegetation in waterlogged ground. Some have yielded amazing archaeological finds such as the Corlea Trackway. Long harvested for fuel, some are now protected habitats for flora and fauna.

Right Copper pot-still at Kilbeggan Distillery, Kilbeggan, established in 1757

exterior highlights include a Victorian walled garden and the Jealous Wall folly – built to block the view of a mansion belonging to the Earl's brother. The Earl believed his brother was conducting an affair with his wife, whom he punished by imprisoning her in her own home for 31 years.

🚗 *From Belvedere, take the L1136 and at the second exit on the roundabout, take the R400 to Mullingar and then the R392 to Ballymahon. Corlea is 6 km (4 miles) after Ballymahon. The Corlea Trackway Centre is to the right.*

⑧ Corlea Trackway Centre
Keenagh, Co Longford
An Iron Age timber bog road believed to have been constructed in 148 BC, the Corlea Trackway is the largest example of its kind to be uncovered in Europe. Its remarkable state of preservation is due to the anaerobic conditions of the bog in which it eventually sank. The Centre *(open Apr–Oct)* has an 18-m (60-ft) stretch of road on display.

🚗 *From Corlea, turn right onto the R392, taking the R371 for Strokestown after Lanesborough and then turning left at the N5. At the roundabout take the third exit onto Bawn Street and drive into Strokestown Park House.*

⑨ Strokestown Park House
Strokestown, Co Roscommon
The splendid Palladian mansion of **Strokestown Park House** *(open daily)*, the finest in County Roscommon, was built in the 1730s. The original furnishings can be seen on guided tours of the interior, while the stable block houses the **Famine Museum**, telling the story of the 1840s Great Famine through documents of the time. The **Garden** includes the longest herbaceous border in Britain and Ireland and a Georgian fruit and vegetable garden.

Above The gently rolling parkland surrounding Belvedere House

Above left Pergola over the long herbaceous border in Strokestown Park Gardens
Above Strokestown Park House, the finest Palladian mansion in County Roscommon

EAT AND DRINK AROUND STROKESTOWN PARK HOUSE

Keenans *moderate*
Modern restaurant built onto a traditional bar in the tiny village of Termonbarry on the River Shannon, 13 km (8 miles) along the N5 east of Strokestown.
Termonbarry, Co Roscommon; 043 332 6098; www.keenanshotel.ie

The Purple Onion *moderate*
Good food using locally sourced ingredients, and cosy booths for discreet dining. There is also an art gallery above the bar. In Termonbarry, 13 km (8 miles) east of Strokestown.
Termonbarry, Co Roscommon; 043 335 9919; www.purpleonion.ie; closed Mon & Tue

---

DAY TRIP OPTIONS
Athlone is an ideal base from which to visit the religious and historic sites of the Lakelands.

The Shannon river
From Athlone ❶, follow the Shannon to Clonmacnoise ❷, an important monastic site, bristling with crosses, a round tower and churches. One of the nicest ways of getting there is on a Viking-style boat. Trips depart from Athlone.

Take a boat from Athlone or follow the drive instructions.

Look and learn
Find out about the industrial history of the Lakelands in Tullamore ❺,

then drive to Kinnitty for a walk in the Slieve Bloom Mountains ❹. Next, head to Georgian Birr ❸ and Birr Castle Gardens with its Science Centre and Great Telescope.

From Athlone, take the M6/N52 to Tullamore, then the R421 to the Slieve Bloom Mountains. Take the R440 to Birr, returning to Athlone on the N62.

TRIP 17

CONNEMARA AND ITS LOUGHS
Clifden to Cong

HIGHLIGHTS

Bustling Clifden
Stroll around the delightful harbour town and "capital"
of Connemara

Coastal beauty
Explore the glorious coastline and take a boat out to
Inishbofin Island

Mountain valleys
Experience the magical atmosphere and sublime beauty
of empty valleys and mountain passes

Lakeland splendour
Drive round, swim in or picnic on the shores of the some
the largest and most spectacular loughs in Ireland

Sunlit birch trees along the striking Lough Mask

CONNEMARA AND ITS LOUGHS

It is said that "for every star God put in the sky, he laid a million stones on Connemara". An exaggeration, yes, but this rocky, mostly treeless terrain is part of what makes up the enigmatic beauty of the region. This drive takes on several facets of Connemara: the bog-mantled moorland and sea-bitten western coastline around Clifden; the dramatic, mountainous landscapes of the north; and, to the southeast, a place of tranquil, watery vistas – for all this wild and hilly terrain drains into some of the most beautiful and majestic loughs in Ireland.

(map of Connemara region, County Galway, showing locations including Clifden, Sky Road, Omey Island, Inishbofin Island, Connemara National Park, Kylemore Abbey, Killary Harbour & Leenane, Delphi Valley, Doolough, Tawny Pass)

ACTIVITIES

Try some of the finest seafood in the vibrant fishing port of Clifden

Take an exhilarating drive along the Sky Road to the western tip of Connemara

Walk round lovely Diamond Hill in the Connemara National Park

Go on a boat trip out into fjord-like Killary Harbour, or to Inishbofin Island, a centre for traditional Irish music

Picnic, swim, walk or drive along the shores of any of the region's lovely loughs

Above River valley at Delphi, named after Grecian Delphi by the Marquis of Sligo, *see p177*

PLAN YOUR DRIVE

Start/finish: Clifden to Cong.

Number of days: 3–4.

Distance: 220 km (137 miles).

Road conditions: Roads are generally in good condition, well paved and signposted. Mountain passes are steep and winding, so take extra care.

When to go: March to October is the best time for good weather on the coast and lakes, and in the mountains.

Opening times: Most shops and attractions open 9 or 10am–5 or 6pm. Shops open Mon–Sat; in large towns also 12–6pm on Sun. Convenience stores in villages open 8am until late.

Main market days: Inishbofin: Farmers' Market, Mon pm.

Shopping: Connemara is famous for its fine tweed and green marble.

Major festivals: Clifden: Arts Week, Sep; Connemara Pony Show, Aug; **Omey Island:** Omey Races, Aug; **Inishbofin:** Arts Festival, May; **Around Connemara:** Connemara Mountain Walking Festival, May; **Cong:** Food Festival, Sep.

DAY TRIP OPTIONS

For **a taste of traditional Irish life** visit Inishbofin Island, or **to explore Irish history** visit the poignant Doolough and Delphi valleys. To experience the **Connemara lakelands**, spend a day driving along the shores of four loughs. For full details, *see p179*.

Below left Stately Ashford Castle in Cong, on the shores of Lough Corrib, *see p179* **Below** Lough Corrib, as seen from Cornamona, *see p179*

KEY

Drive route

Above Clifden, nestled below the imposing Twelve Bens range

VISITING CLIFDEN

Parking
There is a free public car park immediately behind the Tourist Office.

Tourist Information
Galway Road; 095 21163; www.visit clifden.com; open Mar–Oct: Mon–Sat

Shopping
Whitethorn Gallery on Galway Road showcases local artists. **O'Dalaigh Jewellers** on Main Street *(www. celticimpressions.com)* sells Celtic-inspired jewellery. **Millars** on Main Street stocks Irish fashion designers.

VISITING INISHBOFIN ISLAND

Inishbofin Island Discovery makes the 30-minute crossing from Cleggan at least once daily all year *(095 45819; www.inishbofinislanddiscovery.com)*.

WHERE TO STAY IN CLIFDEN

Foyle's Hotel *inexpensive*
Old-fashioned, quirky hotel run by the Foyle family for generations. Attached is Marconi's seafood restaurant.
Main Street; 095 21801; www.foyles hotel.com

Abbeyglen Castle Hotel *moderate*
A 10-minute walk from the centre of town. Views over the Bay and Twelve Bens Mountains and gourmet dining at the hotel restaurant.
Sky Road; 095 21201; www.abbeyglen.ie

The Quay House *moderate*
An award-winning guesthouse with views across the water. Once the harbour master's residence, this is the oldest building in Clifden.
Clifden Harbour; 095 21369; www.thequayhouse.com

❶ CLIFDEN

Co Galway

Situated on a hillside between the Twelve Bens mountain range and the Atlantic, and nestling at the head of a broad bay, Clifden (An Clochán) is blessed with a wonderful setting. Compact and picturesque, it is Connemara's largest town and effectively its capital. It was founded in the early 19th century by John D'Arcy, a Galway sheriff, and still retains much of its Georgian architecture. Boasting a healthy number of good restaurants, pubs and shops, and a bustling atmosphere, this vibrant town deserves more than a cursory glance.

A one-hour walking tour

Begin the walk at the **Tourist Office** ①. Turn uphill on Galway Road and then right into Westport Road and right again, where Clifden's Catholic **Church of St Joseph** ② can be seen. It is from the site of this church that Clifden derives its name, built as it was upon the site of an early Christian monastic beehive hut or *cloghan*. Turn left up Church Hill and, a little further up on the left, the Protestant **Christ Church** ③, built in 1820, holds a silver replica of the Cross of Cong *(see p179)* and has better views than St Joseph's. Carry on along Church Hill, which becomes the beginning of the **Sky Road** ④. From this vantage point visitors can look down and fully appreciate Clifden's majestic setting, with the lofty spires of its churches elegantly set against the looming presence of the Twelve Bens. Continue on Sky Road past the Abbeyglen Castle. A path to the left is the start of a steep, 15-minute climb up to the **D'Arcy Monument** ⑤, which offers spectacular views.

Return by the same route until reaching a right turn down Church Street to Main St and Market Square. **Mullarkey's Bar** ⑥, at the back of Foyle's on the square, often has evening open mic sessions with an eclectic range of music, from Irish traditional to modern folk. From Market Square, follow Beach Road down to the pretty **Harbour** ⑦ – one of Ireland's safest. Look back for a good view of the town and its twin spires. Return to Market Square and turn right down Market Street, lined with interesting shops, restaurants, bars and pubs including **Lowry's** ⑧, another great place to catch a live music session. Turn left into Bridge Street and then right back into Galway Road. Next to the Tourist Office is the **Station House Museum** ⑨ *(open May–Oct: Mon–Sat)* whose exhibitions tell the tale of aviators Alcock and Brown – who ended their transatlantic flight near here in 1919 – and the Connemara pony.

🚗 *From the tourist office car park, turn right up Wesport Road, left up Church Hill and follow Sky Road signs.*

Above View across the green countryside of the Sky Road towards Cleggan

② Sky Road
Co Galway
A rollercoaster of a drive skirting the northern flank of Streamstown Bay, at its summit the Sky Road reaches a height of 152 m (500 ft), affording breathtaking sea views across the islands of Turbot and Inishturk. At the top there is a lay-by ideal for pausing to take in the sweeping views. Follow the road back to the N59 and turn left, then take the next left, signposted **Claddaghduff**. Having safely descended again to sea level at this little village, there may be time to unwind with a drink while waiting for the tide to recede, making it possible to cross the causeway to Omey Island.

🚗 *Drive across the short, sandy causeway via Star of the Sea Church at low tide, following the markers with great care.*

Roller coaster Sky Road

③ Omey Island
Co Galway
For one day each year, in August, this peaceful spot becomes the centre of attention, for the Omey Races, and the beach makes a spectacular setting for a horse race. The rest of the year, the most important site is a 6th-century monastic graveyard and a holy well and chapel dedicated to St Fechin. In the centre of the island is the reedy **Fahy Lough**, around which there are good walking and birdwatching opportunities. Keep an

eye on the time, though, in order not to misjudge the tide, which would mean an enforced wait of six hours.

🚗 *From Claddaghduff it is a 1-km (half-mile) drive north to Cleggan Harbour for ferries to Inishbofin Island.*

④ Inishbofin Island
Co Galway
Inishbofin is a small island with cliffs and sandy beaches, blessed with crystal-clear waters great for swimming, snorkelling and excellent shore angling. At the island's centre is peaceful **Lough Boffin**, home to a range of wading and migrant birds; on its western side are rocky outcrops known as "The Stags", with impressive sea stacks and blow-holes.

Inishbofin ("island of the white cow") is also a centre for traditional Irish music. As well as having its own famous *ceilidh* band, the island plays host to visiting musicians and artists. The shell of a 14th-century chapel – the last vestiges of a monastic settlement established by St Colman in the 7th century – and the remains of a Cromwellian barracks, used to house captured Catholic clergy from all over the country, can be visited too. Near the pier is the small but interesting **Heritage Museum**, dedicated to island history and life.

🚗 *From Cleggan, drive southeast on the R379 to the N59. Turn left onto the N59 to Letterfrack for access to the Connemara National Park.*

Above Ferry to Inishbofin Island from Cleggan Harbour near Claddaghduff

EAT AND DRINK

CLIFDEN
Walsh's Bakery *inexpensive*
This café serves delicious cakes and coffee as well as hot and cold lunches.
Market Street; 095 21283; www. walshsbakery.ie

Connemara Hamper *moderate*
This deli is perfect when stocking up for a picnic, with a superb range of cheeses and cold meats. It specializes in local produce such as Connemara smoked salmon and artisan chocolates.
Main Street, Clifden; 095 21054; www. connemarahamper.com; closed Sun

Mitchell's Restaurant *moderate*
Clifden's premier eating-place; a great dining experience with beautifully presented food. The menu is especially strong on seafood dishes. Good value lunchtime menu.
Market Street; 095 21867; www. mitchellsrestaurantclifden.com; closed Oct–Mar

AROUND INISHBOFIN ISLAND
Oliver's on Cleggan Pier
inexpensive–moderate
Overlooking the harbour in Cleggan, Oliver's is a handy spot for a quick bite while waiting for the ferry to Inishbofin. Unsurprisingly, it specializes in fish and seafood – particularly flatfish, Connemara smoked salmon and Cleggan scallops. The bar serves local oysters. Also has five en suite rooms.
Cleggan Harbour; 095 44640; www.oliversoncleggganspier.ie

Above Diamond Hill, in Connemara National Park, seen from the Visitor Centre

VISITING CONNEMARA NATIONAL PARK

Parking
Park at the National Park Visitor Centre.

National Park Visitor Centre
Letterfrack, Co Galway; 095 41054; www.connemaranationalpark.ie; open daily

Shopping
Cottage Handcrafts at Moyard by park entrance stocks green marble, tweeds and knits.

VISITING KILLARY HARBOUR AND LEENANE

Killary Harbour Boat Trips
Cruises up the fjord depart two or three times daily Apr–Oct.
Leenane, Co Galway; 091 566 736; www.killaryfjord.com

WHERE TO STAY

KILLARY HARBOUR AND LEENANE
Leenane Hotel *moderate*
A former coaching station, this family-run hotel offers beautiful views over Killary Harbour. Now refurbished, it retains its old-world character and has a warm, welcoming ambience.
Clifden Road; 095 42249; www.leenane hotel.com; closed mid-Nov to mid-Mar

DELPHI VALLEY
Delphi Lodge *expensive*
Set in a beautiful secluded location on the shores of Lough Finny and facing the graceful slopes of the Mweelrea mountains, the lodge also offers superb dining in the evening around a communal table.
Delphi Valley; 095 42222; www.delphi lodge.ie; closed mid-Oct to mid-Feb

⑤ Connemara National Park
Co Galway

This protected parkland spreads over 3,000 ha (6,000 acres) of mountains, bogs, heaths and grasslands. The 19th-century Quaker-founded village of **Letterfrack** offers the best access to the park, and is a good opportunity for visitors to leave the car for a while and experience at first hand the unique terrain of Connemara. The excellent **Visitor Centre** provides general information on fauna and wildlife in the park, and maps of the walking trails. One of the best is the circular **Diamond Hill Walk** which offers rewarding views of Kylemore Abbey and its surrounding bays and mountains. It is a looped walk taking about 2–3 hours. For something less strenuous and shorter, there are also three less-demanding trails that skirt the lower slopes of Diamond Hill. All routes are clearly signposted. Along the way, walkers may well glimpse red deer and Connemara ponies, and hear a wide variety of songbirds.

🚗 *From Letterfrack continue east on the N59, along the shores of Lake Pollacappull, to Kylemore Abbey.*

⑥ Kylemore Abbey
Co Galway

One of the most photographed vistas in Connemara is from the shores of Lake Pollacappull. Across this tranquil stretch of water, nestling at the foot of Duchruach Hill, is the castellated form of **Kylemore Abbey** *(open daily; www.kylemoreabbey.com).* Built in the

Below Spectacular Kylemore Abbey, perched on the shoreline of Lake Pollacappull

19th century, since 1922 the abbey has been home to a semi-enclosed order of Benedictine nuns who, until recently, ran a boarding school for girls. Part of the abbey is open to visitors, who can view the dining rooms, library and main hall. The visitor centre recounts the history of the building and the order, and the craft shop sells delicious jams made by the nuns, as well as local pottery. But perhaps the biggest attraction here is the **walled garden** *(open mid-Mar–Oct),* originally laid out in 1860 with no fewer than 21 glass-houses. There is a shuttle bus to the gardens from the abbey.

🚗 *Leaving the abbey, turn left onto the N59 to Leenane for Killary Harbour.*

Above A scenic view of the lovely winding fjord of Killary Harbour

⑦ Killary Harbour and Leenane
Co Galway

Killary Harbour is Ireland's only fjord and the small, picturesque village of Leenane sits at its head. The best view of the fjord is a little way before the village, to the left, as the N59 slopes down towards it. There are several off-road viewpoints for exhilarating panoramas of the glacial valley and, on the opposite shore, the vertiginous dark slopes of Mweelrea mountain plunging into the blue waters. From Leenane, a 90-minute cruise sails the length of the 14-km (9-mile) fjord, offering excellent views. As the waters of the harbour are exceptionally calm, it is rare for passengers to suffer seasickness.

🚗 *Head northeast on the N59. At Aasleagh turn left onto the R335, through the Doolough Pass between the Sheeffry Hills and Mweelrea to the Delphi Valley.*

❽ Delphi Valley
Co Mayo

The Delphi Valley was given its name by the Marquis of Sligo who, on his return from Delphi in Greece in the 1830s, built his country home, Delphi Lodge, on the shores of beautiful Lough Finny, opposite the lower slopes of Mweelrea. It is said that the Grecian landscape reminded him so much of home that he pined for this corner of Mayo.

🚗 *Follow the R335 to Doolough and the Famine Walk Memorial.*

Traditional local road signs

The Famine Walk
During the Great Famine in Ireland (1845–51) a million people died and a further million emigrated. In March 1849, hundreds of starving people walked over the Doolough Pass from Louisburg to Delphi House, where a party of famine relief commissioners were staying, hoping to get food for their families. They were made to wait overnight in harsh conditions before being turned away. Around 400 people died on the trek back. A memorial stone on the shores of Doolough commemorates the tragedy.

❾ Doolough
Co Mayo

Beyond the Delphi Valley, the road skirts the lake of Doolough ("Black Lake" in Irish), reputed to be the second deepest lake in Ireland. Nestled in the midst of the Murrisk Mountains, its enigmatic beauty is further enhanced by the total peace and solitude of its setting. Even in high summer, visitors are few. At the far end of the lake, the small stone **Famine Walk Memorial**, inscribed with a quote from Bishop Desmond Tutu, is on the right. The view back across the lake and the surrounding hills is sublime. For some, the terrible event that took place in this valley in March 1849 to this day reverberates in its sombre beauty.

🚗 *Retrace the route back to the Delphi side of the lake. At the first junction, turn left up the hill, signed Liscarney and Drummin, to reach the Tawnyard Pass.*

❿ Tawnyard Pass
Co Mayo

This mountain road cuts through a remote forested area of the Sheefry. Park at the sign for Tawnyard Forests for superb views over Tawnyard Lough and its surrounding hills as well as the Ben Gorm and Mweelrea mountains. A walking trail leads down to the lough. Once it has reached the head of the pass, the road hairpins down to a stone bridge and levels out on the flatter, fertile plains of South Mayo. At the start of this descent is a small lay-by where, on a clear day, the peak of Croagh Patrick, Ireland's holiest mountain, can be seen *(see p195)*.

🚗 *Stay on this road as far as the junction with the R330, turning right onto it. At Killavally, turn left onto the L1809 for 6.5 km (4 miles) and follow the signs for Ballintubber Abbey.*

Above View over the surrounding hills from the Tawnyard Pass

EAT AND DRINK IN KILLARY HARBOUR AND LEENANE

Gaynor's *inexpensive*
This pub's claim to fame is that many scenes in Jim Sheridan's movie *The Field*, starring Richard Harris, were shot here. It's a very popular and friendly place, serving a good range of well-prepared food.
Leenane, 095 42261

Blackberry Restaurant *moderate*
This family-run restaurant serves reliably good food and takes pride in all its dishes being freshly cooked. Delicious home-made soups and chowders, fish cakes and mussels.
Leenane, 095 42240; www.blackberry restaurant.ie; closed Oct–Mar

Above One of the many little islands that dot the tranquil surface of Lough Corrib

WHERE TO STAY

AROUND BALLINTUBBER ABBEY

Moher House *inexpensive*
This homely bed and breakfast is in the capable hands of owner Marian O'Malley, who ensures all guests are given a warm welcome. Open peat fires and views of Croagh Patrick and Moher Lake add to the friendly, open ambience. Wide choice of breakfasts, and evening meals by arrangement.
Near village of Drummin on the main Leenane–Westport Road (N59); 098 21360; www.moherhousewestport.net; closed Nov–Mar

LOUGH CORRIB

Fairhill House Hotel *moderate*
This refurbished Victorian hotel offers simple but very comfortable country-style accommodation as well as the convivial Eddie's Bar.
Main Street, Clonbur; 094 954 6176; www.fairhillhouse.com

CONG

Ashford Castle Hotel
moderate–expensive
For those who want a truly memorable stay, this dignified hotel is one of Ireland's plushest addresses. The estate offers a wide range of fun acitivities including archery, falconry and golf.
095 9544 6003; www.ashfordcastle.com

⑪ Ballintubber Abbey
Co Mayo

Founded in 1216 by Cathal O'Conner, the King of Connaught, **Ballintubber Abbey** *(open daily)* is often spoken of as "the abbey that refused to die". Remarkably, it is the only church in Ireland where, for coming up to 800 years, Mass has been celebrated without a break and today is still a place of daily worship.

An audiovisual display takes visitors on a journey through Cromwellian burnings, religious persecution, and the actitivies of the notorious "priest hunter" Sean na Sagart ("John of the Priests") who is actually buried in the graveyard. His body was laid facing north instead of the usual practice of burying the dead facing the rising sun. Every year, hundreds of people walk *Tochar Phadraig* ("Pilgrim's Path") from the abbey to Croagh Patrick, and up to the summit of the holy mountain *(see p195).*

🚗 *Join the N84 at Ballintubber and drive south towards Partry. Turn right onto the R300 (signposted Lough Mask Drive) and then left for the tiny hamlet of Srah (An tSraith). Veer left and follow the road that hugs the northern shore of Lough Mask.*

⑫ Loughs Mask and Nafooey
Co Mayo

Lough Mask is a vast limestone lake, etched by rain and river water out of the porous rock, and one of the best spots in Ireland for brown-trout angling. For almost its whole length the road hugs the shoreline, offering lovely lake vistas. The little town of Tourmakeady (Tuar Mhic Éadaigh)

marks the start of the Gaeltacht. From here, the road veers away from the lough and climbs upwards. Stop and look back for a fabulous view. Soon the road dips down into the valley of **Lough Nafooey**. At the end of the lough is a secluded, sandy beach, from where long-abandoned cultivation ridges called "lazy beds", used for growing potatoes until the Famine of 1845–51, can be seen.

🚗 *Climb up the L1601 along Lough Nafooey over Al Dubh Pass to join the R336, turning left towards Maum.*

The Galway Gaeltacht

The Gaeltacht are regions where the Irish language still holds sway. They are found mainly in the more remote communities of western Ireland. The Galway Gaeltacht in Connemara is the most extensive in Ireland, and even the road signs here may be in Irish only. The government actively supports and promotes its continued use, and schoolchildren from other areas often holiday in the Gaeltacht to improve their Irish.

⑬ Maum (An Mám)
Co Galway

The Irish-speaking area around **Maum** is known for the venerable local Joyce family – it is often referred to as "Joyce Country". The village makes a pleasant stop, with the Keane's pub opposite the bridge spanning the River Joyce. From the bridge there are fine views of the Maumturk Mountains.

🚗 *Continue east, taking the R345 along Lough Corrib towards Clonbur and Cong.*

Above Regional architecture of a stone farmhouse on Lough Mask

14 Lough Corrib
Co Mayo and Co Galway

The largest lake in the Republic of Ireland, Lough Corrib is reputed to have an island for every day of the year. One of the largest is **Inchagoil**, which has an important monastic settlement *(see p186)*. Many are wooded, and the dawn chorus in early spring on Lough Corrib is a spectacular natural event.

From Maum to Clonbur there are almost uninterrupted views of this beautiful, island-studded lake. There is a viewing point just before Cornamona (Corr Na Mona). From here it is possible to make a detour onto a tiny peninsula that affords closer views of the Isle of Inchagoil. **Clonbur** (An Fhairche) is a picturesque village on the broad neck of land between Loughs Mask and Corrib. There are forest and lakeside walks in the vicinity and Clonbur Woods are renowned for the variety of butterflies found there. The upper-floor balcony of Burke's pub-restaurant has great views of Mount Gable and the landscape. Its owners also provide maps and advice on local walking trails. One is to the top of Mount Gable, from where the whole of Connemara is spread out below. It is a 3-hour return trek, but it is also possible to drive to within 40 minutes' walk of the summit (ask at Burke's).

🚗 *Take the R346 east to Cong.*

Cong Abbey's 12th-century arched doorway

15 Cong
Co Mayo

Cong was the location for John Ford's 1951 film *The Quiet Man*, starring John Wayne. Movie buffs should head for the **Quiet Man Museum** *(open Apr–Oct daily)*. Nearby, ruined **Cong Abbey** was founded in the 7th century and rebuilt in the 12th and 13th by the last kings of Connaught: Turlough, Rory and Cathal O'Connor. The ornamented 12th-century Cross of Cong once resided here (it is now in the National Museum of Ireland in Dublin, *see p150)*. Behind the abbey, a path leads to **Ashford Castle**, once the home of Arthur Guinness, founder of the Guinness stout brewery in 1756, and now one of Ireland's most luxurious hotels. Take tea here to enjoy the lovely gardens that sweep down to the shores of Lough Corrib.

Above Magnificent mountain scenery between Loughs Mask and Nafooey

EAT AND DRINK

LOUGHS MASK AND NAFOOEY

Maire Lukes *inexpensive*
From the garden at the rear of this landmark pub there are sweeping views of Lough Mask. It serves good light lunches, and helpful staff are knowledgeable about the area. *Toormakeady, Lough Mask; 094 954 4080*

LOUGH CORRIB

Burke's *inexpensive*
This family-run pub and restaurant offers wonderful views of Mount Gable as well as a good variety of meat and fish dishes for hungry walkers. *Clonbur; 094 954 6175; www.burkes-clonbur.com*

CONG

Cullens at the Cottage *moderate*
Located inside the grounds of the Ashford Castle Hotel, this charming thatched cottage serves tempting seasonal bistro dishes. *094 954 6003; www.ashfordcastle. com; closed Nov–Feb*

DAY TRIP OPTIONS

Clifden, Killary Harbour and Cong are all good bases from which to explore the coastline, history and loughs of Connemara.

Island life

From picturesque Clifden ❶ take the lovely drive out on the Sky Road ❷ to Cleggan for the ferry to Inishbofin Island ❹, where traditional Irish music and crafts are still a way of life.

Follow the drive instructions out to Cleggan for the ferry to the island.

History trail

From lovely Killary Harbour ❼, the spectacular, steep and winding route over Bengorm Pass leads to poignant Delphi Valley ❽ and Doolough ❾, the site of a moving monument to Ireland's tragic Famine Trail.

Follow the drive instructions over the pass and through the valley along the lough, continuing to the end of the descent from Tawnyard Pass ❿. When the road reaches the N59, turn right to return to Killary Harbour/Leenane.

Connemara's lakelands

From either Clonbur or Cong ⓯ four loughs – Carra, Mask, Nafooey ⓬ and Corrib ⓮ – can be linked in a day's driving tour that also runs through Joyce Country around Maum ⓭.

Head north to Barna, Ballinchalla and Ballinrobe, then turn left onto the N84 to the shores of Lough Carra. Continue on the N84 up to Partry, then turn left onto the R300 to Srah, and from there follow the drive instructions back to Clonbur or Cong.

TRIP 18

CONNEMARA'S COAST
Galway to Spiddal

HIGHLIGHTS

Vibrant Galway
Join in the "craic" in this fun-loving maritime city

Island-studded lake
Cruise on lovely Lough Corrib, stopping to visit
Inchagoill Island

The heart of Connemara
Explore two achingly beautiful valleys, set against the
Maumturks and Twelve Bens mountain ranges

Dramatic coastline
Be thrilled by the rugged, island- strewn coast
of Connemara

Outposts of Irish culture
Visit the Aran Islands, Irish bastions, and experience a
unique way of life

CONNEMARA'S COAST

When W B Yeats coined the phrase "A terrible beauty" he was describing the whole of Ireland, but it was probably the "water and the wilds" of Connemara that he had in his mind's eye. The name alone conjures up romantic notions of the west of Ireland – a harsh yet utterly entrancing landscape of blanket bogs, lakes and mountains, and a deeply indented coastline strewn with small islands. The region is fringed by the broad sweep of Lough Corrib to the east and the Atlantic to the west, while its northern boundary is defined by Killary Harbour. Dominating the landscape and rarely out of view are the majestic Twelve Bens and Maumturks mountain ranges, whose looming presence lends extra drama to this stunningly beautiful region.

ACTIVITIES

Wash down Galway Bay prawns or oysters with a pint of Guinness in a typical Galway pub

Wander through wild flower meadows in Brigit's Garden

Pack a picnic and hike across the blanket boglands of Connemara

Climb Errisbeg Mountain in Roundstone for the loveliest view in Connemara

Watch traditional Galway hookers (sail boats) race across Galway Bay

Cycle the coastal road of Inishmore, the largest of the Aran Islands

Above Maze-like drystone walls on Inishmore, the most visited of the Aran Islands, *see pp188–9*

PLAN YOUR DRIVE

Start/finish: Galway to Spiddal (An Spiddéal).

Number of days: 3–4, allowing one day on the Aran Islands.

Distance: 240 km (150 miles).

Road conditions: Coastal roads are often narrow and uneven, and signposting can be erratic.

When to go: Mar–Oct is preferable. Most festivals take place in summer, and regional tourist offices are closed Nov–early Mar.

Main market days: Galway: food and craft market (behind St Nicholas Church), all day Sat & Sun pm.

Shopping: Buy a genuine hand-knitted Aran sweater from the Aran Islands or a traditional Claddagh ring.

Major festivals: Galway: International Arts Festival, Jul; Galway Races, late Jul/early Aug; Film Fleadh, early Jul; Galway Oyster Festival, end Sep.

DAY TRIP OPTIONS

Have fun in Galway, with its busy **waterfront**, historic **pubs** and great **restaurants**. For **coastal scenery** and **beaches**, head for Roundstone and follow the **spectacular drive** around Betraghboy Bay. Alternatively, **leave the car behind** and **escape** to Inishmore, the largest of the Aran Islands, and **cycle** around the coast or take in the sights from a **pony and trap**. For full details, *see p189*.

Right A view towards the Twelve Bens across Lough Connemara, *see p187*

Above Galway's brightly painted shopfronts are a feature of the city **Below** Swans by the quayside, Claddagh harbour

VISITING GALWAY

Parking
Most of the city centre is pedestrianized, so it is best to park in the Eyre Square Centre or Forster Street car park opposite St Patrick's Church. There is also a multi-storey car park off Quay Street, next to Wolfe Tone Bridge. Parking discs for on-street parking can be bought at shops, newsagents and the tourist office.

Tourist Information
Aras Failte, Forster Street; 091 537 700; www.galwaytourism.ie; open Mon–Sat

WHERE TO STAY IN GALWAY

Heron's Rest *moderate*
The owner of this boutique B&B near the Spanish Arch has brought the village to the city with her careful attention to detail, individually styled rooms and gourmet breakfasts. She is also a mine of information on events in Galway and its history.
16a The Longwalk, Spanish Arch; 091 539 574; www.theheronsrest.com; open Apr–Oct

The House Hotel *moderate*
Fashionable boutique hotel. Rooms are beautifully appointed and have all the comforts of a top-range hotel. Great location in the Latin Quarter.
Spanish Parade; 091 538 900; www.thehousehotel.ie

The Hardiman *moderate*
Formerly a traditional Victorian railway hotel, this landmark building has been given a contemporary facelift but retains its large, graceful bedrooms. The Oyster Bar is well worth a visit.
Eyre Square; 091 564 041; www.thehardiman.ie

❶ GALWAY

Co Galway

Situated on a narrow neck of land between Galway Bay and Lough Corrib, Galway is the only maritime city in Ireland that actually looks out across the sea and has a tang of salt about it. Despite being one of the fastest growing cities in Europe, it has a village atmosphere and is famous for its summer festivals, thriving arts scene, historic pubs and painted shopfronts. It is also where Irish is most widely spoken – a reminder that it is the cultural hub for the broader hinterland of Connemara and the Aran Islands, Ireland's largest Gaeltacht. From Eyre Square, the main drag leads to the riverfront, a Continental-style promenade where locals come to enjoy the "craic" – fun.

A two-hour walking tour

From Eyre Square Centre car park exit onto **Eyre Square** ①, a former market square and jousting ground, once located outside the old city walls, and now a pleasant green space. In the fountain in the centre, Galway's maritime traditions are celebrated by the sculpture of a hooker – the traditional Galway fishing boat, examples of which can be seen sailing in Galway's harbour.

Lynch family crest, Lynch Castle

Leaving the square, stroll down William Street and Shop Street, Galway's main drag. On the right is **Lynch's Castle** ②, the home of one of Galway's ruling families in the 16th century. Further down Shop Street, fork left for High Street. On the corner of Cross and Quay streets is **Dillon's Jewellers** ③, which has a quaint museum *(open daily; pm only Sun)* dedicated to the history of the Claddagh ring *(see box)*. Continue down to the river and turn left to the **Spanish Arch** ④, the remnants of the city wall extension (1584), built to protect the river

quays, and a reminder of Galway's once extensive trading links with the rest of Europe. Behind the arch is the glass-fronted **Galway City Museum** ⑤ *(open Tue–Sat, Sun pm)*, which has exhibitions on Galway themes, an eclectic permanent collection – a Victorian child's tricycle, an 18th-century reliquary of St Ursula – and good views over the river. Under the arch is Nimmo's *(see right)*, a good spot for lunch. Look across to the far bank of the River Corrib at this point to see Claddagh, the oldest fishing village in Galway, which gives its name to the Claddagh ring *(see right)*.

From the Spanish Arch, follow **Fishery Walk** ⑥ – the wooden walkway is clearly marked – upstream. Continue past Wolfe Tone Bridge towards the Salmon Weir Bridge, following the river as it curves right onto Waterside. On the opposite bank is the Roman Catholic Cathedral of St Nicholas, an imposing modern structure built of local limestone and Connemara marble,

Lynch's Window ⑨, carved with a skull and crossbones, from which James Lynch, nobleman and mayor, reputedly hanged his own son, Nicholas Lynch, for murdering a Spanish guest in a pique of jealousy. The official executioner had refused to carry out the deed, no doubt heeding the people's pleas for clemency. Galwegians claim this event gave rise to the term "'lynching". From here return to the main drag of Shop Street and turn left back to Eyre Square.

🚗 *Leaving Galway, cross Wolfe Tone Bridge and follow the signs for Salthill, a resort suburb 1 km (half a mile) southwest. With Galway Bay on the left, follow the promenade. Just before the Black Rock diving board, turn right at a mini roundabout. Drive up the hill and through a series of roundabouts, eventually descending to the N59. Turn left here onto it. After 10 km (6 miles), turn right to the Connemara Marble Visitor Centre in Moycullen.*

and beyond that the spires of Galway University, which has an 1849 Gothic Revival quad. In summer, look out for salmon ascending to their spawning grounds upstream. At Waterside, the River Corrib, opens out into Lough Corrib – the largest lake in the Republic of Ireland. Beyond the weir are the remaining stanchions of the Galway–Clifden railway bridge.

Traditional Claddagh wedding ring

Just past a slipway on Waterside, turn right down St Francis Street and walk back towards the centre. At the junction with Eglinton Street, turn right and follow Mary Street into Bowling Green. Here is **Nora Barnacle House** ⑦ (open summer for guided tours), the family home of Nora Barnacle, muse and long-suffering spouse of the writer James Joyce, who visited Nora here. Now a museum, it houses Joycean memorabilia and holds readings of Joyce's work.

Around the corner, on Lombard Street, is the **Collegiate Church of St Nicholas** ⑧. Founded in 1320, it is the largest functioning medieval church in Ireland. Legend has it that Christopher Columbus prayed here prior to his voyage to the New World. Behind the church, in Church Lane, is

The Claddagh Ring
A traditional wedding ring featuring two hands holding a heart with a crown on top, the Claddagh ring takes its name from the oldest fishing village in Galway, on the west bank of the River Corrib. It is said to have been designed in the 1730s by goldsmith Richard Joyce, who presented it to William III as a mark of gratitude for securing his release from Moorish pirates. If the heart on the ring is pointing towards the body, it means the wearer's heart is taken; if it points outwards, the heart is open. Internationally famous, the Claddagh ring has been worn by such diverse figures as John Wayne and Queen Victoria.

EAT AND DRINK IN GALWAY

Corrib House Tea Rooms & Guesthouse *inexpensive*
This charmingly restored Georgian townhouse with views over the river offers breakfast and lunch, as well as teas and coffees. The weekend brunches are superb.
3 Waterside, Woodquay; 091 446 753; www.corribhouse.com

Goya's *inexpensive*
Great place for coffee and cakes. Vibrant and friendly atmosphere.
2–3 Kirwan's Lane; 091 567 010; www.goyas.ie; closed Sun

McDonaghs Seafood House *moderate*
Busy eatery famed for its chowders – the measure of a good restaurant on the western seaboard – it is everything from a take-away fish bar to a boulevard seafood restaurant.
22 Quay Street; 091 565 001; www. mcdonaghs.net; restaurant: closed Sun

Tigh Neachtain *inexpensive*
A landmark pub, reputed to be Galway's oldest (the interior has barely changed since 1894). Open fires create a warm, inviting atmosphere, and there are often impromptu music sessions.
17 Cross Street; 091 568 820; www.tighneachtain.com

Ard Bia at Nimmo's *moderate*
Top-drawer cooking and great atmosphere. Popular with local foodies. Particular favourites are the Galway mussels and haddock chowder. More informal dining available downstairs in the daytime.
Spanish Arch; 091 561 114; www.ardbia.com

Below A *currach*, or traditional sailing boat, in Galway City Museum

Above Fishing boat on lovely Lough Corrib
Above right Brigit's Celtic-inspired garden

WHERE TO STAY

AROUND OUGHTERARD

Camillaun Lodge and Angling Centre *inexpensive*
Family-run guesthouse on the banks of the River Owenriff, with direct access to Lough Corrib. Facilities include a billiards room and a garden hot tub.
Oughterard (turn right down Camp Street at the Boat Inn); 091 552 678; www.camillaun.com; closed Oct–Mar

Currarevagh House *moderate*
Country house from 1842, set in beautiful woodland. Good restaurant (open to non-residents for dinner).
Oughterard (7 km/4 miles outside the town on the Glann road); 091 552 312; www.currarevagh.com; closed early Nov–mid-Mar

AROUND INAGH VALLEY

Ballynahinch Castle Hotel *expensive*
Grand 4-star hotel in extensive woodland. Terrific dining options are available in the restaurant and the Fisherman's Pub.
Recess (on the R341 to Toombeola); 095 31006; www.ballynahinch-castle.com

Lough Inagh Lodge *expensive*
This former hunting lodge with a lakeside setting is a perfect retreat.
Recess (on the R344 towards Leenane and Letterfrack); 095 34706; www.loughinagh-lodgehotel.ie; closed mid-Dec–mid-Mar

AROUND DERRIGIMLAGH BOG

Ardagh Hotel *moderate*
Family-run hotel overlooking Ardbear Bay. The restaurant specializes in locally caught seafood.
Ballyconneely Road, Clifden (just south of town); 095 21384; www.ardaghhotel.com

ROUNDSTONE

St Josephs B&B *inexpensive*
Cosy and welcoming with good breakfasts, in the heart of the village.
Roundstone; 095 35865; www.stjosephs roundstone.com

② Connemara Marble Visitor Centre
Moycullen, Co Galway
Connemara is famous for its marble. Sometimes referred to as Irish jade, it is valued for its subtle shades of green, the result of large copper deposits in the area. The process of turning it into jewellery, ashtrays and chess sets can be seen at the Connemara Marble Visitor Centre *(open May–Oct: daily; Nov–Apr: Mon–Fri)*. Items can be bought in the showroom.
🚗 *Take Chapel Road out of Moycullen and turn right onto the N59 towards Oughterard. After 7 km (4 miles), turn right at a sign pointing to Brigit's Garden (2 km/1 mile off the N59).*

③ Brigit's Garden
Rosscahill, Co Galway
This is a contemporary garden *(open Feb–Dec)* dedicated to the four seasonal Celtic festivals. Cynics might find it a bit new-agey but there is a real sense of wonderment here and children generally love it. The large grounds feature sculptures, standing stones, ring forts, nature trails and pools, and the excellent café uses produce from the garden. Particularly attractive are the ancient woodland and wild flower meadows.
🚗 *Return to the N59, turn right and continue northwest to Oughterard (7 km/4 miles). There is a large car park on the right on the way into town.*

④ Oughterard
Co Galway
The gateway to Connemara, this is a lively town and an important angling centre. Its main attraction is **Lough Corrib**, Ireland's second largest lake, 2 km (1 mile) north of the town itself.

In spring, when the mayflies hatch, Oughterard becomes a magnet for trout fishermen. The best way to see the lake is to take a boat trip with Corrib Cruises, who operate boats year-round *(www.corribcruises.com)*. In the summer, you can sail to – and take a guided tour of – the lovely **Inchagoill Island**, which is the site of a ruined monastery and Romanesque church.
For information on fishing, call by Thomas Tuck's tackle shop on Main Street.
🚗 *From Oughterard, continue north along the N59, and turn right onto the R336 at Maam Cross.*

⑤ Maam Valley
Co Galway
This scenic drive along the R336 through the Maam Valley is an opportunity to enjoy the splendours of Connemara in relative isolation. The blanket bog (thinner and flatter than the raised bog of the Midlands) imbues the area with a desolate beauty, and if the light is right, the vivid yellow gorse and pale green reeds yield a rich palette of colours. It is worth stopping the car for a closer look and a walk. Eventually the road skirts the billowing curves of the **Maumturk Mountains** and enters the village of **Leenane**. Follow the road uphill onto the N59 west to Clifden. Look out for splendid views of **Killary Harbour** *(see pp176–7)* on the right.
🚗 *Continue on the R336 and turn left onto the N59 towards Clifden. Just before Kylemore Abbey turn left onto the R344, signposted Recess (Sraith Salach; 16 km/10 miles) The signpost is tucked in tight on a sharp corner, so be careful not to miss it.*

⑥ Inagh Valley
Co Galway

This stretch of the route passes through one of the most scenic valleys in Connemara, with broad swaths of blanket bogland on either side of the road. It eventually squeezes through the Maumturk and Twelve Bens mountains. There are wonderful views of Lough Inagh to the right.

🚗 *Regaining the N59, turn right and drive into Clifden (21 km/13 miles). Entering Clifden (see p174), turn left onto the R341 coast road, signposted Ballinaboy and Ballyconneely. In Ballinaboy, ignore the left turn for Toombeola and instead take the next left, a narrow road leading through Derrigimlagh Bog for 2 km (1 mile) and ending in a cul de sac.*

Above The pretty fishing village of Roundstone, clustered around its harbour

⑦ Derrigimlagh Bog
Co Galway

This area of bogland on the western fringes of Europe was once at the forefront of modern technology, for it is the site of the world's first transatlantic radio station, built by Guglielmo Marconi and opened with a staff of 150 in 1907. The concrete block and rusty chain by the small lough at the end of the road are the remains. Nearby, a white cairn marks another historic event. On 15 June 1919 John Alcock and Arthur Whitten Brown crash-landed their Vickers Vimy bomber biplane here after completing the first non-stop flight across the Atlantic.

🚗 *Return to the R341 and cut straight across onto a narrow well-paved road. Drive up the hill and pull into the car park (1 km/half a mile). Below is the official Alcock and Brown Monument. There are also wonderful views across the broad sweep of Mannin Bay. Return to the R341, turn right, following the signs for Ballyconneely and Roundstone.*

⑧ Roundstone
Co Galway

Eventually the coast road loops around to Roundstone (Cloch na Ron – "Seal Rock"). Perched high above the fishing harbour and looking out across island-studded Bertraghboy Bay, this is the most picturesque village on the Connemara coast. In the distance, framing the expanse of water, are the Twelve Bens and Maumturks; behind the village, Errisbeg (300 m/984 ft), a 2-hour hike (follow the road past O'Dowd's pub), affords some of the finest views in all Connemara.

Culturally vibrant, Roundstone has become a magnet for craftsmen and artists, and in summer holds a regatta of traditional Galway hookers. It also has a couple of good bars and restaurants, including O'Dowd's (see right). 3 kilometres (2 miles) southwest of town, off the R341, the beautiful white sandy coves of **Gorteen Bay** and **Dog's Bay**, lie back-to-back on a headland.

🚗 *Follow the R341 coastal road to Toombeola (7 km/4 miles) and turn right onto the R342. Continue past Cashel and take the first right onto the R340, signposted Glinsce and Carna, skirting Bertraghboy Bay.*

Above A Connemara pony, a sturdy breed suited to the rugged landscape

EAT AND DRINK

OUGHTERARD
Kelly's Bar *inexpensive*
Country pub with good home cooking and live music sessions.
Camp Street; 091 866 721

AROUND DERRIGIMLAGH BOG
Keoghs Bar *moderate*
Popular family-run bar/restaurant. Wide range of dishes from sirloin steak to warm crab claws with lemon butter. On the R341 south of Clifden. *Ballyconneely; 095 23522; www. keoghsballyconneely.com*

ROUNDSTONE
O'Dowd's *inexpensive–moderate*
In business since 1906, this harbourfront pub has superb food, wood-panelled walls and open fires. *Harbour; 095 35809; www.odowds seafoodbar.com*

Below Gorteen Bay, one of two idyllic beaches near Roundstone

Above Pearse's Cottage, the summer home of the revolutionary Pádraig Pearse

WHERE TO STAY

THE ARAN ISLANDS (OILEÁIN ARANN)
An Dún Guest House *inexpensive*
Welcoming guesthouse at the foot of Connor's Fort on Inishmaan. Five en suite rooms with lovely views, and dinner available too.
Inishmaan; 087 680 6251; www. inismeainaccommodation.ie; open Mar–Nov only

Kilmurvey House *inexpensive*
Situated between Kilronan and Bun Gowla on the west side of the island, at the foot of Dun Aengus, this 150-year-old stone house has en suite bedrooms with fine views. Dinner served in summer.
Kilmurvey, Inishmore; 099 61218; www.aranislands.ie

Pier House Guesthouse *moderate*
Located right next to the jetty, with splendid views, this small yet charming guesthouse has a handful of simple, pine-furnished rooms.
Kilronan, Inishmore; 099 61417; www.pierhousearan.com

SPIDDAL (AN SPIDÉAL)
An Cruiscin Lan Hotel and Restaurant *inexpensive*
Popular, modern hotel in the middle of Spiddal. Rooms are spacious and en suite. Restaurant attached.
Spiddal; 091 553148; www.cruiscin.ie

⑨ Bertraghboy Bay
Co Galway
Rugged and windswept, and littered with tiny islands, Betraghboy Bay is breathtakingly beautiful. On the far side of the bay is **Carna**, an important lobster fishing centre, from where it is a short hop of 5 km (3 miles) to **Mweenish** (Maoinis), an island linked by bridge to the mainland and with beautiful sandy beaches. Due west of Maoinis is isolated **St Mac Dara's Island** (Oileán Mhic Dara), one of the many uninhabited islands in this area. It has the remains of a church and the bed (grave) of St Mac Dara. The island is so sacred that fishermen used to dip their sails three times as a mark of respect when passing.
🚗 *From Carna turn right onto the coastal R340 and follow it around the headland, with views of Kilkieran Bay on the right. Pass through the village of Kilkieran and just before Glinn Chatha turn right, following the sign for Ros Muc and Pearse's Cottage.*

⑩ Pearse's Cottage (Teach an Phiarsaigh)
Rosmuck Peninsula, Co Galway
Located just off the R340, Pearse's Cottage *(open daily)* was the summer residence of the Dublin school teacher, revolutionary and writer Pádraig Pearse (1879–1916). Following the collapse of the 1916 Uprising, Pearse and 14 other leaders were executed, thus becoming martyrs to the cause. Pearse used this cottage to run a summer school for his students. It was also where he penned his graveside oration for the nationalist hero Jeremiah O'Donovan Rossa in 1915. The closing words of the speech, "Ireland

unfree shall never be at peace" became the rallying cry for many Irish patriots. The cottage contains mementos of Pearse's life.
While here, it is worth exploring the Rosmuck Peninsula on foot to appreciate the fabulous setting.
🚗 *Drive back to the R340 and continue east. Around 5 km (3 miles) past Glencoh turn right onto the R336 for Rossaveel (signposted Rós an Mhíl), the main port for the Aran Islands. Cars cannot be taken onto the islands, so park in the port.*

Above Traditional red-sailed Galway hookers catch the breeze in Galway Bay

⑪ The Aran Islands (Oileáin Arann)
Co Galway
This trio of islands on the western fringes of Europe – Inishmore (Inis Mor; Great Island), Inishmaan (Inis Meáin; Middle Island) and Inisheer (Inis Oírr; Eastern Island) – are a continuation of the limestone base of the Burren in North Clare *(see p127)*. Far out in Galway Bay, they act as a bulwark, helping to protect the city of Galway from the driving force of the Atlantic.
For many Irish people, the islands symbolize a Celtic Eden, where Irish traditions, from language to dress, as

Right The blanket bogland of Connemara, long harvested for peat

well as farming and fishing methods, persist. The playwright J M Synge (1871–1909) put the islands on the map with the publication of *Playboy of the Western World* in 1907. A fraught tale of love and murder, it was inspired by time he spent on Inishmaan.

The largest island, **Inishmore** is the most visited. Boats arrive at **Kilronan** (Cill Rónáin), where bicycles can be hired and jaunting cars (pony and traps) wait to give island tours. The **Aran Heritage Centre** *(Apr–Oct daily)* in Kilronan is worth a visit.

Inishmore's main attraction is **Dun Aengus** (Dun Aonghasa), an Iron Age promontory fort, located on the edge of granite cliffs. It has four concentric stone walls and is protected by a *chevaux de frise*, a ring of razor-sharp stone stakes. Further along the coast, **Dún Duchathair**, known as the Black Fort, has dry-stone ramparts.

Other sights include **Teampall Chiaráin**, a ruined 12th-century church with striking doorways, and **Na Seacht d'Teampaill**, the "Seven Churches", a monastery built between the 9th and 15th centuries.

Inishmaan is the chief bastion of Aran culture and is much quieter than the other islands. Among its main sights are **Dún Chonchúir**, a pre-Christian fort, and **Synge's Cottage**, where the playwright stayed during his time here.

Sights on the smallest of the three islands, **Inisheer**, include the ruined **Church of St Gobnait** and the 15th-century **O'Brien's Castle**.
🚗 *From Rossaveel, continue along the R336 to Spiddal.*

Aran Sweaters

These thick woollen jumpers with elaborate patterns on the front are traditionally worn by Aran Island fishermen. Knitted from unscoured wool that retains its natural lanolin, they protected the fishermen from the worst of the elements. Each pattern was unique to a family or village, and would help identify the wearer in case of a fatality at sea.

🚗 Spiddal (An Spidéal)
Co Galway
This long coastal village marks the end of the Gaeltacht region. It has a Blue Flag beach (Silver Strand), and curragh races along the shore in summer. Next to the beach, the **Spiddal Craft Village** *(open year-round)*, a complex of small craft studios, sells high quality textiles, musical instruments, ceramics, jewellery and leatherwork.

Above left Looking over the cliff edge at Dun Aengus, Inishmore **Above centre** A jaunting car on the Aran Islands **Above** Kilmurvey Beach, Inishmore

VISITING THE ARAN ISLANDS (OILEÁIN ARANN)

Tourist Information
For information on accommodation, which is very limited and needs to be booked, contact the tourist board. *Kilronan; 099 61263; www.visit aranislands.com; open daily*

Aran Island Ferries
Aran Island Ferries operates a year-round passenger service to the Aran Islands (cars are not allowed), with several boats a day. The crossing takes about 40 minutes. *37–9 Forster Street, Galway (main office); Rossaveel (ferry terminal); 091 568 903; www.aranislandferries.com*

EAT AND DRINK ON THE ARAN ISLANDS (OILEÁIN ARANN)

Joe Watty's *inexpensive*
Lively music pub with a lovely, shaded beer garden and good food too. *Kironan, Inishmore; 086 049 4509; www.joewattys.ie*

DAY TRIP OPTIONS
Spend a day in Galway, drive around island-studded Betraghboy Bay or escape to the Aran Islands.

Vibrant Galway
Galway ❶ is a great place to spend a day. Stroll on the waterfront, visit Nora Barnacle's House and sample some of Ireland's best pubs.

Galway is easily reached from the rest of Ireland, including the N6 (linking with M4 from Dublin and N18 from Shannon) and the N17 from the north.

Island-studded Betraghboy Bay
Stroll around the picturesque village of Roundstone ❽, then head for Betraghboy Bay ❾ to experience the beauty of coastal Connemara.

Follow the drive instructions.

Celtic Eden
Take a ferry to the Aran Islands ⓫. At 13 km (8 miles) long and 3 km (2 miles) wide, Inishmore is easy to explore by bike or jaunting car.

Rossaveel is 32 km (20 miles) west of Galway along the R336/R372. The ferry companies operate shuttle buses between Galway and Rossaveel to coincide with ferry crossings.

TRIP 19

MAYO'S COASTAL SPLENDOUR
Westport to Doogort

HIGHLIGHTS

Georgian elegance
Browse the galleries and bookshops of
"pretty little" Westport

A holy mountain
Trek to the summit of Croagh Patrick and be rewarded
by stupendous views over Clew Bay

Rugged coastline
Head along the south coast of Achill Island and be
thrilled by dramatic headlands lashed by crashing waves

Sandy beaches
Escape to one of the county's many idyllic beaches for
crystal-clear seas, white sand and water sports

The picturesque landscape of Achill Island

MAYO'S COASTAL SPLENDOUR

Mayo lies in the far west of Connaught. Gloriously beautiful, it has never had it easy. The land here can be grudging and the wild seas unforgiving. During the Great Famine the county experienced the highest levels of emigration and its sense of isolation is a legacy of this. Many visitors bypass Mayo, drawn by the rugged beauty of Connemara or the romance of Sligo. They miss much – heather-mantled bog lands, majestic mountains and a stunning coastline. If you could eat scenery, a local saying goes, Mayo would be the richest county on earth. Nowhere is this wealth more evident than in the broad sweep around Clew Bay – from Westport to Achill Island.

Above The Atlantic Drive through spectacular coastal scenery, on Achill Island, *see p196*

ACTIVITIES

Explore the hundreds of islands in Clew Bay by kayak

See the fortified towers built by a 16th-century pirate queen

Stroll along the sands of Keel beach framed against the dramatic backdrop of Minaun Heights

Visit the Deserted Village at the foot of the Slievemore Mountains

0 kilometres 5

0 miles 5

KEY

Drive route

Above The white sandy beach at Keel, backed by the soaring sea cliffs of Minaun Heights, *see p196*

PLAN YOUR DRIVE

Start/finish: Westport to Doogort.

Number of days: 2–3, allowing one day on Clew Bay and two on Achill Island.

Distance: 84 km (51 miles).

Road conditions: Well paved and signposted. Some steep terrain with hairpin bends.

When to go: The best time to visit is March to early November. Many tourist facilities are closed in winter.

Opening times: Most shops and attractions are open from 9 or 10am to 5 or 6pm. Shops are usually open from Mon to Sat, however in large towns and shopping centres, shops usually stay open late one night, usually Thu or Fri, and also open from 12 to 6pm on Sun. In most villages there are small convenience stores which open from 7 or 8am until late in the evening.

Main market days: Westport: Sat, food and crafts; Thu, Country Market (food).

Shopping: Westport has a couple of good bookshops, craft shops and galleries selling books and prints on Irish themes.

Major festivals: Westport: Croagh Patrick Pilgrimage, last Sun in July; Westival Arts & Music Festival, Oct; Achill Island: Walking Festival, Mar/Apr; Heinrich Böll Weekend, early May; Yawl Sailing Festival, Jul/Aug.

DAY TRIP OPTIONS

For a day of **gentle pottering**, spend the morning browsing the bookshops and galleries of **Westport**, before an invigorating **hike** up **Croagh Patrick** for the outstanding **views**. For beach-lovers, Achill Island is the highlight of Mayo. Follow **Atlantic Drive** around its southern tip to the beaches at **Dooega** and **Keel**. End either day with a **music session**, in **Westport** or **Dooagh**. For full details, *see p197*.

ⓘ WESTPORT

Co Mayo

Set on the shores of Clew Bay, Westport is one of the prettiest and most congenial towns in Ireland, with an understated Georgian elegance. The English satirist William Thackeray, visiting in 1842, wrote in his book *Irish Sketch Book*: "Nature has done much for the pretty little town of Westport; and after Nature, the traveller ought to be thankful to Lord Sligo, who has done a great deal too." This is a fair appraisal. Sligo commissioned planners and the English architect James Wyatt to design his mansion, its grounds and the town bordering his estate in the 1770s.

Above Westport House, the home of Lord Sligo, who planned the town of Westport

VISITING WESTPORT

Parking
All parking in Westport is metered. You can park in most streets for free for up to 1 hour. The best place to park is on the Mall at the end of James Street.

Tourist Information
Bridge Street, Westport. Co Mayo; 098 25711; www.westporttourism.com

KAYAKING

Clew Bay Bike Hire & Outdoor Adventures
Explore the islands of Clew Bay by kayak. Small excursions set out from Westport regularly in summer. *098 24818; www.clewbaybikehire.com*

WHERE TO STAY IN WESTPORT

Clew Bay Hotel *inexpensive*
Family-run hotel with well-appointed rooms and helpful staff. Guests have free access to the leisure centre next door. *James Street; 098 28088; www.clewbayhotel.com*

Wyatt Hotel *inexpensive*
Small, stylish hotel with an unbeatable location on the Octagon and an excellent gastro pub. *Octagon; 098 25027; www.wyatthotel.com*

A two-hour walking tour

Westport is one of a handful of planned towns in Ireland, its carefully arranged streets forming a neat square. From the Mall, walk down James Street to the **Octagon** ① for the start of the walk. The town's oldest buildings are arranged around this striking octagonal main square. In the middle, perched on a lofty plinth, is a statue of St Patrick, under whose benign gaze the town sits.

From the Octagon, walk back down James Street towards the Mall. Look out on the right for the **Sea Sky Shore Gallery** ②, featuring local artists' work. The Mall, a popular promenade, flanks the Carrowbeg River, its two sides, South Mall and North Mall, linked by a series of bridges – Wyatt changed the course of the river in order to accommodate his grand designs for the town. Cross the river at James Street and take the second left by

Beer barrels stacked up outside a pub

the church onto New Road to the **Linen Mill** ③, which sells homeware made in the adjoining 1960s weaving factory. Trace your steps back to the turn for the North Mall and head down it, taking in the Anglican church. Cross back over the bridge and walk up Bridge Street, the town's other main thoroughfare, with several good restaurants. Halfway up the street is **Matt Molloy's** ④, owned by the eponymous Chieftains' flautist. It has traditional Irish music sessions every night. Westport's music scene really comes alive every year during its Arts and Music Festival *(late Oct; www.westival.ie).* Walk back down Bridge Street, to South Mall and the car park.

To get to the town's main attraction, Georgian **Westport House and Gardens** *(open Mar–Oct: daily; Nov–Dec & Feb: Sat & Sun)*, drive down James Street to the Octagon, forking right up Quay Hill, off Peter Street, for 2 km (1 mile). The former home of the Earls of Altamont has a sweeping marble staircase and is adorned with family portraits. It has embraced tourism, with a pirate adventure park, ziplines and a miniature railway. The gardens are peaceful and worth a wander. The harbourfront near the entrance has restaurants, pubs and craft shops.

🚗 *Turn right onto Quay Road, signposted Louisborough, then R335. Drive 8 km (5 miles) west to Murrisk. Park by the Croagh Patrick Information Centre.*

Mayo's Pirate Queen
In the 16th century, a pirate called Grace O' Malley, or "Granuaile", pretty much ruled the roost from her power base on Clare Island. With her fleet of 20 ships, she belligerently defied Elizabethan forces, eventually gaining the respect of Elizabeth I herself. The remains of her strongholds can be seen around Clew Bay and on Achill Island. She died in Newport in 1603.

---

② Croagh Patrick
Co Mayo
Ireland's most sacred mountain, Croagh Patrick occupies a peculiar place in the Irish psyche. St Patrick, who is credited with bringing Christianity to Ireland in the 5th century, is said to have fasted and prayed on its summit for 40 days. Every year on the last Sunday in July – known as Reek Sunday – up to 40,000 pilgrims trek up its rocky slopes, many in bare feet.

The ascent of the 765-m (2,510-ft) summit is steep, with a scramble over loose, shifting scree on the upper half. However, the sweeping view over Clew Bay, with its confetti of islands, is ample reward. Pick up a stout walking stick from the **Croagh Patrick Information Centre** at the base of the mountain to make the ascent, which takes about two hours, followed by a 90-minute descent.

At the foot of Croagh Patrick, on the other side of the R335, is the **National Famine Memorial**, a harrowing depiction of one of the so-called "coffin ships" that carried Irish emigrants to North America as they fled the Great Famine (1845–52). The terrible conditions on the ships often led to death and disease.

🚗 *Return along the R335 towards Westport. Just before Westport, turn left onto the N59 (north). A few kilometres (miles) after Westport look for a sign pointing left to Rosscahill Pier (7 km/4 miles).*

③ Rosscahill Pier
Co Mayo
A narrow but well-paved road leads to an inlet on Clew Bay. Across the tranquil stretch of water is one of the best views of Croagh Patrick – magical on a clear summer's evening.

🚗 *Return to the N59 and continue north to Mallaranny. Keep left on the R319 signposted Achill, passing through Polranny to Achill Sound.*

Above left Matt Molloy's in Westport **Above centre** Statue of St Patrick at the foot of Croagh Patrick overlooking Clew Bay **Above** *Madonna and Child* icon on Croagh Patrick

EAT AND DRINK

WESTPORT
McCormack's at the Andrew Stone Gallery *inexpensive*
Above McCormack's butcher shop. The menu includes quiches, cakes, bacon and cabbage, soups and Irish stew.
Bridge Street; 098 25619; closed Wed & Sun

An Port Mór *moderate*
Classy food at affordable prices made by a French-trained patron/chef.
Brewery Place; 098 26730; www.anportmor.com

The Pantry & Corkscrew *moderate*
Run by a husband-and-wife team, with scrummy food; try Irish fish tempura.
Peter Street, The Octagon; 098 26977; www.thepantryandcorkscrew.com

CROAGH PATRICK
The Tavern Bar and Restaurant *inexpensive–moderate*
Family-run restaurant at the foot of Croagh Patrick. The food is excellent.
Murrisk; 098 64060; www.tavern murrisk.com

Above View across Clew Bay towards Clare Island from Atlantic Drive

Above Keem Bay, beneath the Croaghaun Heights on the west side of Achill Island

VISITING ACHILL ISLAND

Tourist Information
Davitt Quarter, Achill Sound; 098 20400; www.achilltourism.com

WHERE TO STAY

ACHILL SOUND

Achill Island Hotel *inexpensive*
Just before the causeway for Achill Sound. Rooms have good views.
Achill Sound; 098 45138; www. achillislandhotel.com

ATLANTIC DRIVE

Lavelle's Seaside House *inexpensive*
Good-value B&B. Mickey's, the bar next door, serves sublime crab claws.
Dooega; 098 45116; www.lavelles seasidehouse.com

KEEL

Achill Cliff House Hotel *moderate*
Family-run hotel with sweeping views, spacious rooms and a good restaurant.
Keel; 098 43400; www.achillcliff.com

Bervie *moderate*
Guesthouse in the former coastguard station. Has direct access to the beach.
Keel; 098 43114; www.bervieachill.com

Below Stopping the traffic on the Slievemore Mountain **Below right** The Deserted Village

④ Achill Sound (Gob an Choire)
Co Mayo

Islands in the west of Ireland have a special allure for the Irish. Often seen as the repository of a lost way of life, they remain potent symbols of the past. **Achill Island** is no exception. Ireland's largest island at 24 km (15 miles) long and 19 km (12 miles) wide, it is connected to the mainland by a causeway. It has sandy beaches, dramatic cliffs, boglands and heathery slopes. Over the years it has inspired artists and writers, including German writer Heinrich Böll, American painter Robert Henri and painter Paul Henry.

The road bridge spans the narrow, winding strait at **Achill Sound** – a good place to stock up. Facilities here include an ATM, post office, a supermarket, hotels and restaurants.

🚗 *On the island side of Achill Sound, proceed for about 500 m (500 yards), then turn left off the R319, following signs for Atlantic Drive and Cois na Farraige ("Road by the Sea").*

⑤ Atlantic Drive
Achill Island, Co Mayo

After 6 km (4 miles) the road skirts the southern tip of the island and the remains of an 18th-century church and holy well, named after St Damhnait, an early Christian saint. The graveyard looks across to **Little Achill Island** (Achill Beg). Nearby is **Carrick Kildavnet**, an almost intact example of a 15th-century tower house, built by the O'Malley clan *(see p195)*. From the pier there are fine views across the sound to Corraun Hill.

At **Cloughmore**, as the still waters of Achill Sound give way to Atlantic breakers, some of Ireland's most spectacular coastal scenery unfolds. For 6 km (4 miles) the road rises

steadily to a viewing bay overlooking Ashlean Bay and north to Achill Head, then descends into a series of hairpin bends, looping around the small pebbly beach of **Portnahally** before climbing the other side of the valley. At the next T-junction, turn left to continue along Atlantic Drive and into **Dooega**, a picturesque, fishing village with a Blue Flag beach.

🚗 *Minaun Heights loom large above Dooega – to drive to the top, turn left immediately after Mickey's Pub.*

⑥ Minaun Heights
Achill Island, Co Mayo

The road to Minaun Heights climbs steadily. Pass a school, take the next left and follow the road as it swings right over a small bridge, skirting the slopes of Mweelin Hill. Turn left at the junction and drive up for views of Clare Island to the southwest and Black Sod Bay to the north.

🚗 *Return to junction, turn left and go along Mweelin road to R319. Follow it to Cashel and Keel 3 km (2 miles) on.*

⑦ Keel
Achill Island, Co Mayo

Keel is known for its white sandy beach, framed by the soaring sea cliffs of Minaun Heights, and is backed by a large lake, popular for water sports.

🚗 *Continue west on the R319 for a couple of kilometres (miles) to Dooagh.*

⑧ Dooagh
Achill Island, Co Mayo

Just west of Keel is the tiny village of Dooagh, which has a nice beach and several good cafés. Gielty's, a popular pub at the west end of the village, hosts traditional music sessions.

🚗 *Continue on the R319 to Keem Bay (3 km/2 miles).*

Left Carrick Kildavnet, a 15th-century base of the pirate Grace O'Malley

OUTDOOR ACTIVITIES

Achill Outdoor Activity Centre provides an extensive programme of outdoor activities and water sports, with a strong emphasis on education. It caters for small and large groups, and also provides accommodation (*Cashel-Bunacurry; 098 47253; www.achilloutdoor.com*). **Blackfield Watersports** rents out surfboards, wetsuits and equipment, and offers surfing instruction at all levels (*Keel Beach; 089 422 1553; www.blackfield. com*). For individuals, **Keel's seasonal tourist information office**, by the beach, can provide information on lake water sports as well as scuba diving, pony trekking and sea kayaking (*contact details as for Achill Sound tourist information office, see left*).

EAT AND DRINK

KEEL

Beehive Café *inexpensive*
Informal café-cum-craft shop in Keel. Menu includes home-made soups, sandwiches and seafood. Full licence. *Keel; 086 854 2009; open Feb–Nov*

DOOAGH

Gielty's Bar and Restaurant *moderate*
As the road rises up towards Keem Strand, this is the last opportunity for refreshments. The busy, family-run establishment incorporates a restaurant serving great comfort food, a bar hosting regular traditional music sessions and a coffee shop. *Dooagh; 098 43119; www.gieltys.com*

DOOGORT

The Cottage Coffee Shop *inexpensive*
Just opposite the beach in Doogort, this excellent, family-run café provides inexpensive home cooking. *Doogort; 098 43966; open Easter–Sep*

9 Keem Bay
Achill Island, Co Mayo

After Dooagh the road rises dramatically. At the peak is a lay-by with views of the pincer-shaped beach at Keem Bay, nestling at the foot of the Croaghaun Heights, and across to Achill Head. Descend to the blissfully unspoiled sandy beach – the furthest west you can drive on the island. Bring provisions.

🚗 *Retrace the R319 to Keel. In the village is Minaun View Bar and petrol station. Fork left just before here and then left again. Continue for 3 km (2 miles) to the Deserted Village.*

Above The secluded Golden Strand at Bulls Mouth, between Doogort and Bunacurry

10 The Deserted Village
Achill Island, Co Mayo

This is an eerie village, strung along the southern slopes of the Slievemore Mountain. The Great Famine almost certainly played a part in its abandonment, which was hastened when grants for fishing boats became available at the end of the 19th century, and its villagers were enticed away from the land to the sea.

🚗 *Retrace the route to the bridge and turn left. Keeping the slopes of Slievemore to the left, follow signs to Doogort (4 km/2 miles).*

11 Doogort
Achill Island, Co Mayo

Nestling in the shadow of Slievemore Mountain, the island's highest point, this tiny village overlooks another fine Blue Flag beach. Opposite the Cottage Coffee Shop, the Red Fox Press sells hand-printed books and prints of Achill Island. Seals can be spotted in the waters around the northern tip of Achill, while amethyst is found in the mountains here. From Doogort, follow signs for Bunacurry but turn left for **Bulls Mouth** 3 km (2 miles) before it for a secluded beach. From Bunacurry, the R319 leads back to Achill Sound.

DAY TRIP OPTIONS

For a gentle day laced with books, art and music, spend some time in and around Westport. To make the most of Mayo's beaches, spend a day on Achill Island, starting at Achill Sound.

Culture and conviction
Spend a day exploring the perimeter of island-dotted Clew Bay. Start at Westport ❶, where it is easy to while away a morning browsing in bookshops and galleries. After lunch, drive west for an afternoon hike up Croagh Patrick ❷ for views over the bay. Return to Westport for a drink and a traditional music session.

Follow the drive route from Westport to Croagh Patrick and back again.

Beach life
From Achill Sound ❹, take Atlantic Drive ❺ to the beach at Dooega, carrying on via Minaun Heights ❻ to Keel ❼ and its beach, ending up at Dooagh for drinking and music.

Follow the drive route from Achill Sound, taking the R319 along the spine of the island for a direct route back.

TRIP 20

LEGENDS AND LAKES
Mullaghmore to Lough Key

HIGHLIGHTS

Majestic Ben Bulben
See the majestic mountain that dominates much of the county, changing mood with the weather

Literary landscapes
Trace the places mentioned in the poems of Irish poet W B Yeats, and visit his grave in Drumcliffe

Seaside Sligo
Potter around pretty Mullaghmore, surf the waves at Strandhill, and enjoy a walk and pub lunch at Rosses point

Legendary burial site
Scale the mountain-top burial place at Knocknarea attributed to Celtic warrior Queen Maeve

LEGENDS AND LAKES

County Sligo is an enchanting place to visit, full of stories, poetry and legend. Two dramatic mountains – mighty Ben Bulben and cairn-topped Knocknarea – overlook much of the county, a landscape that inspired the poetry of William Butler Yeats, who spent his childhood here. Sligo Town is an upbeat city, with a small-town friendliness and a lively river front. South of here are the surfing resorts of Strandhill and Enniscrone, also known for their seaweed baths, and the Ox Mountains, where Lough Easkey and Lough Talt offer good trout fishing and walks. For a feel of ancient Ireland, visit the passage tombs at Carrowmore, the largest megalithic burial site in Ireland, or remote Carrowkeel overlooking Lough Arrow.

ACTIVITIES

Imagine the life of a 17th-century colonist at Parke's Castle on the shore of Lough Gill, then take a boat to Yeats' beloved isle of Innisfree

Read the letters and other writings of W B Yeats in Sligo County Library

Relax in a seaweed bath at Enniscrone or Strandhill, perhaps after a round of golf or a surfing lesson

Cast for trout or even salmon in River Ballysadare or Lough Easkey

Pet the equine inmates at a donkey and pony sanctuary at Castlebaldwin or watch a bird-flying display at the Irish Raptor Centre at Ballymote

Above The fishing village of Mullaghmore, a springboard for boat trips to Inishmurray, *see p202*

PLAN YOUR DRIVE

Start/finish: Mullaghmore to Lough Key.

Number of days: 4–5, allowing 1–2 days north of Sligo Town, half a day in the town and 2 days to its south.

Distance: Approx 200 km (125 miles).

Road conditions: The drive includes some unclassified roads, which are narrow and may not have markings. Take care on these roads, especially on bends. You may encounter sheep or other wildlife on rural roads.

When to go: Spring to autumn is best, but it can be wet and windy at any time of year. The winter months, when mountain roads may be impassable, are not as suitable for hill walking and other outdoor activities.

Opening times: Most shops and attractions open 9 or 10am–5 or 6pm. Shops open Mon–Sat; in large towns also 12–6pm on Sun.

Main market days: Sligo Town: Fri, Market Yard, (9am–3.30pm); Farmers' Market, Sat, Institute of Technology, (9am–1pm).

Shopping: Sligo Town has a variety of shops on O'Connell Street, Wine Street and Grattan Street, and The Quayside and Johnston's Court shopping centres.

Major festivals: Sligo Town: Cairde Summer Festival, Jul; Yeats International Summer School, Jul and Aug; Jazz Festival, Jul; Sligo Live, Oct; **Around Carrowkeel Megalithic Cemetery**: Riverstown Vintage Festival, Jun; James Morrison Traditional Music, Riverstown, Aug.

DAY TRIP OPTIONS

Sligo Town makes a good base for day trips to both north and south. **Poetry lovers** might enjoy a trip around **Yeats country**, visiting the places that inspired the poet. To get a feel of **ancient Ireland**, visit the megalithic tombs at Carrowmore and Carrowkeel. For full details, see p209.

Left W B Yeats' grave in the churchyard of St Columba's, Drumcliffe, see p203

WHERE TO STAY AROUND DRUMCLIFFE

Ardtarmon House *inexpensive*
This lovely country house has been in the same family since 1852 and is surrounded by its own wooded grounds and a farm. It is a 500-m (500-yard) walk to a safe swimming beach from the house, which offers four B&B rooms as well as self-catering accommodation in the old outhouses.
Raghly Road, Ballinphull (Take minor road towards Raghly from beside the Yeats Tavern in Drumcliffe and drive for 2 km/1 mile to Carney. Turn left again towards Raghly and drive 4 miles/6 km to Dunleavy's shop. Turn left again towards Raghly for 3 km/ 2 miles until the wooden Ardtarmon House sign with a shamrock symbol among trees on left); 071 916 3156; www.ardtarmon.com; closed for two weeks at Christmas and New Year

Above Lissadell House, once the home of Constance Markeivicz, a leader of the Easter Uprising of 1916

❶ Mullaghmore
Co Sligo
The picturesque fishing village of Mullaghmore is pleasant to visit both for its harbour setting and for moody Classiebawn Castle nearby. Both castle and harbour were built from local stone. In the 20th century, the castle was the residence of British earl Lord Louis Mountbatten – killed when his boat was blown up off the coast in 1979. The headland has stunning views and a sandy beach.

The tiny, mystical island of **Inishmurray** lies offshore 7 km (4 miles) northwest of Streedagh Point. Weather permitting, boat trips to the island run from Mullaghmore pier from March to October *(087 254 0190)*. Founded by St Molaise in the 6th century, Inishmurray was a secluded monastic retreat and has remains including cursing stones, beehive cells and engraved altars. The island is also an important bird and wildlife sanctuary.

🚗 *Take the R279 out of Mullaghmore but follow the Bundoran sign after 1 mile (1.5 km). Go straight across the N15, then straight over a further three*

small crossroads. Turn left at the sign for the Gleniff Horseshoe Drive, 3 miles (5 km) from the N15.

The Legend of Diarmuid and Gráinne
Gráinne, daughter of the High King Cormac Mac Airt, was betrothed to the warrior and leader Fionn Mac Cumhaill, but she fell in love with and eloped with another warrior called Diarmuid. For years they were pursued around the country by Fionn. While the couple were staying in a cave on Ben Bulben Diarmuid was killed by a boar on the slopes of the mountain and Gráinne died of grief. The cave was their last hiding place and they are said to be buried together inside it.

❷ Gleniff Horseshoe
Co Sligo
This circular drive through country roads leads to a magical spot behind **Ben Bulben**, the distinctive mountain that rises abruptly out of the plain. This beautifully austere valley is one of the most peaceful places in the county. The dark mouth of a cave can

Below A thatched cottage between Bundoran and Mullaghmore **Below centre** The Round Tower at Drumcliffe **Below right** The scenic drive around Gleniff Horseshoe be seen high up in the mountainside. According to mythology, this was the last refuge of ill-fated lovers Diarmuid and Gráinne *(see box)*.

🚗 *Follow the drive back to the N15 and turn left onto it, through Mount Temple and Grange. Turn right at a signpost for Carney and follow the road for 3 miles (5 km) to Lissadell village. Follow signs for Lissadell House.*

③ Lissadell House
Ballinfull, Co Sligo

This early 19th-century estate was the childhood home of Constance Markievicz, the first woman to be elected to the British House of Commons and one of the leaders of the Easter Rising of 1916 by Irish republicans. Her friend W B Yeats was a visitor here. The house, which overlooks the ocean, was built in Greek Revival style. Now beautifully restored, it houses an eclectic collection of furnishings and paintings, while the grounds are a delight to wander round *(open mid-Apr–mid-Oct: daily; www.lissadellhouse.com)*.

🚗 *Retrace the route to Carney. Head south to Orchard Grove and continue straight on. Turn right at the N15 for Drumcliffe, then left onto Drum Road.*

④ Drumcliffe
Co Sligo

In St Columba's churchyard in Drumcliffe, below the rocky hulk of Ben Bulben, is the **grave of W B Yeats**, one of Ireland's greatest poets *(see box)*. He was laid to rest here in 1948, nearly 10 years after his death, when his body was moved from the South of France. The poet had asked his wife to "dig me up and plant me in Sligo".

The village also has a **round tower**, damaged by lightning in 1396, and a **High Cross**, remnants of a monastic settlement founded in AD 574.

🚗 *Continue south on the N15, then, in Rathcormac, take the second left and immediately left again. Turn left at the N16, then left again for Glencar Lough. There is a car park on the right, and a path leads to the waterfall.*

⑤ Glencar Lough and Waterfall
Glencar, Co Leitrim

Surrounded by great, sweeping mountains carved out by ancient glaciers, **Glencar Lough** is fed by waterfalls and streams that descend from the slopes behind. These are even more spectacular after heavy rain. In particular, one waterfall sometimes gets blown upwards by the wind, giving the dramatic and unusual appearance that it is actually flowing upwards.

The main **Glencar Waterfall** (50-ft/15-m high) crashes noisily into a rocky pool. "There is a waterfall ... that my childhood counted dear," wrote W B Yeats of Glencar (*Towards the Break of Day*, 1919).

🚗 *Turn right as you exit the car park and left onto the N16. Turn right onto the R286 and follow the signs for Parke's Castle.*

W B Yeats (1865–1939)
Although born in Dublin, Nobel Laureate poet William Butler Yeats spent much of his youth in Co Sligo, forming a deep attachment to the county and calling it "The land of heart's desire". He returned many times and is buried in Drumcliffe churchyard. Sligo locations found in his poetry include Glencar, Innisfree (on Lough Gill), Dromahair (Leitrim), Lissadell House, Coole Park and Ben Bulben. A signposted tour of Yeats Country features many of these. Details are available from the Sligo Town Tourist Information office *(071 916 1201; northwestinfo@failteireland.ie)*.

Above Yeats Country: the landscape that inspired W B Yeats' poetry

EAT AND DRINK

DRUMCLIFFE

Yeats Tavern *inexpensive*
This is a large lively pub with the adjoined Davis's Restaurant offering a variety of seafood as well as poultry and game. It is popular at weekends for roast lunches and weather permitting, you can also dine alfresco.
Drumcliffe (5 minutes' walk from the churchyard, along the N15); 071 916 3117; www.yeatstavernrestaurant.com

AROUND DRUMCLIFFE

Lang's Bar and Restaurant *inexpensive*
As well as offering beautiful views of Ben Bulben, this traditional bar and restaurant incorporates a grocery shop. It is located a mere 10-minute walk from Streedagh Beach.
Grange; 071 916 3105; www.langs.ie; restaurant: closed Tue

Above Glencar Waterfall, one of several waterfalls tumbling into Glencar Lough

Above Parke's Castle, a splendid fortified manor house overlooking Lough Gill

VISITING SLIGO TOWN

Parking
Park in Quay Street car park on Lower Quay Street or in the Quayside Shopping Centre underground car park, which is just opposite.

Tourist Information
Fáilte Ireland Northwest, Old Bank Building, O'Connell Street; 071 916 1201; www.sligotourism.ie; open Mon–Sat 9am–5pm (Nov–Apr: closed Sat)

WHERE TO STAY IN SLIGO TOWN

The Clayton Hotel *moderate*
Large hotel in a historic building with an Elizabethan façade. Houses a leisure centre and spa, as well as a kids' club, making it particularly popular with families. There are also some apartments to rent.
Clarion Road; 071 911 9000; www.claytonhotelsligo.com

The Glasshouse *moderate*
This stunning glass building overlooking the Garavogue River is in an ideal location for exploring the city. Quirky interior in bright colours designed to reflect Sligo's vibrancy.
Swan Point, Hyde Bridge; 071 919 4300; www.theglasshouse.ie

⑥ Parke's Castle and Lough Gill
Co Leitrim
Set on the shore of Lough Gill in spectacular countryside, **Parke's Castle** *(open Apr–Oct)* is a fortified manor house with wide mullioned windows built in 1609 by Captain Robert Parke. The house was built over the site of the original 15th-century castle, home to a prominent local clan, the O'Rourkes (Uí Ruairc). The stones of O'Rourke's tower were used to build the three-storey manor on the eastern side. It has been carefully restored using Irish oak and traditional crafts-manship, and is a fine example of the plantation style of architecture favoured by the 17th-century settlers. Boat trips around **Lough Gill** *(Easter–Oct)* leave from a jetty outside the castle walls.

The lake itself is the location of Yeats' beloved **Isle of Innisfree** – "There midnight's all a glimmer, and noon a purple glow". It is possible to visit the tiny island. There is not much to see, though visitors may, like the poet, "hear lake water lapping with low sounds by the shore".

The bell of Sligo Abbey is said to be at the bottom of Lough Gill. According to legend, it was sunk when the abbey was demolished in 1642. It is said that those pure of heart can still hear it tolling.

🚗 *Continue on the R286 to Sligo. On the way there is a viewing point overlooking Lough Colgagh.*

⑦ Sligo Town
Co Sligo
Although technically a city, Sligo is locally referred to as Sligo Town. A gateway to the northwest, it is an attractive blend of quaint charm and modern verve. Striking new buildings like the Glasshouse sit side by side with characterful older ones such as the Yeats Memorial Building, both overlooking the Garavogue River, a popular focal point whose banks are lined with shops and restaurants. Sligo's main street is O'Connell Street.

A two-hour walking tour
From the Lower Quay Street car park cross to the riverside to see the **Famine Memorial ①**, which commemorates the thousands who died in the Great Famine of 1845. Many others emi-grated from Sligo's quays. Turn left into Quay Street for **City Hall ②**, an

Above Curiosities in one of the cosy pubs on Sligo Town's Rockwood Parade

Italian Renaissance-style building dating from 1865. On the corner is the **Post Office ③** built in 1901 and the traditional shop front of Henry Lyons and Co, a Sligo landmark since 1878.

Across Wine Street, beside Douglas Hyde Bridge, is the **Yeats Memorial Building ④**, erected in 1895 and now home to the Yeats Society and venue for the annual Yeats International Summer School.

Cross five-arched Hyde Bridge into Stephen Street. In front of the Neo-Classical building commissioned for Ulster Bank in 1863 is a **statue of W B Yeats ⑤**. Next door are the **County Library** and **County Museum ⑥** *(both closed Sun and Mon; museum closed lunchtime)*. The museum's Yeats section contains the poet's Nobel Prize medal and letters.

Continue along Stephen Street and into the Mall for **The Model ⑦** *(closed Mon)*, home to the Niland collection and works by Jack B Yeats. Retrace the route

Above Altar by the holy well at Tobernalt on the north shore of Lough Gill

along Stephen Street and turn left onto Bridge Street to cross **New Bridge** ⑧ – built in 1682 – over the river. Turn left down Kennedy Parade and right into Abbey Street for **Sligo Abbey** ⑨ *(open Apr–Oct: daily)* built in 1252, destroyed by fire in 1414 and rebuilt with Gothic and Renaissance carvings and cloisters. It has the only 15th-century high altar to survive in an Irish monastic church.

Pass the sandstone **Court House** ⑩ at the end of Abbey Street, cross over to Castle Street and continue up Grattan Street and John Street to **St John's Cathedral** ⑪ *(closed to visitors)*, where the parents of W B Yeats were married in 1863. Further along John Street is the

Yeats statue, Sligo Town

Cathedral of the Immaculate Conception ⑫ *(open daily)*, built in 1858–95 and noted for its stained glass.

Turn left onto Temple Street for the **Hawk's Well Theatre** ⑬. Take a left down "The Lungy" and Charles Street back to John Street and turn right. Take the first left down O'Connell Street and then first right down Tobergal Lane to riverside **Rockwood Parade** ⑭, a hub of cafés, restaurants and shops. Turn left onto the parade towards Hyde Bridge, left again, then right onto Quay Street to return to the car park.

🚗 *Take the N15 north, signposted Lifford, and first left onto the R291 for Rosses Point, 8 km (5 miles) from Sligo.*

EAT AND DRINK

AROUND PARKE'S CASTLE AND LOUGH GILL
Riverbank Restaurant *moderate*
Rustic-style restaurant in a picturesque location on the banks of the River Bonet in pretty Dromahair, where the chef serves creative cuisine using fresh local ingredients.
Dromahair (from Parke's Castle return towards Manorhamilton but turn right onto the R288, and follow the road south to Dromahair); 071 91 64934; www.riverbankrestaurant.ie; open Fri–Sun eves and Sun lunch

SLIGO TOWN
Fureys *inexpensive*
This is an old-style pub with regular traditional music sessions, right in the heart of Sligo Town.
Bridge Street; 087 943 4744

Bistro Bianconi *moderate*
Informal Italian restaurant that is popular with locals. Large menu, with pizza, pasta, steak and seafood.
Tobergal Lane; 071 914 1744; www.bistrobianconi.ie

Coach Lane *moderate*
Traditional food and a cosy atmosphere in this restaurant above Donaghy's bar. Buffalo wings, seafood, poultry and organic produce feature on the menu. There is a terrace for outdoor eating, weather permitting.
1–2 Lord Edward Street; 071 916 2417; www.coachlanesligo.com

Fiddlers Creek *moderate*
Lively pub with food served in the bar or in the more formal restaurant. Options include spicy chicken wings, grilled steak and tasty seafood bakes.
Rockwood Parade; 071 914 1866

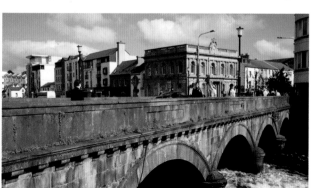

Above Five-arched Douglas Hyde Bridge over the River Garavogue in Sligo Town

Above Fishing at Rosses Point **Above top right** An open fire in the Strand Bar, Strandhill **Above right** Native seaweed, used as a spa treatment at the seaweed baths at Strandhill and Enniscrone

WHERE TO STAY AROUND BALLYSADARE

Castle Dargan *expensive*
Set in a vast, mature landscape, this hotel also has an 18-hole golf course which was designed by former Open champion Darren Clarke and a spa with a hydrotherapy pool and oxygen bar. *From the N4, take the R284 exit and follow signs to Ballygawley. Castle Dargan is on Dromahair Road; 071 911 8080; www.castledargan.com*

⑧ Rosses Point
Co Sligo

After the bustle of Sligo, drive out to the quiet peninsula of Rosses Point, ideal for a relaxing beach walk. The village has pubs and restaurants and at the end of the peninsula there are beaches, sand dunes, an 18-hole links golf course and a yacht club. In the harbour stands the "Metal Man", a giant statue of a sailor, pointing ships safely into the channel for Sligo. **Oyster Island** and **Coney Island** are both visible from here.

🚗 *Retrace the route back into Sligo. Take the R292 at the bus and train station, for Strandhill, about 8 km (5 miles) from Sligo. In Strandhill, park in the seafront car park.*

⑨ Strandhill
Co Sligo

This small seaside resort, overlooked by the brooding Knocknarea Mountain, is a popular surfing destination. The beach is unsafe for swimming (it is prohibited), but the strands are great for leisurely walks in both directions – at low tide it is possible to walk over Dorrin's Strand to **Coney Island**. The village has a surf club, two surf schools and a challenging 18-hole links golf course. It is also home to the **Voya spa**, which specializes in Ireland's only indigenous therapy – seaweed baths *(open daily; book in advance in summer 071 916 8686; www.voyaseaweedbaths.com)*.

🚗 *Leaving Strandhill, keep to the right at the Y-junction at the pink church. There is a sign for Ballysadare and Carrowmore. Continue along the R292 until a left turn signposted for Knocknarea. Park in the car park.*

⑩ Knocknarea
Co Sligo

This enormous cairn atop Knocknarea is 55 m (180 ft) in diameter and 10 m (33 ft) high. According to folklore, it was built as a burial place for the legendary Queen Maeve (Medbh in Irish), an Iron Age queen. She is supposed to have been buried standing up, in full battle uniform. Archaeologists believe the cairn actually dates from around 3000 BC, much earlier than the legend suggests. Maeve's cairn is a 45-minute walk from the car

Above Surfers on the beach at Strandhill, one of Ireland's best beaches for surfing

park. On a clear day there are fine views over Sligo and the surrounding five counties.

🚗 *Return to the R292 and turn left. Continue straight on at the roundabout to Carrowmore. Park in the car park.*

⑪ Carrowmore Megalithic Cemetery
Co Sligo

The largest megalithic burial ground in Ireland, **Carrowmore** is also one of the most significant sites of its kind in Europe. There are in excess of 60 tombs here – a fascinating mixture of small passage-tombs and dolmens (a type of single-chamber tomb enclosed by boulders). Some archaeological research suggests that Carrowmore's oldest tombs are more than 5,000 years old. The visitor centre (*Apr–Oct daily; last admission 5pm*) offers informative guided tours of the cemetery in season.

🚗 *Turn right out of the car park and right again. Return to the R292 and turn left. Turn right onto the N59 and continue straight on into Ballysadare. Park in the centre of the village.*

Above View from Knocknarea, the last resting place of the legendary Queen Maeve

⑫ Ballysadare
Co Sligo

This picturesque village, where the River Ballysadare flows into the sea is a prime location for salmon fishing. W B Yeats spent a lot of time in this area as a child and it is believed to have inspired his poem *Down by the Sally Gardens.*

🚗 *Cross the bridge and turn right onto the N59 for Ballina. Pass a turn for Glen Wood to the left, good for walks and picnics. Continue on the N59 until a signpost for Easkey. Turn right here, onto the R297.*

⑬ Easkey
Co Sligo

The small village of Easkey and the slightly larger seaside resort of **Enniscrone** (also Innishcrone), further around the coast, are set on a beautiful rocky shoreline. The main attraction here is the **surfing** (*see right*) and the Irish Surfing Association is based here. Enniscrone has a sweeping 3-km (2-mile) Blue Flag beach. Other attractions there include Kilcullen's Seaweed Baths (*www.kilcullenseaweedbaths.net*), established in 1912, and proud of its Edwardian ambience, and Enniscrone Golf Course.

🚗 *From Easkey or Enniscrone follow the R297 south towards Newtown. After Newtown turn onto the N59 and continue for Ballina.*

Queen Maeve of Connaught

Maeve (or Medbh), the Celtic warrior Queen of Connaught, was a character in the mythological tale *The Táin*. Although she was powerful, she was jealous of her husband Ailill's white bull. Searching for an equal, she found the Brown Bull of Cooley in Ulster. But its owners refused to lend it to her, so she and her army invaded Ulster and stole it. Legend says that when she got the bull home, it fought and killed her husband's white bull and then died on its way home to Ulster.

Above The River Ballysadare and Lough Easkey are popular with anglers

SURFING AT EASKEY

Easkey Surf Information Centre is based on Main Street and posts daily surf reports on its noticeboard (*096 49428; www.irishsurfing.ie*). Lessons are also available from the **Seventh Wave Surf School** in Easkey and Enniscrone (*087 971 6389; www.surfsligo.com*).

EAT AND DRINK AT STRANDHILL

The Venue *inexpensive–moderate*
A traditional-style pub and a large, friendly restaurant, with everything from shrimp to steaks, make this a popular spot in Strandhill. *Top Road; 071 916 8167; www.venuestrandhill.ie*

The Strand Bar & Restaurant *moderate*
A lively bar, popular with surfers, serves bar meals all day and has live music at weekends. Upstairs, a separate restaurant, the Jade Garden serves Chinese and Thai food in elegant surroundings. A third restaurant, Stoked, occupies the top floor. *Strand Bar: 071 916 8140; www.thestrandbar.ie, Jade Garden: 071 916 8935, Stoked: 071 912 2734*

Above View from Carrowkeel Megalithic Tombs over Lough Arrow

WHERE TO STAY

BALLINA

The Ice House Hotel *moderate*
This stunning boutique hotel overlooks the River Moy and blends country style and contemporary chic. *The Quay; 096 23 500; www.icehouse hotel.ie*

AROUND CARROWKEEL MEGALITHIC CEMETERY

Gyreum Ecolodge *inexpensive*
Set in great surroundings near Lough Arrow and the Bricklieve Mountains, Gyreum has small rooms, large dorms and "tent" capsules in the central hall. *Corlisheen, Riverstown (from Carrowkeel take N4 to Castlebaldwin and turn right, following signs for Bow & Arrow crossroads and through Killadoon crossroads. Take first turn after Killadoon on left (on steep hill) and continue for 1 km (half a mile). Entrance to Gyreum is on the right); 087 328 0789 ; www.gyreum.com*

Coopershill House *expensive*
This beautiful Georgian mansion has been the home of the O'Hara family for seven generations and offers visitors a warm welcome, with open fires, candlelit dinners, acres of lovely grounds and four-poster beds. *Clearly signed 2 km (1 mile) from Riverstown (from Carrowkeel take N4 to Drumfin and take right turn to Riverstown); 071 916 5108; www. coopershill.com; closed Nov–Mar*

⑭ Ballina
Co Mayo
The largest town in the county, Ballina is a charming market town, set on the River Moy. It is famous for its hospitality with plenty of shops and cafés, and good fishing along the river. Among Ballina's attractions are the ruins of **Moyne Abbey** and **Rosserk Friary** dating back to the 15th century, and the impressive **St Muredach's Cathedral** (completed in 1831). Every July the town hosts a popular street festival with many events and live music.

Take the R294 east towards Gleneask and turn right into the car park at Lough Talt.

⑮ Lough Talt
Co Sligo
This magical place is a favourite spot with trout fishermen. There is an easy walk around the shore (6 km/4 miles) and it is also the start for the much longer Sligo Way walk. Lough Talt has two *crannógs* – small man-made islands inhabited in the Iron Age. Continue along the road through the rolling countryside of the Ox Mountains to reach **Lough Easkey**. With its wide open skies and a spare beauty, it is popular with anglers and walkers. A few kilometres (miles) beyond Lough Easkey, at Mass Hill, is the **Shaking Rock**, a massive boulder which can be rocked by hand, but amazingly, has never fallen.

Return to the R294 and continue, signposted Boyle. Carry on into Tobercurry and turn left onto the N17 for Sligo. Then after 14 km (19 miles) turn right and follow the signs for "Eagles Flying".

⑯ Irish Raptor Centre
Portinch, Ballymote
Watch eagles, hawks and falcons swooping overhead at the centre *(071 91 89310; www.eaglesflying.com; open Apr–Oct: daily; closed lunchtime),* which has two daily flying demonstrations and interactive shows about the lives and habits of the various birds of prey. Visitors are allowed to touch some of the birds. There is also a petting zoo with goats, sheep, rabbits, guinea-pigs and donkeys.

Return to the main road, turning left for Ballymote. Crossing the town on the R293, follow signs for Castlebaldwin L1604. After 10 km (6 miles) turn right and follow the signs for Carrowkeel.

⑰ Carrowkeel Megalithic Cemetery
Co Sligo
Overlooking Lough Arrow in the scenic Bricklieve Mountains, the remote cemetery at **Carrowkeel** *(open daily)* dates back to around 3800 BC. The site comprises 14 hill-top passage tombs with an additional six to the west. Excavated in 1911, the tombs, which differ in

Above The 19th-century St Muredach's cathedral, on the banks of the River Moy in the attractive market town of Ballina, seen from one of the town's bridges

Above Ponies enjoy the good life at the Sathya Sai Sanctuary Trust, a charity founded to take care of elderly and abandoned ponies and donkeys

style and size, are particularly good examples of Irish passage tombs. One of them is similar to Newgrange (see p160), except that in Carrowkeel the inner chamber is lit by the sun on the summer solstice (21 June), rather than on the winter solstice as happens at Newgrange.

Children might enjoy a visit to the **Sathya Sai Sanctuary**, a rest home for neglected ponies and donkeys (www.donkeys.ie; 086 103 1932; open Apr–Oct: weekends, other times

Above The entrance to one of the passage tombs at Carrowkeel

phone ahead for appointment). From Carrowkeel, follow the signs for the equine sanctuary a little further down the same road.

🚗 **Leaving the sanctuary, head south on the N4. At the first exit for Boyle, continue on the N4 for approximately 8 km (5 miles). The entrance to Lough Key Forest Park is on the left. Go down the driveway to enter the car park.**

18 Lough Key
Boyle, Co Roscommon
Lough Key Forest Park (park: open daily; visitor centre and attractions: check website; www.loughkey.ie) is one of Ireland's most extensive parks. It comprises some 350 hectares (530 acres) of stunning forest and mixed woodland, with walking trails including a tree canopy walk suspended 9 m (30 ft) above the ground. Among the park's lakes and islands, Trinity Island houses the remains of an ancient abbey. Boats are available for hire, and there are also picnic areas, a lakeside visitor's centre and a well-equipped children's playground.

OUTDOOR ACTIVITIES
Ballina-based **Paddle and Pedal Adventures** offers guided kayaking trips on the River Moy run by one of Ireland's leading kayakers. There are also bikes for hire here (The Quay, Ballina; 087 680 8955; paddle andpedal.ie).

EAT AND DRINK AROUND CARROWKEEL MEGALITHIC CEMETERY

Coopershill House
moderate–expensive
Have a drink by the fire before enjoying a superb gourmet meal served in the elegant, authentic Georgian dining room of this country-house hotel. Clearly signed 2 km (1 mile) from Riverstown; 071 916 5108; www.coopershill.com; closed Nov–Mar

DAY TRIP OPTIONS
Sligo Town is an ideal base for exploring Yeats Country and the ancient cemeteries.

Yeats country
Poetry lovers and romantics could take a trip around the places that inspired W B Yeats. In Sligo Town ❼, pay homage to the poet's statue, and see his Nobel Prize medal

in the County Museum. Drive to Drumcliffe ❹, where the poet is buried. Continue to dramatic Glencar Lough and Waterfall ❺, and return to the town via Lough Gill ❻, where boat trips to Yeats' beloved Isle of Innisfree are available from Parke's Castle jetty.

Take the N15 to Drumcliffe, then follow the drive's instructions to Glencar Lough and Lough Gill.

Ancient Ireland
Drive south to Carrowmore Megalithic Cemetery ⓫ for a guided tour of the passage tombs. Continue south to Carrowkeel Megalithic Cemetery ⓱.

Follow the drive's instructions to Carrowmore. From there, take the R292 to the N3, then N4, and turn off at Castlebaldwin for Carrowkeel.

TRIP 21

DRAMATIC DONEGAL
Newmills to Rossnowlagh

HIGHLIGHTS

Rugged Glenveagh National Park
Spot wild deer and golden eagles and explore mountains, lakes, glens and Glenveagh Castle

Scenic Horn Head
Watch puffins, guillemots and storm petrels, and hike over the headland

The rocky Rosses
Meander through this pretty corner of Donegal, a landscape dotted with lakes and fringed with secluded bays

Old-world Glencolmcille
Time travel to 18th-century rural Donegal in the Folk Village Museum

Breathtaking Slieve League
Brave the sheer drops of Slieve League, some of the highest sea cliffs in Europe

DRAMATIC DONEGAL

A rugged hinterland and dramatic headlands give Donegal a fierce beauty. Cliffs battered by fierce Atlantic storms shelter unspoiled coves and beaches; remote inland valleys harbour wild deer and pairs of golden eagles. But the wild is tempered by the human: Glenveagh Castle has one of Ireland's finest gardens and The Rosses is the birthplace of several of Ireland's leading musicians. Everywhere, there's a warm Irish welcome, especially in the good seafood restaurants and pubs. This coastal drive provides a rich and varied experience, from braving the heights of Slieve League to enjoying simple seaside pleasures in Rossnowlagh on Donegal Bay.

Above The dramatic sea cliffs of Slieve League, *see p220*

ACTIVITIES

Soak in an outdoor hot tub with views of Sheephaven Bay

Explore the hiking trails and beaches of Ards Forest Park

Play a round of golf on the superbly sited Cruit Island Golf Club

Shop for Donegal tweed in the weaving town of Ardara

Tuck into locally caught seafood while looking out over Donegal Bay

Build sandcastles or learn to surf in family-friendly Rossnowlagh

KEY

Drive route

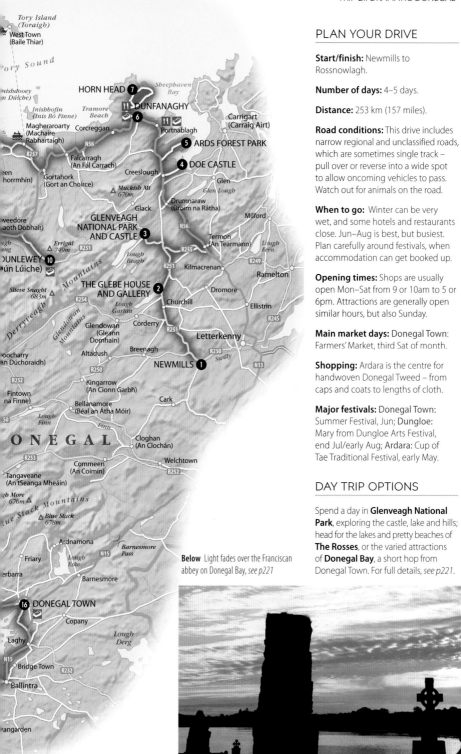

PLAN YOUR DRIVE

Start/finish: Newmills to Rossnowlagh.

Number of days: 4–5 days.

Distance: 253 km (157 miles).

Road conditions: This drive includes narrow regional and unclassified roads, which are sometimes single track – pull over or reverse into a wide spot to allow oncoming vehicles to pass. Watch out for animals on the road.

When to go: Winter can be very wet, and some hotels and restaurants close. Jun–Aug is best, but busiest. Plan carefully around festivals, when accommodation can get booked up.

Opening times: Shops are usually open Mon–Sat from 9 or 10am to 5 or 6pm. Attractions are generally open similar hours, but also Sunday.

Main market days: Donegal Town: Farmers' Market, third Sat of month.

Shopping: Ardara is the centre for handwoven Donegal Tweed – from caps and coats to lengths of cloth.

Major festivals: Donegal Town: Summer Festival, Jun; **Dungloe**: Mary from Dungloe Arts Festival, end Jul/early Aug; **Ardara**: Cup of Tae Traditional Festival, early May.

DAY TRIP OPTIONS

Spend a day in **Glenveagh National Park**, exploring the castle, lake and hills; head for the lakes and pretty beaches of **The Rosses**, or the varied attractions of **Donegal Bay**, a short hop from Donegal Town. For full details, *see p221*.

Below Light fades over the Franciscan abbey on Donegal Bay, *see p221*

Above Doe Castle, overlooking Sheephaven Bay **Above top right** The waterwheel at Newmills Corn and Flax Mills **Above right** Creeslough, on the road to Dunfanaghy

VISITING NEWMILLS

Newmills Corn and Flax Mills are 5 km (3 miles) outside Letterkenny using R250. *Off Churchill Road; 074 912 5155; open mid-May–Sep*

VISITING GLENVEAGH NATIONAL PARK

Glenveagh National Park Visitor Centre
The visitor centre is on the northern end of Lough Veagh, on the R251. A shuttle bus runs to castle and gardens. *Churchill; 076 100 2537; www.glenveagh nationalpark.ie; open daily*

WHERE TO STAY

DUNFANAGHY

Arnolds Hotel *moderate*
Family-run hotel with a restaurant, burger bar and cocktail bar, as well as riding stables offering treks along beaches. *Dunfanaghy; 074 913 6208; www.arnoldshotel.com*

AROUND DUNFANAGHY

Shandon Hotel and Spa *expensive*
Luxury hotel on a hillside overlooking Sheephaven Bay, east of Dunfanaghy (N56 towards Letterkenny and third left for Marble Hill). Sea views from bedrooms and spa, and an outdoor hot-tub. *Marble Hill Strand, Port na Blagh; 074 913 6137; www.shandonhotelspa.com*

① Newmills
Co Donegal

Newmills Corn and Flax Mills, on the banks of the River Swilly, are fine relics of Ireland's industrial heritage, with some parts of the complex dating back 400 years. The corn mill is driven by one of the largest waterwheels in the country, while a smaller wheel powers the machinery for extracting the fibre in flax. There are working models and demonstrations that show how flax is turned into linen cloth.

🚗 *Leaving Newmills, turn left at main road and continue on R250, then on R251 to Churchill. Drive on, passing*

Lough Gartan on the left. Turn left at a sign for Glebe House and Gallery; it is a short distance off the main road.

② The Glebe House and Gallery
Churchill, Co Donegal

Once the home of English-born landscape and society portrait artist Derek Hill (1916–2000), this red-brick Regency-style house *(open Jul & Aug: daily; Jun & Sep–Oct: Sat–Thu)* on the shore of Lough Gartan was built in 1828 as a rectory. Guided tours of the well-preserved interior reveal William Morris wallpapers, Islamic ceramics, paintings by Tory Island artists *(see p217)* and objects collected by Hill over the years – etchings and ceramics by Picasso, and paintings by Renoir, Kokoschka and Jack B Yeats. The adjacent Glebe Gallery stages changing exhibitions.

🚗 *Continue on the R251 to Glenveagh National Park Visitor Centre.*

③ Glenveagh National Park and Castle
Churchhill, Co Donegal

This spectacular national park *(open daily)* covers 16,000 hectares (61 sq. miles) of mountains, lakes, bogs and woodlands, home to red deer and golden eagles – the latter reintroduced to Ireland in 2001.

In the centre of the park is the castellated **Glenveagh Castle**, a 19th- century structure set beside Lough Veagh, while dome-shaped **Mount Errigal** (749 m/2,457 ft), the

Above Moody view of Glenveagh National Park, with Lough Veagh at the centre

Above Errigal Mountain, the highest in Donegal, marks the western end of Glenveagh National Park

highest mountain in Donegal, overlooks the park to the west. The **Visitor Centre** supplies information, maps, and tickets for the shuttle bus to the castle (every 15 minutes) for guided tours of the late-Victorian interior, walks in the gardens – particularly notable for their rhododendrons from March to May – tea rooms, and nature trail leading to a viewpoint over Lough Veagh. It is also possible to walk the 7 km (4 miles) to the castle.

Regular guided walks are offered by park rangers and there are serious walking trails for experienced hikers.

🚗 *Leaving Glenveagh Visitor Centre, turn right onto the R251 and take the second left onto the R255 towards Termon. Turn left at the N56 for Creeslough and Dunfanaghy. In Creeslough, turn right at the sign for Doe Castle, 3 km (2 miles) off the main road.*

❹ Doe Castle
Creeslough, Co Donegal
Sixteenth-century Doe Castle is worth seeing for its lovely setting on a promontory on Sheephaven Bay, with sea on three sides. It was originally the seat of the MacSweeneys, a family of Scottish mercenaries who were outlawed in 1691. The grounds are open daily but the castle itself can only be visited on a guided tour.

🚗 *Drive back along the same road to the N56 and continue north, turning right at the sign for Ards Forest Park. Park in the marked car park.*

The Rock of Doon
A right turn off the R255 to Termon from Glenveagh leads to Garton and the **Rock of Doon** (Carraig a Duin), where chieftains of Donegal's leading clan, the O'Donnells, were inaugurated from 1200 until 1603. A path leads up to the rock from a small car park, next to which is the **Well of Doon**, one of Ireland's many healing wells. Another path leads to the **Mass Rocks**, where Catholics held Mass in secret after the introduction of anti-Catholic penal laws in 1691.

❺ Ards Forest Park
Creeslough, Co Donegal
With woodlands, lakes, rivers, bogs and good sandy beaches, this forest park offers signposted hiking trails, 3–13 km (2–8 miles) in length. Points of interest include megalithic tombs and four Iron Age ring forts.

🚗 *Rejoin the N56 and continue north to Dunfanaghy.*

❻ Dunfanaghy
Co Donegal
The gateway to the Horn Head Peninsula, this attractive holiday resort has a fine 18-hole links golf course. Its other attraction is **The Workhouse** (*open Apr–Oct: daily; Nov–Mar: Mon–Fri*), once the last refuge of the desperate poor and now a heritage centre documenting life in the area during the Great Famine.

🚗 *Follow Horn Head signs out of town for the scenic drive, and park at Horn Head Bridge for walk to Tramore Beach.*

Below Heather-strewn hills around the Rock of Doon, beyond Glenveagh National Park

Above Horn Head and the holiday resort of Dunfanaghy

VISITING HORN HEAD

Parking
As you leave Dunfanaghy for the scenic drive around Horn Head you pass Horn Head Bridge 1 km (half a mile) west of the town, where you can park for the walk to Tramore Beach.

WHERE TO STAY

AROUND HORN HEAD
Corcreggan Mill *inexpensive*
This unique property offers en suite B&B rooms as well as camping and glamping facilities, including bell tents, a railway carriage and a trawler.
Corcreggan, Dunfanaghy; 078 080 3564; www.corcreggan.com

BUNBEG (AN BUN BEAG)
Bunbeg House *inexpensive*
Occupying a wonderful spot down by the tiny harbour, this pleasant guesthouse has cosy rooms, all with water views; in warmer weather breakfast is taken out on the terrace.
Bunbeg; 074 953 1305; www.bunbeghouse.com

❼ Horn Head
Dunfanaghy, Co Donegal

A scenic 13-km (8-mile) drive around Horn Head offers panoramic views of the northwest coast, from the Rosguill Peninsula off to the east to Tory Island and the Bloody Foreland to the west. The lonely, heather-covered headland rises sheer from the sea, its ledges an ideal habitat for guillemots, gulls, puffins and storm petrels. At the tip of the headland, walk to the viewpoint at Faugher for the best views of the 180-m (600-ft) high cliffs, as well as the ruins of a 17th-century signal tower. Afterwards enjoy a walk to Tramore Beach from Horn Head Bridge.

A two-hour walking tour to Tramore Beach

It is possible to walk all the way round Horn Head (13 km/8 miles), but for a shorter walk (8 km/5 miles), concentrate on the area just north of Tramore Beach, the beautiful dune-fringed arc of sand that stretches along the western side of Horn Head.

The beach can be accessed along a public footpath from **Horn Head Bridge** ①. At the far end of the bridge a public footpath runs for nearly 3 km (2 miles) through the sand dunes. **Tramore Beach** ② has rock pools to explore as well as a Celtic **stone circle** ③ on the hill overlooking the beach – to reach it, follow the sheep track north. Don't miss **McSwine's Gun** ④, near the edge of the cliff – a sea cave with a blow hole that noisily spouts water when the northwesterly winds blow. On a calm day it is possible to peer down the blow hole to the sea, about 30 m (100 ft) below (take

extra care around here, especially in inclement weather).

To complete the short walk, retrace the path back to Horn Head Bridge.
🚗 *Continue along the N56 through the Gaeltacht town of Falcarragh, and follow the signs for Bloody Foreland. Keep right on Station Road and turn onto the R257 after Gortahork.*

Above Flock of sheep clustered on a rugged green Donegal hillside

8 Bloody Foreland
Co Donegal

This most northwesterly corner of Ireland is said to have been named for the red glow of its rocks at sunset, though more sinister rumours claim it refers to past battles. Though fairly built up, parts of it remain wild and windswept, and from the north side of the headland there are superb views out to **Tory Island** and back to Horn Head and **Muckish Mountain**. The beaches here attract surfers. As the road turns the corner and heads south to **Bun na Leaca**, there are views to **The Rosses** and **Arranmore Island**.

🚗 *Continue along the R257 south through Derrybeg to Bunbeg.*

9 Bunbeg (An Bun Beag)

Visitors are likely to hear Irish spoken in this long, narrow village, which has views of the sea on one side and towards conical Mount Errigal on the other. On the way through, take a right turn at the brown "*Trá*" (beach) sign and drive to the tiny harbour. Ferries serve Tory Island year round and nearby **Gola Island** in summer.

🚗 *Leaving Bunbeg, take the R258 to Gweedore, then turn left on the N56. At the junction with the R251, fork right, driving alongside Lough Dunlewey. Dunlewey is at the far end of the lake, below Mount Errigal.*

Visiting Tory Island

Ferries to Tory Island, 15 km (9 miles) off Donegal's coast, leave from **Magheroarty** (which has a good crafts shop) on the road to Bloody Foreland, and the village of **Bunbeg**, and take about an hour. The island is famous for its artists, drawn here by the quality of its light since the 1950s, and 6th-century **monastic ruins** with a **round tower**. Bikes can be hired to explore the island and coastal paths offer good walking. The main village is **West Town**.

Above left Craggy rock formations on Tory Island **Above** The hilly lanes around the village of Bunbeg

VISITING TORY ISLAND

The **Tory Ferry** makes the crossing two to three times daily depending upon the season and the weather. *087 199 3710; www.toryferry.com*

EAT AND DRINK

AROUND HORN HEAD

The Mill Restaurant *moderate*
Very popular family-run restaurant on the shores of New Lake on the N56 west of Dunfanaghy, soon after the turning for Horn Head. Serves modern Irish cuisine using fresh, local produce. Also has seven en suite guest rooms. Book well ahead, especially in summer. *Figart, Dunfanaghy, Co Donegal; 074 913 6985; www.themillrestaurant.com; closed Nov–Feb*

BUNBEG (AN BUN BEAG)

Teach Hiudái Beag *inexpensive*
Traditional pub with a folk music session every Monday night; it pulls in some big names. Also hosts smaller Friday night music sessions, plus a lively cabaret on the last Saturday of each month. *Bunbeg; 074 953 1016*

Above Bunbeg's attractive harbour, departure point for ferries to Tory and Gola islands

Above Isolated cottage near Burtonport in The Rosses **Above top right** Grassy landscape around the village of Ardara, the start of the Glengesh Pass **Above right** Low tide exposes the mudflats at The Rosses

VISITING ARRANMORE ISLAND

Ferries make the 15-minute crossing from Burtonport to Arranmore Island several times daily throughout the year.
Arranmore Fast Ferry; (087) 317 1810; www.arranmorefastferry.com

WHERE TO STAY

DUNLEWEY

Errigal Youth Hostel *inexpensive*
This hostel enjoys a spectacular location at the foot of Mount Errigal in Dunlewey. It's an ideal base for exploring Glenveagh National Park or Mount Errigal itself.
Dunlewey; 074 953 1180; www. anoige.ie; open Mar–Sep

THE ROSSES

Donegal Thatched Cottages *inexpensive–moderate*
A selection of attractive cottages on Cruit Island, set in the midst of some of the most breathtaking scenery in Donegal.
Cruit Island, Kincasslagh; 087 236 4963; www.donegalthatchedcottages.com

⑩ Dunlewey (Dún Lúiche)
Dunlewey, Co Donegal
The 30-m (100-ft) high round tower of the Church of the Sacred Heart – a 19th-century take on early Christian forms – signals the approach to Dunlewey, set on the shores of Lough Dunlewey under Donegal's highest mountain, Mount Errigal. The various attractions of **Dunlewey Lakeside Centre** (Ionad Cois Locha), *(open Apr–Oct daily)* include a recreated 19th-century weaver's cottage, a farm with animals to pet, and boat trips on the lake. There is also a crafts shop, which sells Donegal Tweed.

🚗 *Drive back to Gweedore, but carry on along the N56 to Crolly, then turn right onto the R259 to Annagry (signposted Donegal Airport).*

⑪ The Rosses (Na Rosa)
Co Donegal
This Irish-speaking region is a pretty, hilly corner of Donegal, with a hinterland full of small lake-filled valleys and a jagged coast with sandy coves. Almost every brown sign for a *Trá* (beach) leads to an idyllic stretch of sand, very often deserted. Many well-known musicians have roots in the area, including the popular Irish music group Clannad and the singer Enya.

The famous Irish country singer Daniel O'Donnell is from the small village of **Kincasslagh** (Cionn Caslach). From the village, follow the signs for the airport and head for the car park behind the airport; from here a short walk leads to a lovely beach backed by dunes.

Just offshore, joined to the mainland by bridge, is scenic **Cruit Island** (An Chruit), which has one of the most scenic links golf courses in the country. To get to the island, turn right just after Kincasslagh's Viking House Hotel. Drive to the end of the island to take in the outstanding views on all sides.

Ferries for nearby **Arranmore Island** (Árainn Mhór), a large, populated island, leave from **Burtonport** (Ailt an Chorráin), a small fishing port

Above The spectacular Glengesh Pass between Glengesh Hill and Common Mountain

which was once one of the most important ports in the country and has a couple of excellent seafood restaurants. **Dungloe** (An Clochán Liath), the last stop on the peninsula, is the main town of The Rosses. It has a seasonal tourist office (in the converted church at the top of the village) and is a good place to stock up on provisions. For 10 days every year at the end of July the Mary From Dungloe Festival takes place, a busy programme of music, parades and children's activities culminating in a beauty pageant to elect the new "Mary from Dungloe" from young contenders representing the counties of Ireland.

🚗 *Drive straight through Dungloe but instead of turning left with the main road at the top of the hill, keep straight, leaving the church on your left. The road will become narrower and bumpier, but the drive is worth it for the scenery. After rejoining the N56, turn right for a detour to the beach at Dooey Point, then rejoin the N56 and travel south to Ardara.*

Above Handloom weaver at work on a traditional loom in Ardara

12 Ardara
Co Donegal

Ardara is an attractive, hilly village and a good place to buy hand-woven tweeds, handknits or crafts, with long-established names such as Kennedy of Ardara, John Molloy, Campbells and Trióna Design for sale. See the weavers' looms in action in some of the larger shops or visit the **Ardara Heritage Centre** *(open Easter–Sep)* on the main street, to learn about the history of the tweed industry in Donegal since the 1900s, from sheep shearing to spinning and weaving.

The drive from Ardara to Glencolmcille west of the town passes through the spectacular **Glengesh Pass**, a steep mountain road winding between Glengesh Hill and Common Mountain, with viewpoints along the way.

🚗 *Leaving Ardara take the N56 to Donegal and then turn right onto the R230 for Glencolmcille through the Glengesh Pass. In Glencolmcille drive straight through the village to An Cláchan, the Folk Village Museum. There is a car park at the museum.*

13 Glencolmcille (Gleann Cholm Cille)
Co Donegal

One of the most westerly points of Donegal, on a peninsula reaching far into the Atlantic, the quiet village of Glencolmcille has a remote feel. The area, named after St Columba (Colm Cille) was hit hard by emigration after the 1950s. The **Folk Village Museum** (An Cláchan) *(open Easter–Oct)* recaptures life in rural Donegal through the centuries, with three cottages representing the 1700s, 1800s and 1900s. The village is also the base of Oideas Gael, a respected provider of courses in Irish language and culture.

🚗 *From Glencolmcille take the L1025 to Carrick (11 km/7 miles). Follow signs for Bunglas and Slieve League, turning right at Carrick for Teelin. In Teelin, turn right just before the school. Proceed to the first car park and then walk the 2 km (1 mile) to the cliffs (if feeling brave – the road ahead is rough with no barriers and sheer drops – drive on to the top car park).*

Above Gweebarra Bay, on the scenic coastal road from Dungloe in The Rosses to Ardara

SHOPPING IN ARDARA

The factory shop of **John Molloy** *(07495 41133; www.johnmolloy.com)* sells hand-knitted Aran fisherman's jumpers, contemporary knitwear designs and classic Donegal tweeds, including traditional caps. **Trióna Design** *(07495 41422; www triona design.com)*, based in the old Mart building, which used to house one of Donegal's original tweed makers, was reopened by the Mulhern family in the 1980s and now makes stylish handwoven tweed coats and suits.

EAT AND DRINK AROUND THE ROSSES

Danny Minnie's *moderate*
This family-run restaurant in Annagry, The Rosses, serves modern cuisine, with seafood a speciality. Log fires, tapestries and antiques create a cosy atmosphere. Also has a small number of en suite guest rooms.
Annagry, Co Donegal; 074 954 8201; www.dannyminnies.ie; closed Sun

The Lobster Pot *moderate*
Seafood is a speciality of this pub and restaurant near the pier in Burtonport, with lobster a particular favourite. Open fires and a warm welcome characterise this friendly spot.
Burtonport, Co Donegal; 074 954 2012; www.lobsterpot.ie

Above Killybegs' busy fishing harbour Above centre Stone-fronted pub in Donegal Town Above right Rossnowlagh's wide sandy beach, popular with families and surfers

VISITING DONEGAL TOWN

Parking
Park on the street near the castle.

Tourist Information
The Quay, Donegal Town; 074 972 1148; www.govisitdonegal.com; open Mon–Sat

WHERE TO STAY

AROUND KILLYBEGS

Castle Murray House Hotel *moderate*
This hotel is situated on a narrow headland jutting into McSwynes Bay, 8 km (5 miles) east of Killybegs. The rooms here are superbly appointed and all have spectacular views over the bay and the hills. A romantic treat.
St John's Point, Dunkineely; 074 973 7022; www.castlemurray.com

AROUND DONEGAL TOWN

Harvey's Point *expensive*
A country hotel on the shores of Lough Eske, this is a peaceful haven a few kilometres north of Donegal Town. Rooms are huge and luxurious, with king-size beds and Italian marble bathrooms.
Lough Eske, Donegal Town; 074 972 2208; www.harveyspoint.com

ROSSNOWLAGH

The Sandhouse Hotel *expensive*
Imposing hotel on the waterfront. Watch the sunset from the deck, fall asleep to the gentle sounds of the Atlantic rolling, and in the morning take in sea views from the hotel's drawing room or outdoor terrace.
Rossnowlagh, 071 985 1777; www.sandhouse.ie

⑭ Slieve League (Sliabh Liag)
Bunglas; Co Donegal
At 600 m (2,000 ft) high, the cliffs at Slieve League are among the highest sea cliffs in Europe. It is possible to walk to their summit, but the walking trail, One Man's Pass, has several narrow ledges and sheer drops and is only suitable for extremely experienced hikers. The full 4½-hour walk has far-reaching views, including to the beautiful crescent-shaped strand at Malin Beg. Perhaps the best way to view the cliffs is to take a boat trip, departing from Teelin pier.
🚗 *Rejoin the R263 and follow signs for Killybegs and Donegal Town.*

⑮ Killybegs
Co Donegal
A major fishing port, Killybegs harbour is always packed with trawlers. It is also home to the **Carpet Making and Fishing Centre** *(open Mon–Fri)*, which tells the story of the area's history. The centre has the longest hand-knitting loom in the world. There are

demonstrations of the town's hand-knotted carpet industry, famous since Donegal Carpets was established in Killybegs in 1898. The company's carpets grace some of the world's finest houses, from Dublin Castle to the White House.
🚗 *Continue on the R263 and turn right onto the N56 to Donegal Town and park on the street near the castle in the centre.*

⑯ Donegal Town
Co Donegal
The county town of Donegal is a good base for exploring the southern part of the county. Its name means "Fort of the Foreigners", possibly after the Vikings, who built a garrison here in the 9th century.
    Its main sight is **Donegal Castle** *(Easter–mid-Sep: daily; mid-Sep–early Apr: Thur–Mon)*, built on a loop in the River Eske in the town centre. Restored in the 1990s, it was originally the seat of the O'Donnell clan, rulers of Donegal until 1607

Above The soaring cliffs of Slieve League, among the highest in Europe when they fled Ireland for Spain in the misguided hope of rallying Catholic support against the English. The castle was granted to Sir Basil Brooke, an English captain, who remodelled it in the Jacobean style, retaining the original tower. Guided tours of the castle reveal interiors representative of these two eras.

Brooke also laid out the town's market square, known as the **Diamond**. An obelisk in the centre commemorates four Franciscan monks from Donegal Abbey who wrote the *Annals of the Four Masters* (1630s), a history of Gaelic people from 40 days before the Great Flood until the end of the 16th century. The ruins of the **Franciscan Abbey** (1474) – a few cloister arches and Gothic windows – lie on the mouth of the River Eske.

🚗 *From Donegal Town, follow the signs for Sligo, turning right onto the N15. At Ballintra, turn right onto the R231 for Rossnowlagh.*

Above Lake in the craggy, boulder-strewn mountains around Slieve League

Lough Derg

Thirty-three kilometres (20 miles) southeast of Donegal, Lough Derg is the site of an annual pilgrimage known as St Patrick's Purgatory, marking the 40 days St Patrick spent in prayer here, trying to rid Ireland of evil spirits. Between June and August thousands of pilgrims descend on **Station Island** for a three-day fast and 24-hour vigil. Only pilgrims can attend, but it is atmospheric to go to the jetty and view the basilica from the shore. There is also an exhibition in the **visitor centre** on the lakeshore.

⓱ Rossnowlagh
Co Donegal

The main attraction here is the long sandy beach. There is a surf school and a surf club, and the gently sloping beach offers suitable conditions for beginners, as well as good swimming. Another attraction is the **Sandhouse Hotel** on the seafront. Dating from the 1830s, it is a nice spot for afternoon tea.

🚗 *Return via the R231 to the main N15 to Sligo.*

Above Teelin Bay, departure point for boat trips around Slieve League

SHOPPING IN KILLYBEGS

Donegal Carpets, inside the Carpet Making and Fishing Centre *(074 974 1944; www.visitkillybegs.com)*, produces world-famous hand-knotted rugs, many of which grace stately homes across the world. There is also a crafts shop at the centre.

EAT AND DRINK

ROSSNOWLAGH

Smugglers Creek *moderate*
Tuck into bar food or dine at the restaurant at this cosy pub near Rossnowlagh. Accommodation is also available. *Rossnowlagh; 071 985 2367; www.smugglerscreekinn.com*

AROUND ROSSNOWLAGH

Creevy Pier Hotel *moderate*
Remote location 5 km (3 miles) south of Rossnowlagh on the R231, with superb views of Donegal Bay. Seafood is a speciality and you can either dine in the restaurant or eat in the bar. *Kildoney Glebe, Ballyshannon; 071 985 8355; www.creevypierhotel.com*

DAY TRIP OPTIONS

If time is short, three places are relatively easy to access – Glenveagh National Park, The Rosses and Donegal Bay.

Outdoor activities

Glenveagh National Park ❸ runs a wide programme of free events and activities, including ranger-led walks through the park. *For information about events, contact 074 913 7090; www.glenveaghnationalpark.ie.* The gardens at Glenveagh Castle within the park are known for their rhododendrons and walled garden.

Get there on the N56, turning off onto the R255 before Termon.

Rocky coasts and Irish music

A Gaeltacht area, The Rosses ⓫ is one of the loveliest corners of Ireland, with a rocky coast enclosing sandy bays, easily accessed islands such as Aran and Cruit, and a hinterland with many lake-filled valleys. It also has a strong musical tradition, evident in its pubs, and good seafood restaurants.

Access The Rosses on the N56, turning onto the R259 at Crolly.

Clifftop walks and winter woollies

Starting from Donegal, head to the western end of the peninsula for the towering cliffs at Slieve League ⓮, stopping at Killybegs ⓯ for a walk around its busy harbour and to shop for hand knits and tweeds. Returning to Donegal, stop for dinner at Castle Murray Hotel on St John's Point, a slender finger of land with lovely views on all sides.

Donegal is quickly accessed on the N15. From there, the N56 links up with the R263 to Slieve League.

TRIP 22

THE FANAD PENINSULA

Ramelton to Rosguill Peninsula

HIGHLIGHTS

Historic departure

Learn about the Flight of the Earls,
a landmark in Irish history, at the old battery fort
in Rathmullan

Sweeping bays

Discover some of northwest Ireland's loveliest bays, such
as Warden Beach and Tranarossan

Georgian lighthouse

Visit Fanad Head, one of Ireland's most northerly points,
for stirring Atlantic views and its lighthouse

Scenic Atlantic Drive

Take a memorable cliffside drive around the
Rossguill Peninsula

THE FANAD PENINSULA

The Fanad (Fanaid) Peninsula and neighbouring Rosguill Peninsula feature some of Ireland's finest seascapes. Magnificent golden beaches are backed by a mix of rolling farmland and heathland, threaded by empty roads affording panoramic views over Lough Swilly and Sheephaven Bay. A series of rocky headlands culminate in Fanad Head itself, a dramatic spot topped by a whitewashed lighthouse. Stride or ride along near-deserted beaches, explore heather-lined coastal paths, enjoy fishing, golf or watersports in Rathmullan or Portsalon, or simply sit on the sands or eat locally caught seafood in the pretty resort towns that dot the coast.

Above The Flight of the Earls Visitors Centre, Rathmullan, see p226

ACTIVITIES

Gallop along the shores of Lough Swilly at Rathmullan Strand

Jump on a ferry to Buncrana, a 10-minute trip across Lough Swilly from Rathmullan

Take a walk on the golden sands of Warden Beach

Spin for mackerel off a pier, wrestle with a bluefin tuna, or learn to fly-fish for rainbow trout at Portsalon or Downings

Paddle a kayak or hire a pedalo from Portsalon Pier

Get into the swing at Portsalon Golf Club or Rosapenna's spectacularly sited 18-hole links courses

KEY

Drive route

Above Boats in the bay just off the pier at Portsalon, *see p228*

PLAN YOUR DRIVE

Start/finish: Ramelton to Rosguill Peninsula.

Number of days: 2 days.

Distance: 116 km (72 miles).

Road conditions: Some regional roads are narrow, and some unclassified roads have no central dividing line, so it is often necessary to slow down when approaching oncoming traffic. On minor roads, watch out for sheep and wildlife.

When to go: The north west of Ireland can be harsh in winter with cold Atlantic winds, so spring to autumn are the best times to visit. Be prepared for rain at any time of year. Plan carefully around festivals, when accommodation can be hard to find.

Opening times: Most shops and attractions are open from 9 or 10am to 5 or 6pm. Shops are usually open Mon–Sat. In large towns and shopping centres, shops usually stay open late one night on Thu or Fri and open from 12 to 6pm on Sundays. In most villages there are small convenience stores which open from 7 or 8am until late.

Main market days: Ramelton: country market (Town Hall), Sat.

Major festivals: Rathmullan: Community Festival, Jul/Aug; Eargail Arts Festival (throughout Donegal), Jul; **Rosguill Peninsula:** Downings, Jul/Aug.

DAY TRIP OPTIONS

Families will enjoy a leisurely day in Rathmullan, trying out the **watersports**, **golf courses** and **horse riding**, just sitting on the **beautiful beach**, or perhaps taking the **ferry to Buncrana** for a change of scene. Alternatively, focus on the Atlantic Drive, a **thrilling ride** round the Rosguill Peninsula with **dramatic views** on all sides. For full details, *see p229*.

Above The gentle waves at Portsalon Beach, Lough Swilly, *see p228*

1 Ramelton
Co Donegal

Set on the banks of the River Leannan, this pretty heritage town was once a prosperous trading port and linen market. Georgian townhouses and cottages line the streets and stone mills and 19th-century warehouses with red doors create an attractive quayside. The arrival of the railway in Letterkenny led to Ramelton's decline in the 19th century. Rugby Union aficionados might be interested to know that the famous player Dave Gallaher, captain of New Zealand's All Blacks from 1903 to 1906, was born here.

🚗 *From Ramelton, take the R247 to Rathmullan. Turn right at Pier Road and park in the car park by the pier.*

Above and **above top right** The old mill buildings and warehouses lining Ramelton's quay **Above right** Brightly painted houses in the seaside resort of Rathmullan

VISITING RATHMULLAN

Ferry to Buncrana
In summer (Jul–Sep), a car ferry operates seven to eight times a day between Rathmullan and Buncrana on the Inishowen Peninsula. The crossing takes about 20 minutes. *Rathmullan; 087 211 2331; www.swillyferry.com*

WHERE TO STAY IN RATHMULLAN

Rathmullan House *expensive*
Luxury country house hotel on Lough Swilly, with direct access to the beach. Facilities include tennis courts, a spa with a long list of pampering treatments, a heated indoor pool, log fires in winter, and an excellent restaurant, which uses produce from its own walled garden. *Lough Swilly; 074 915 8188; www.rathmullanhouse.com*

2 RATHMULLAN
Co Donegal

This seaside resort on the shores of Lough Swilly has a magnificent setting, with sweeping views across the lough to Inch Island and Buncrana on the Inishowen Peninsula. It has a pier with a marina and a long sandy beach, backed by trees. The resort offers angling, sailing, kayaking, kite-surfing, pony trekking and a 9-hole golf course. This circular walk combines historical interest, fine views, a ruined friary and an invigorating stretch along the beach.

A three-hour walking tour

From the car park by the pier, walk to the **Flight of the Earls Visitor Centre** ① *(open Jun–Sep: daily; Easter–Jun: weekends only)* in the old battery fort (1810). It was from this spot that the earls of Tyrone and Tyrconnell and some 90 supporters fled to France in 1607 with the aim of proceeding to Spain to rally support for the overthrow of the English in Ireland. Their failure led to the confiscation of great tracts of Irish land by the British Crown and the Plantation of Ulster – colonization by English and Scots. The visitor centre tells the story of the earls and the events that followed, an important episode in Irish history, which effectively ended its old aristocracy.

Turn north along the beach (with the sea on the right), for a lovely walk along Rathmullan Strand past the rocky outcrop of **Kinnegar Head** ② and carry on along Kinnegar Strand to the end of the beach, where a stream flows under a bridge. Cross

Right the lush green headlands of fjord-like Lough Swilly

Above Horse riders on Rathmullan Strand, with the Inishowen Peninsula beyond

HORSE RIDING IN RATHMULLAN

Golden Sands Equestrian Centre
Specializes in beach rides. Half or full-day outings with picnic included, as well as rides by the hour.
Rathmullan; 074 915 8124

EAT AND DRINK IN RATHMULLAN

Belle's Kitchen *inexpensive*
Superb modern restaurant offering a top-drawer menu featuring dishes such as peppered steak baguette and Donegal crab linguini, alongside good old-fashioned fish 'n' chips; breakfast served until noon.
Pier Road; 074 915 8800; www. rathmullanrestaurants.com; closed Wed

The Tap Room *inexpensive*
This terrific little cellar bar, down in the original basement kitchens of Rathmullan House, offers a winning combination of wood-fired pizzas and craft beers.
Rathmullan House, Lough Swilly; 074 915 8188; www.rathmullanhouse.com

Killygarvan Bridge and turn left. To shorten the walk, return along the road to Rathmullan, through pretty copses, to the friary. For the hardy, continue up Glen Road, a long, steep climb with spectacular views of Lough Swilly. The land on the left is known as The Flats. The route passes between an abandoned **lime kiln and lime quarry** ③, once used to make whitewash for the cottages and farmhouses of the area. Turn left at Glencross, just after the farmhouse, and walk through Carnafeagh, turning sharp right at the top of the hill. Look out for a **Standing Stone** ④ on the right. At the T-junction, turn left down the Red Brae, back to Rathmullan. The route passes the ruins of a 15th-century **Carmelite Friary** ⑤, with a church that was converted to a bishop's private residence in the 17th century. Follow the road along the seafront and back to the pier. In summer, there is a car ferry to Buncrana *(see left)*, an attractive resort, with two castles and sandy beaches, on Inishowen Peninsula.
🚗 *From Rathmullan, head north on the R247 towards Portsalon. This becomes the R268, signposted Fanad Drive.*

③ Ballymastocker Bay
Co Donegal
North of Rathmullan, the Fanad Drive coast road becomes progressively more scenic as stunning views across Lough Swilly unfold. A series of viewing points along the way offer opportunities to stop and take in the

glorious panorama. Just after the road starts climbing, look down to the right. The circular cages in the water below are used to farm salmon, an important (though sometimes controversial) industry on Lough Swilly.

A little further on, the slopes of **Knockalla Mountain** rise to the left. 5 kilometres (3 miles) before Portsalon, the road rounds on a view over **Ballymastocker Bay** and its golden strand, **Warden Beach**, one of the best beaches in Ireland. The winding drive down to the bay is one of the prettiest in Donegal.
🚗 *Continue north along the R268/ Fanad Drive to Portsalon.*

Above Spectacular view from the slopes of Knockalla Mountain

Above Winding country road on the hillside near Portsalon **Above centre** A typical thatched cottage on the roadside near Portsalon **Above right** Portsalon's long, wave-washed Stocker Strand

HORSE RIDING ON ROSGUILL PENINSULA

Carrigart Riding Stables
Pony trekking on the beach.
Carrigart; 074 915 3583; info@carrigart horseridingcentre.ie; open Easter–Nov

WHERE TO STAY

FANAD HEAD (CIONN FHANADA)

Rockhill Holiday Park *inexpensive*
Log cabins and mobile homes to rent in Kerrykeel, between Milford and Fanad Head. Offers children's activities including arts, crafts and cookery classes, as well as go-kart racing, watersports, climbing, tennis and football, and organizes children's day trips and summer camps. On the R246 on the outskirts of Kerrykeel.
Kerrykeel; 074 915 0012; www.rockhill.ie

ROSGUILL PENINSULA

Tra na Rosann Hostel *inexpensive*
Hostel set in pretty countryside with views of the coast and Tory island. Near several quiet beaches and Tranarossan Bay.
Downings; 074 915 5374; www. anoige.ie; open Jun–Aug

Downings Bay Hotel *moderate*
This three-star hotel overlooks the bay and is a good base for exploring the area. It also has a leisure centre with an indoor pool 1 km (half a mile) down the road.
Downings; 074 915 5586; www. downingsbayhotel.com

Rosapenna Hotel and Golf Resort *moderate*
Four-star hotel on Sheephaven Bay with three superb links golf courses, a leisure centre and a pool.
Downings; 074 915 5301; www. rosapenna.ie; open Apr–Oct

④ Portsalon
Co Donegal

This tiny seaside resort on the east side of Fanad Head is a hive of activity in summer, with kayaks, sailing boats and pedalos bobbing in the water, and children building sandcastles on the strand. The action centres on **Portsalon Pier** (take a right turn in the village), where a small watersports shop hires out wet suits, kayaks and diving equipment, charters boats and runs boat trips around the bay. Anglers can spin for mackerel from the pier; high tide or night-time are best. Just along the coast, **Portsalon Golf Club**, an 18-hole links course established in 1891, has an outstanding setting with panoramic views.

🚗 *Take the coast road out of Portsalon, passing through Doagh Beg and on to Fanad Head. At Fanad Head, turn right along the road to Fanad lighthouse (1 km/half a mile). Park on right at lighthouse gates.*

The Gaeltacht
Fanad Head is in the Donegal "Gaeltacht", the name given to the Irish-speaking areas of Ireland. Until the 16th century Irish was the main language of Ireland, but under British rule English was enforced and Irish was outlawed. Today, some 75 per cent of people in the Gaeltacht speak Irish. Children are taught Irish in schools, and road signs are in Irish; cultural traditions are also preserved. The Donegal Gaeltacht is one of the largest in the country, stretching almost unbroken along the coast from Fanad Head to Slieve League.

⑤ Fanad Head (Cionn Fhanada)
Co Donegal

Piled on a rocky outcrop at the tip of Fanad Head, **Fanad Lighthouse** (now self-catering accommodation) is an attractive ensemble of whitewashed buildings clustered around a classic

Above The picturesque 19th-century lighthouse atop a rocky outcrop at Fanad Head

lighthouse tower. It was built in 1818, in response to the tragic sinking of the *Saldana* in Lough Swilly – it is said that all lives were lost save that of the ship's parrot, whose silver collar bearing the ship's name identified the vessel. The view from the grounds of the lighthouse takes in Tory island to the west and Dunaff Head to the east.

Leaving the lighthouse, take the main road back through Fanad Head. Instead of following the R247 to Kerrykeel follow the coast road around **Ballyhiernan Bay**, where there's a picnic area, south to **Milltown** and back. This detour is a lovely drive with views over **Mulroy Bay** and across to the **Rosguill Peninsula**.
🚗 *Take the R246 to Kerrykeel (An Cheathru Chaol). Continue to Milford and turn right onto R245 for Carrigart.*

Above The treacherous rocks of Fanad Head, one of Ireland's most northerly headlands

6 Rosguill Peninsula
Co Donegal
Known as the Atlantic Drive, the road around Rosguill Peninsula, from Mulroy Bay to Sheephaven Bay, is an exhilarating route, with outstanding views of rocky headlands and white sandy bays around every hairpin

bend. The 11-km (7-mile) drive starts in **Carrigart** (Carraig Airt), a Victorian village that once formed part of the estate of the Earls of Leitrim. The gateway to the Rosguill Peninsula, it benefits from tourism in summer. Behind the main street, Strand Park looks over the dune-backed shoreline. Take the R246 out of Carrigart. After 6 km (4 miles), there is a stunning view over **Tranarossan Bay**, a perfect arc of fine white sand.

Follow the road round to **Rosapenna**, which has a long beach, two 18-hole links golf courses – the Old Tom Morris course dating from 1891 and Sandy Hills, a challenging modern links – and on to **Downings** (Na Dúnaibh) in Sheephaven Bay. In autumn, Downings is the launching point for game fishing charters in search of giant bluefin tuna.

From Downings, follow the road around the peninsula through a wild and stony landscape. The road is narrow and bumpy in places, but this is the most thrilling part of the drive, a succession of scenic inlets and dramatic seascapes. On the run back to Carrigart, there's a great viewpoint at **Clontallagh** (Cluain tSalach).

Above Rolling farmland and heathland on the Fanad Peninsula

FISHING ON FANAD HEAD AND ROSGUILL PENINSULA

Central Fisheries Board
For information on sea angling, including big game fishing off Downings, contact the Central Fisheries Board. Its website lists charter boats and skippers in the area. *01 884 2600; www.fisheriesireland.ie*

EAT AND DRINK AROUND FANAD HEAD (CIONN FHANADA)

Ripples Restaurant *moderate*
Overlooking Mulroy Bay, at the entrance to Kerrykeel village, this family-friendly restaurant offers steaks, duck, fish and chips, and much more. *Kerrykeel; 074 915 0110; www. ripplesrestaurant.com*

DAY TRIP OPTIONS
Seaside Rathmullan, is a lovely base for outdoor activities or following the Atlantic Drive around Rossguill Peninsula.

Historic Rathmullan
Make the most of the great beach and outdoor activities at Rathmullan 2 for an ideal day trip. Visit the

Flight of the Earls Visitor Centre, play golf or enjoy a walk in the surrounding area. In summer, take the Lough Swilly Ferry from the pier to Buncrana on the Inishowen Peninsula, a 10-minute hop.

Rathmullan is 20 km (12 miles) from Letterkenny, which links with the N56 and N14. See p226 for details of ferries to Buncrana.

The Atlantic drive
For dramatic seascapes and unspoiled beaches, drive around the Rossguill Peninsula 7. Don't miss Tranarossan Bay, one of Ireland's best beaches.

From the N56, take the R245 to Carrigart (15 km/9 miles), the start of the drive.

TRIP 23

CLASSIC NORTHERN IRELAND

Carrickfergus to Lough Neagh

HIGHLIGHTS

Bushy glens
Drive through some of the nine forested Glens of Antrim

Geological marvel
Explore the dramatic and mythic splendour of the
Giant's Causeway

Spectacular views
Enjoy panoramic seascapes from the heights of Bishop's
Drive Road

Romantic castle
See the breathtaking clifftop ruins of Dunluce Castle

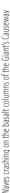

Waves crashing on the basalt columns of the Giant's Causeway

CLASSIC NORTHERN IRELAND

A drive along the Causeway Coast and through the Glens of Antrim takes in spectacular scenery, from dramatic coastal cliffs and unspoiled beaches and bays to romantic glens, hillside waterfalls and forest parks. This tour begins just north of Belfast and follows a dramatic and breathtaking coastal route dotted with pretty villages, historic castles and stunning natural wonders to discover, including the Giant's Causeway, a place steeped in myth and legend. At the southern end it turns inland through the lovely Sperrin Mountains to reach tranquil Lough Neagh, at the heart of Northern Ireland.

ACTIVITIES

Take a walk high above the sea across the Carrick-a-Rede rope bridge

Sample Irish whiskey and learn the secrets of how it is made, at the Old Bushmills Distillery

Stroll through centuries of history along the walls of Derry

Take a boat trip on the calm waters of lovely Lough Neagh

Above Far-reaching views and sheer cliffs add drama to the coastline around the Giant's Causeway, Co Antrim, *see p238*

0 kilometres 10

0 miles 10

KEY

Drive route

PLAN YOUR DRIVE

Start/finish: Carrickfergus to Lough Neagh.

Number of days: 5, allowing half a day at the Giant's Causeway.

Distance: Approx. 340 km (210 miles).

Road conditions: Roads are generally in good condition, although some mountain and glen roads may be impassable in winter.

When to go: Spring, summer and autumn offer the best weather, and most visitor attractions are open. The weather is always changeable, so be prepared for rain at any time of year.

Opening times: Most shops and attractions open 9 or 10am–5 or 6pm. Shops open Mon–Sat; in large towns also 12–6pm on Sun. Convenience stores in villages open 8am until late.

Main market days: Coleraine: second Sat of month; Limavady: Fri; Derry: first Sat of month; Dungannon: first Sat of month; Strabane: last Fri of month.

Shopping: Coleraine's Causeway Speciality Market (see above) is a vibrant gathering of artists and craftspeople, while Derry has shops selling traditional Irish linen, crystal and tweeds.

Main festivals: Waterfoot (Glenariff): Féis of the Glens, Jul; Ballycastle: Rathlin Sound Maritime Festival, May/Jun; Aul Lammas Fair, Aug; Derry: Jazz and Big Band Festival, May; Foyle Film Festival, Nov; Omagh: Bluegrass Festival, May.

DAY TRIP OPTIONS

Bird watchers should pack a picnic and take the ferry from Ballycastle to Rathlin Island to see the puffin colony. Lovers of **nature and history** could easily spend a day exploring Glenarm and Glenariff, the "Queen" of the Glens of Antrim. For full details, see p241.

Left Fishing vessels moored at the harbour at Carnlough, Glenarm, see p235

Above Sturdy walls of Carrickfergus Castle, overlooking the harbour and Belfast Lough

WHERE TO STAY

AROUND CARNFUNNOCK COUNTRY PARK

Ballygally Castle Hotel *moderate*
Facing the sandy beaches of Ballygally Bay, 3 km (2 miles) on the A2 coastal road from the country park, this castle dates back to 1625 and reputedly even has its own friendly ghost. Original beamed ceilings and period rooms add to the charm and character.
Causeway Coastal Route, Ballygally, BT40 2QZ; 028 2858 1066; www. hastingshotels.com

AROUND GLENARM

The Londonderry Arms Hotel *moderate*
This is a friendly, historic hotel in the village of Carnlough (5 km/3 miles on the A2 from Glenarm) at the foot of Glencoy, restored to its original Georgian style by the current owner. Rooms are very comfortable, and are individually furnished. There is an excellent bistro and bar too (*see Eat and Drink, opposite*). Curiously, Sir Winston Churchill once owned the Londonderry Arms.
20 Harbour Road, Carnlough, BT44 0EU; 028 2888 5255; www.londonderryarmshotel.com

① Carrickfergus
Co Antrim

The oldest city in County Antrim, predating even Belfast, of which it is now almost a district, Carrickfergus is a pretty seaside town set on Belfast Lough. Dominating the waterfront is **Carrickfergus Castle** (*open daily*), a striking Norman edifice built for defence in the 12th century and used for this purpose as recently as World War II. It is possible to take a guided tour of the castle, the best-preserved of its kind in Northern Ireland, and from its ramparts there are good views of the harbour and marina and across Belfast Lough. Nearby on Antrim Street is the **Carrickfergus Museum and Civic Centre** (*open Mon–Sat*) with exhibitions on local history. Carrickfergus is known worldwide as the subject of a haunting Irish ballad that begins, "I wish I was in Carrickfergus".

🚗 *Follow the A2 north to reach the Causeway Coastal Route. There are great sea views en route to Whitehead; the road then follows the western shore of Larne Lough. After the port town of Larne itself, the best of the Causeway Coastal Route begins, with spectacular cliffs and sea views over to Scotland. Continue on the A2, passing through Black Cave tunnel and along Drains Bay. The entrance to Carnfunnock Country Park is just after the bay, on the left. Drive through the entrance (marked with a pyramid) and park in the car park.*

② Carnfunnock Country Park
Drains Bay, BT40 2QG; Co Antrim

A perfect place for families to enjoy, **Carnfunnock Country Park** (*open daily*) is a lovely country park of 190 ha (470 acres) filled with woods, gardens and walking trails, parts of which are set on the coastal shore. Many of the estate's original features, such as the walled garden and the ice house, remain. There are plenty of activities, including a mini-golf course, geocaching, an activity centre and adventure playground (with sensory play area) and a maze. There are also picnic areas and a café.

🚗 *Continue along the A2 coastal road through Ballygally and Milltown to Glenarm village, gateway to Glenarm. Follow its main street to the glen.*

Above The Gothic stone Barbican Gate, the main entrance to Glenarm Castle

③ Glenarm
Co Antrim

This lovely forested glen stretches along the Glenarm river, which is fed by streams gushing down from the glen. The Glenarm Scenic Route runs from the village of Glenarm, up the B97 through the glen itself, back down

Right The Glenarm river skirting the walls of noble Glenarm Castle, seat of the Earls of Antrim

Above View over the beautiful forested slopes of Glenariff towards the sea

to the coast through the next glen, Glencoy, and along the A42 to **Carnlough**. Along the way is Gothic **Glenarm Castle**, seat of the Earls of Antrim. Its extensive grounds include a delightful 18th-century **Walled Garden** (open mid-Mar–Oct: daily) and tea rooms in the old Mushroom House. The Walled Garden is especially lovely in spring when a sea of spring bulbs and clouds of apple and pear blossom are a breathtaking sight.

🚗 *Continue on the A2 via Carnlough to Waterfoot.*

4 Waterfoot

Co Antrim

Waterfoot (also known as Glenariff), the village at the mouth of Glenariff, is set on Red Bay, so-named for its sandstone cliffs and the resulting shade of the sand on its long stretch of beach. Glenariff is known as the "Queen of the Nine Glens of Antrim". It is a U-shaped valley bounded on either side by precipitous hills, and the landscape really is spectacular, with everything from seashores and cliffs to dense forest and waterfalls. **The Glenariff Forest Park Scenic Route**, along which the route runs, is typical of the wonderful glen scenery that is a highlight of driving in Antrim.

🚗 *At the end of Waterfoot village, turn left at the T-junction onto the A43, signposted for Glenariff Forest Park. Follow this road; the entrance to the forest park is on the left.*

5 Glenariff Forest Park

BT44 0QX; Co Antrim

This stunning **forest park** (open daily) in the upper part of the glen, has many scenic, circular, waymarked trails and walks that lead through mixed woodlands, along the Inver and Glenariff rivers, past waterfalls and to viewpoints with panoramic views down the mountainsides and all the way to the Mull of Kintyre in Scotland. Especially well worth seeing are two of the park's largest and most spectacular waterfalls, Ess na Larach, which has a viewing-point bridge, and Ess na Crub.

🚗 *Leaving the Forest Park, turn left onto the A43, then right onto the B14 along the glen of Glenballyeamon to Cushendall.*

EAT AND DRINK

AROUND CARNFUNNOCK COUNTRY PARK

Garden Restaurant *moderate*
The restaurant at the Ballygally Castle Hotel is the most attractive place for a meal in these parts. It is located inside the castle walls and looks out over the gardens. The chefs pride themselves on their use of local produce resulting in dishes such as rump of Mourne lamb with curry and cumin puree. Enjoy afternoon tea (from €20), or choose from the informal lunch menu available in the lounge.
Causeway Coastal Route, Ballygally, BT40 2QZ; 028 2858 1066; www. hastingshotels.com

AROUND GLENARM

Coach House Bistro *moderate*
Part of the Londonderry Arms Hotel, this warm and welcoming bistro serves up good-quality favourites including various steaks, seared salmon and confit of duck. There's also the convivial Arkle Whiskey Bar, named after the legendary racehorse.
20 Harbour Road, Carnlough, BT44 0EU; 028 2888 5255; www. londonderryarmshotel.com

Below left St Patrick's Church, Glenarm
Below Pretty fishing village of Carnlough

GETTING TO RATHLIN ISLAND

Rathlin Island Ferries depart year-round from Ballycastle for the short crossing to the island. Advance booking is advised. *Ballycastle Ferry Terminal, 8 Bayview Road, Ballycastle; 028 2076 9299; www.rathlinballycastleferry.com*

WHERE TO STAY

BALLYCASTLE
Colliers Hall *inexpensive*
This guesthouse offers both B&B-style and self-catering accommodation in an old converted stone barn. *50 Cushendall Road; 028 2076 2531*

AROUND BALLYCASTLE
Manor House *moderate*
This 18th-century Georgian house – a ferry ride away from the mainland – overlooks the sheltered harbour at Rathlin Island, and every room has a sea view. The Island restaurant is the top draw, while the café is a great spot to idle away an hour or so. *Rathlin Island, BT54 6RT; 028 2076 0046; www.manorhouserathlin.com*

Whitepark House *moderate*
This is a beautiful guesthouse set on picturesque Whitepark Bay, with three gorgeous double rooms as well as a friendly welcome and personal service. *150 Whitepark Road, Ballintoy, BT54 6NH; 028 2073 1482; www.whitepark house.com*

Below Torr Head, with its dramatic landscape and stunning sea views

Above Wild and rocky shoreline near the popular seaside resort of Ballycastle

Glens of Antrim
The coastline of Antrim is marked by nine glens, each full of natural wonders such as rivers, waterfalls and forests. The nine are Glenarm, Glencloy, Glencorp, Glendun, Glenballyeamon, Glenaan, Glenshek, Glentaisie and Glenariff. The last is known as the "Queen of the Glens" because of its particular majesty and beautiful waterfalls. The glens are full of myths, legends and stories of fairies, which were once a large part of local folklore.

6 Cushendall
Co Antrim
Cushendall is an attractive little conservation village and resort. Much of the activity centres on the waterfront, with its pier and sailing club. There is a golf course and beach, and the ruined Layde Church has some lovely Celtic crosses. Caves in nearby Tiveragh Hill are said to be occupied by the "little people". *Follow the A2 north, then turn right onto the B92 (also signed to Torr Head Scenic Route) through Knocknacarry and on to Cushendun.*

7 Cushendun
Co Antrim
This tiny, picturesque fishing village is known for its quaint, whitewashed houses built in Cornish style. It was designed for Lord Cushendun by the architect Clough Williams-Ellis, best known for his Italianate town of Portmeirion in Wales. The waterfront and sheltered harbour are perfect for a stroll. On a clear day there are superb views across to Scotland. *Take the Torr Road, following signs for Torr Head. Turn right for Torr Head.*

Above Traditional shopfront in the pretty village of Cushendall

8 Torr Head
Co Antrim
The road to **Torr Head** ascends steeply and there are some spectacular coastal views over the North Channel to the Mull of Kintyre in Scotland, north to Rathlin Island and down over stunning **Murlough Bay**. The ruined buildings below Torr Head used to be customs houses and a lookout station that recorded the passage of transatlantic ships. The small lane down to Murlough Bay from Torr Head passes a megalithic

tomb and a group of old radio masts and outbuildings that were once a transmission and listening station for the Royal Air Force.

🚗 *Leaving Torr Head or Murlough Bay, turn right onto Torr Road and, on reaching the village of Ballyvoy, turn right onto the A2 for Ballycastle. Park on the seafront in Ballycastle.*

Above The lookout station at Torr Head

🟡 Ballycastle
Co Antrim

Ballycastle is a busy market town and a popular seaside resort. From the harbour here, ferries leave for the 40-minute crossing to **Rathlin Island**. It is in a cave on the island that, in 1306, the fugitive Robert the Bruce is said to have seen the struggling spider that prompted him to "try again" and return to win Scottish independence from the English. Scattered with ancient ruins, the island is now home to a puffin colony. Ballycastle – at the

head of glens Glenshesk and Glentaisie – has a small heritage trail taking in churches, monuments and the ruins of a Franciscan friary.

🚗 *Take the B15 coastal road west to Carrick-a-Rede Rope Bridge.*

🔟 Carrick-a-Rede Rope Bridge
BT54 6LS; Co Antrim

The famous **Carrick-a-Rede Rope Bridge** *(open daily, weather permitting)* runs across a chasm 20 m (66 ft) wide and 23 m (75 ft) deep. It was originally used as a working bridge enabling salmon fishermen to cross to the small rock outcrop, but nowadays it is primarily a tourist attraction, as much for the beauty of the site as for the challenge of crossing the wobbly bridge itself. Arrive early in peak season to avoid queues, and wear sensible footwear and warm clothes to cross the bridge. The bay of **Larrybane**, below, was used as a limestone quarry for much of the 1950s, and visitors can walk to the old quarry area and view the fine stalactite cave in the cliffs.

🚗 *From Carrick-a-Rede, turn right onto the B15. As a short detour, turn right for Whitepark Bay, a pristine crescent-shaped beach, sheltered below cliffs and backed by sand dunes (strong currents make it unsuitable for swimming). Returning to the B15, go through Ballintoy and turn right onto the A2, signed to Bushmills. Then turn right onto the B146 for the Giant's Causeway. There is paid parking next to the Visitor Centre, although the site itself is free.*

Above The hair-raising rope-bridge crossing at Carrick-a-Rede

EAT AND DRINK

CUSHENDALL

Johnny Joe's *inexpensive*
This is a lively pub with traditional music and singing every weekend, and impromptu music sessions on other nights, especially in summer. A wide range of classic and inventive dishes are served in the friendly first-floor restaurant, Upstairs at Joe's.
23 Mill Street, BT44 0RR; 028 2177 1992 (bar); 028 2177 2849 (restaurant); www.johnnyjoes.co.uk

CUSHENDUN

Mary McBride's Bar *inexpensive*
This tiny bar is big on character and atmosphere, with fabulous Saturday evening and Sunday afternoon music sessions. The Little Black Door bistro upstairs is one of the best places to eat along this stretch of coast.
2 Main Street, BT44 0PH; 028 2176 1511

BALLYCASTLE

Central Wine Bar *inexpensive*
Come to this family-run restaurant for a great evening out. The menu changes according to the season.
12 Ann Street; 028 2076 3877

Cellar Restaurant *moderate*
Cosy and atmospheric restaurant with slate walls and low-hanging lights; whole lobster is the house speciality.
11B The Diamond, BT54 6AW; 028 2076 3037; www.cellarballycastle.com

Above The jagged, quarried limestone cliffs, concealing fine stalactite caves, of Larrybane

Above Giant's Causeway on a stormy day
Below right Visitor admiring the view from the cliffs around Giant's Causeway

VISITING GIANT'S CAUSEWAY

Giant's Causeway Visitor Centre
A shuttle bus runs from the Centre to the rock formations, 1 km (half a mile) away. Wear appropriate shoes and raincoats, as it can be wet and slippery on the stones. *44 Causeway Road, BT57 8SU; 028 2073 1855; www.nationaltrust.org.uk/ giants-causeway*

WHERE TO STAY

GIANT'S CAUSEWAY

The Smuggler's Inn *inexpensive*
This is a small, family-run hotel with great sea views, ideally situated down the road from the Giant's Causeway. There is also a restaurant. *306 Whitepark Road, BT57 8SL; 028 2073 1577; www.smugglersinnireland.com*

BUSHMILLS

The Bushmills Inn *moderate*
This cosy hotel, with open peat fires and gas lighting, describes itself as "a living museum of Ulster hospitality". However, every modern luxury is also present in the charming rooms. The restaurant is excellent, too *(see opposite)*. *9 Dunluce Road, BT57 8QG; 028 2073 3000; www.bushmillsinn.com*

AROUND BUSHMILLS

Bayview Hotel *moderate*
This quiet hotel in the small harbour village of Portballintrae, just north of Bushmills, overlooks the sea and is a great base for exploring the area. *2 Bayhead Road, Portballintrae, BT57 8RT; 028 2073 4100; www.bayview hotelni.com*

⑪ Giant's Causeway

BT57 8SU; Co Antrim

This natural geological phenomenon consists of around 40,000 polygonal basalt columns, forming a huge causeway that juts out into the sea. Scientists believe that the columns were created some 60 million years ago by volcanic activity. However, local legend tells it better, with the story that they were created by the Irish giant, Finn McCool, who was fighting a rival Scottish giant, Benandonner. McCool is said to have created a pathway of stepping stones from Ireland to Scotland, so he could walk across the sea to confront his rival. There are similar stones on the island of Staffa in the Hebrides.

A two-hour walking tour

From the car park and **Visitor Centre** ①, follow the cliff path to the right. There are great views as the path ascends. Descend the **Shepherd's Steps** ② carefully (there are 162 in total, and they are steep). At the bottom, follow the path towards the **Giant's Organ** ③, an impressive set of columns in the cliff face, that resemble 12-m (39-ft) organ pipes. Walk past the Organ towards the **Amphitheatre** ④. On turning the corner into the Amphitheatre, the **Giant's Eyes** ⑤ are on the right – eye-shaped sockets in the red iron ore layer, where basalt boulders have fallen out. Turn and follow the path back past the Organ, then take the path that descends towards the Causeway itself. Look out for the **Giant's Boot** ⑥ rock on the shore of Port Noffer to the right. Before passing through the **Giant's Gate** ⑦, turn and look back for a view of the Giant's Chimney Tops, chimney-stack-like columns protruding from a headland to the east. Through the Gate are the main "stepping stone" rock formations.

Any wish made while sitting in the **Wishing Chair** ⑧ in the Middle Causeway is said to come true. Return up the path to the Visitor Centre. From here there is a good view of the hunched form of the **Giant's Granny** ⑨. Continue past Port Ganny to see the **Camel** ⑩, which "sits" in Portnaboe, before heading back to the Visitor Centre. 🚗 *From the car park, turn right on the B146, then turn right again onto the A2. Drive through Bushmills to the Distillery.*

12 Old Bushmills Distillery
BT57 8XH; Co Antrim
Ireland's oldest whiskey distillery, the **Old Bushmills Distillery** *(open daily)*, was founded in 1608 when a royal licence was granted by King James I to Sir Thomas Phillips to distil *uisce beatha* (Irish for "water of life"), or whiskey as it is now known. Old Bushmills is still a fully operational distillery, where brands such as Bushmills, Black Bush and Bushmills Malt are made, using unpeated malted barley. Guided tours for visitors explain the craft of Irish whiskey-making, including the Irish triple-distillation process, and looking at the warehouses full of barrels. There's a chance to taste the product at the end of the tour.

🚗 *Leave Bushmills on the A2, signed for Portrush. Dunluce Castle is a short distance along this road on the right.*

Irish Whiskey
Irish whiskey is made from three ingredients: barley, yeast and water. The barley is milled to a grist, which is then steeped in Mash Tuns with hot water, to produce fermentable sugars. The addition of yeast converts these sugars into alcohol. The raw spirit is then distilled in a pot still. Irish whiskey is distilled three times, giving it its unique flavour. It is then matured in oak casks. Bushmills is aged for five years in sherry and bourbon casks, which refines the spirit and adds complexity, colour and more flavour, but some whiskies are aged for much longer, such as Bushmills 21-Year-Old Malt.

13 Dunluce Castle
BT57 8UY; Co Antrim
The romantic ruins of **Dunluce Castle** *(open daily)* have a dramatic clifftop setting, jutting out into the sea. A short audiovisual presentation on the history of the castle can be viewed before exploring the ruins. Most of the present castle building dates from the 16th and 17th centuries and there are breathtaking (if scary) views down to the water crashing onto the rocks far below.

🚗 *Continue on the A2 towards Portrush. From a car park on the right-hand side there are sweeping coastal views. After the following bend, there is a space on the left just large enough*

for one car. If it is empty, park and cross the road. Look back towards Dunluce to see the Giant's Head, a huge face eroded into the cliffs. At Portrush, turn right onto Causeway Street and drive to Ramore Head for more sea views.*

14 Portrush
Co Antrim
Portrush is a large seaside town and one of Northern Ireland's most popular family holiday destinations. It gets very busy in the summer, especially on bank holiday weekends. There are plenty of outdoor activities and the beach is very good for surfing. **Waterworld** *(open Jun–Sep: daily)*, the water park on the seafront, and other amusements provide plenty of family entertainment.

🚗 *Continue on the A2 to Portstewart. Follow signs for the Promenade, turn right onto Atlantic Circle and drive along Kinora Terrace to Portstewart Point and Harbour Hill, affording lovely views over to the Inishowen Peninsula.*

15 Portstewart
Co Derry
Portstewart is another very busy seaside holiday resort with a lengthy beach and promenade. The long golden strand is the main focal point, popular with walkers and surfers.

🚗 *From Portstewart take the B185 in the direction of Coleraine but, at the roundabout, take the A29 (second exit) for the Coleraine ring road. At Greenmount Roundabout, take the B201 (third exit) for Castlerock. Turn left onto the A2. Turn right onto the B119, Sea Road, signed for Castlerock. Hezlett House is on this road just before Castlerock village.*

Above Surfers enjoying the waves at Portrush Beach, a popular family holiday destination

EAT AND DRINK

BUSHMILLS
The Bushmills Inn *moderate*
The award-winning restaurant at this hotel *(see left)* is housed in its 17th-century stables, overlooking a garden courtyard. The mix of traditional and new Irish cuisine at the restaurant might feature pan-fried peppered fillet of beef flamed in Bushmills whiskey. The Gas Bar here is a lively spot. The inn even has its own cinema.
9 Dunluce Road, BT57 8QG; 028 2073 3000; www.bushmillsinn.com

PORTRUSH
Ramore Wine Bar *inexpensive*
Part of the Ramore complex, which includes the classy Neptune & Prawn restaurant and the Spanish-influenced Basalt.
The Harbour, BT56 8BN; 028 7082 4313; www.ramorerestaurant.com

Below Ruined Dunluce Castle, breathtakingly perched on its rocky promontory

Above Mussenden Temple, perched on the clifftop Above centre Glenelly Valley in the Sperrins Above right River Foyle in Derry

WHERE TO STAY

AROUND DOWNHILL DEMESNE

Downhill Beach House *inexpensive*
Overlooking the beach to Donegal, this grand Victorian building has a mix of double and family rooms, and dorms. A lounge, dining room and kitchen are available for use to guests.
Glenhassen Hall, 12 Mussenden Road, Downhill, Castlerock, BT51 4RP; 028 7084 9077; www.downhill beachhouse.com

DERRY~LONDONDERRY

Beech Hill Country House Hotel *moderate–expensive*
A charming and elegant hotel, set in mature gardens southeast of Derry's city walls, which has hosted some of the world's top politicians, actors and musicians. There's even a museum in the hotel. Home cooking is a speciality.
32 Ardmore Road, BT47 3QP; 028 7134 9279; www.beech-hill.com

City Hotel *moderate*
This large, 4-star hotel with a heated pool overlooks the River Foyle.
Queen's Quay, BT48 7AS; 028 7136 5800; www.cityhotelderry.com

AROUND DERRY~LONDONDERRY

Carrick Lodge *inexpensive*
Unassuming but welcoming guesthouse with just two rooms – one for families – overlooking meadows.
138 Ballyquin Road, Limavady, BT49 9EZ; 028 7776 7194; www.carrick-lodge.com

AROUND LOUGH NEAGH

Ardtara Hotel *moderate*
A delightful 19th-century country house hotel, Ardtara is full of character with lots of old-style charm and decor.
8 Gorteade Road, Upperlands, Maghera, BT46 5SA (on A29 north of Desertmartin); 028 7964 4490; www.ardtara.com

16 Hezlett House

BT51 4TW; Co Derry
Pretty **Hezlett House** *(open May–Jun & Sep: Sat–Sun; Apr & Jul–Aug: Fri–Tue)* is a picture-postcard traditional thatched Dower House and farmyard owned and run by the National Trust. It is thought to be one of the oldest buildings in Northern Ireland, with timber frames dating from 1690. Visitors can take a guided tour of the simply furnished, Victorian-style interior to learn more about life in 18th-century rural Ireland. There is also a small museum of historic farm equipment.

🚗 *Return to the A2 and turn right. The entrance to the Downhill Estate is on the right before the road begins to descend down a hill.*

Above Symbolic statue "Hands Across the Divide", in the city of Derry

17 Downhill Demesne

BT51 4RP; Co Derry
The lovely **Downhill Demesne** *(open daily)* was built between 1774 and 1778 by the Earl of Bristol. Downhill House itself is now a ruin, but its gardens remain and there are spectacular clifftop walks. Clinging to the top of the cliffs, the picturesque **Mussenden Temple** *(028 7084 8728 for opening details)* was originally used as a library. Saved from collapsing over the edge when the site was taken over by the National Trust, it is now a popular wedding venue.

🚗 *Follow the road to Downhill and turn left here, just after the row of buildings, for the Bishops Road Drive. There are spectacular elevated views over Lough Foyle to the Inishowen Peninsula and, further along, to the Sperrin Mountains. Continue on this road, turning right onto the B201 Windyhill Road and rejoining the A2 for Limavady. From here the road skirts the edge of Lough Foyle for part of the way to Derry. Park on the street or in one of two multi-storey car parks at Quayside and Foyle Road.*

18 Derry~Londonderry

Co Derry
Derry is a large, commercial city with a historic walled centre lying along the banks of the River Foyle. The walls, forming an elevated walkway, date back to the early 17th century. "The Troubles" *(see p246)* had a huge impact on the city of Derry and, like Belfast, it has powerful murals representing the feelings of both sides of the community. However, since the 1998 Good Friday Agreement that launched the peace process, the city is more optimistic. The Museum of Free Derry *(open Jul–Sep: daily; Oct– May: Mon–Sat)* tells the story of the city's turbulent history.

🚗 *From Derry, take the A5 towards Omagh, passing through Strabane. After 48 km (30 miles) turn left onto Mellon Road for the Ulster American Folk Park.*

⑲ Ulster American Folk Park

BT78 5QY; Co Tyrone

This fascinating **Folk Park** (open Jul & Aug: daily; Sep–May: Thu–Sun) tells the story of emigration from Ireland to America in the 18th and 19th centuries. Visitors move around the site through a series of traditional buildings ranging from an Irish weaver's cottage to a period American street, and there is even a full-sized reconstruction of a 19th-century sailing ship, of the kind in which the emigrants crossed the Atlantic, that can be boarded in order to experience the hardships they endured. In these authentic settings, costumed characters perform traditional crafts and go about their daily routine, bringing the past to life, while tours and exhibitions provide fascinating background information.

🚗 *Leaving the Park, turn left onto the A5 south, then left onto Gortnagarn Road and left again onto the B48. The entrance to the Gortin Glen Forest Park is on the right hand side. To reach the Forest Drive, drive through the car park and follow the signs.*

Above Pennsylvania log farmhouse at the Ulster American Folk Park

⑳ Sperrin Mountains

Co Tyrone/Co Derry

The Sperrins are a designated Area of Outstanding Natural Beauty and the largest mountain range in Northern Ireland. There are numerous scenic drives, cycle trails and walking routes in the area. The **Gortin Glen Forest Park** (open daily) covers part of the 1,500-ha (3,700-acre) forest. The park has a range of delightful walking trails, including one that follows the pretty Pollan Burn, as well as an 8-km (5-mile) Forest Drive that includes a number of "vista parks" en route, where motorists can stop to enjoy magnificent views. The coniferous woods are home to plenty of wildlife including red squirrels and Sika deer.

🚗 *Turn right out of the Park on the B48 to Gortin and then Plumbridge. Turn right at Plumbridge onto the B47, passing through the Glenelley Valley. At Draperstown, turn right onto the B40 for Magherafelt and, from there, head south on the B160 to Ballyronan village on the shores of Lough Neagh.*

㉑ Lough Neagh

Co Derry

Lough Neagh, in the very centre of Northern Ireland, is the third-largest lake in Europe, and five of the six counties border it. It is a popular place for bird-watching (around 1,000 whooper swans settle around the lake in winter) and fishing, and there are many visitor attractions all around the lough. Boat trips run from **Ballyronan Marina** to sites of interest around the lake, such as the beautiful Celtic High Cross at Ardboe, while an evening cruise with live folk music offers the chance to see the sun set over the Sperrins.

Above Tranquil Lough Neagh, a popular spot for boat trips and bird-watching

EAT AND DRINK IN DERRY~LONDONDERRY

Browns in Town *moderate*
A smart, contemporary restaurant, popular for its consistently great cooking and stylish atmosphere. *21 Strand Road, BT48 7BJ; 028 7136 2889; www.brownsintown.com*

La Sosta Ristorante *moderate*
A buzzy, authentic, family-run Italian restaurant serving delicious food. Friendly service. *45/a Carlisle Road, BT48 6JJ; 028 7137 4817; www.lasostaderry.com; open eves only; closed Sun & Mon*

The House *moderate*
This landmark 19th-century building is now a fine-dining establishment serving mouthwatering dishes such as whiskey-cured salmon and pan-seared monkfish. *Custom House Street, BT48 7AS; 028 7137 3366; www.thehousederry.com; closed Mon & Tue*

DAY TRIP OPTIONS

Glenarm and Ballycastle are ideal bases to see rich birdlife and visit lovely glens.

A trip to puffin island
Take the ferry (40 mins, booking essential) from Ballycastle ⑨ to Rathlin Island – bring a picnic and explore this tranquil haven for birds and other wildlife. Puffins are in residence from April to August. If it's

not picnic weather there is a pub and a restaurant (the Manor House, *see p236*) on the island.

Only island residents can bring cars to the island. Leave the car at the ferry terminal or seafront in Ballycastle.

A day in the glens
Combine several lovely glens in a day's tour, starting at Glenarm ❸, pausing to visit Glenarm Castle with its delightful gardens and

tea room. Then drive down Glencoy before heading back up along the coast to Waterfoot (Glenariff village) for Glenariff ❹ and the lovely woodland walking trails of Glenariff Forest Park ❺.

Head south on the A2 to Glenariff Glen, and then from here follow the drive's instructions to Glenariff Forest Park.

TRIP 24

THE LAND OF ST PATRICK
Belfast to the Mountains of Mourne

HIGHLIGHTS

Buzzing Belfast
Discover the historic Titanic Quarter, the colourful Cathedral Quarter and the vibrant Queen's Quarter

Outstanding gardens
Stroll through beautiful Mount Stewart Gardens, laid out by Lady Londonderry in the 1920s

Coastal wildlife
Explore the myriad small bays and inlets at Strangford Lough, rich in wildfowl and marine life

Majestic mountains
Head through the high passes of the Mountains of Mourne, pausing near the Spelga Dam for superb views

THE LAND OF ST PATRICK

With Strangford Lough at its centre and the open sea to the east, County Down has more than 320 km (200 miles) of coastline, with good beaches and nature reserves to enjoy. In the south of the county, the magnificent Mountains of Mourne dominate the horizon. The county is also rich in historic monuments and stately homes, while St Patrick's Trail traces the footsteps of Ireland's patron saint. From the hustle and bustle of Belfast in Co Antrim, along the Ards Peninsula flanking the eastern shores of Strangford Lough, and through the pretty seaside villages on Dundrum Bay, this drive ends with a spectacular trip through the Mountains of Mourne.

Above The peaceful waters of Strangford Lough, the UK's largest sea inlet and designated an Area of Outstanding Natural Beauty, *see p248*

0 kilometres   6

0 miles   6

KEY

▬ Drive route

ACTIVITIES

Discover the epic story of the *Titanic* at the excellent Titanic Belfast

Explore the fascinating open-air Ulster Folk and Transport Museum and step back to the 18th century

Wander around the classical house and gardens of lovely Castle Ward

Hike up Slieve Donard, the highest mountain in Northern Ireland

PLAN YOUR DRIVE

Start/finish: Belfast to the Mountains of Mourne.

Number of days: 3 days.

Distance: 150 km (93 miles).

Road conditions: Generally good, but some mountain roads may be impassable in winter.

When to go: Spring, summer or autumn when the weather is milder and most attractions are open.

Opening times: Most shops and attractions open 9 or 10am–5 or 6pm. Shops open Mon–Sat; in large towns also 12–6pm on Sun. Convenience stores in villages open 8am until late.

Main market days: Belfast: Fri (variety) and Sat (food and craft), Sun (food, craft and antiques), St George's; **Newtownards:** Sat; **Portaferry:** Sat.

Major festivals: Belfast: Film Festival, Apr; *Titanic* Maritime Festival, May; International Arts Festival, Oct; **Hillsborough:** Oyster Festival, Sep; **Castlewellan:** Celtic Fusion, Jun; **Newcastle:** Mourne International Walking Festival, Jun.

DAY TRIP OPTIONS

Nature lovers can experience the area's natural splendour and diverse wildlife by hiring a canoe on Strangford Lough, or hiking through the Tollymore Forest Park in the foothills of the Mountains of Mourne. **Families** with children will enjoy visiting the Exploris Aquarium in Portaferry. For full details, *see p249*.

Below left Belfast's Crown Bar, *see p246*
Below Newcastle, a 19th-century resort beneath the Mourne Mountains, *see p249*

VISITING BELFAST

Parking
There are several car parks close to City Hall, including Bedford Street, Dublin Road and Great Victoria Street, and metered parking around Ulster Hall.

Tourist Information
Belfast Welcome Centre, 9 Donegall Square North, BT1 5AD; 028 9024 6609; www.visitbelfast.com; open 9am–5:30pm Mon–Sat, 11am–4pm Sun.

WHERE TO STAY

BELFAST

Malmaison *moderate–expensive*
Funky and stylish hotel in an old seed warehouse. Period features mix with contemporary decor.
34–8 Victoria Street, BT1 3GH; 028 9600 1405; www.malmaison.com

Ten Square *moderate–expensive*
Boutique luxury hotel with stylish bedrooms and a superb, central location on Donegall Square.
10 Donegall Square South, BT1 5JD; 028 9024 1001; www.tensquare.co.uk

The Merchant Hotel *expensive*
Set in a historic listed building in the Cathedral Quarter, and elegantly decorated with antiques.
35–9 Waring Street, BT1 2DY; 028 9023 4888; www.themerchanthotel.com

AROUND THE ULSTER FOLK AND TRANSPORT MUSEUM

The Old Inn *moderate*
Charming hotel that offers an old-fashioned welcome with open fires and beamed ceilings.
15 Main Street, Crawfordsburn, BT19 1JH (15 km/9 miles after the Ulster Folk Museum on the A2, turn left on B20, signposted Crawfordsburn); 028 9185 3255; www.theoldinn.com

❶ BELFAST

Co Antrim

A bustling trading port in the 18th and 19th centuries, Belfast has a rich heritage. The city built and launched the RMS *Titanic* in 1912, making it a global centre for ship-building; it is also famous for its linen and tobacco industries. However, the Troubles, from the 1960s to the 1990s, led to decline. Regeneration projects in the wake of the peace process have helped the economy recover and there is a buzz about the city, especially in the arty Cathedral Quarter, Queen's Quarter (around Queen's University) and the Gaeltacht Quarter, which promotes Irish language and culture.

A two-hour walking tour

Start at City Hall on **Donegall Square** ①, a classical masterpiece completed in 1906. Take a look inside at the palatial marbled entrance. From the north side of the square walk along Donegall Place and continue before turning right into Castle Lane, taking one of the narrow "Entries" to join High Street. Turn right here to see **Albert Clock** ②, a curious tower, built in 1867 as a memorial to Prince Albert. Turn left along Victoria Street, left into Waring Street and right into Donegall Street to reach the period Cathedral Quarter and **St Anne's Cathedral** ③ *(open*

Above Political mural, West Belfast, the frontline of the sectarian conflict known as the Troubles

Mon–Sat, Sun pm). Work began in 1899 on St Anne's, which contains some beautiful mosaics of St Patrick. From the cathedral, turn left at Royal Avenue, then right into Castle Street and left into Fountain Street. At No. 52 is Belfast's oldest library – the **Linen Hall Library** ④ *(open Mon–Fri)*, with superb archives on Irish history and culture. Walk along Wellington Place, turn left at the end onto College Square and continue along Great Victoria Street. On the right is the **Grand Opera House** ⑤, a handsome building dating from 1895. No. 46 is Belfast's most famous pub – the **Crown Bar** ⑥ – with its fabulous high Victorian interior. Continue to University Road and the University Quarter around prestigious **Queen's University** ⑦, founded in 1845. The Visitor Centre *(www.qub.ac.uk; 028 9097 5252)* holds exhibitions and can arrange guided tours of the campus. From

University Square, turn right onto College Park and continue to Botanic Avenue and the **Ulster Museum** ⑧ *(www.nmni.com; open Tue–Sun)*, which has a fine collection of art, craftwork and archaeological finds. Next door are the **Botanic Gardens** ⑨ *(open daily)*, opened in 1827. The early Victorian wrought-iron and glass palm house was added soon after. To return to City Hall, follow Botanic Avenue onto Dublin Road and Bedford Street.

🚗 *From Donegall Quay, take Victoria Street leading to A2 for Bangor, crossing Queen Elizabeth Bridge. Continue on A2 to Holywood, following the signs for the museum (11 km/7 miles from Belfast).*

Taxi and Boat Tours
To see West Belfast's political murals, symbols of the city's past and present sectarian divisions, take a Black Taxi tour from City Hall. Or tour the *Titanic* Quarter by boat, visiting landmarks connected with the building of the RMS *Titanic*. Tours leave from the Lagan Lookout on Donegall Quay.

② Ulster Folk and Transport Museum
Cultra, Holywood, BT18 OEU; Co Down
This outdoor museum-village *(open Tue–Sun)* has a collection of early 20th-century buildings from all over Ulster, reconstructed here. A transport section commemorates local ship- and aircraft-building, and a miniature railway runs on Saturday afternoons, weather permitting.

🚗 *Rejoin the A2 in the direction of Bangor. Leave it at Crawfordsburn*

and take the B20 (Ballyrobert Road) for Bangor and then the A21 to Newtownards. Take the A20 for Portaferry, driving beside Strangford Lough, and turn left for Mount Stewart after 8 km (5 miles).

③ Mount Stewart House and Gardens
Portaferry Road, Newtownards, BT22 2AD; Co Down
Created by Lady Londonderry in the 1920s, these gardens contain a vast range of plants and trees, set off by architectural features such as the octagonal **Temple of the Winds** and outstanding views across Strangford Lough. Highlights include the **Italian and Spanish Gardens**, the **Shamrock Garden** and the **Sunken Garden**. The house has an eclectic collection of furniture and artwork – including a painting of the celebrated racehorse Hambleton by George Stubbs – and information about the statesmen who have lived or stayed here.

🚗 *Leaving Mount Stewart, turn left onto the A20. Greyabbey is just over 3 km (2 miles) from Mount Stewart.*

Above left The wrought-iron and glass palm house in Belfast's Botanic Gardens **Above** An old-fashioned picture house recreated at the Ulster Folk Museum

EAT AND DRINK IN BELFAST

The Crown Bar *inexpensive*
The interior of Belfast's most famous pub, built in 1895, is ornately tiled, with etched glass, polished brass and cosy snugs. The menu includes baguettes and burgers plus traditional Irish stew and beef and Guinness pie.
46 Great Victoria Street, BT2 7BA; 028 9024 3187; www.nicholsonspubs.co.uk

The Cellar Restaurant *moderate*
This is one of the city's best-kept secrets. Set on the slopes of Cave Hill, it has great views over the city. Expect dishes such as venison, guinea fowl, pan-fried salmon, lamb and one or two vegetarian options.
Belfast Castle, Antrim Road, BT15 5GR; 028 9077 6925; www.belfast castle.co.uk

Deane's EIPIC *expensive*
Michelin-starred restaurant run by chef Michael Deane and known for its high-quality cuisine using locally sourced produce. Sleek, modern decor.
28–40 Howard Street, BT1 6PF; 028 9033 1134; www.deaneseipic. com; open Wed–Sat

Above The Neo-Classical façade of Mount Stewart House, with a grand stairway leading to its gardens

VISITING STRANGFORD LOUGH

Tourist Information
Portaferry: *The Stables, Castle Street, BT22 1NZ; 028 4272 9882; www. visitardsandnorthdown.com; open Easter–end Sep*

Boat Trips
From Portaferry to Strangford, **ferries** run at quarter past and quarter to the hour. **Boat trips** on the lough from Portaferry can be arranged through *Ards Boat Tours, 028 9182 6846*

WALKING IN THE MOURNE MOUNTAINS

The Newcastle Visitor Information Centre at 10–14 Central Promenade *(0330 0137 4046)* has stacks of material on walks in the Mournes. Twenty guided walks are also available *(www. visitmournemountains.co.uk).*

WHERE TO STAY

STRANGFORD LOUGH
The Cuan Inn *inexpensive*
This small, friendly family-run hotel in Strangford village has an intimate feel; decent restaurant too.
The Square, Strangford, BT30 7ND; 028 4488 1222; www.thecuan.com

DOWNPATRICK
The Mill at Ballydugan *moderate*
Just outside Downpatrick, this 18th-century flour mill has been turned into a small hotel, bistro and restaurant.
Drumcullen Road, Ballydugan, BT30 8HZ; 028 4461 3654; www. ballyduganmill.com

NEWCASTLE
Harbour House *inexpensive*
Bright, simply furnished rooms in this welcoming guesthouse south of town, which also has a decent restaurant.
4 South Promenade, BT33 0EX; 028 4372 3445; www.harbourhouse newcastle.com

Slieve Donard Resort & Spa
expensive
Built as a luxury Victorian hotel and still oozing class in its unrivalled setting, this resort overlooks the Royal County Down golf course.
Downs Road, BT33 0AH; 028 4372 1066; www.hastingshotels.com

AROUND NEWCASTLE
Burrendale Hotel *moderate*
A relaxed hotel and country club on the A50 just outside Newcastle, with a cosy bar, two restaurants and pool.
51 Castlewellan Road, BT33 0JY; 028 4372 2599; www.burrendale.com

Above Kilkeel Harbour, a major fishing port **Above right** Gothic arches of Cistercian Grey Abbey

4 Greyabbey
Co Down
The attractive village of Greyabbey takes its name from **Grey Abbey**, a Cistercian abbey founded in 1193. The remains of its Gothic buttresses and arches nestle in parkland on the north of the village. A museum in the gatehouse documents its history.
🚗 *Return to the A20 and drive south to Portaferry, following the signs to the Strangford Ferry (see left).*

5 Strangford Lough
Strangford, Downpatrick, BT30 7LS; Co Down
This Area of Outstanding Natural Beauty forms the UK's largest sea inlet and is rich in wildlife. It is almost landlocked except for a gap between **Portaferry** and **Strangford** known as the "Narrows". The lough can be accessed from either side. Arrange a canoe trip or take a boat tour around its waters from Portaferry *(see left).*
🚗 *From Strangford, take the A25 towards Downpatrick for 2 km (1 mile). At the crossroads there is a sign for the entrance to Castle Ward pointing to the right.*

6 Castle Ward
Strangford, Downpatrick, BT30 7LS; Co Down
A wonderfully eccentric building, Castle Ward *(open mid-Mar–Oct: daily pm)* was built in the 1760s. It famously combines two contrary architectural styles. The front of the house is Neo-Classical, while the rear, overlooking Strangford Lough, is Neo-Gothic. Inside, the decor is similarly mixed. An extensive walled area surrounds the house, with woodland trails and lovely views of the lough. Much of *Game of Thrones* was filmed here; visitors can pick up a map of all the filming locations at the reception.
🚗 *Return to the A25 and turn right to Downpatrick, 13 km (8 miles) away. In the town, follow signs for the Saint Patrick Centre and park opposite it.*

7 Downpatrick
Co Down
St Patrick (c. AD 390–461), Ireland's patron saint, landed in Strangford Lough in around AD 428. He is strongly linked with Downpatrick.
The Saint Patrick Centre *(open*

Above The Neo-Classical front of Castle Ward, which gives no clue to its Neo-Gothic rear

Mon–Sat; Jul & Aug: also Sun pm) on Market Street, traces his footsteps in the area. He is said to be buried in the graveyard of **Down Cathedral**, on English St (turn left out of the St Patrick Centre and walk up the steps by the building), where a stone slab marks the spot. However, Armagh also claims to be his burial place.

🚗 *From Downpatrick, take the A25 to Clough and join the A2 for Newcastle.*

The Powers of St Patrick

Inspired by a vision, St Patrick came to Ireland to convert the pagan population to Christianity. Legend credits him with many supernatural deeds, including ridding the country of snakes.

Above Portaferry, departure point for the ferry across the "Narrows" to Strangford

⑧ Newcastle
Co Down

This seaside resort has a magnificent setting, with the **Mourne Mountains**, dominated by **Slieve Donard** (852 m/ 2,796 ft), the highest mountain in Northern Ireland, rising behind the town and Dundrum Bay. It is known for its two golf courses, including the links course at the **Royal County Down Golf Club**, and the splendid **Slieve Donard Hotel**, a spa hotel

set between sea and mountains. Newcastle has a pleasant **beach**, but for more privacy drive 5 km (3 miles) south of town, where the **Mourne coastal footpath** gives access to secluded coastline. There is a car park, picnic table and walks.

🚗 *Continue south along the A2 to the pretty town of Kilkeel and then turn right onto the B27 to Hilltown. This leads up into the Mourne Mountains.*

⑨ Mountains of Mourne
Co Down

The Mourne Mountains lie in an area of outstanding natural beauty. There are many popular walking trails *(see far left)* including those up **Slieve Donard** and its slightly smaller neighbour **Slieve Commedagh**, with views as far as the Isle of Man on a clear day. The highlight of this area is the **Silent Valley** (after 6.5 km/4 miles on the B27, turn right onto Head Road for the Visitor Centre), a reservoir flanked by the Mourne Wall, a 35-km (22-mile) dry-stone wall linking 15 mountain peaks. To experience its magical silence take the 5-km (3-mile) walk around the reservoir. Return along Head Road to the B27 and turn right to reach the **Spelga Dam**.

The **Silent Valley Visitor Centre** *(open daily; 08457 440 088; www. niwater.com)* has an exhibition about the area and a café with stunning views. As the valley is closed to traffic, a **shuttle bus service** runs between Ben Crom and the car park *(runs Jul–Aug: daily)*.

It is possible to continue to pretty **Rostrevor**, staying on the B27 to Hilltown and turning left onto the B25. Rostrevor is known for its mild micro-climate and has parks and picnic areas with views across to Carlingford on the Cooley Peninsula.

Above Gothic flying buttresses at the ruined abbey in the pretty village of Greyabbey

EAT AND DRINK

NEWCASTLE

Sea Salt Café & Bistro *inexpensive*
Tasty lunches daily and a varied bistro-style menu Thu–Sat eve.
51 Central Promenade, BT33 0HH; 028 4375 8261; www.seasaltnewcastle.com

Hugh McCanns *moderate*
Terrific all-rounder with a restaurant, beer garden and live music Saturday afternoons, all in a great setting near the promenade.
119 Central Promenade, BT33 0EU; 028 4372 6622; www.hughmccanns.com

AROUND NEWCASTLE

The Buck's Head Inn *moderate*
In an 18th-century building, this is a friendly spot with imaginatively cooked seafood and other local produce.
77 Main Street, Dundrum, BT33 0LU (6 km/4 miles) north of Newcastle on the A24); 028 4375 1868

Mourne Seafood Bar *moderate*
Delicious, fresh, locally caught seafood with unusual as well as well-known species appearing on the menu.
10 Main Street, Dundrum, BT33 0LU (6 km/4 miles) north of Newcastle on the A24); 028 4375 1377; www.mourne seafood.com

---

DAY TRIP OPTIONS

Newcastle makes a good base to explore the various attractions in this area. Here are two day trips, with an option for rainy weather.

Sea and mountains

Take a canoe trip on Strangford Lough ⑤ to spot the abundant

wildlife. Or head to Tollymore Forest Park for a scenic hike at the foothills of the Mountains of Mourne ⑨. There are several hiking trails (the longest is 13 km/8 miles), through forests and along the River Shimna.

The park can be found 3 km/2 miles south of Newcastle.

Family fun

A great option on rainy days is the Exploris Aquarium *(open daily)* in Portaferry, near Strangford Lough ⑤. There is a marine discovery lab and a seal rescue centre.

Retrace the drive on the A2/A25 to Strangford and Portaferry.

TRIP 25

FERMANAGH LAKELANDS
Belleek to Boa Island

HIGHLIGHTS

Spectacular views
Contemplate one of the finest views in Northern Ireland
from the Cliffs of Magho

Spellbinding caverns
Wonder at the stalactite-filled caverns and subterranean
pools of the Marble Arch Caves

Neo-Classical stately homes
Experience the 18th-century grandeur of Florence Court
and Castle Coole

Tranquil waterways
Savour the peaceful waters of Lough Erne, a paradise for
nature-lovers, bird-watchers and anglers

A boathouse situated along the still waters of Lough Erne

FERMANAGH LAKELANDS

The inland county of Fermanagh in Northern Ireland is known as the Lakelands, for more than a third of its total area lies under water. The scenic waterways of Lough Erne, divided into Upper and Lower Lough Erne, are the county's main feature. Lower Lough Erne, set against a hilly backdrop, is dotted with islands and flanked by castles, stately homes, walks and forest parks. This tour includes all the highlights of Lower Lough Erne – exploring the lake by land and water, and taking in its main sights, loveliest views and most interesting activities. For outdoor enthusiasts there are underground rivers, caves, forests and ruined castles, while others can visit stately homes, a lace museum and a china workshop.

Above The still waters of Lough Macnean, near Marble Arch Caves, *see p254*

ACTIVITIES

Explore Enniskillen Castle, a stronghold that guarded the main pass to Ulster in medieval times

Enjoy a cruise on Lough Erne or rent a boat and visit some of the islands

Walk or cycle the scenic trails of Castle Archdale Country Park

Search for the mysterious stone figures that inspired Seamus Heaney in Caldragh Cemetery on Boa Island

0 kilometres 4
0 miles 4

KEY
Drive route

Car
Pettig
Belalt
Stonefort
BOA ISLA 9
Larkhill
Rossharbour
Dreenan
Carrickacottia
Leggs
Lustyr Isla
BELLEEK 1
A47
Rosscor
Drumbadmeen
Lowe
Earrancassidy
Church
B52
FERMANAGH
Glen
Derryg
Lough Melvin
Garrison
Slisgarrow
Buggan
Rossinver
Scribbagh
Tullybrack 358m
R281
Tullyskeherhy
Kiltyclogher
Tullintloy
Tullyrossmearan
R281
B52
Glenkeel
Lough Macnean Upper
Laghty Barr
Mul
Belcoo
Glenfarne
Blacklion
N16
Termon
Barran
Cornagee
Gowlan

Above The main house, Castle Archdale Country Park, *see pp256–7*

PLAN YOUR DRIVE

Start/finish: Belleek to Boa Island.

Number of days: 2 days.

Distance: 108 km (67 miles).

Road conditions: Mostly good although there are some uneven surfaces along the A46. Some of the smaller roads around Monea and Boho are liable to flooding. Lough Navar Forest Drive is one-way and uneven in parts.

When to go: Spring through to autumn, when most attractions are open and the weather is best.

Opening times: Most shops and attractions open 9 or 10am–5 or 6pm. Shops open Mon–Sat; in large towns also 12–6pm on Sun. Convenience stores in villages open 8am until late.

Main market days: Belleek: third Tue of month; **Enniskillen:** Tue and Thu; Farmers' Market, every second Sat.

Shopping: Belleek is renowned for fine Parian China. Enniskillen is a centre for many crafts, including jewellery, ceramics and textiles. Handmade lace and linens are on offer in Bellanaleck.

Major festivals: Enniskillen: Drama Festival, Mar; Happy Days Beckett Festival, Aug; Festival Lough Erne, Sep; Fermanagh Live Arts Festival, Oct; **Upper and Lower Lough Erne:** Classic Fishing Festival, May; **Lower Lough Erne:** Vintage Car Rally, Aug.

DAY TRIP OPTIONS

For a first-rate **family attraction** visit the Marble Arch Caves Geopark. **Nature-lovers** will enjoy walking, boating or cycling around the shores of Lower Lough Erne. For full details, *see p257.*

Above Walkway down to the Marble Arch Caves, one of Europe's top show caves

WHERE TO STAY

AROUND MARBLE ARCH CAVES

Customs House Inn & Restaurant
inexpensive–moderate
This country hotel is at Belcoo, on the drive route from Belleek to Marble Arch Caves and 20 km (12 miles) from the caves off the N16. It offers a warm welcome, good food and lovely views over Lough Macnean.
25–7 Main Street, Belcoo, BT93 5FB; 028 6638 6285; www.customs houseinn.com

Knockninny Country House
inexpensive–moderate
Lovingly restored Victorian hotel, complete with marina, situated on Upper Lough Erne's shoreline, 14 miles/ 23 km from the caves on the A509.
Knockninny Quay, Derrylin,BT92 9JU; 028 6774 8590; www.knockninny countryhouse.com

AROUND ENNISKILLEN

Killyhevlin Hotel
moderate
A peaceful place set in extensive grounds on the shores of Lough Erne just 1 km (half a mile) from Enniskillen along the A4 to Castle Coole. The pool and Jacuzzi are good places to unwind after a day's driving.
Killyhevlin, BT74 6RW; 028 6632 3481; www.killyhevlin.com

① Belleek
Co Fermanagh
This quiet village on the banks of Lough Erne has quaint, hand-painted shop fronts. It is famous for its fine parian china, an industry introduced to the village by the local landowner in 1857, in the wake of the potato famine. At the **Belleek Pottery Visitor Centre** (*Jan–Feb: Mon–Fri; Mar–Dec: daily, Sun pm only*), guided tours take visitors to see the delicate Belleek china being crafted and decorated. A museum displays Belleek ware from the company's earliest days, including an urn-shaped vase made for the 1900 Paris Exhibition, and there is a showroom and tearoom.

🚗 *Cross the bridge by the Pottery, veer left then turn left and follow signs for the A46, a lovely drive alongside Lower Lough Erne. After 21 km (13 miles), just after Tully Castle, turn right onto the B81 at Binmore Road for Derrygonnelly. Continue to Monea and 2 km (1 mile) after Monea turn right at the crossroads, then right again after another 1 mile (2 km) at a T-junction. Follow the signs to Belcoo, then turn left in Blacklion for Florence Court. Turn right for the Marlbank Scenic Loop. The entrance for Marble Arch Caves is 8 km (5 miles) along this drive, on the left.*

② Marble Arch Caves
Marlbank, Co Fermanagh; BT92 1EW
These unique show caves are among Europe's finest and are part of an area of outstanding geological interest recognized by UNESCO. They were sculpted out of limestone, and formed when Ireland was covered by ocean some 330 million years ago. Guided tours (*Mar–Oct: daily, last tour*

4pm, Nov: Wed–Sun, last tour 3pm; book ahead during peak times, 028 6634 8855) begin with an underground boat ride through a mesmerizing landscape of stalactite-filled caverns, stone pools, streams and cascades, each feature atmospherically lit. The 9-m (30-ft) Marble Arch itself stands in a glen at the confluence of three streams. Tours last 75 minutes and are suitable for anyone of reasonable fitness (wear walking shoes and a warm sweater). Facilities include a restaurant and exhibition area.

🚗 *Leaving Marble Arch Caves, drive down the entrance road and turn left. At the next T-junction, turn right. Drive through the small hamlet of Florence Court and turn right into Florence Court.*

Lough Navar Forest Drive
This is an extensive area of woodland with a diverse array of habitats. A 7-mile (11 km) scenic tour, known as the Forest Drive (*open daily, 10am–sunset*), begins off the Glennasheevar Road between Derrygonnelly and Garrison, and emerges at the spectacular 300-m (1,000 ft-) high Magho Cliffs, with an outstanding viewpoint over Lower Lough Erne, Donegal and the surrounding mountains. From the main forest drive there are many short walks signed to various points of interest.

③ Florence Court
Enniskillen, Co Fermanagh; BT92 1DB
A beautiful stately home dating from the early 18th century, Florence Court (*grounds open daily; house open Mar, Apr & Oct: weekends; Map–Sep: daily pm weekends only; call in*

Right Setting a gentle pace on a back road in County Fermanagh

advance on 028 6634 8249), was occupied by the Earls of Enniskillen until the early 1950s, when it was acquired by the National Trust. A guided tour reveals rich Rococo plasterwork – especially on the ceilings of the dining room, Venetian room and staircase – all restored following a fire in 1955, and fine Irish furniture. The grounds have a water-powered sawmill, an ice house, a forge, a walled garden and a forest park with walking trails.

🚗 *At the exit, turn right, signposted Enniskillen/A4. Then turn left onto the A32 for Enniskillen and after 3 km (2 miles), turn right on the road signposted as Arney/Bellanaleck. Continue for 4 km (2 miles) to reach Bellanaleck. Park at the lace museum.*

4 Bellanaleck
Co Fermanagh
The quirky **Sheelin Antique Irish Lace Museum** (open Mon–Sat) in Bellanaleck has around 700 examples of lace made in Ireland between 1850 and 1900. It also sells vintage lace and linen, including wedding dresses and veils, baby bonnets, lace coasters and more. There is a sweet little tea shop next door.

🚗 *From Bellanaleck, take the A509 north and turn right onto the A4 for Enniskillen. For Enniskillen Castle, keep left through the town and park at the free car park beside the castle.*

5 Enniskillen
Co Fermanagh
This county town is situated on an island between Lower and Upper Lough Erne. Its main sight is **Enniskillen Castle** (open Mon–Sat; Jun–Sep: daily), built in the

early 15th century by the Maguire family. Standing at the narrowest crossing point between the two loughs, it has had an interesting history and has been used as an English garrison fort and military barracks. The castle's most stunning feature is the Watergate, a fairy-tale twin-turreted tower, best admired from the far bank of the river. It now houses the **Fermanagh County Museum** and the **Inniskilling Museum**.

Also in Enniskillen is the **Buttermarket**, a delightful enclave of small art galleries, craft studios and coffee shops set in the restored 19th-century dairy market.

🚗 *Leaving Enniskillen, follow signs for Belfast/A4. Castle Coole is just over 2 km (1 mile) from Enniskillen. An admission charge per car is taken on the driveway.*

6 Castle Coole
Enniskillen, Co Fermanagh; BT74 6JY
One of Ireland's finest Neo-Classical houses, Castle Coole (grounds: open daily; house: open Apr–Sep daily), was commissioned by the first Earl of Belmore in the 1790s. Its expense nearly bankrupted him. The splendid Regency furnishings can be appreciated on a guided tour, highlights of which include the State Bedroom, the Oval Saloon and the servants' quarters. There is a lovely lakeside walk in the grounds.

🚗 *Take Castle Coole Road (A4) back towards Enniskillen. Keep left at the mini roundabout and then turn right at the lights. At the roundabout, take the 4th exit for the A32 for Irvinestown and Kesh. After 5 km (3 miles), turn left at the roundabout onto the A47 for Killadeas.*

Above left Monea Castle ruins, near Belcoo
Above Enchanting setting of Enniskillen Castle

EAT AND DRINK

BELLEEK
The Thatch *inexpensive*
Pretty thatched tea room in the centre of Belleek, with daily specials, great coffee and home baking.
20 Main Street, BT93 3FX; 028 6865 8181

Fiddlestones *inexpensive*
Traditional-style pub with an open fire and regular music sessions.
15–17 Main Street, BT93 3FY; 028 6865 8008

AROUND MARBLE ARCH CAVES
MacNean House and Restaurant *expensive*
Run by award-winning chef Neven Maguire. Outstanding food prepared with local ingredients and great ambience in a village location 19 km (12 miles) west of Enniskillen on N16.
Main Street, Blacklion; Co Cavan; 071 985 3022; www.nevinmaguire.com; open eves only; closed Mon & Tue

ENNISKILLEN
The Jolly Sandwich *inexpensive*
Buzzy daytime café/deli serving all-day breakfast, toasties, cupcakes and coffee.
3 Darling Street, BT74 7DP; 028 6632 2277; closed Sun

Blake's of The Hollow/Café Merlot *moderate*
Blake's, the pub, is full of character, with an original Victorian bar. Below the pub, Café Merlot serves tasty European dishes, slow-roast meats and seafood.
6 Church Street, BT74 7EJ, 028 6632 2143, www.blakesofthehollow.com; Café Merlot: 028 6632 0918

Franco's Restaurant *moderate*
Seafood is the speciality, but there is also rib-eye steak, rack of lamb and duck, as well as pasta and pizza.
Queen Elizabeth Road, BT74 7DY; 028 6632 4424; www.francos restaurant.co.uk

VISITING LOUGH ERNE

Exploring by boat
Boats can be rented for the day or half-day *(Mar–Oct; 028 6862 8100; www.manormarine.com)*. No experience required as instructions are given. Trips around the lake, on the *Lady of the Lake* cruise boat, passing Devenish, depart from Rossclare Jetty at Killadeas *(Jul & Aug: daily, mid-Apr–Sep: Sat only, weather permitting); 079 4032 7129; www.ladyofthelaketours.com*

WHERE TO STAY

LOWER LOUGH ERNE

Manor House Country Hotel *moderate*
Situated 11 km (7 miles) from Enniskillen on the shores of Lough Erne along the B82 drive route, this 18th-century manor house combines period elegance and modern comforts including a pool and sauna. Boats for hire by the day or take a leisurely cruise around the lake *(see above)*.
Killadeas, BT94 1NY; 028 6862 2200; www.manorhousecountryhotel.com

Lough Erne Resort *expensive*
Five-star resort in the shape of luxury rooms and loughside lodges, a spa and two championship-quality golf courses.
Belleek Road, Enniskillen BT93 7ED; 028 6632 3230; www.lougherne resort.com

BOA ISLAND

Lusty Beg Island *moderate*
A private ferry takes visitors and their cars to this idyllic 30-ha (75-acre) island complete with a B&B, lakeside cabins, self-catering chalets and spas.
Lusty Beg Island, Boa Island, Kesh, BT93 8AD; 028 6863 3300; www.lustybegisland.com

⑦ Lower Lough Erne
Co Fermanagh

Lough Erne is divided into two distinct water systems. Upper Lough Erne is a maze of small channels and joins the mighty Shannon river, while Lower Lough Erne is a vast lake set in unspoiled countryside, closer to the sea. It is the perfect location for activities such as water sports, bird-watching, boating and fishing, while on land there are numerous trails for hiking and cycling, as well as pony-trekking. There are over 150 small islands and inlets to explore, and some of the larger islands boast their own resorts.

To explore Lower Lough Erne, join a cruise on board the comfortable *Lady of the Lake* from Killadeas or rent a boat independently from Manor House marina *(see left)*. One of the most interesting islands is **Devenish Island**, once called Ox Island. It has the remains of a monastic settlement founded by St Molaise in the 6th century, including a superb 25-m- (82-ft-) tall,

12th-century round tower. Notice the human faces carved above the four windows, the only instance of such embellishment on an Irish round tower.

White Island also has the remains of a 12th-century church, with eight enigmatic figures along the interior north wall. They are believed to date from the 6th–9th centuries.

🚗 *Leaving Killadeas, turn left onto the A47. After 2.5 miles (4 km), look for the entrance to Castle Archdale Country Park and park at the Visitor Centre.*

⑧ CASTLE ARCHDALE COUNTRY PARK
Irvinestown, Co Fermanagh; BT94 1PP

This large country park on the shores of Lough Erne has mature woodlands, a marina and a slipway, as well as many walking and cycling trails and a red deer enclosure and butterfly garden. The castle, built in the early 1600s, is now a ruin, accessible through Castle Archdale Forest. The Visitor Centre, in the courtyard buildings of the old manor house, has information on walks and wildlife. A heritage trail links points of interest, including evidence of the park's use by the RAF in World War II. In summer, boats are available for hire to explore Lough Erne, and a ferry runs to White Island *(see right)*.

A two-hour walking tour

Start this 6-km (4-mile) walk at the **Visitor Centre** ① and continue towards the **walled garden** ②, where the road leads to the marina and caravan park. Enter the forest here and at the first junction turn left towards the castle. Continue straight on to a cottage and a signpost for **Tom's Island** ③. Turn left here (if the path is waterlogged, take the forest road and then rejoin the path after the jetty). Cross the causeway onto Inish Beg or Tom's Island, keeping left. The lakeside path has excellent views over to White Island (there is a ferry to the island from the marina, see right) and of Lough Erne, stretching into the distance. Keep walking along the path past the jetty and then inland slightly, following the river. Continue along this and cross the access road. At the bridge and tarmac road into the Forest Service car park, turn right. The ruins of **Castle Archdale** ④ are here. In the summer this area is particularly enchanting with colourful wild flowers in bloom. Turn left uphill and take the path behind the castle. At the junction turn left, then left again at the next forest road, and then right. To return to the visitor centre, trace the route back to the forest and follow the road past the walled garden.

🚗 *Return to the A47 and turn left for Kesh. After 2 km (1 mile) turn left for the Kesh scenic route. The road surface is uneven but there are lovely views of Lough Erne, with a viewpoint about 1 km (half a mile) along. At Kesh, turn left at the junction and then left again at the T-junction for Pettigo/Belleek, crossing the bridge. Take the next left onto the A47 for Boa Island. On the island, there is a signposted turn for Lusty Beg Island. About 2 km (1 mile) after this, turn*

left for Caldragh Cemetery. Park at the bottom of the road and access the graveyard through the turnstile on the left.

9 Boa Island
Co Fermanagh
The largest of Lough Erne's islands, Boa is joined to the mainland by bridges at both ends. It is notable for two mysterious stone figures, to be found in the centre of **Caldragh Cemetery**, an early Christian graveyard at the western end of the island. The first, the **Boa Island Figure**, is a carved stone, 1 m (3 ft) high, with two faces, back to back; it is also known as the Janus Figure after the Roman god with two faces. It is believed to represent a Celtic deity and symbolize fertility, but its true significance is uncertain. It is said to have inspired Seamus Heaney's poem "January God".

The second, smaller figure beside it, the **Lusty Man**, was originally discovered in a cemetery on Lusty Mor Island, just south of Boa Island, and was moved to its present location in 1939. It is thought to be older than the Janus figure, but is similarly shrouded in mystery.

Above far left Turret-like lodges of the Lough Erne Resort **Above left** The tranquil waters of Lower Lough Erne, a haven for wildlife **Above** Courtyard buildings of the old manor house at Castle Archdale

VISITING CASTLE ARCHDALE

Visitor Centre
Castle Archdale Country Park, Irvinestown, is 17 km (11 miles) northwest of Enniskillen; 028 6862 1588; open Easter–Oct daily, Nov–Easter Sun 10am–4pm only

Boat and Bike Hire
Boats, kayaks, hydrobikes and bikes can be hired at weekends from Easter to the end of September, daily in June to August. Boats take up to six or eight people and instructions are provided. *028 6862 1156; www.castlearchdale boathire.com*

Ferry Trips
The White Island ferry makes the 20-minute crossing to White Island *(Easter–Sep weekends only, Jul–Aug daily)*. There is also a ferry from **Trory Point** to Devenish Island *(6 km/4 miles from Enniskillen on A32; Apr–Sep daily)*.

EAT AND DRINK

The hotels in the area offer several options for drinking and dining *(see Where to Stay, left)*.

DAY TRIP OPTIONS
Enniskillen is an ideal base, the area's best sites being within easy reach. The first trip takes in Marble Arch Caves, followed by a visit to pretty Bellanaleck. The second option is a day on Lower Lough Erne – choose to explore by boat, bike or on foot.

Caverns and lace
Marble Arch Caves ② are a global geopark and a popular attraction

for families. Book ahead for the tour, which includes a boat ride and walk through immense caverns. On the way back to Enniskillen, stop at the Sheelin Antique Irish Lace Museum in Bellanaleck ④ (vintage items for sale), and have lunch or afternoon tea in the tea room.

Follow the A32 southwest for 17 km (11 miles) to reach the caves. Return on the A32/A509 via Bellanaleck.

A day on Lough Erne
Take one of the access points for a lakeside walk along Lower Lough Erne ⑦ or hire a boat to do some independent island-hopping. Alternatively, rent a bike from Castle Archdale Country Park ⑧ and cycle around the shoreline.

Head north from Enniskillen on the A32/B82 for Castle Archdale Country Park and Killadeas.

INDEX

Page numbers in **bold** refer to main entries

ACKNOWLEDGMENTS

Dorling Kindersley would like to thank the many people whose help and assistance contributed to the preparation of this book.

Photography
Brian Daughton, Stephen Power

Additional Photography
Joe Cornish, Tim Daly, Steve Gorton, Jamie Marshall, Ian O'Leary, Rough Guides/Roger Mapp, Antony Souter, Clive Streeter, Alan Williams

Maps
John Plumer, JP Map Graphics Ltd, www.jpmapgraphics.co.uk

Picture Credits
Every effort has been made to trace the copyright holders of images, and we apologize in advance for any unintentional omissions. We would be pleased to insert the appropriate acknowledgments in any subsequent edition of this publication.

The Publishers would like to thank the following individuals, companies and picture libraries for their kind permission to reproduce their photographs:

t=top; tc = top centre; tl=top left; tr=top right; c=centre; cl=centre left; cr=centre right; bc = bottom centre; bl=bottom left; br=bottom right.

Alamy Stock Photo: Buiten-Beeld / Johan van der Wielen 170; Holger Burmeister 26bx; Ian G Dagnall 50; Dennis Flaherty 92bc; Eye Ubiquitous / Hugh Rooney 138; Chris Howes / Wild Places Photography 120; Brian Jannsen 250; JoeFox CountyMayo 208br; David T. Kavanagh 162; Fabrice Lambert 206br; David Lyons 128; Mira 226ca; Tony Mullen 94; George Munday 34ca; Keith Nuttall 227tr; scenicireland.com/Christopher Hill Photographic 214ca; Republic of Ireland 198; Robertharding / Richard Cummins 70; Stuwdamdorp 10tr; Peter Titmuss 10bl. **AWL Images:** Shaun Egan 2-3; Shaun Egan 210. **Barberstown Castle:** 142tl. **Borris House:** 85clb. **Corbis:** Richard Cummins 125tr; Destinations 73t, 75tl, 227bc; **Michael Diggin:** 15tl. **Dreamstime.com:** Barry32 26bl; Gabe9000c 34tl; Giuseppemasci 78; John Holmes 110; Laurentiu Iordache 146; Miroslav Liska 28-29; MNStudio 86; Stefano Valeri 180. **Dublin Mountains Partnership:** Karen Woods 143br. **Mark Fearon**/www. photographersdirect.com: 207bl. **Flickr.com:** www.flickr.com/photos/jule_berlin/560207760/ 218ca; www.flickr.com/photos/dnlbyl/2213073893 Donal Boyle 218br. **Galway City Museum:** 185br. **Getty Images:** Axiom Photographic Agency/Richard Cummins 9br; 136br, 183br, 183tl, 192cl, 225bl; Lonely Planet Images/Gareth McCormack 217tl; Lonely Planet RF/Trish Punch 38; Moment/© Marco Bottigelli 222; Photographer's Choice/Andrew Holt 16br, 26tr; Robert Harding World Imagery/Gary Cook 193tl; Robert Harding World Imagery/Richard Cummins 76tl; Stephen Rafferty 245bc; Robert Harding World Imagery/Roy Rainford 7cl; Universal Images Group / Eye Ubiquitous 154. **iStockphoto.com:** BestTravelPhotography 102; JanMiko 60; Kevin Mclaughlin 190; Susanne Neumann 30, 242; Paul Withers 230. **The National Trust Photo Library** ©NTPL: 247bc, 248br. **Newmills Corn and Flax Mills:** David Armour 214tc. **Photolibrary:** Design Pics Inc/The Irish Image Collection 77tr. **Sathya Sai Sanctuary Trust for Nature:** 209tl. **Strokestown Park:** 169tl, 169tr. **Tipperaryphotos.com:** 13tl.

Sheet Map
iStockphoto.com: miroslav_1.

Jacket
Front and Spine: iStockphoto.com: miroslav_1; **Back:** 4Corners: Maurizio Rellini crb; Alamy Stock Photo: scenicireland.com / Christopher Hill Photographic tl; Getty Images: Moment / © Marco Bottigelli cla; iStockphoto.com: gianliguori tr, miroslav_1 b.

All other images © Dorling Kindersley For further information see: www.dkimages.com

Illustrators
Arun Pottirayil , Pallavi Thakur, Dev Datta

DK | Penguin Random House

THIS EDITION UPDATED BY
CONTRIBUTORS Brian Daughton, John S Doyle, Yvonne Gordon, Darren Longley
SENIOR EDITOR Alison McGill
SENIOR DESIGNER Stuti Tiwari
PROJECT EDITORS Parnika Bagla, Rada Radojicic
EDITORS Avanika, Nayan Keshan
PICTURE RESEARCH COORDINATOR Sumita Khatwani
ASSISTANT PICTURE RESEARCH ADMINISTRATOR Vagisha Pushp
JACKET COORDINATOR Bella Talbot
JACKET DESIGNER Ben Hinks
SENIOR CARTOGRAPHIC EDITORS Mohammad Hassan, Casper Morris
CARTOGRAPHY MANAGER Suresh Kumar
DTP DESIGNER Tanveer Abbas Zaidi
SENIOR PRODUCTION EDITOR Jason Little
SENIOR PRODUCTION CONTROLLER Stephanie McConnell
DEPUTY MANAGING EDITOR Beverly Smart
MANAGING EDITORS Shikha Kulkarni, Hollie Teague
MANAGING ART EDITORS Bess Daly, Priyanka Thakur
ART DIRECTOR Maxine Pedliham
PUBLISHING DIRECTOR Georgina Dee

First edition 2010
Published in Great Britain by Dorling Kindersley Limited, DK, One Embassy Gardens, 8 Viaduct Gardens, London SW11 7BW
Published in the United States by DK Publishing, 1450 Broadway, Suite 801, New York, NY 10018
Copyright © 2010, 2021 Dorling Kindersley Limited
A Penguin Random House Company
21 22 23 24 10 9 8 7 6 5 4 3 2 1
Reprinted with revisions 2013, 2018, 2021
All rights reserved.

A CIP catalogue record for this book is available from the British Library.
A catalogue record for this book is available from the Library of Congress.
ISSN 1542 1554
ISBN 978 0 2414 3669 1
Printed in China
www.dk.com